PageMaker® 6.5 For Dummies®, Internet Edition

Cheat Sheet

Attention Macintosh users:

Substitute the ⌘ key for Ctrl and the Option key for Alt in the shortcuts.

Getting Around

To Do This:	Press This:
Zoom to 100%	Ctrl+1
Zoom to 200%	Ctrl+2
Fit in Window	Ctrl+0
Zoom to 50%	Ctrl+5
Zoom in (magnify)	Ctrl+plus
Zoom out (reduce)	Ctrl+hyphen
Magnify beyond 400%	Drag around area with Zoom tool
Go to previous page	Page Up
Go to next page	Page Down
Go to specific page	Ctrl+Alt+G

Palette Commands

To Choose This Command:	Press This:
Hide/Display all active palettes	Tab
Hide/Display Control palette	Ctrl+ apostrophe
Hide/Display Colors palette	Ctrl+J
Hide/Display Styles palette	Ctrl+B
Open Define Styles dialog box	Ctrl+3
Hide/Display Layers palette	Ctrl+8
Hide/Display Master Pages palette	Ctrl+Shift+8
Hide/Display Hyperlinks palette	Ctrl+9

Toolbox Shortcuts

Tool:	Press This:
Toggle between last tool used and Arrow tool	F9
Text tool	Alt+Shift+F1
Rotate tool	Shift+F2
Crop tool	Alt+Shift+F2
Line tool	Shift+F3
Orthogonal Line tool	Alt+Shift+F3
Rectangle tool	Shift+F4
Rectangle Frame tool	Alt+Shift+F4
Ellipse tool	Shift+F5
Ellipse Frame tool	Alt+Shift+F5
Polygon tool	Shift+F6
Polygon Frame tool	Alt+Shift+F6
Grabber tool	F10 or Shift+F7
Zoom tool	Alt+Shift+F7

Cheat Sheet $2.95 value. Item 0126-7.
For more information about IDG Books, call 1-800-762-2974.

For Dummies®: Bestselling Book Series for Beginners

PageMaker® 6.5 For Dummies®, Internet Edition

Attention Macintosh users:

Substitute the ⌘ key for Ctrl and the Option key for Alt in the shortcuts.

Commands

To Choose This Command:	*Press This:*
Get help	F1
Save	Ctrl+S
Save As	Ctrl+Shift+S
Print	Ctrl+P
Undo	Ctrl+Z
Place	Ctrl+D
Document Setup	Ctrl+Shift+P
Links Manager	Ctrl+Shift+D
Group	Ctrl+G
Ungroup	Ctrl+Shift+G
Lock	Ctrl+L
Unlock	Ctrl+Alt+L
Enter/Exit Story Editor	Ctrl+E
Spell-check	Ctrl+L
Replace	Ctrl+H
Find	Ctrl+F
Find next	Ctrl+G

Special Characters

Note: Not all Web browsers can display these characters.

To Choose This Character:	*Press This:*
© Copyright	Alt+G
® Registered trademark	Alt+R
¶ Paragraph	Alt+7
§ Section	Alt+6

Supported HTML Styles

Note: All PageMaker styles must be set to translate to one of the following HTML styles during HTML export.

HTML Style:	*Suggested Use:*
Body Text	General content
Blockquote	Long quotations or other indented text
Address	Addresses, captions, or legal matter
Preformatted	Directory listings or software code
Heading 1	Main titles
Heading 2	Section heads
Heading 3	Subsection heads within text
Heading 4	Bylines, captions, or labels
Heading 5	Not recommended for headlines
Heading 6	Not recommended for headlines
Unordered List	Bulleted lists
Ordered List	Numbered lists
Menu List	Menus, such as a list of keywords hyperlinked to other sections
Directory List	Table of contents or menus with long entries
Definition List	Definitions, glossaries

Text-Formatting Commands

To Choose This Formatting Supported on the Web:	*Press This:*
Bold	Ctrl+Shift+B
Italics	Ctrl+Shift+I
Plain	Ctrl+Shift+spacebar

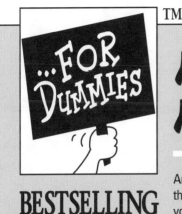

PageMaker® 6.5 for Dummies®

INTERNET EDITION

by Galen Gruman

Foreword by Lori Birtley

IDG Books Worldwide, Inc.
An International Data Group Company

Foster City, CA ♦ Chicago, IL ♦ Indianapolis, IN ♦ New York, NY

PageMaker® 6.5 For Dummies®, Internet Edition

Published by
IDG Books Worldwide, Inc.
An International Data Group Company
919 E. Hillsdale Blvd.
Suite 400
Foster City, CA 94404
www.idgbooks.com (IDG Books Worldwide Web site)
www.dummies.com (Dummies Press Web site)

Library of Congress Catalog Card No.: 97-70370

ISBN: 0-7645-0126-7

Printed in the United States of America

10 9 8 7 6 5

1O/SV/QU/QQ/IN

Distributed in the United States by IDG Books Worldwide, Inc.

Distributed by CDG Books Canada Inc. for Canada; by Transworld Publishers Limited in the United Kingdom; by IDG Norge Books for Norway; by IDG Sweden Books for Sweden; by IDG Books Australia Publishing Corporation Pty. Ltd. for Australia and New Zealand; by TransQuest Publishers Pte Ltd. for Singapore, Malaysia, Thailand, Indonesia, and Hong Kong; by Gotop Information Inc. for Taiwan; by ICG Muse, Inc. for Japan; by Intersoft for South Africa; by Eyrolles for France; by International Thomson Publishing for Germany, Austria and Switzerland; by Distribuidora Cuspide for Argentina; by LR International for Brazil; by Galileo Libros for Chile; by Ediciones ZETA S.C.R. Ltda. for Peru; by WS Computer Publishing Corporation, Inc., for the Philippines; by Contemporanea de Ediciones for Venezuela; by Express Computer Distributors for the Caribbean and West Indies; by Micronesia Media Distributor, Inc. for Micronesia; by Chips Computadoras S.A. de C.V. for Mexico; by Editorial Norma de Panama S.A. for Panama; by American Bookshops for Finland.

For general information on IDG Books Worldwide's books in the U.S., please call our Consumer Customer Service department at 800-762-2974. For reseller information, including discounts and premium sales, please call our Reseller Customer Service department at 800-434-3422.

For information on where to purchase IDG Books Worldwide's books outside the U.S., please contact our International Sales department at 317-596-5530 or fax 317-572-4002.

For consumer information on foreign language translations, please contact our Customer Service department at 1-800-434-3422, fax 317-572-4002, or e-mail rights@idgbooks.com.

For information on licensing foreign or domestic rights, please phone +1-650-653-7098.

For sales inquiries and special prices for bulk quantities, please contact our Order Services department at 800-434-3422 or write to the address above.

For information on using IDG Books Worldwide's books in the classroom or for ordering examination copies, please contact our Educational Sales department at 800-434-2086 or fax 317-572-4005.

For press review copies, author interviews, or other publicity information, please contact our Public Relations department at 650-653-7000 or fax 650-653-7500.

About the Author

Galen Gruman is executive editor at *Macworld* magazine in charge of news and features, as well as a frequent reviewer of desktop publishing software for *Macworld* and *InfoWorld*. A pioneer user of desktop publishing in professional magazine production, Galen adopted the technology in 1986 for a national engineering magazine, *IEEE Software*.

Galen's honors include the finals of the Computer Press Awards for best computer-oriented news story in a general-interest publication (1986) and winning best in-depth technical feature in the American Society of Business Press Editors Awards (1993), which he shared with Lon Poole and Arne Hurty of *Macworld*. He was president of the Computer Press Association from 1992 to 1995.

Galen is co-author with Deke McClelland of *PageMaker 6 For Windows For Dummies, PageMaker 5 For Windows For Dummies, PageMaker 6 for Macs For Dummies,* and *PageMaker 5 For Macs For Dummies.* With Barbara Assadi he co-authored the critically praised *QuarkXPress 3.1 For Windows Designer Handbook, Macworld QuarkXPress 3.2/3.3 Bible,* and *QuarkXPress 3.3 For Dummies,* all from IDG Books Worldwide, Inc.

ABOUT IDG BOOKS WORLDWIDE

Welcome to the world of IDG Books Worldwide.

IDG Books Worldwide, Inc., is a subsidiary of International Data Group, the world's largest publisher of computer-related information and the leading global provider of information services on information technology. IDG was founded more than 30 years ago by Patrick J. McGovern and now employs more than 9,000 people worldwide. IDG publishes more than 290 computer publications in over 75 countries. More than 90 million people read one or more IDG publications each month.

Launched in 1990, IDG Books Worldwide is today the #1 publisher of best-selling computer books in the United States. We are proud to have received eight awards from the Computer Press Association in recognition of editorial excellence and three from Computer Currents' First Annual Readers' Choice Awards. Our best-selling ...*For Dummies*® series has more than 50 million copies in print with translations in 31 languages. IDG Books Worldwide, through a joint venture with IDG's Hi-Tech Beijing, became the first U.S. publisher to publish a computer book in the People's Republic of China. In record time, IDG Books Worldwide has become the first choice for millions of readers around the world who want to learn how to better manage their businesses.

Our mission is simple: Every one of our books is designed to bring extra value and skill-building instructions to the reader. Our books are written by experts who understand and care about our readers. The knowledge base of our editorial staff comes from years of experience in publishing, education, and journalism — experience we use to produce books to carry us into the new millennium. In short, we care about books, so we attract the best people. We devote special attention to details such as audience, interior design, use of icons, and illustrations. And because we use an efficient process of authoring, editing, and desktop publishing our books electronically, we can spend more time ensuring superior content and less time on the technicalities of making books.

You can count on our commitment to deliver high-quality books at competitive prices on topics you want to read about. At IDG Books Worldwide, we continue in the IDG tradition of delivering quality for more than 30 years. You'll find no better book on a subject than one from IDG Books Worldwide.

John Kilcullen
Chairman and CEO
IDG Books Worldwide, Inc.

Eighth Annual Computer Press Awards 1992

Ninth Annual Computer Press Awards 1993

X WINNER

Tenth Annual Computer Press Awards 1994

Eleventh Annual Computer Press Awards 1995

IDG is the world's leading IT media, research and exposition company. Founded in 1964, IDG had 1997 revenues of $2.05 billion and has more than 9,000 employees worldwide. IDG offers the widest range of media options that reach IT buyers in 75 countries representing 95% of worldwide IT spending. IDG's diverse product and services portfolio spans six key areas including print publishing, online publishing, expositions and conferences, market research, education and training, and global marketing services. More than 90 million people read one or more of IDG's 290 magazines and newspapers, including IDG's leading global brands — Computerworld, PC World, Network World, Macworld and the Channel World family of publications. IDG Books Worldwide is one of the fastest-growing computer book publishers in the world, with more than 700 titles in 36 languages. The "...For Dummies®" series alone has more than 50 million copies in print. IDG offers online users the largest network of technology-specific Web sites around the world through IDG.net (http://www.idg.net), which comprises more than 225 targeted Web sites in 55 countries worldwide. International Data Corporation (IDC) is the world's largest provider of information technology data, analysis and consulting, with research centers in over 41 countries and more than 400 research analysts worldwide. IDG World Expo is a leading producer of more than 168 globally branded conferences and expositions in 35 countries including E3 (Electronic Entertainment Expo), Macworld Expo, ComNet, Windows World Expo, ICE (Internet Commerce Expo), Agenda, DEMO, and Spotlight. IDG's training subsidiary, ExecuTrain, is the world's largest computer training company, with more than 230 locations worldwide and 785 training courses. IDG Marketing Services helps industry-leading IT companies build international brand recognition by developing global integrated marketing programs via IDG's print, online and exposition products worldwide. Further information about the company can be found at www.idg.com.

1/26/00

Author's Acknowledgments

No book is done by one person, despite what the cover byline may indicate. My thanks to the following people for helping me make this book come alive: my partner Ingall W. Bull III; my frequent colleague and even more frequent *Macworld* writer Deke McClelland; Nancy DelFavero, the project editor at IDG Books; and the staff at *Macworld* magazine.

Publisher's Acknowledgments

We're proud of this book; please register your comments through our IDG Books Worldwide Online Registration Form located at `http://my2cents.dummies.com`.

Some of the people who helped bring this book to market include the following:

Acquisitions, Development, and Editorial

Project Editor: Nancy DelFavero

Acquisitions Editor: Michael Kelly, Quality Control Manager

Associate Permissions Editor: Heather H. Dismore

Copy Editors: Michael Bolinger, Tamara S. Castleman

Technical Editor: Lee Musick

Editorial Manager: Mary C. Corder

Editorial Assistant: Chris H. Collins

Production

Project Coordinator: Sherry Gomoll

Layout and Graphics: Cameron Booker, Linda M. Boyer, Elizabeth Cárdenas-Nelson, Dominique DeFelice, Kelly Hardesty, Angela F. Hunckler, Brent Savage, Kate Snell, Michael A. Sullivan

Proofreaders: Kathy McGuinness, Joel K. Draper, Rachel Garvey, Dwight Ramsey, Robert Springer, Karen York

Indexer: Ty Koontz

General and Administrative

IDG Books Worldwide, Inc.: John Kilcullen, CEO

IDG Books Technology Publishing Group: Richard Swadley, Senior Vice President and Publisher; Walter R. Bruce III, Vice President and Publisher; Joseph Wikert, Vice President and Publisher; Mary Bednarek, Vice President and Director, Product Development; Andy Cummings, Publishing Director, General User Group; Mary C. Corder, Editorial Director; Barry Pruett, Publishing Director

IDG Books Consumer Publishing Group: Roland Elgey, Senior Vice President and Publisher; Kathleen A. Welton, Vice President and Publisher; Kevin Thornton, Acquisitions Manager; Kristin A. Cocks, Editorial Director

IDG Books Internet Publishing Group: Brenda McLaughlin, Senior Vice President and Publisher; Sofia Marchant, Online Marketing Manager

IDG Books Production for Branded Press: Debbie Stailey, Director of Production; Cindy L. Phipps, Manager of Project Coordination, Production Proofreading, and Indexing; Tony Augsburger, Manager of Prepress, Reprints, and Systems; Laura Carpenter, Production Control Manager; Shelley Lea, Supervisor of Graphics and Design; Debbie J. Gates, Production Systems Specialist; Robert Springer, Supervisor of Proofreading; Kathie Schutte, Production Supervisor

Packaging and Book Design: Patty Page: Manager, Promotions Marketing

♦

The publisher would like to give special thanks to Patrick J. McGovern, without whom this book would not have been possible.

♦

Contents at a Glance

Cartoons at a Glance

By Rich Tennant

page 207

"FOR OBVIOUS REASONS WE DECIDED NOT TO USE AN ACRONYM."

page 101

page 47

"HONEY! OUR WEB BROWSER GOT OUT LAST NIGHT AND DUMPED THE TRASH ALL OVER MR. BELCHER'S HOME PAGE!"

page 251

"SINCE WE GOT IT, HE HASN'T MOVED FROM THAT SPOT FOR ELEVEN STRAIGHT DAYS. ODDLY ENOUGH THEY CALL THIS 'GETTING UP AND RUNNING' ON THE INTERNET."

page 9

page 313

"Would you like Web or non-Web?"

Fax: 978-546-7747

E-mail: richtennant@the5thwave.com

World Wide Web: www.the5thwave.com

Table of Contents

Foreword

Adobe PageMaker has long been heralded as a great print publishing program. Now, many of us are creating pages for both print and online distribution. Internal networks, corporate intranets, and the World Wide Web have changed the way page designers think and work.

The PageMaker development team in Seattle has been working hard to deliver Adobe PageMaker 6.5 with a focus on solutions for online publishing. This book is the ideal companion, and Galen Gruman is the perfect guide to help you achieve your best electronic publishing results.

PageMaker 6.5 features new tools and techniques for creating publications for both the Internet and the printed word. You can give your current PageMaker documents new life in electronic form or create all-new pages for both print and the Web.

If you want to take the kinks out of your hyperlinks, spread your GIFs nice and thin, and reign as the duke (or duchess) of URLs, this is the book to help send you on your way.

Lori Birtley
PageMaker Senior Product Marketing Manager
Adobe Systems

Introduction

PageMaker is synonymous with desktop publishing and with good reason. Back in 1985, when Aldus first demonstrated PageMaker 1.0 running on that cute little Mac, the world was in awe of this brilliant new program. Apple Computer suddenly found itself with a new market, thanks to the desktop publishing industry that PageMaker, Adobe Systems PostScript printing language, and the Apple LaserWriter printer jointly spawned.

Other programs were around before PageMaker, such as Studio Software FrontPage for the PC (before Windows even!) and Manhattan Graphics Ready!Set!Go! for the Macintosh, but they're mere historical footnotes today (although Ready!Set!Go! is trying to stage a comeback). PageMaker hung around and soon became the DTP standard for a simple reason: PageMaker is designed to work like real layout artists do — except without the wax and X-Acto knives.

PageMaker has grown to be a lot more than an electronic galley-waxer. It provides the tools you need so that you can make your words attractive, integrate your prose with pictures, and put together a whole document on your own — whether it's a single-page ad, a 16-page newsletter, a 30-page annual report, a 100-page technical manual, or a 400-page book (such as this one). And now it's bringing those qualities to the new frontier of publishing for the Internet.

Why a Book ...For Dummies?

Gee, you're going to produce all sorts of print and Web documents with just one little program? Don't be fooled. The program's not so little. PageMaker is stuffed with features and options, plus plug-in programs that add even more choices to your menus. You aren't going to need most of the PageMaker tools on any single project, and you'll probably be able to live your life not using a third of them. So how do you know which tools to use for your particular kind of project and which are best left for that whiz-bang artist down the hall who produces 3-D posters? Just continue what you're doing now: reading this book.

These pages show you how to create the kind of documents that a novice Web publisher can produce fairly easily. The real fancy stuff is best left to the design gurus who do that kind of work all day long, and they can spend plenty of time reading someone else's book. This book is for you: the person who does more than just use PageMaker.

Why PageMaker for the Web?

With the excitement surrounding the World Wide Web, PageMaker is making the move to be not only a popular desktop publishing tool, but also a versatile tool for online publishing. PageMaker joins the seemingly dozens of Web-publishing tools now available as a widely used program that's been around for more than a decade.

The Web began to develop into a publishing medium — not just a place for electronic mail and all-text correspondence — several years ago, but it was only in 1995 that traditional publishing tools started to be used to create publications for the Web. PageMaker 6.01 had a rudimentary Web export plug-in, and several companies developed Web plug-ins for QuarkXPress. But most of the tools used to publish documents on the Web have had nothing to do with the traditional publishing programs — they're as different as a page-layout program like PageMaker and presentation software like Persuasion or PowerPoint.

Instead of being built with the help of a full-fledged page composition program, most Web pages have been produced from scratch by using HTML (HyperText Markup Language), which is essentially a bunch of computer coding. Before PageMaker 6.5 came along, Web-publishing tools were really just special-purpose programming that produced Web pages instead of software. They forced you to grapple with the somewhat arcane HTML and use it as you would a computer programming language such as C or BASIC. With PageMaker 6.5, you still need some familiarity with HTML, but you no longer need to be a programmer (which leaves you more time for your creative expression).

The best way to create a page layout is in a layout program, and PageMaker is one of the most versatile tools around for doing that kind of work. So, with the layout strengths of PageMaker and its newfound Web-export features, you can do the bulk of your page makeup using a tool that works like you think, and then tweak the results later in an HTML editor. PageMaker 6.5 bridges the gap between the worlds of print publishing and publishing to an audience on the Internet. This opens up Web publishing to artists, designers, and other nonprogrammers. Plus, the enhanced layout and Web publishing capabilities of PageMaker enable you to take existing PageMaker page designs and rework them for the Web rather than starting from scratch.

About This Book

You can approach this book in any one of several ways, depending on how you like your information served up:

- If you're an avid reader — which you probably are if you're reading this part of the book — you can follow the book from cover to cover, building up your expertise as you progress.
- If you're looking for a specific reference on how something works, and you can't find any mention of it in your PageMaker manual (which, like most manuals, is well-intentioned but falls short of being completely helpful), look here. The *...For Dummies* people kindly provide a thorough index to all the wonderful tips and techniques in this book.

- If you already know PageMaker but want a quick refresher on a seldom-used feature, information on this latest version, or a quick take on a feature you've never had to use, flip through the book to see what tidbits are here. Look for the little margin icons, such as the one next to this paragraph. They point out information to make you a more effective PageMaker user. And don't forget to check out the contents pages.
- If you already know PageMaker but are new to the World Wide Web, the book you need is in your hands. The print and online publishing worlds are very different, and an introduction to the Web can help you chart this new territory.
- If you're looking for chitchat to impress your colleagues while you're standing around the water cooler, check out Part VII, which is full of trivia and factoids about PageMaker. The information is even useful for when you get back to your desk.

No matter which way you read the book, enjoy it. Publishing (whether for print or for the Web) is a creative experience, often fun but sometimes frantic. When the fun stops, take a break, read a chapter, learn a neat trick; then go back to your project with renewed vigor.

A Book for the Both of Us

This book is for both Windows and Macintosh users. Just about two-thirds of all Web pages are now created on the Macintosh and the rest on Windows, although Windows 95 users are jumping onto the Web in increasing numbers. Approximately 60 percent of PageMaker users are Macintosh-based and 40 percent are Windows-based, at least among registered customers in the United States.

Some software tools (such as Adobe PageMill) are Mac only, while others (such as Asymetrix WebPublisher) are Windows only. But most of the popular tools — including Adobe PageMaker, QuarkXPress, SoftQuad HoTMetaL Pro, Microsoft Internet Explorer, Netscape Navigator, ClarisWorks, Microsoft Word, Corel WordPerfect, CorelDraw, Macromedia FreeHand, Adobe Photoshop, Microsoft Excel, Qualcomm Eudora Pro, Macromedia Director, Adobe Persuasion, Microsoft PowerPoint, Microsoft FoxPro, and Claris FileMaker Pro — are on both platforms in compatible versions.

What this all means is that no matter which computer you use, PageMaker 6.5 and the techniques in this book apply to you directly. Much fuss has been made over which system works better — Macintosh or Windows — but this years-old rivalry doesn't matter here. The system for some of us and the one for the rest of us both do the job when you need to create layouts for the Web. So, why don't we all just get along? We've got Web pages to make!

How to Use This Book

To make sure that you understand what I'm talking about, this book uses several conventions to indicate what you're supposed to type, which menus you're supposed to use, and which keys you're supposed to press.

If I describe a message or something you type on screen, it looks like this:

> **Insert Disk 2 into the internal drive**

Menu commands are listed like this:

> File⇨Print

This means you pull down the File menu (with your mouse) and then choose the Print command.

Keyboard shortcuts are listed like this:

> Option+⌘+P (Macintosh)
>
> Ctrl+Alt+P (Windows)

This means you hold the Option key, the ⌘ (Command) key, and the P key simultaneously with a Mac. (Use the Ctrl key, the Alt key, and the P key simultaneously with Windows.) An easy way to use the keyboard shortcut is to hold the Option and ⌘ keys and then press P. Whichever way you type a keyboard shortcut, don't press the + key. (In the PageMaker manual, the Mac keyboard shortcut is indicated as Command + Option + P.)

The Mac and Windows keyboards are almost the same, as are the shortcuts for most functions in most programs. The Ctrl key on Windows is usually the same as the ⌘ (Command) key on the Macintosh, even though the Mac has its own separate Ctrl key that is rarely used. The Alt key on Windows is usually the same as the Option key on the Mac. (This book gives both Mac and Windows shortcuts.)

How This Book Is Organized

I've divided *PageMaker 6.5 For Dummies, Internet Edition* into seven parts, not counting this introduction, to make it easy for you to find the material you need right away. Each part has no more than three or four chapters, so you don't have to worry about making a lifelong commitment to finding out something.

Part I: Welcome to Publishing for the Internet

Web publishing is a new field — it's been just a couple of years since the Internet became a popular communications medium — so there's a lot to learn about publishing for the Web, no matter which tools you use. The two chapters in this part help you understand how the Web differs from the printed word and how to make sense of the many tools you can use to create your Web pages.

Part II: Getting Started with PageMaker 6.5

Once you're introduced to the basic Web-publishing issues, you're primed to use PageMaker to create your Web documents. This part explains exactly what you need to do to get PageMaker 6.5 up and running and then how to set up your page parameters.

Part III: Putting Words in Print and Online

Once you're actually in PageMaker, you have a blank screen to fill up. Here's where the fun starts: You can begin creating your document! This part delves into the most fundamental component of your Web page: the text it contains. You find out how to get text on your page, how to format it, modify it, and correct it.

Part IV: Pumping Up Your Layout Power

The most important — but most challenging — part of creating a Web page (or a printed page for that matter) is designing an effective layout, something the reader can easily follow. This part explains how to make your Web pages the envy of your competition and how to master PageMaker to get more of your work done in less time.

Part V: Say It with Pictures

Text is nice, but images are what grab the reader's attention (just cruise the Web for proof of that). In this part, you find out how to import and work with pictures, as well as how to pick the best colors for the Web.

Part VI: Weaving a Web Page

Whether you're an experienced print designer new to the Web, or someone new to desktop publishing, this part gives you the essential lowdown on managing hypertext links, fine-tuning your pages in an HTML editor, and other Web-publishing tasks I bet you've never heard of.

Part VII: The Part of Tens

This section of the book is the shop-talk part you can use to impress friends and family. It's chock-full of tidbits, advice, trivia, and other information about PageMaker and how to use it. Some of this stuff may seem obvious, and some not so obvious, but all of it is based on remembering those little details and lessons that only experience can provide. Save yourself some bumps along the road and check out this part.

Icons Used in This Book

To alert you to special passages of text that you especially may want to read (or avoid), a bunch of modern hieroglyphics (proudly known as *icons*) pop up throughout the book to help guide you.

Here's some information that you may want to scribble on a sticky note and glue to your monitor, because you never know when the information is going to come in handy and save you some time or effort. Look for these in your spare time.

If you know PageMaker 6.0, you already know much of PageMaker 6.5. This icon alerts you to something that works differently or is new in Version 6.5.

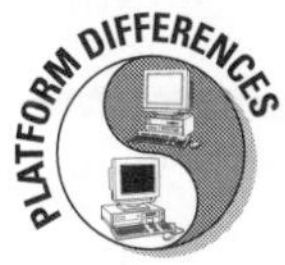

Adobe has done a great job of making PageMaker for the Macintosh and for Windows work as much alike as possible. That's why both Mac and Windows users can glean useful information from this book and why I was able to alternate illustrations of Mac and Windows screens. But not everything can be made identical between the two platforms, and this icon alerts you to such differences.

Throughout this book is information on how Web publishing and print publishing are alike and how they are different. When those variations really matter, you see this icon to help you reorient your thinking from print to the Web.

Here's something you need to remember but may easily forget, because the information may seem unimportant at first but turns out to be needed later on.

Here's an example of something you may want to avoid. (Not that this icon is bad or anything.) This icon highlights one of those nitty-gritty techno-details that you don't have to know but may come in handy if (a) something goes wrong and you have to ask an expert for advice or (b) you want to impress your boss.

Not everything works the way you want it to, or at least the way you expect. These icons let you know when an action (or lack thereof) may cause a problem, such as losing your data.

Not everything works. . . . Oh, I already said that. Anyhow, these icons are a cross between tips and warnings; they describe ways in which PageMaker acts oddly or incorrectly. You're in no danger of losing data, but you may be unnecessarily perplexed. This information shows you how to get things back to normal or work around the oddity.

Where to First?

This book is designed to appeal to a variety of reading styles. So, where should you start? Wherever you want. What if you have a question about a specific topic? Go to the Index and track down the answer that way. What if you want to know more about one type of feature? Use the Table of Contents to steer you to the appropriate chapter. What if you're experienced in print layout but face the new challenge of creating Web documents? Start with Chapters 1 and 2, and jump to Chapter 6. And, if you're new to the whole shebang, just move on to the next page and read at a comfortable pace.

Part I

Welcome to Publishing for the Internet

"SINCE WE GOT IT, HE HASN'T MOVED FROM THAT SPOT FOR ELEVEN STRAIGHT DAYS. ODDLY ENOUGH THEY CALL THIS 'GETTING UP AND RUNNING' ON THE INTERNET."

In this part . . .

Imagine that you're taking a cross-country trip. You aren't going to just hop in the Rav4 or on your moped and toddle off. No, first you want to figure out what you need to take with you, and then you want to figure out how to get there — maybe by taking a taxi to the airport or simply piling your camping gear into the Westfalia. Likewise, before you launch into creating a Web page, spend a few minutes to figure out exactly what you want to accomplish and then how you want to do it.

The World Wide Web is, after all, a new frontier. In just a couple of years, Web publishing has gone from a little-known computer gimmick for geeks to the hottest communications ticket around. It's a brave new world out there, and fortunately, an old standby like PageMaker is ready to help. The first part of this book describes the similarities and differences between print and Web publishing, acquaints you with terms like *HTML* and *browser,* and talks about the tools you need to create pages bound for the Web.

Chapter 1

So, You Want to Be a Web Publisher?

In This Chapter

- How Web and print pages are alike
- How Web and print pages are different
- How HTML works to create Web pages
- How to plan the length of your Web document
- How browsers affect the look of your Web pages

Face it. You're a print junkie. You crave the written word. Heck, you've got this book in your hands right now. It all probably started with bedtime fairy tales, then progressed to Dr. Seuss (*the* twentieth century master of the rhyming couplet). The next thing you know you're hiding comic books in your underwear drawer (okay, so maybe you still do). Sure, you read sometimes because you *have* to. You cram for exams. You answer those memos, review those reports, look to see if Publishers Clearing House has already Made You a Winner! You discovered magazine racks are the new singles spot of the '90s. Why, you might even be responsible for producing some of this printed stuff.

Now the Internet has you hooked and it's come time for you to join the expanding ranks of World Wide Web publishers. But unless you're among the very techno-hippest residents of the online universe, you probably don't know the Web anywhere as well as you know print. The notion of publishing in cyberspace can be intimidating, and you may end up trying to fit a square peg (print) into a round hole (the Web) when you begin to design your Web pages (which is not to say that the printed word is for squares).

Although the Web may seem new and strange, in many ways it should seem familiar. The process of learning how to publish for the Web isn't as difficult as, say, venturing from magazine design to TV production. You're still dealing essentially with text and pictures that people read and digest, even though the information appears on a computer screen, not on the printed page, and can include animation and sound effects as part of the package.

The World Wide Web (or Web for short) is a hypermedia system that lets you cruise through the many words, pictures, and sounds on the Internet. Other systems exist for accessing information through the Internet, but the Web has become the most popular, largely because of Web *browsers* that enable you to simply point and click to link to other places on the Internet.

Planning Your Publication

Many of the fundamentals of creating a publication are the same for the Web as they are for print. I'm thinking of the nuts-and-bolts publication planning and organization that's invisible to the reader but is the skeleton upon which the publication is built.

- The first step in planning any publication is deciding what you're trying to communicate. Whether you're writing the Great American Paperback, a letter to Grandma, or publishing a Web page for the whole wide world — you still have to sit down and figure out what it is you want to say.
- Next, you have to decide who it is you're writing for. What you tell an audience of engineers about a new product, for instance, is going to be very different from what you tell a group of teenage consumers. The group to which you focus your publication is called your *target audience,* and identifying that group is essential to communicating successfully. For both print and the Web, this step is vital.
- You need to organize your information in some sort of logical sequence, with the broadest information at the top of your document and more detailed information following in order by importance (such as for news stories or business announcements), by time (for events or schedules), alphabetically (for a directory or listing), or by some other appropriate order (such as by region for a cookbook). Try scratching out an outline first on paper; it might seem old-fashioned, but it works for me.

- Finally, you need to determine just how much information you want to provide. This decision affects the length of the entire publication, as well as the length of each section (whether it's a sidebar, a series of paragraphs, a book chapter, or a linked page on a Web site). Figuring out how long each part of your document needs to be will help you better organize your material visually. It may sound obvious, but this step is critical, and many a publication in print and online failed because no one figured out how long the darn thing should be.

Planning a Web publication involves this same sort of process. Each page of your Web document needs a message worth communicating, a target audience, a logical organization, and a defined level of detail.

I'll use something near and dear to me (this book) as an example of how to organize information. Notice how the major sections, called *parts*, group together related information based on a particular topic (such as starting out, dealing with text, planning layouts, and so forth). Several chapters exist within each part, each detailing an aspect of the part's bigger topic. Then, within each chapter are sections and subsections that further distinguish related components. This kind of *hierarchy* (now, there's word to throw around at your next clambake) is typical in almost any publication — print or Web.

Because this book has to communicate lots of information on a number of areas, I grouped similar information together to make it easier to digest one big concept at a time. I also broke big pieces of information into smaller, more focused topics to make them less overwhelming and to make finding specific information easier.

Just as there's more to an animal's innards than its skeleton, a publication's fundamentals are more than this high-falutin'-sounding hierarchy. Consider this book again. I've used some other devices to help keep the information distinct yet related — icons in the page margins that help you find specific kinds of information that appear throughout the book, sidebars on topics not directly related but still relevant to the subject at hand, and the index and table of contents to help you navigate around this book quickly and read it in any order you want.

Now compare a Web page with a print page (shown in Figures 1-1 and 1-2) to see how organizing a document for either medium is accomplished in similar ways. The pages aren't too fancy, so you can focus on fundamentals.

The organization of Figures 1-1 and 1-2 is basically the same: general information up front and more specific information following, bulleted lists, a title and subtitles, and information grouped by topic. (More information was crammed into the print page, obviously; I explain that in the sidebar "How long should a Web page be?") Many other ways to create a print or a Web version of this example exist, but the basic principles apply for either.

Web and Print Pages: Just Alike or Way Different?

Before you dive in and start creating Web pages, you need to be aware of the basic differences between print and online publications to create the most effective and interesting Web pages you can. If you're making the transition from print to Web, you may need to get some of your old assumptions out of

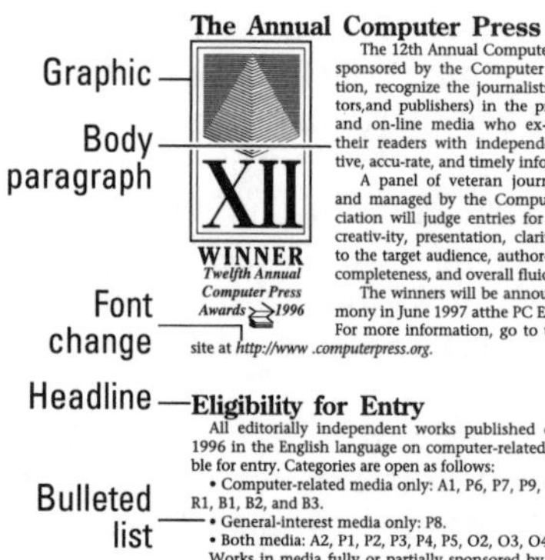

The Annual Computer Press Awards

WINNER
Twelfth Annual Computer Press Awards 1996

The 12th Annual Computer Press Awards, sponsored by the Computer Press Association, recognize the journalists (authors, editors,and publishers) in the print, broadcast, and on-line media who ex-cel in serving their readers with independent, authoritative, accu-rate, and timely information.

A panel of veteran journalists selected and managed by the Computer Press Association will judge entries for the following: creativ-ity, presentation, clarity, significance to the target audience, author-ity, timeliness, completeness, and overall fluidity.

The winners will be announced at a ceremony in June 1997 atthe PC Expo show.

For more information, go to the CPA's Web site at *http://www .computerpress.org*.

Eligibility for Entry

All editorially independent works published or broadcast in 1996 in the English language on computer-related topics are eligible for entry. Categories are open as follows:

- Computer-related media only: A1, P6, P7, P9, O1, O5, O6, T3, R1, B1, B2, and B3.
- General-interest media only: P8.
- Both media: A2, P1, P2, P3, P4, P5, O2, O3, O4, T1, and T2.

Works in media fully or partially sponsored by a vendor, work whose content is commissioned or determined by a vendor, or work produced by a vendor is *not* eligible. NOTE: Having technical reviews by a vendor or, in the case of a book, a vendor's "official"endorsement does not disqualify an entry if the author or publisher retains full editorial control.

Entry Packaging Instructions

To be eligible for judging, entries must follow these packaging guidelines. Photocopies of the entry form are acceptable. NOTE: In no cases will ring-bound, plastic-bound, board-mounted, covered, folder-bound, sheathed, or other such packaged entries be accepted.

All entries must be submitted as two copies, with one entry form per copy. The CPA cannot make copies for you, either of the submissions themselves or of entry forms.

Individual Works: For print-based media, submit 2 copies each of all articles (tearsheets or photocopies), such as newspaper reports or magazine reviews. Staple (preferred) or clip an entry form to each copy. For online media, submit 2 copies each of all articles (on 3.5-inch disk in HTML format). For broadcast media, submit 2 copies each of all segments (on VHS tape for TV or audio tape for radio).

Overall Works: Submit 2 copies each of any 3 different issues of, for example, a magazine, radio series, or on-line publication. Attach an entry form with a rubberband to each set.

For categories P6 (magazine) and P9 (newsletter), the 3 issues must be consecutive.

For category A1 (new publication), the 3 issues must be consecutive if the entry is from the print medium. Online and broadcast entries in this category must be sites/shows or regular segments focused on computer-related issues.

For category A2 (columnist), submit 2 copies each of 5 different columns. Entries may contain material from multiple publications if written by the same columnist.

Print: Photocopies and tear sheets are equally acceptable; however, we prefer photocopies rather than newsprint clips, especially for stories with multiple jumps (since the thin newspaper columns combined with newsprint's flimsiness increase the risk of an entry being damaged or lost during judging). Cross out unrelated material that is clearly not an advertisement. Stapled entries are preferred; use binder clips or large paper clips rather than small paper clips if staples are unavailable or insufficient for binding.

Broadcast: These mav be stand-alone shows or regular segments in a larger show. Submit 2 copies of each entry on VHS videotape or standard audiocassette. Follow the instructions for Individual Works or Overall Works, as appropriate, except rubberband the entry forms to entries. For individual works, do not combine multiple entries on one tape.

On-Line: Submit 2 copies of entries on 3.5-inch disks in HTML format. Follow the instructions for Individual Works or Overall Works, as appropriate. Use a binder clip to attach the entry form to each copy. For individual works, do not combine multiple entries on one disk. For category O5 (site), provide free access from February 1 to April 1, and indicate the URL or location on your entry forms.

Books: Submit 2 copies of the book with an entry form taped or stapled to the front of each copy's title page. Each book may be entered in only one category. Books must have a copyright date of 1996, no matter when released.

Entry Fees

CPA members: Individual members may submit 5 entries at no charge; corporate members may submit 20 entries at no charge. Additional entries cost US$35 (CDN$55) each. The entry form must include your CPA member ID (which is found on your CPA membership card) or a CPA membership application with 1997 dues (US$75 or CDN$105); contact the CPA administrator for corporate membership dues and applications.

Non-CPA members: Entries cost US$35 (CDN$55) each.

Payment methods: U.S. or Canadian funds on a check drawn on a U.S. or Canadian bank or via international money order.

Categories

ALL MEDIA

A1. Overall New Publication

The best new publications (in any medium) are those that find an unmet need and fill it better than their competitors. Winners will display a balance of fresh perspective, editorial excellence, and outstanding design. To be eligible, the publication, show, or site must have first appeared on or after January 1, 1996.

A2. Overall Columnist

This category, which includes print, broadcast, and online en-tries, recognizes a regularly appearing column by a single author in either computer-related or general-interest publications. Personality and style, knowledge, integrity, and impact on the audience and industry are all key considerations. The author is judged for merit as an overall columnist, and not for individual submissions. (A columnist who writes for multiple publications may send entries from more than one publication as separate entries.)

do submit: The best of a columnist's regularly appearing work.

do not submit: Editorials, guest editorials, or opinion columns that appear irregularly or that appeared only once.

PRINT

P1.Individual News Story

News stories are almost always triggered by a recent or unique event, and are judged on their accuracy, newsworthiness, and relevance to the audience. While the News Story category is not limited to breaking news, all entries should introduce new information and

Questions on the Awards or the CPA? Contact Michele Zatorski, CPA administrator, at 631 Henmar Dr., Landing, NJ 07850; phone (201) 398-7300, fax (201) 398-3888. Because of the volume of inquiries, the CPA may not be able to respond to inquiries in the week before the entry due date. http://www.computerpress.org

Figure 1-1: Components of a simple print page. A Web version of this appears in Figure 1-2.

the way. Those old assumptions about producing print publications often don't work on the Web, and using them can turn off potential Web readers. Two examples follow:

- Print publishers assume that people read text from beginning to end, at least within sections of a book or article. But, on the Web, readers jump around, using "hot spots" (called *hypertext links*) within text that let them move to entirely different stories from the one they were just reading. So the assumption of a top-to-bottom read just doesn't fly on the Web.
- Print publishers often use devices like multiple columns to make text easier to read. But, on the Web, multiple columns are often harder to read for a couple of reasons: If the columns extend past the bottom edge of the screen, the reader has to scroll down to finish the column and then back up to start the next one — and that's way too much of a

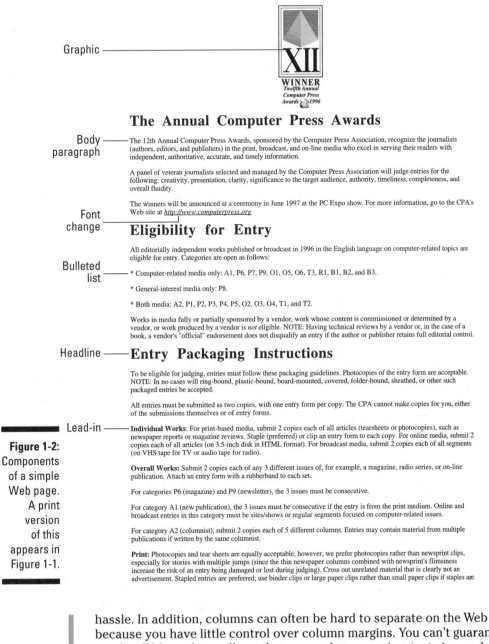

The Annual Computer Press Awards

The 12th Annual Computer Press Awards, sponsored by the Computer Press Association, recognize the journalists (authors, editors, and publishers) in the print, broadcast, and on-line media who excel in serving their readers with independent, authoritative, accurate, and timely information.

A panel of veteran journalists selected and managed by the Computer Press Association will judge entries for the following: creativity, presentation, clarity, significance to the target audience, authority, timeliness, completeness, and overall fluidity.

The winners will be announced at a ceremony in June 1997 at the PC Expo show. For more information, go to the CPA's Web site at http://www.computerpress.org

Eligibility for Entry

All editorially independent works published or broadcast in 1996 in the English language on computer-related topics are eligible for entry. Categories are open as follows:

* Computer-related media only: A1, P6, P7, P9, O1, O5, O6, T3, R1, B1, B2, and B3.

* General-interest media only: P8.

* Both media: A2, P1, P2, P3, P4, P5, O2, O3, O4, T1, and T2.

Works in media fully or partially sponsored by a vendor, work whose content is commissioned or determined by a vendor, or work produced by a vendor is *not* eligible. NOTE: Having technical reviews by a vendor or, in the case of a book, a vendor's "official" endorsement does not disqualify an entry if the author or publisher retains full editorial control.

Entry Packaging Instructions

To be eligible for judging, entries must follow these packaging guidelines. Photocopies of the entry form are acceptable. NOTE: In no cases will ring-bound, plastic-bound, board-mounted, covered, folder-bound, sheathed, or other such packaged entries be accepted.

All entries must be submitted as two copies, with one entry form per copy. The CPA cannot make copies for you, either of the submissions themselves or of entry forms.

Individual Works: For print-based media, submit 2 copies each of all articles (tearsheets or photocopies), such as newspaper reports or magazine reviews. Staple (preferred) or clip an entry form to each copy. For online media, submit 2 copies each of all articles (on 3.5-inch disk in HTML format). For broadcast media, submit 2 copies each of all segments (on VHS tape for TV or audio tape for radio).

Overall Works: Submit 2 copies each of any 3 different issues of, for example, a magazine, radio series, or on-line publication. Attach an entry form with a rubberband to each set.

For categories P6 (magazine) and P9 (newsletter), the 3 issues must be consecutive.

For category A1 (new publication), the 3 issues must be consecutive if the entry is from the print medium. Online and broadcast entries in this category must be sites/shows or regular segments focused on computer-related issues.

For category A2 (columnist), submit 2 copies each of 5 different columns. Entries may contain material from multiple publications if written by the same columnist.

Print: Photocopies and tear sheets are equally acceptable; however, we prefer photocopies rather than newsprint clips, especially for stories with multiple jumps (since the thin newspaper columns combined with newsprint's flimsiness increase the risk of an entry being damaged or lost during judging). Cross out unrelated material that is clearly not an advertisement. Stapled entries are preferred; use binder clips or large paper clips rather than small paper clips if staples are

Figure 1-2: Components of a simple Web page. A print version of this appears in Figure 1-1.

hassle. In addition, columns can often be hard to separate on the Web because you have little control over column margins. You can't guarantee that Web readers will see the same column spacing, text size, and other key visual guideposts that you see when creating the page. (Later in this chapter, I explain why Web pages can look different depending on what you're using to read them.)

Web documents differ from print documents in two main ways that seem almost contradictory:

- Web documents are dynamic. When you click into hypertext links (your connections to other Web pages), you can instantly hopscotch throughout the document or around the Internet to points of interest, a process akin to plucking out cue cards. Printed publications, on the other hand, are bound, self-contained units that lend themselves to a linear read.
- The average Web document (at least the do-it-yourself kind, not the Web-page-designer-as-animator kind) tends to be static, often with long columns of text, interrupted with only a limited variety of graphics, and not much in the way of layout, which makes it seem more like a newsletter than a magazine. The text and graphics styling of printed publications, by comparison, are limited only by the boundaries of their pages.

How can this contradiction be true? Read on.

How long should a Web page be?

Many Web pages, especially the early ones, were no more than long lists of information. Until recently, the Web didn't easily support multicolumn documents, graphics with text wrapping around them, and all that other layout razzmatazz because large numbers of these elements increased the *downloading* time (the time it takes to get a document off the Web and on to your screen). This was so much the case that Web readers gave up and went and surfed elsewhere. Pages of text tended to look like the one in Figure 1-2, which shows about a sixth of an entire page contained in that particular Web document. (The print version is about twice as space-efficient as the Web version because Web text has to be made bigger because small text is hard to read on a computer monitor.)

Look again at Figures 1-1 and 1-2: You can actually see more information in Figure 1-1 than in Figure 1-2, even though the pages are the same size. The reason is that you can get away with using smaller type (such as 8 or 9 points) on paper and still keep the text legible. (On the Web, 10 or 12 points is a typical font size.)

Studies have shown only 5 percent of people who read newspapers get past the first few paragraphs of a story. You can blame television, or you can just say paragraph after paragraph of textual matter just isn't that exciting. The situation isn't much different on the Web. Because people hate to read long lists, smart Web-page designers break information into small chunks. These smaller pieces of information are connected by a chain of hypertext links that let you hop from connection to connection as the mood suits you. Print documents, on the other hand, use lots of headlines, titles, graphics, and other elements to keep you moving through lengthy text in either a linear fashion or by skipping around (like the elements do in this book).

The upper-left window in Figure 1-3 shows the page from Figure 1-2 redone in a style that's much more "hyperlink-y" (which has nothing to do with the adorable metal spring that rolls down staircases). The information provided in each document is largely the same, but Figure 1-3 presents it in a way that more greatly resembles a typical Web page. Neither the Figure 1-2 or Figure 1-3 style is inherently better than the other, they're simply used differently. The following are the strengths and weaknesses of the two approaches shown in Figures 1-2 and 1-3:

- In Figure 1-2, the designer assumes that the information is critical enough that people need to read through the whole document, or at least scroll through the text. If a specific piece of information is needed (in this case, the instructions for entering stories for a specific award), this format can be a bit frustrating to use because the reader has to scroll through pages and pages of material to reach the bit of information needed.

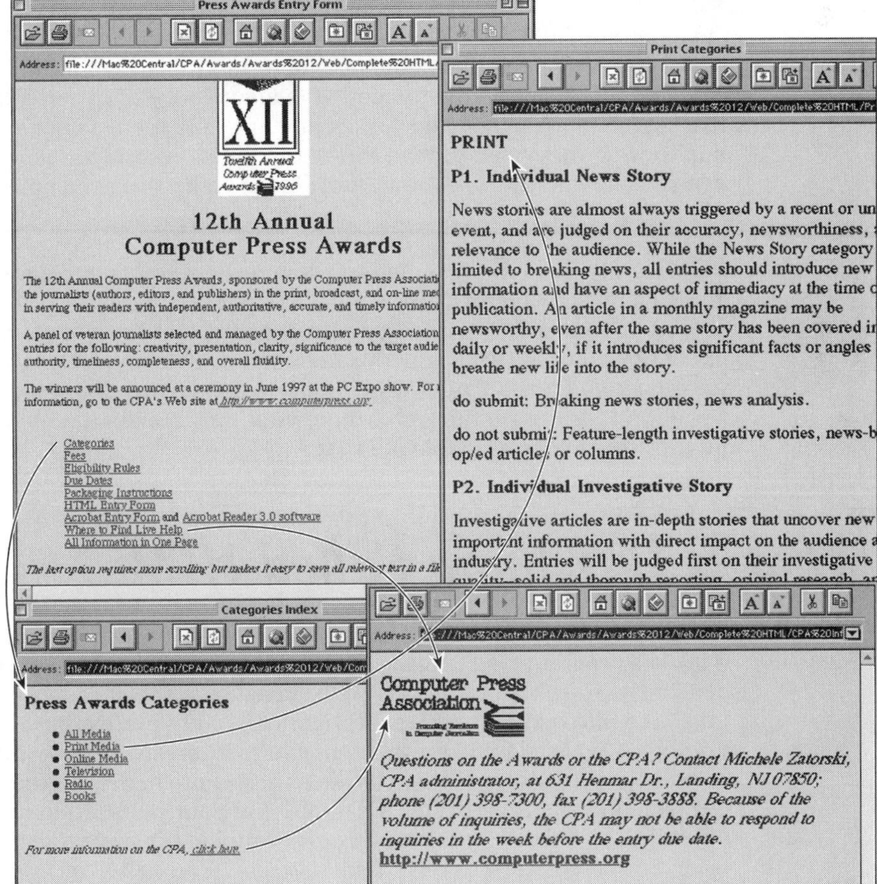

Figure 1-3: The same basic information from Figure 1-2 as it looks with a sequence of hypertext links.

- In Figure 1-3, the designer assumes that readers may want to jump to the specific information relevant to them rather than scroll through all the instructions. In this example, that's great if most people are applying for only a couple of awards, but what if readers are greedy and want to enter for a whole bunch of awards? All that jumping around just for a few wall plaques can become tedious. In which case, they'd probably prefer to scan the entire text in order. What's shown in Figure 1-3 isn't just one page — the document consists of several Web pages linked together; you're seeing just a few of them (a reader, of course, would see one page at a time).

The entry form shown in Figures 1-1 through 1-3 is a real one. The print version (Figure 1-1) was mailed to entrants to fill out. The headlines make this version pretty easy to use and the layout is compact and linear. But for the Web, the awards committee posted two versions: an HTML version with hyperlinks, and a downloadable version designed to be "pulled down" from the Web, read, and printed out from the user's computer. From there, the document could be mailed back with the entry.

Wait a minute. Did I say two versions were posted? I meant three. The page creators later decided that some people would prefer one big file to scroll through on the Web. So the document in Figure 1-2 was hyperlinked to the main screen (shown in Figure 1-3), giving online readers a choice to either jump to what they need or read the whole thing on screen. See, you can have your nonfat cake and eat it, too! (More on how to accomplish this is in Part VI.)

Web documents can be designed to allow readers to acquire information through a line-by-line read, or by a hop, skip, and a jump, so you can choose the best approach for your message. Although print documents have this kind of flexibility — that's why this book has a table of contents and an index to let you turn to specific sections — this mixing of formats isn't as easy in print as it is on the Web, where your only real limitations are time and the size of your available file space.

What Is This Thing Called HTML?

Web documents rely heavily on the *HT* in HTML (*HyperText Markup Language*). HTML is a programming language that makes it possible for your pages to be used on the World Wide Web. HTML is based on a special set of codes embedded into text that add text formatting and hypertext links. When you click into a hypertext link for the item you're interested in, the information you want pops up from a Web document anywhere in the Internet. Within your own document, it divides the content of your publication into many separate pieces that you can connect by jumping from one link to another.

Imagine going to an art museum with a separate room for each artist. Every room has four doors, each leading into an adjoining room. The path you take through the museum isn't necessarily the same as someone else's chosen path, so you are likely to end up seeing a different set of paintings and artists in a different order than another person. You may see some of the same artists another person sees, or you may not. (If you've ever been to the Chicago Art Institute, you'll know exactly what I mean!) It's numerous options like these that make "surfing" the Web the ultimate in customized reading, although you might not realize you're customizing what you see.

In a hypertext document (such as on the Web), you're traveling along your own personalized reading path.

Who's the Fairest Browser of Them All?

Much of the text formatting you rely on when designing print documents does a disappearing act when it comes time for its journey to the Web. Chapter 6 provides examples of formatting that runs into trouble along the way to the Web — the mixed results of using columns, the lack of choice of specific fonts, and the inability to do sophisticated formatting like text wraps.

Part of the reason for this is that HTML is a primitive formatting language — more primitive than that of even very early PageMaker. Another reason is that each Web *browser* interprets HTML differently (a browser is the software that lets you view Web documents). This means that what you see on your browser doesn't necessarily look exactly like what I see on my browser, or what your Uncle Samson sees on his browser.

Even on the newest versions of the three most popular browsers — Netscape Navigator, Microsoft Internet Explorer, and America Online (which uses a version of Internet Explorer) — the same page is going to look different on each one. The page is also going to look different in Windows than on a Mac. Older versions of browsers display pages differently than newer ones. Not only are some newer features like table formatting not going to display correctly on older browser versions, but the look of text may vary from one version of the browser to another. The width of the browser window also affects column widths and how text lines *wrap* (move from line to line). To make the whole process even more complicated, many browsers let individual users set their own preferred fonts and sizes.

What this all means is that Web-page font sizes are going to change, columns are going to shift, and text may appear in different fonts depending on the equipment being used to cruise the Internet. That means your documents probably won't look exactly like what you create in PageMaker, or after you tweak them in an HTML editor, once those documents are on the Web.

These discrepancies are unavoidable. My advice is to avoid spending too much of your time fine-tuning type sizes and column placements. Instead, focus on the organization of your content and making your arrangements simple so that your publication can survive the trip to the Web.

Notice that I haven't said anything about graphic images changing in appearance depending on where they're viewed. Pictures also can look different from browser to browser and platform to platform, although the difference is usually confined to varying color hues (see Chapter 15 for more on this). Because Web graphics are *bitmapped images* — made up of a predefined, fixed series of dots — the likelihood of your browser making your images look any different than they do in PageMaker, Photoshop, or Corel Photo-Paint is practically impossible.

A tour of differences

How different can the same page look from browser to browser? Examine Figures 1-4 through 1-9. They show the same page as it appears in America Online 3.0, Netscape Navigator 3.0, and Internet Explorer 2.0 for both Windows 95 and Macintosh, all at their default settings. These browsers are updated over time, so the version you own may be a more current one than was available when this book was written.

If you look carefully at Figures 1-4 through 1-9, you'll notice that the formatting varies somewhat from browser to browser and platform to platform. (I scrolled up or down a bit on each screen to better point out the differences.) You can see that the text size varies, as well as the positioning of the columns.

- The size of the text and the font it's displayed in differ widely. Some browsers display text at a larger, more readable size — but at the price of showing less information. The most efficient at displaying text are America Online and Navigator for Mac, while the least efficient at text display are America Online and Navigator for Windows.
- The width of the index column varies significantly, from too skinny (such as America Online for Windows 95 and Internet Explorer for both Mac and Windows) to pleasantly wide (such as Navigator for Windows).
- Column spacing varies a little from browser to browser, and in all cases columns are a bit too close to each other.
- The text efficiency noted earlier is really noticeable in America Online for Mac and Navigator for Mac — you can actually see an extra story on your screen, plus much more of the index than in other browsers.
- The spacing around graphics varies, with America Online for Mac and Navigator for Mac and Windows adding more space above graphics than the other browsers. The extra space helps to separate stories a little better.

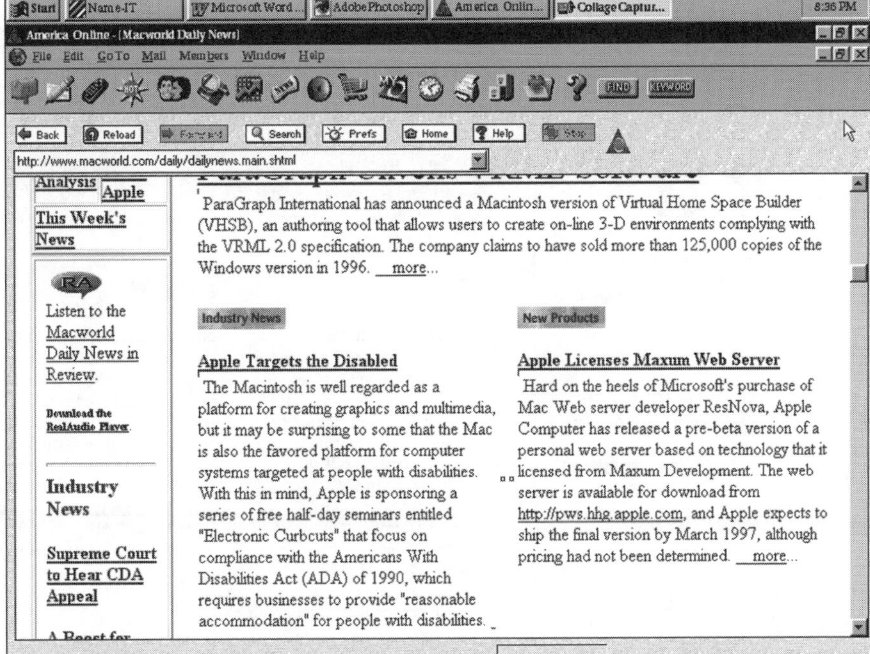

Figure 1-4: The view of a Web page in America Online 3.0 for Windows 95.

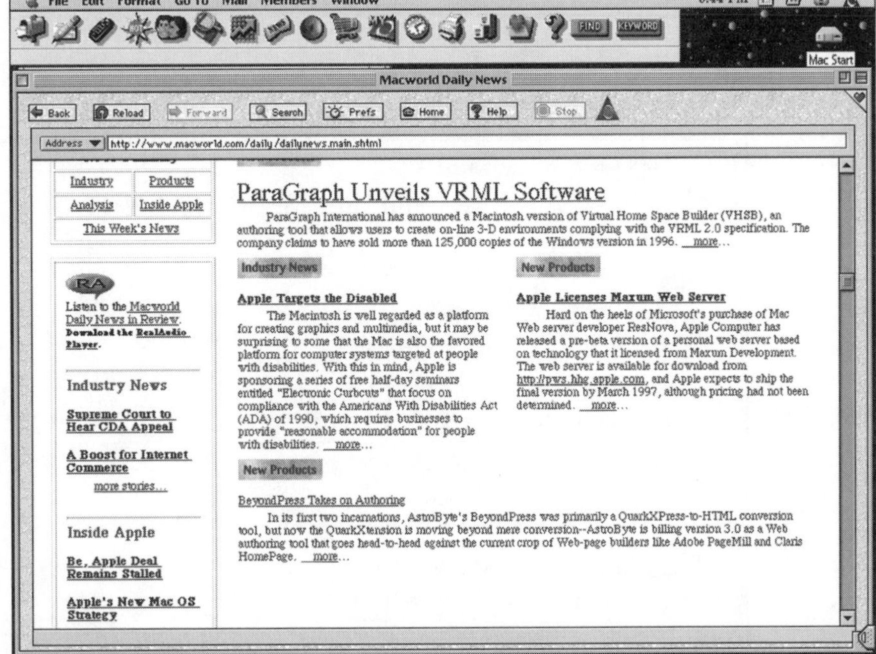

Figure 1-5: The view of a Web page in America Online 3.0 for Macintosh.

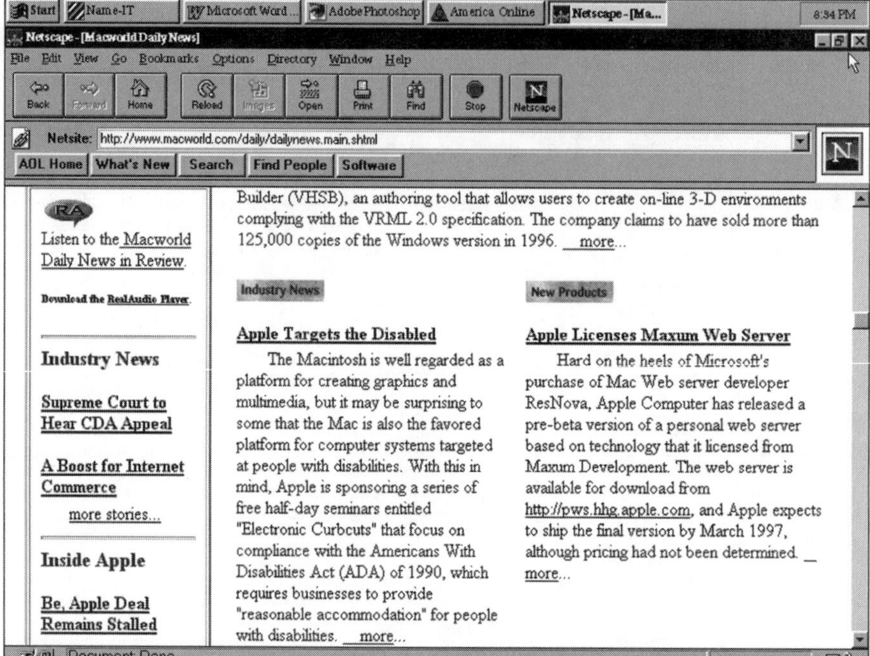

Figure 1-6: The view of a Web page in Netscape Navigator 3.0 for Windows 95.

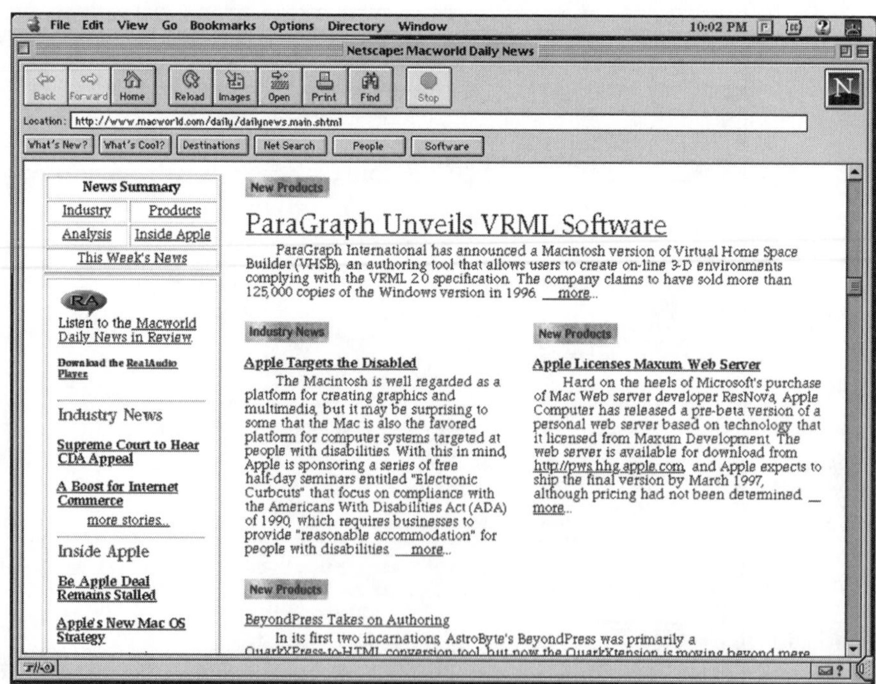

Figure 1-7: The view of a Web page in Netscape Navigator 3.0 for Macintosh.

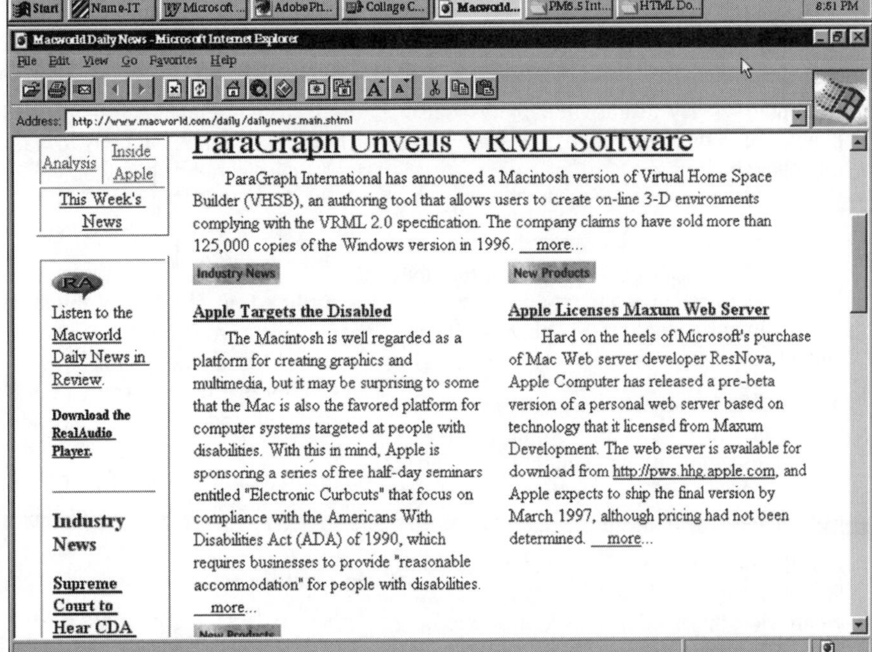

Figure 1-8: The view of a Web page in Microsoft Internet Explorer 2.0 for Windows 95.

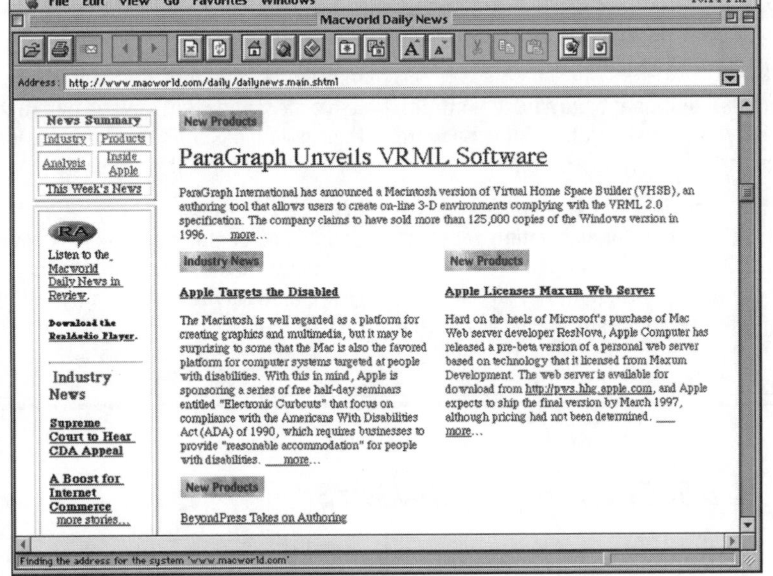

Figure 1-9: The view of a Web page in Microsoft Internet Explorer 2.0 for Macintosh.

You, too, can use Web publishing lingo

To become savvy to the vocabulary used in publishing to the Internet, just cruise through the following terms:

Browser A program that lets you view, deliver, and receive information and files over the Internet. A *browser plug-in* is a program that the browser uses to add functionality, such as the display of animation (Shockwave, for example) or motion video (such as QuickTime).

Internet The global network of computers that supports the means for computer users around the world to communicate. It includes the World Wide Web, Internet Relay Chat, Gopher, news groups, and FTP.

World Wide Web *The Web* for short, this portion of the Internet lets computer users anywhere view information and exchange data. It is based on the Internet's *HyperText Transfer Protocol* (HTTP), which allows for the display of documents on the Web. The `http://` at the start of a Web address signals a computer's browser that the person is using the Web portion of the Internet.

Web page A document viewed on screen through a Web browser, rather than in a word processor or page-layout program.

HTML The *HyperText Markup Language* is a set of specifications for formatting text and inserting graphics on a Web page. The HTML language is fairly primitive (it doesn't support fonts and symbols that PageMaker users take for granted) because the first Internet users in the 1970s were on mainframes, DOS PCs, and UNIX workstations, and HTML was written to take their limited display capabilities into account. Now that Windows and the Mac rule the PC world, HTML is slowly evolving to support richer formatting.

Hyperlink One of the cool things about Web pages is that you can create hypertext, which creates links to other pages or even other Web sites. The text usually appears in blue and is underlined, and clicking it just once with your mouse immediately transports you to a new location (the hyperlink's destination). You can navigate the Web quickly, jumping from one place to another with the click of your mouse.

Internet Relay Chat This part of the Internet allows a form of live conferencing among groups of people, who can simultaneously read each other's text messages.

Gopher The Internet's search function, which lets you find files on the Internet.

News groups These are essentially bulletin boards on the Internet, where people can leave messages that anyone can read and add their own messages to. The news groups are arranged by topical interest.

FTP The *File Transfer Protocol* is one way that people and companies make files available for transfer from their computer to your computer. (The other way is to have a hyperlink to a file on their computer.)

Customizing browsers

If you've read the preceding sections of this chapter, you know that browsers can make Web pages look a little different than what their creators intended. Here's a chance to get even — you can call some of the shots on how your browser displays pages. The following shows you some options to customize the way the three major browsers display pages.

America Online 3.0

American Online allows you really only one custom option: You can ask for images to be drawn after the entire page has been downloaded to your computer. This is a more efficient process than watching the graphics files gradually materialize on screen as they arrive. You can do this through the Prefs button in the AOL browser, which is located just below the box for the URL line (the Internet address box). This takes you to the Preferences dialog box shown in Figure 1-10.

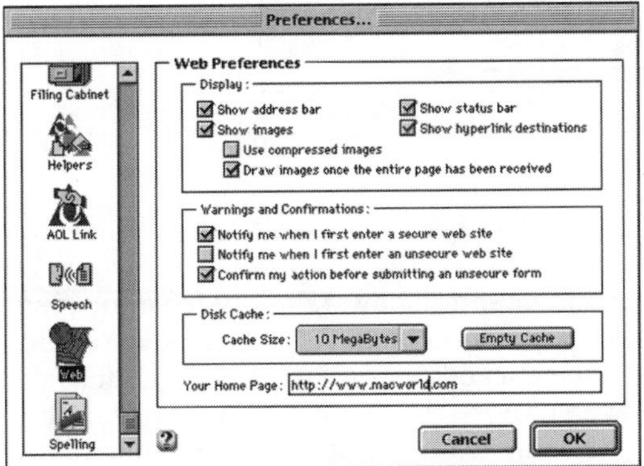

Figure 1-10: Use this dialog box to specify America Online 3.0 screen preference settings.

Netscape Navigator 3.0

Netscape Navigator gives you a number of choices to individualize your screen viewing. To select your custom preferences, use Options⇨General Preferences to open the dialog box shown in Figure 1-11.

In the Appearance pane, check the Underlined option in the Link Styles section (Windows) or Followed Links Expire (Mac) to specify that *hypertext links* (words or phrases you click to get to other spots on the Web) are underlined.

In the Fonts pane (shown in the figure), select the font you want for your text. You need to specify fonts for two types of text: *fixed text* and *proportional characters*. Fixed text is used for some lists and commands on the Web, to indicate file names, and to show what you need to type into your computer. Generally, you want to choose a font that looks like typewriting (Courier is a good example). Proportional characters are pretty much all the rest of the type fonts you see on the screen.

You can also change the size of the text in the Appearance panes. So, if you're not seeing enough of the text in your browser window, you can reduce the size of the text to fit more on your screen. Figure 1-12 provides an example of reformatted text and how it can change the appearance of your Web page. Compare it to Figure 1-6, which displays the same information with a different text size and font.

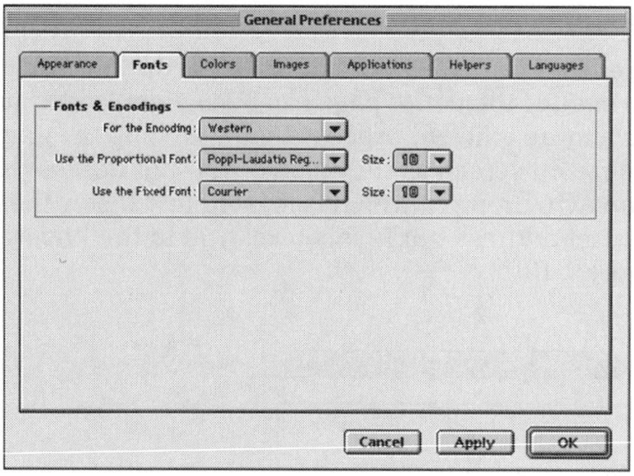

Figure 1-11: Use this dialog box to select your viewing preferences in Netscape Navigator 3.0.

In the Colors pane, choose the color you want the hyperlinks to appear in. Hyperlinks are the connections to other material within your Web document or to material in other documents. They stand out from the rest of the text through the use of color or underscores. You can pick colors both for read hyperlinks (ones you have clicked on) and unread hyperlinks (not yet clicked on). You can even choose the color of regular text, although I suggest you leave the regular-text color at a safe, readable black.

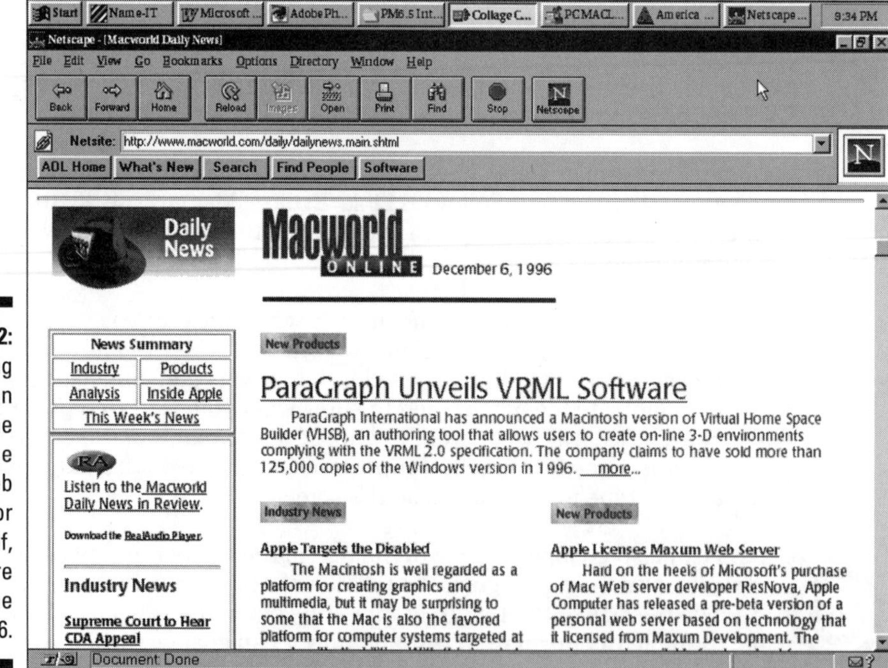

Figure 1-12: Changing the font can improve the appearance of your Web pages. For proof, compare this image to Figure 1-6.

In the Images pane, you can tell Navigator how to deal with colors that may have been specified in a Web document but that your monitor can't display. I recommend you leave this on the default setting, which is Automatic. You can also choose to have graphics display while the page is downloading or after it's done. I prefer to have this set at After loading (so you can read the text while the images are still loading), but either preference works.

Don't worry about the other panes; they don't affect what you see on screen.

Microsoft Internet Explorer 2.0

Internet Explorer fans are well aware that Explorer 3.0 is the most recent version now available. However, at the time this book was written, Microsoft had not yet released Explorer 3.0 for Macintosh, so I'm covering just Explorer 2.0 here.

You can exercise your options on a number of Internet Explorer settings to suit your personal taste. Use View⇨Options to open the set of tabbed panes that control the Internet Explorer preferences. Figure 1-13 shows the Options dialog boxes for Mac and Windows 95 (obviously, they look very different).

In Windows 95, limit your dabbling with Options to just the Appearances pane, which lets you set everything from fonts to link colors.

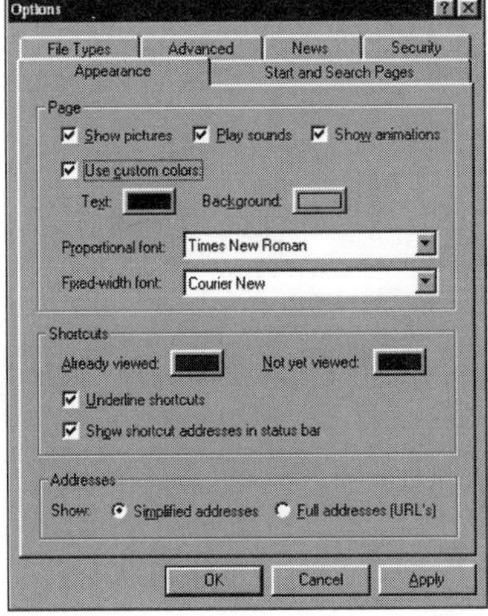

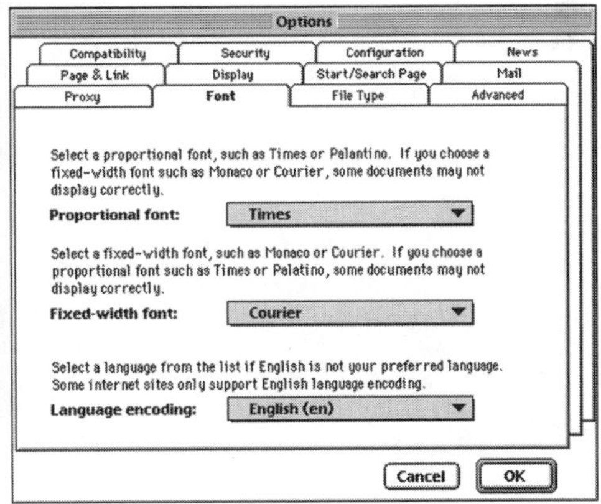

Figure 1-13: The Internet Explorer 2.0 Options dialog boxes for Windows 95 (left) and Macintosh.

On the Mac, use the following panes (Windows users should follow the Mac steps but look for all the options in the Appearances pane):

- In the Font pane, choose the font you want for the majority of your text (that's called the *Proportional* font) and the font for command examples and some lists (called the *Fixed-width* font because they default to fit in a set width, like a typewriter font).
- In the Page & Link pane, you can set the text and background colors, tell Explorer the best quality to use for image display (lower quality images display faster), and specify what kinds of sound files to play if a Web page happens to use them. You can also determine the colors for hyperlinks that are *unread* (not yet clicked on) and *read* (clicked on), as well as whether links are underlined.

- In the Display pane, you select when the full screen is displayed — either before graphic images are downloaded, or after Explorer figures out image dimensions (my preferred setting, because you can then read the text while the graphics are loading), or after images are downloaded. Note that Internet Explorer for Windows 95 has no equivalent for this option setting — a rare occasion when the Mac version outdoes the Windows version of a Microsoft product.

Chapter 2

PageMaker, Word Processors, and HTML Editors. Oh, My!

In This Chapter

- What PageMaker does best to create Web pages
- Where word processors come in handy
- When to use an HTML editor
- What types of formatting survive export to the Web
- What all that HTML document coding means

Whether you use Microsoft Word, WordPerfect, or some other popular word processor, you may think that you have all the tools you need to produce your Web documents, right? More and more word processors are adding basic export and editing capabilities to create Web pages, so what the heck do you need another program for? Well, to put it in layman's terms, to keep you from going bonkers.

Sure, you can create a rudimentary layout with a word processor, but using one of these tools to publish a Web site is like using a bicycle to go from San Francisco to Boulder, Colorado. The work is slow, it's exasperating, it requires a large amount of preparation, and you probably can't make it. If you're working on Web pages, Microsoft Word is a bicycle with a flat tire, WordPerfect is a tricycle with streamers on the handlebars, and an HTML editor (a specialized program for creating Web-page code) is a compact car you inherited from your uncle.

And then there's PageMaker. If HTML editors are so much better than a word processor for creating Web pages, why would you use PageMaker to create Web pages? Because, comparatively speaking, PageMaker is a corporate jet with all the amenities of home. It transforms making page layout into a relatively painless and sometimes even pleasurable experience. Best of all, you'll find yourself trying things that you'd never dare attempt in a word processor or HTML editor (and would regret if you did).

When Do I Use PageMaker?

Most of the work in creating a Web page or series of pages is in deciding what to do with the layout. Where should the elements go? How should they relate to each other? What part of the contents should be on which page? What kinds of headers and cross-references (or, *hyperlinks* in Web-speak) are needed? What elements should be the same within a Web site or within a section on a site? How much should the page look like a real layout versus a scrolling list?

I cover these specific issues in Part IV, but you're probably asking a more basic question: When is it right to use PageMaker and when is it right to use another tool? This may seem to be an odd question. PageMaker is a layout program after all, so what's the issue? The issue is that PageMaker is designed for print publications, not for the Web. Adobe has added Web export capabilities to PageMaker, as well as other Web-specific features, but PageMaker still is designed primarily for print.

In a nutshell, PageMaker is not as high powered as a dedicated HTML editor, like Adobe PageMill, for some Web-publishing needs such as precise positioning and support for table formatting. On the other hand, HTML is a very limited language, compared to the sophisticated PostScript printing language that PageMaker is designed to use. (*PostScript* is found in many desktop printers and is the standard language for commercial printing equipment.)

A longtime PageMaker product manager, Lori Birtley, once told me (and it's absolutely true) that HTML is more limited in what it supports than even ancient PageMaker 1.0. So when PageMaker has to create material for the relatively primitive HTML from a document designed for versatile PostScript, some things just don't work as well as you want them to.

Don't let this put you off — PageMaker is a great tool for many Web pages, but you are almost certainly going to need to do some work elsewhere to get exactly what you want. PageMaker is easier to use than an HTML editor for most of the work, but an HTML editor offers greater precision and control over the HTML code that hides behind every Web page in the world.

The bottom line is this: It's easier to take existing PageMaker layouts and convert them to HTML than to start from scratch in an HTML editor.

Earlier, I likened PageMaker to a corporate jet and an HTML editor to an economy car. You'll definitely want to fly the jet to go from San Francisco to Boulder, but when you arrive in Boulder, a car is just fine for getting to your hotel. You'll find that you need both PageMaker and an HTML editor to create the best Web pages. In a nutshell, you use PageMaker to build your pages and an HTML editor to fine-tune them. Therefore, it's key to understand what PageMaker can and can't do before launching into your own Web-page designs.

So, when should you use PageMaker?

When you want to avoid the ugly code that underlies Web pages

First, let me show you why PageMaker is better than a word processor or a basic HTML editor. They say that seeing is believing, so perhaps the best way to find out why you should use PageMaker is to discover what's really behind a Web page. Figure 2-1 shows you the ugly truth: A bunch of code underlies the great-looking layout of a recent *Macworld* home page design, which you can see in Figure 2-2.

Using a WYSIWYG (what-you-see-is-what-you-get) program like PageMaker is easier and more intuitive than coding your page in a word processor (see Figure 2-1) or an HTML editor (see Figure 2-3). As you can see in the HTML code in Figure 2-3, this HTML editor, Adobe PageMill 2.0 — one of the better HTML editors on the market — is much more intuitive than word-processing code (such as in Figure 2-1) but still not as WYSIWYG as PageMaker (as shown in Figure 2-4).

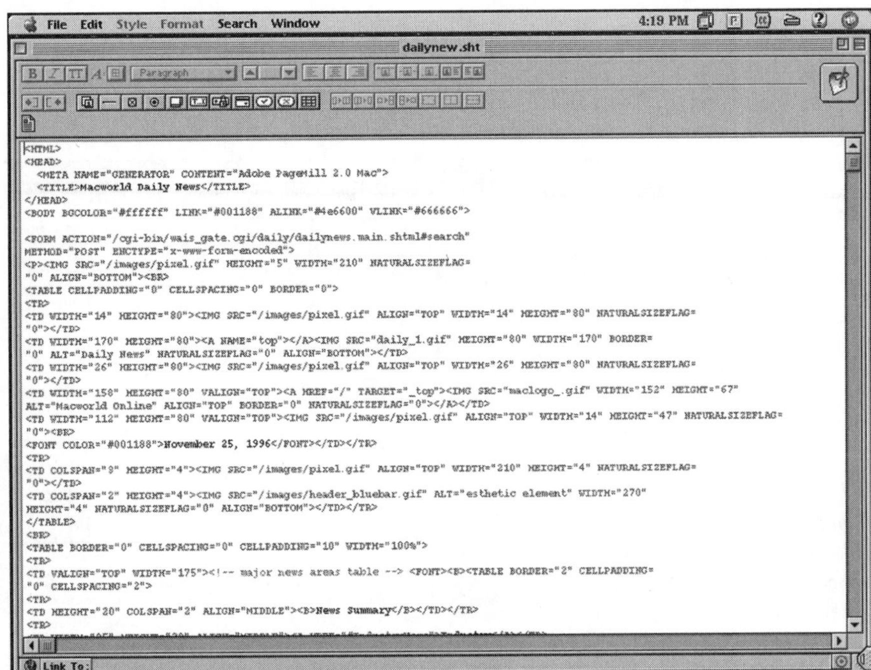

Figure 2-1: Thankfully, PageMaker hides all this ugly code from you.

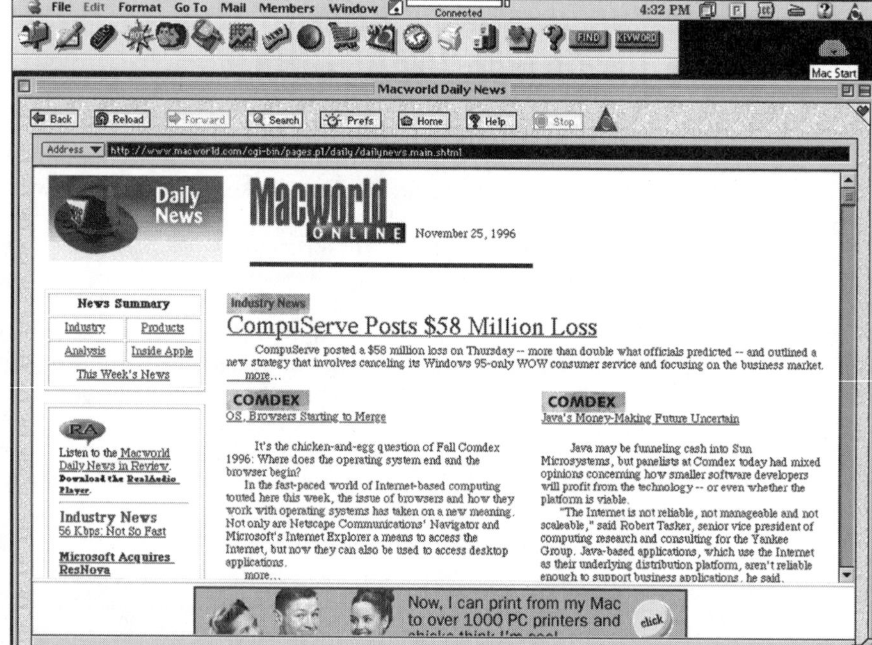

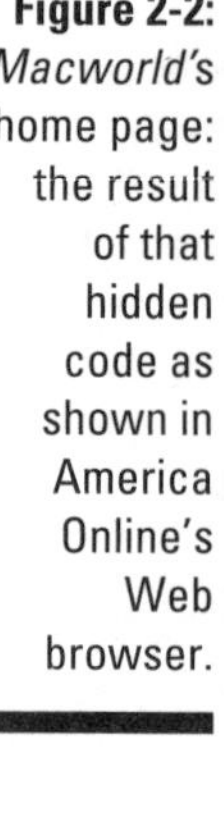
Figure 2-2: *Macworld's* home page: the result of that hidden code as shown in America Online's Web browser.

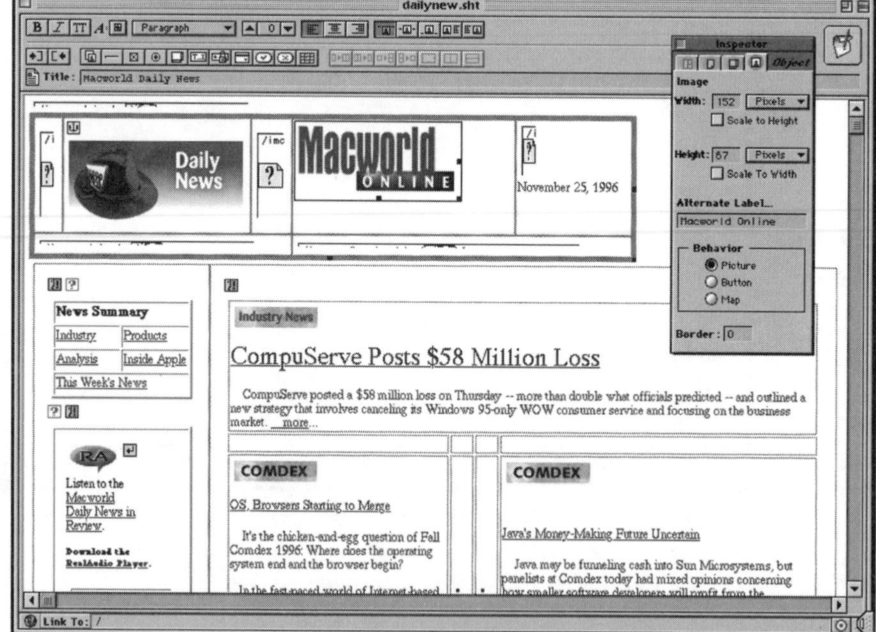

Figure 2-3: How HTML code for a Web page looks in the HTML editor, Adobe PageMill 2.0.

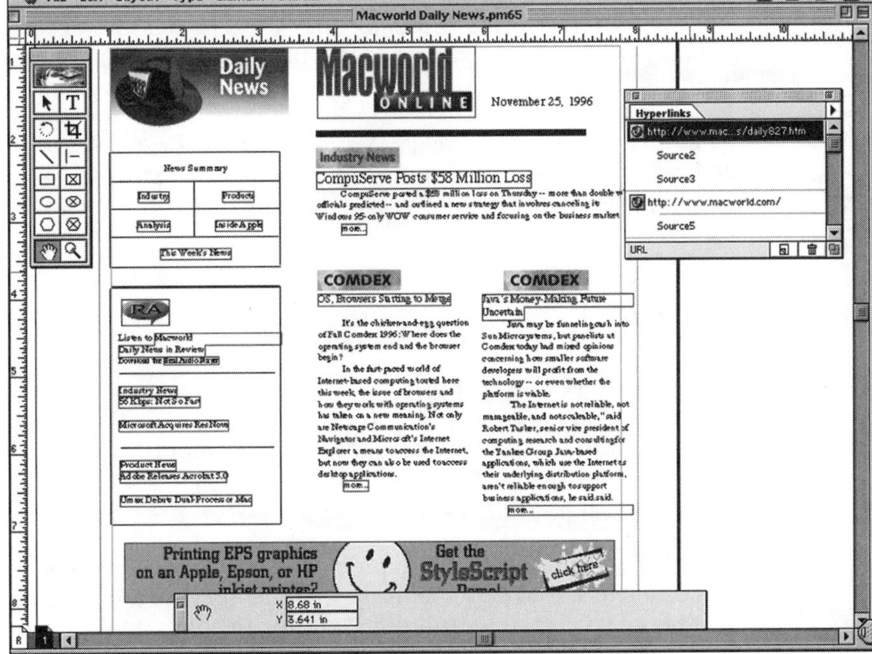

Figure 2-4: This PageMaker layout was used to create a Web page similar to the one in Figure 2-3.

For straightforward Web pages

For more straightforward Web pages, PageMaker is a great tool. What's straightforward? One or two columns of information, for starters. The less exacting you get with the placement of elements relative to each other, the better PageMaker can handle your Web-page design.

As a starting point for sophisticated Web pages

PageMaker simply doesn't support some of the features found in the latest version of HTML, including *frames* (independent areas on a page that can be scrolled without affecting other areas, similar to *panes* in Microsoft Excel) and some graphics such as vertical lines.

That's why if you want to create sophisticated Web pages like that in Figure 2-2, you are going to find PageMaker to be a great starting point, but not the end of the journey. You still need a good HTML editor like PageMill and a working knowledge of HTML language. Two good resources are *HTML For Dummies Quick Reference* by Deborah S. Ray and Eric J. Ray, and *PageMill 2.0 For Dummies* by Deke McClelland and John San Filippo (both published by IDG Books Worldwide, Inc.).

PageMaker is designed from the ground up to do layout in a visual way, while most HTML editors work more like word processors or text editors, requiring you to switch back and forth between a layout preview and a non-layout editing mode.

To put it simply, the new PageMaker converts the PageMaker files you know and love into HTML files. And it adds some tools so you can take advantage of Web-specific features, like hyperlinks, which are discussed later in this chapter.

For filling in the content

Word processors are great for writing and editing a lot of prose, but because voluminous text isn't something you need too often on the Web, launching a word processor for a few paragraphs and then importing the file into PageMaker for use in a Web layout is just too much work. Just type the text into PageMaker as you create it.

It's natural to launch your word processor when you have something to write. But check that impulse. Too much text on your Web pages is a sure way to bore your readers and reduce traffic to your site. The online medium is about connections — its *hyperlinks* — and quick access to information. A lengthy document is usually not suited to the Web because the longer it is, the slower it is (and many people pay for their online time), plus it means lots of scrolling for the reader. Sometimes length makes sense — such as for online news stories, but for most Web work, excessive text is a bad idea.

Don't get me wrong. There's nothing wrong with word processors. There's nothing wrong with bikes, either, but you don't use them for a cross-country business trip. So how do you know when to use PageMaker and when to use a word processor? The answer depends on what sort of document you're creating.

When you have multiple columns

Take a look at a professionally produced magazine or newsletter. Chances are the text is organized into multiple columns. Even the text in this book — which is laid out in PageMaker by the way — features one wide column and a second, much slimmer column on the left side of the page for icons and the like.

What does that have to do with the Web? Well, now that HTML Version 3.2 has been widely adopted — the latest versions of Netscape Navigator, Microsoft Internet Explorer, and America Online all support it — you are

Who needs columns?

You never understood why anyone used them in the first place, and you certainly don't need them now. Well, think again. Multiple columns are part and parcel of publishing because they simplify integrating elements — both graphics and stories — into a layout.

Using multiple columns means that you can change the width of a graphic freely without wreaking havoc on your layout. Multiple articles (an article is also known as *a story* in PageMaker) can fit on a page without interfering with each other. Each page is a balancing act, and columns provide the structure needed to keep your work from flying apart at the seams (and you thought columns are used because artists like to do things that the rest of us can't). Check out Figures 2-2 and 2-4 for example. The first figure shows a fine-tuned multicolumn page and the second a raw page created in PageMaker (both use columns).

In the early days of PageMaker, the ability to create multiple columns was reason enough to invest in it. Today, you can create multiple columns in a word processor or HTML editor. But the process is awkward, even in powerful programs such as Word, WordPerfect, or PageMill, given all the formatting that goes on in dialog boxes. With all the mousing and clicking required, you begin to feel like you're at the gym doing hand workouts.

PageMaker lets you drag columns around, repositioning and resizing them at will, just as if they were physical objects floating above the surface of your page. Clearly, PageMaker wins the multiple-column contest.

going to start seeing more and more Web pages that have multiple columns, rather than the single-column look most Web sites have had in the past. If you're creating multiple-column pages, use the tool that knows through and through how to do multiple columns: PageMaker.

The final Web page exported from PageMaker probably won't match the PageMaker document's layout precisely. During export, PageMaker needs to move things around to go from the printed page dimensions to the screen dimensions, and PageMaker makes its best guess when doing so. You can help out PageMaker by designing your Web pages to be the same size as they will appear on-screen. (Chapter 5 covers Web-page sizes.)

For working with graphics

In PageMaker, you can rotate graphics to any angle with a couple swift clicks of your mouse button. And you can just as easily skew, resize, and crop graphics. In a word processor, you can resize graphics and, maybe, crop. But forget the rest.

Many of the fabulous PageMaker graphic capabilities don't mean a thing to a Web page. PageMaker can't export any graphic elements created within it to HTML format, with the single exception of horizontal lines. So don't waste your time drawing boxes or circles. Also, some effects you do on imported images — like skewing and rotating — are ignored.

The most widely used effects — resizing, scaling, and cropping — are kept, so you can modify an image in your PageMaker Web document with these tools. But don't assume that everything you do to a graphic in PageMaker will survive the journey to the Web. Figures 2-5 and 2-6 show examples of what gets exported and what doesn't.

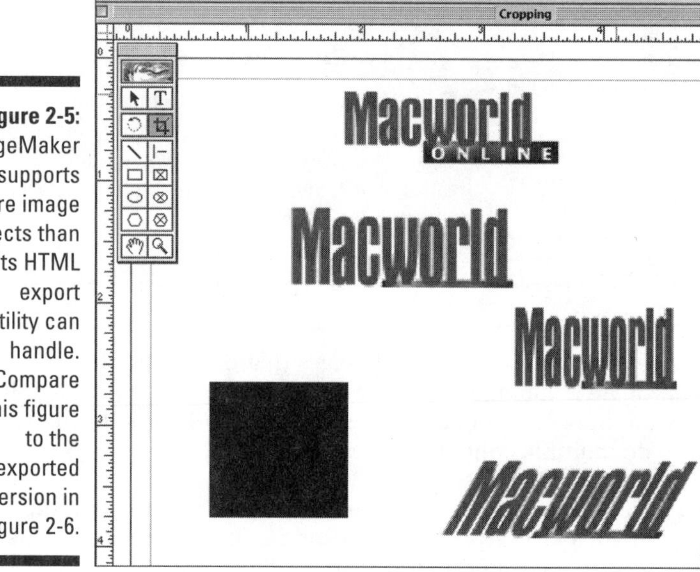

Figure 2-5: PageMaker supports more image effects than its HTML export utility can handle. Compare this figure to the exported version in Figure 2-6.

PageMaker does accomplish one thing that most word processors and HTML editors can't. It translates your standard-format images (like those in TIFF and EPS formats) into the Web's GIF and JPEG formats for you automatically, picking the best format of the two for each image. (I cover what those formats mean and when to worry about them in Chapter 13.) That means you can use the images directly, rather than having to first open them in a program like Adobe Photoshop or Corel Photo-Paint and then saving them as GIF or JPEG files.

PageMaker can also import graphics from your word processor and export them to HTML. That means you can place a drawing you created in CorelDraw, for example, into your text inside your word processor and then

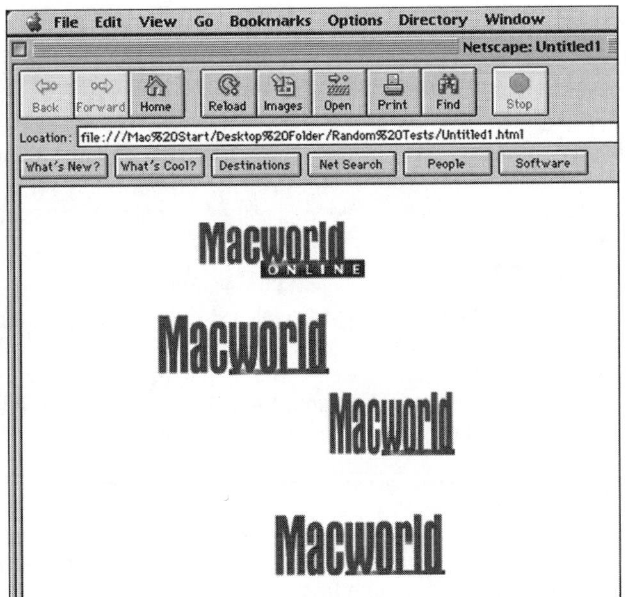

Figure 2-6: Compare this figure to Figure 2-5. The skewed graphic didn't stay skewed when exported to HTML and the black box drawn in PageMaker was dropped completely.

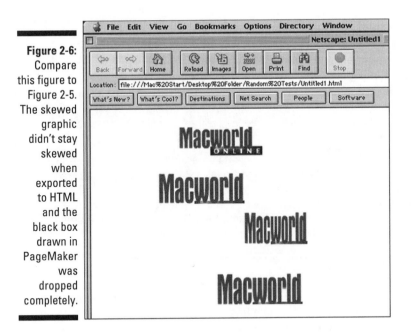

bring the whole enchilada into PageMaker. The program supports these so-called *embedded graphics* (PageMaker refers to them as *in-line graphics* because they are inside lines of text), which it considers to be basically special symbols in your text.

The quality of embedded graphics may deteriorate during importing. It's sort of like making photocopies. Copy a copy and you get what's politely called a *second-generation* copy — something yucky and fuzzy that you give to someone else only in desperation because you lost the original. Well, a similar thing can happen when using second-generation embedded graphics. Make sure that you experiment by previewing your Web pages to see how any embedded graphics survive the trip from your word processor to PageMaker to HTML.

The reason graphics can lose quality when imported into PageMaker as part of a text document is similar to why making photocopies of a photocopy leads to poor image quality: You're not working with the original. Programs like Word don't always copy the original file when you import a graphic. When you print a document, a high-quality original is sent to your laser printer, but when you import a text file into PageMaker, a lower-resolution *placeholder* is imported, not the higher-resolution original. For the Web this isn't so critical, because your monitor displays images at 72 dots per inch, much coarser than any printer or even a fax machine. But you can still get *jaggies,* color shifts, or weird scaling when using embedded graphics.

Why PageMaker is the pick for graphics

In print publishing, the gap between word processors on one side and PageMaker on the other is expanding into a chasm. The latest versions of Word, WordPerfect, and some other word processors are capable of importing graphics, but try working with them.

For example, say you want to reposition a graphic at the beginning of a paragraph and have the text wrap around it. In PageMaker, you can just drag the graphic to where you want it and turn on the text wrap feature. You can even make the wrap follow the shape of the graphic. If you want to do the same thing in a word processor, get ready for some major work. It will take you so much time that you may as well draw each character by hand.

PageMaker also lets you draw lines, squares, and circles, of course, as well as apply shades of gray to boxes and other elements. You can also accomplish these feats with a well-equipped word processor, but the process is time consuming and difficult.

Although word processors and HTML editors are constantly adding more graphics controls, you need a page-layout program like PageMaker if you really want to use graphics effectively in your document.

For defining Web-page colors

Defining colors is another big disappointment in a word processor. You can't do it, or only in a limited way. Many HTML editors let you define almost any color you want — even though most Web browsers don't support more than 256 colors (216 of which are supported by both Mac and Windows, so those are the ones you want to stick with). PageMaker has a special Web color palette with just those Web-safe colors to prevent you from creating something at your computer your readers won't see correctly. (Chapter 15 provides more information on Web colors.)

For combining multiple stories

Word processors are really good at handling a long, single document, whether or not the document has headlines and bullets. But word processors are very bad at combining multiple *stories* (articles or other chunks of text) onto a page or across pages. HTML editors are better at managing multiple stories, but their layout features are often not as straightforward as PageMaker's WYSIWYG approach.

So, if your pages have a number of different elements and stories of varying lengths, you're better off using PageMaker.

For creating hypertext links

A big part of creating your Web site is the linking of pages to one another, both within your site and to others. *Hypertext links* (*hyperlinks* for short) — the (usually) blue underlined text or boxed graphics on a Web page that when clicked open a new page — are the online equivalent to turning to another page in print.

An HTML editor knows all about managing hyperlinks. In that regard, the advantage of using PageMaker over an HTML editor seems to be nil. PageMaker is no better or no worse than an HTML editor at managing hyperlinks, but why do the linking in an HTML editor after you've created the rest of the page in PageMaker? Make it easy on yourself: You're already working in PageMaker, so it makes sense to use the tools already at your disposal.

Although PageMaker can import hyperlinks from word-processing documents, you have to know in advance what hyperlinks you want to create before even doing your layout. It makes more sense to make those hyperlinks all at once when you set up your Web site, rather than do some in your word processor and the rest in PageMaker.

You are likely to find that as you create your pages in PageMaker, the relationships among them that you first envisaged change. Just as graphic designers modify their layouts after they see them take shape, you'll also probably modify your Web layouts. In short, save hyperlinking for the final version.

When Do I Use a Word Processor?

PageMaker, word processors, and HTML editors are all good tools. Depending on what you're doing, one type of program is clearly better than the other, but you don't always have to choose between them. You can do some work in your word processor and then import that work into PageMaker for further refinement, especially for layout. Then you can export your PageMaker pages to HTML format and fine-tune them in an HTML editor.

Think of the advantages: Layout artists can keep editors from messing in the PageMaker layouts by restricting them to creating text in Word or WordPerfect, and editors can make sure that layout artists don't skip over text formatting to focus on the graphics. (Some artists consider text to be the stuff that holds graphics together, sort of like the way white bread holds together the meat of the sandwich.)

For text-intensive projects and formatting

If you're working on a text-heavy layout, use your word processor to create and edit the text. Save the PageMaker Story Editor, the built-in word processor explained in Chapter 8, for touch-ups, minor edits, and those documents that are mostly graphics with little text.

Use *style sheets* (a shortcut method to apply formatting with a couple keystrokes) in your word processor if you're using styles in your layout. (Styles are explained in depth in Chapter 9.) The styles don't have to look the same in your word processor as they do in PageMaker. In fact, don't even try to make them the same — styles on the Web are more limited than what your word processor or PageMaker can format, so you lose most of your formatting anyhow. Because styles on the Web aren't as sophisticated as those in PageMaker or a word processor, don't spend a lot of time doing fancy formatting that won't show up on the Web.

Although styles on the Web are limited, they remain essential, because they are the primary way that you specify text's appearance. The issue is not whether you should use styles — you should — but where you should create and apply them. The answer is easy: Create and apply your styles in whatever program you're doing the writing and editing.

You have to do this kind of localized formatting work in one place or the other, and it's easier to do formatting in the place where the editing happens. Why? Because most character formatting (like indicating boldface and italics, or specifying a headline) almost always relates to the content of the text, and it's the writer or editor who's familiar with its meaning. Sure, whoever is doing the layout can apply the formatting in PageMaker, but that person won't know what should be stressed through italics, underlining, or whatever.

If you're the person who's doing both the Web page writing and layout, do any character formatting (such as boldface or italics) that relates to the meaning of your text in your word processor. When you get to the layout stage in PageMaker, you have more things on your mind than content — such as how many columns of text you want and whether the headlines fit properly.

Even if you have remarkable powers of concentration and coordination — you can chew gum and dance the Macarena at the same time — it's still not a good idea to work on layout and meaning and editing and drawing all at once. You have more luck if you keep these different elements of the page-production process separate. Another good reason to concentrate on one operation at a time is that it's usually easier to edit in your word processor because that's what it's designed to do.

Formatting that works (and doesn't) on the Web

Most special text formatting — from small caps to underlining to fancy fonts — is lost on the Web because every *browser* (a program, such as Internet Explorer or Netscape Navigator, that lets you view what's on the Web) can be set to use a different default for text fonts and type sizes. Don't bother using non-HTML formatting styles in your word processor or in PageMaker, and be stingy about using special characters, because not all browsers support them. Symbols often differ on Macs and PCs, so a character you use in your layout may not be what the browser shows the reader.

On the Web, you're pretty much limited to basic type styling. For example, it's safe to apply the following text formatting to your document (complete tables of formatting that survive HTML coding are in Chapter 6):

- Boldface
- Italics
- A limited number of common special symbols, such as the paragraph symbol (¶), some foreign language symbols (for example, Ç), or a copyright mark (©)

The following type-styling selections don't survive export to the Web, so avoid using them in either your word processor or in PageMaker:

- **Drop caps:** Don't bother trying to import drop caps from your word processor into PageMaker for Web pages. HTML simply doesn't support them.
- **Precision Typography:** Kerning, the use of fonts and point sizes, and other typographic attributes (except the very basics like boldface and italics) don't survive HTML formatting. Although HTML does allow some text and paragraph formatting, it doesn't support precision in typography.
- **Most Special Symbols:** Except for some commonly used ones, special symbols (such as most mathematical symbols) and non-Western European language symbols (such as those in Slavic languages) usually don't display properly on the Web. Chapter 6 lists the ones that do.

Each browser controls how text is displayed, so any fine-tuned typography in the original file would be useless. Therefore, rely on styles to specify size, and use HTML coding tags in your HTML editor for increasing and decreasing text size (see Chapter 9 for more information on HTML text styles).

Because text formatting on the Web is so straightforward, where you do your text editing — in a word processor or PageMaker — is up to you. My advice: Use a word processor for editing large stories and PageMaker for the rest. What is large? A good rule of thumb is: Any story that scrolls off your screen may require word processing, and any story that takes up more than two screens is a definite word-processing candidate.

For simple layout and formatting

Length is not the only consideration, of course. You bought PageMaker because it has extensive formatting and layout options, so you should save PageMaker for when you need those capabilities. For example, both PageMaker and any best-selling word processor or HTML editor let you format text with little effort.

Switching to italics in a word-processing program is as simple as pressing Ctrl+I (Windows) or ⌘+I (Mac), while switching to boldface is as simple as Ctrl+B (Windows) or ⌘+B (Mac). In PageMaker, you just press Ctrl+Shift+I or Shift+⌘+I, or Ctrl+Shift+B or Shift+⌘+B. (You can use the same keystrokes to switch off italics or boldface.) You can also use the menus or palette options provided in either program to format text.

So if all that you're doing is writing a simple Web page that uses very little text formatting and a very basic layout, don't bother with PageMaker — a word processor or HTML editor is fine. Going back to the bicycle and airplane analogy, simple formatting tricks amount to no more than a jaunt to the corner store. Taking a plane is hardly the solution, even if one is parked in the driveway.

Because HTML is a less-sophisticated formatting tool than your word processor or PageMaker, you're forced to give up a bunch of typographic effects that don't translate to the Web. For experienced PageMaker users who have grown accustomed to having sophisticated formatting options at their disposal, this is the single biggest adjustment to make when moving from print to online publishing.

When Do I Use an HTML Editor?

The screen image back in Figure 2-2 was *not* created in PageMaker 6.5 — it was created in an HTML editor by experienced Web-page designers and programmers. Although the layout shown in Figure 2-4 shows you can create a page like Figure 2-2 in PageMaker, I'd be lying if I said that PageMaker by itself can create a Web page that complex.

If you take the PageMaker layout in Figure 2-4 and have PageMaker create an HTML page from it, you get a Web page that looks like the one in Figure 2-7. Pretty different, huh? (Chapter 17 shows you how to convert your PageMaker layout into an HTML document.) PageMaker is a good way to get you started on creating a professional-looking Web page, but to complete the task you may need another tool.

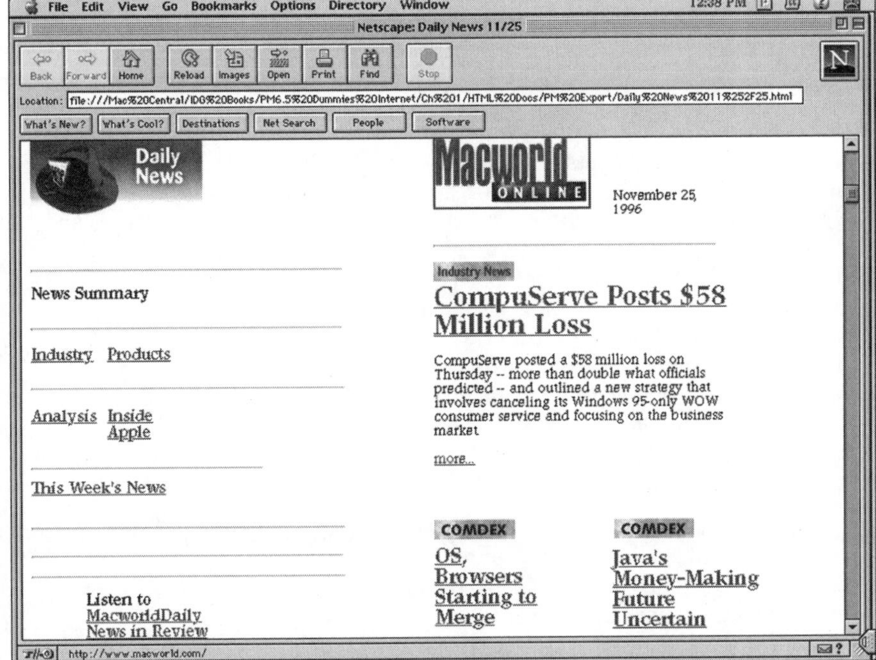
File Edit View Go Bookmarks Options Directory Window
12:38 PM
Netscape: Daily News 11/25
Back Forward Home Reload Images Open Print Find Stop
Location: file:///Mac%20Central/IDG%20Books/PM6.5%20Dummies%20Internet/Ch%201/HTML%20Docs/PM%20Export/Daily%20News%2011%252F25.html
What's New? What's Cool? Destinations Net Search People Software
Daily News
Macworld ONLINE
November 25, 1996
Industry News
CompuServe Posts $58 Million Loss
CompuServe posted a $58 million loss on Thursday -- more than double what officials predicted -- and outlined a new strategy that involves canceling its Windows 95-only WOW consumer service and focusing on the business market.
more...
News Summary
Industry Products
Analysis Inside Apple
This Week's News
COMDEX
OS, Browsers Starting to Merge
COMDEX
Java's Money-Making Future Uncertain
Listen to MacworldDaily News in Review
http://www.macworld.com/

Figure 2-7: The results of an HTML Web page created in PageMaker. Obviously, it could benefit from some refining in an HTML editor.

To place elements precisely

The page shown in Figure 2-2 resulted from extensive tweaking to get the elements laid out just right. No automated export feature, including the one in PageMaker, can do that kind of fine-tuning. For that you need a human brain and a tool (such as an HTML editor) designed to tweak HTML pages.

To edit HTML files after you've exported them from your PageMaker layouts, you can use two basic kinds of tools: text editors and HTML editors. Although the line is blurring a bit between HTML editors and text editors, the key difference remains: Only an HTML editor is designed specifically for working with Web pages, and it has the full set of commands and functions needed to manage the Web pages on your site.

- Text editors are programs like Microsoft Word and Corel WordPerfect, or even a basic editor like SimpleText for the Macintosh or NotePad for Windows 95. HTML documents are text-only files (also called ASCII) composed of commands that Web browsers translate into what you see on-screen. Because it's such a basic format, any browser on any type of computer can read an HTML file, and any program that can edit text can be used to edit the HTML file.

The secret world of coding languages

Behind the scenes of PageMaker, hidden well away, is a set of computer code that translates what you create on-screen into what is viewed on a Web browser. If you think about it, the same holds true for a print publication: Behind your great-looking print publication is the PostScript or PCL code (the language used by many PC printers) that PageMaker generates to tell your printer how to create your masterpiece. HTML does the same for the Web by telling browsers how to display your document the way you want your readers to see it.

Three coding languages lie under the surface of a document, which tell the printer or browser all the steps to take to faithfully render your document on paper or online:

- *PostScript,* the printing language used by most Macintosh printers, all imagesetters (the devices used to create film negatives for professional printing), and many PC printers
- *PCL,* the Printer Control Language created for Hewlett-Packard printers that's all but standard on PC printers and is now found on many Mac printers
- *HTML,* the HyperText Markup Language created for the Web that tells your browser what to display, just as PostScript and PCL tell your printer what to print

PageMaker translates your layout to PostScript or PCL when you print, based on the target printer. It's all automatic, so you never see it happen or ever see the PostScript or PCL code — only the printer sees that. Likewise, when you are done with a PageMaker layout and want to create a Web page from it, you can use an export command to translate the PageMaker layout to HTML. (Exporting to HTML is covered in Chapter 17.)

- HTML editors are a new kind of program that are designed to specifically create and edit HTML files for Web pages. Just as publishing programs are specialized editors for layout files, HTML editors are specialized editors for Web files. There are dozens of HTML editors available today, including Adobe PageMill, SoftQuad HoTMetaL Pro, Claris HomePage, Bare Bones Software BBEdit, NetObjects Fusion, Gonet Communications Golive Pro, Miracle Software World Wide Web Weaver, Corel Web Designer, DeltaPoint QuickSite, and Microsoft FrontPage.

For creating tables

If there's an Achilles' heel in PageMaker-based Web publishing, it's the lack of a real tables feature that survives HTML export as an HTML table. The truth is you must do your tables in an HTML editor if you want them to look and feel like the rest of your Web page.

Why is that? When you import a table from your word processor, PageMaker strips out the formatting. So, don't bother creating fully functioning tables with individual cells and the whole rigmarole. You can place tabs between table elements and then do the table formatting in PageMaker with your imported text, but even that formatting won't translate to HTML.

So what can you do? PageMaker includes a separate utility called Adobe Table that creates tables. You can bring those tables into PageMaker and export them into your Web page as if they were graphics, and that's precisely how they are treated — as a graphic, not as a text table. That means their text font won't match that of the surrounding text when displayed on someone's browser. The browser determines the font and size for the story but, because the table is converted into a graphic, that table will look exactly like it did in your PageMaker document.

When dealing with code

Whether in PostScript, PCL, or HTML format, the code is critical to correct output or display. Luckily, PageMaker handles all that code for you. Well, at least it does for print documents. When was the last time you worried about PostScript or PCL code in your PageMaker file? For HTML, you have to think about it for three reasons:

- The HTML language is new, so it's constantly changing, with new functions added every year. PageMaker 6.5 knows about the functions up through HTML 3.2, but not all browsers know about Version 3.2. And some browsers have additional features not covered by the official HTML standard; either way, you might want to adjust the HTML file created by PageMaker to take into account the capabilities (and lack of capability) of the browsers you expect your readers to use.
- HTML is very limited when it comes to layout and formatting. The very first version of PageMaker could put it to shame. HTML was designed for use on older computers that couldn't display graphics and multicolumn layouts. HTML is being revised each year to be more visually oriented, but just as it took ten years for DOS to evolve into Windows 95, HTML has a ways to go on its similar journey. PageMaker does its best when exporting to HTML, but you can expect to do additional work in an HTML editor that knows the limits of the language.
- PageMaker 6.5 does its best to convert your PageMaker layouts into HTML Web pages, but it's not perfect. The way it handles multipage export often doesn't match what you want, and it can only approximate the positions of columns, not match them exactly. (Chapter 18 covers these kinds of issues in detail.)

Along with showing you how to create Web pages in PageMaker, this book covers what HTML can and cannot do for the specific kind of content you might want in your Web page — from typography to graphics, or from columns to hyperlinks. Chapter 17 walks you through all the steps to creating an HTML Web page. Chapter 18 explains the work you'll do on a Web page exported from PageMaker in an HTML editor. Chapter 22 lists the most useful HTML codes — the commands that you'll use in an HTML editor. When you export your PageMaker pages to HTML format, PageMaker automatically inserts these (and other) HTML codes into the exported HTML file, but if you want to edit them, change them, or add new ones in an HTML editor, read Chapter 22.

HTML is the standard format for Web pages, but new formats are starting to appear as well. Because of the way the Web was designed, a Web page must use the HTML format, but other types of formats can be included in Web pages. The most popular of these is the Adobe Portable Document Format (PDF), also known as Acrobat format, which PageMaker can also export. (Chapter 19 covers how to create Acrobat pages for use in your Web site.)

Acrobat files retain all the rich typographic settings — fonts, kerning, and so forth — and precise layout placement that print publishers have long taken for granted thanks to programs like PageMaker. A drawback to Acrobat files is their size, which makes downloading times unbearable for most readers. But sometimes that downloading time is worth the payoff.

Four Things PageMaker Does Best

Don't let any comparison of word processing, HTML editing, and page layout obscure the strengths that PageMaker offers, which is the reason you bought the program in the first place. Here's a quick rundown of what you get for your PageMaker investment:

- You can combine multiple stories and images to present complex information in a way that's easy for the reader to grasp — and you can perform this task more easily than you could in a word processor or HTML editor.
- You can add Web-safe colors (those certain to go over to the Web) to your documents.
- You can reuse existing PageMaker layouts and reformat them for use on the Web. You can even create dual-purpose documents for print and online use.
- You can add *hypertext links* (a system of quick connections) to other pages in your PageMaker document as well as to other Web addresses.

In other words, you get a lot of bang for your buck! The rest of this book tells you how to start taking advantage of your investment.

Part II

Getting Started with PageMaker 6.5

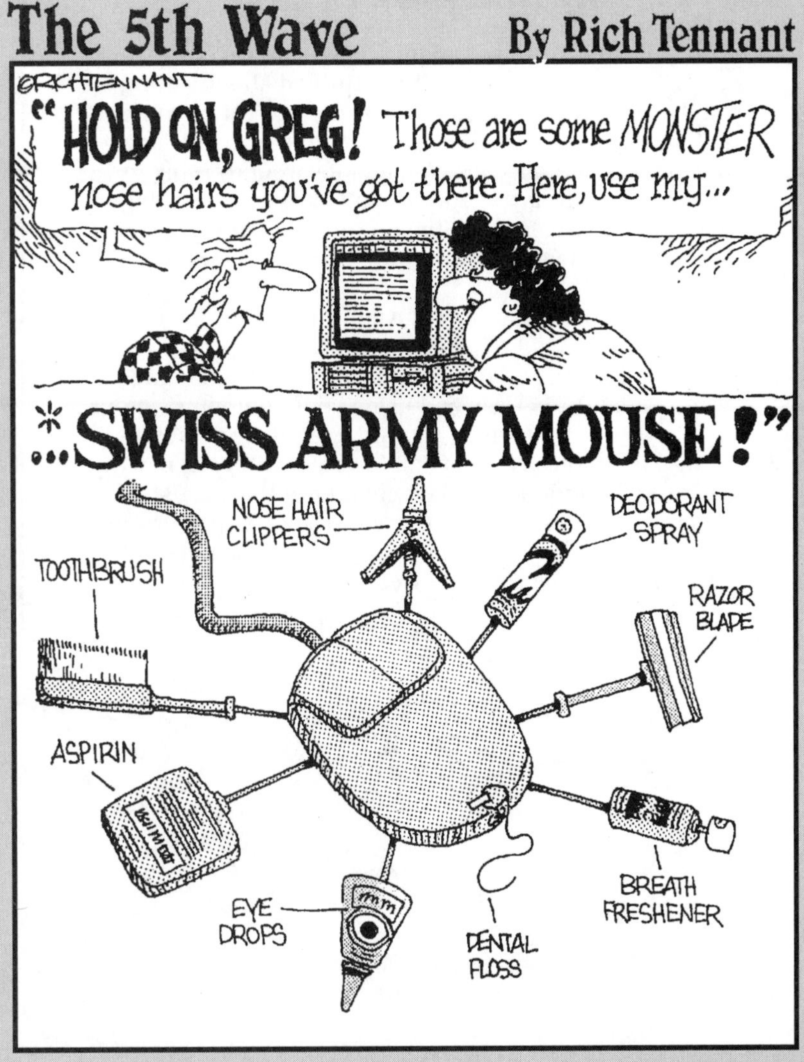

In this part . . .

No one likes to get up on the wrong side of the bed (and some of us aren't too thrilled about getting up on the right side). It really throws off the rest of your day. Before you know it, you're in the middle of an avalanche of mistakes and miscues. You fumble around trying to shut off the buzzing telephone and answer the ringing alarm clock. You bring in the dog and let out the ferret. You turn on the coffee maker but forget the carafe.

Getting off to a lousy start is what this part of the book can help you avoid. The next three chapters cover the basics of starting up the PageMaker program, finding your way around the screen, and using your computer's mouse and keyboard to get the program to actually do something. Once you're feeling comfortable with your new digital surroundings, the last chapter of this part shows you how to set up your document pages. With everything under control, you're ready to begin creating nifty publications for the World Wide Web.

Chapter 3

Starting, Mousing, and Other Vital Stuff

In This Chapter

- Starting PageMaker 6.5 with Windows 95 or Macintosh
- Adding a shortcut icon (or alias) to your desktop
- Clicking, dragging, double-clicking, and other mouse tricks
- Working with program and document windows

The good news about PageMaker 6.5 is that it lets you create Web pages with a minimum of bother (plus the full assortment of print documents, brochures, newsletters, and so forth with less effort and in less time than ever before). The bad news is that you have to use a computer to do it. And that means that you have to fling yourself headlong into the world of computer geekdom. You have to learn such terms as *click, drag, taskbar, dialog box,* and *submenu.* You even have to shake hands with a *mouse,* for heaven's sake.

If this is your first encounter with a desktop publishing program, or if you invested in PageMaker 6.5 to dabble in creating your own Web pages, you may feel a little overwhelmed at first. But after a few days of working with PageMaker, you are likely to discover that things really aren't as complicated as they seem. The process is simply a matter of learning some basic lingo and becoming familiar with what you see on your monitor's screen. To that end, this chapter walks you gently through the initial steps of bringing PageMaker to life, moving around on the screen, and using your mouse and computer keyboard to make the program actually do something. By the end of the chapter you, too, can confidently toss about phrases like "navigating the interface" and "maximizing the open window" — thereby qualifying yourself for a seat at the Web-head lunch table. And if that's not something to look forward to, what is?

If you're already familiar with PageMaker, you may just want to skim through this chapter and read the sections marked with the Version 6.5 icon. Then again, you may want to read the whole chapter carefully — you may discover a few tricks and techniques you didn't know or may have forgotten.

Powering Up PageMaker 6.5

Assuming that you've installed PageMaker on your hard drive (if you haven't, see the Appendix at the back of this book for installation instructions), you can start PageMaker through a pretty simple process. Just do the following:

Do not install Version 6.5 over Version 6.0. Doing so overwrites several custom files. For information on installing PageMaker 6.5, see the Appendix of this book.

1. **Turn on your computer.**

   Unless you believe in Zen computing, flicking your computer's On switch is essential. On a PC, the switch or button could be anywhere: on the front, on the side (usually on the right), or on the back (often reachable with your right hand if the PC's front is facing you). On most Macs, a special button on the keyboard turns the computer on and off; it's usually labeled with a left-pointing triangle.

2. **Wait for Windows 95, Windows NT, or the Macintosh operating system (OS) to start up.**

   You *cannot* run PageMaker 6.5 on a computer using Windows NT 3.5 or Windows 3.1. (PageMaker 6.0 is the last version that can run under Windows 3.1; no version runs under NT 3.5.)

3. **Start PageMaker.**

   On the Macintosh, move your mouse until the *pointer* (the white, mobile, on-screen arrow controlled by your mouse) is hovering over the icon for your disk drive. *Double-click* (press the mouse button twice rapidly) on the icon to open up its contents. Look for a folder called Adobe PageMaker 6.5 and double-click on the folder to open the folder. Look for an icon called Adobe PageMaker 6.5 (it looks like a page layout with the PageMaker logo and the number 6.5) and double-click on it to launch the program. You may see a stopwatch icon when your Mac is busy opening the program. Figure 3-1 illustrates what you see when you start PageMaker.

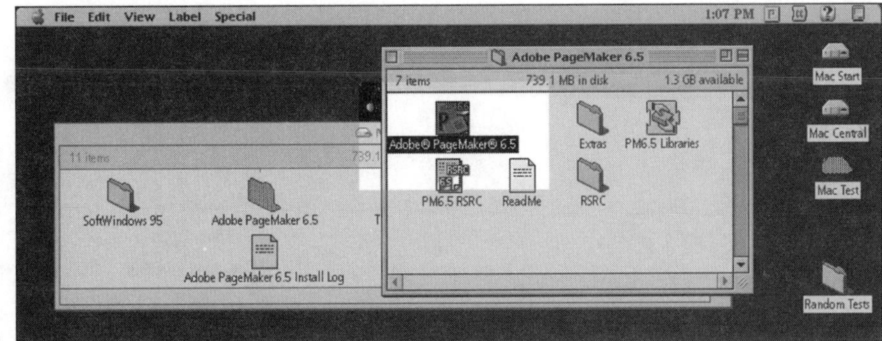

Figure 3-1: Launching PageMaker 6.5 on the Mac.

To start PageMaker in Windows 95 or NT 4.0, move your mouse until the *cursor* — that's the little arrow that moves around on-screen when you move your mouse — is hovering over the Start button in the lower-left corner of your screen. Now *click* (press the left mouse button) on that button. Next, move your cursor up to the Programs item and click on it to display another list of options. Click on the Adobe option to display yet another list of options and then click on the PageMaker 6.5 option. You see a little hourglass icon while Windows opens the program, and then the PageMaker opening screen appears. Figure 3-2 illustrates the process of starting PageMaker by using the Start menu.

All references to running Windows 95 or PageMaker under Windows 95 also cover operations under Windows NT 4.0, unless I give separate instructions for Windows NT. Usually, I just say "Windows" so you know I mean either one. Note that the new NT 4.0 looks and acts almost the same as Windows 95.

I find working with the Start button at the top of my screen to be easier than at the bottom, so I moved up my Start button. To do this, just click anywhere on the bar that contains the Start button with the left mouse button. Keep the left mouse button depressed, and *drag* the bar to the top of the screen. Let go when the bar snaps to the top. You can also do this to move the Start button to the right or left side of your screen, if that's your druthers.

Menus and submenus work differently in Windows than on the Mac. In Windows, after you click on the Start button, submenus appear as you simply "hover" your mouse cursor over the various menu items; you don't have to keep clicking your way through layers of menus as you do with earlier versions of Windows. If you find yourself getting frustrated by this setup (because menu items seem to keep hiding or changing as you move the mouse), you can still click your way through the submenus, and Windows locks those menus in place in the process.

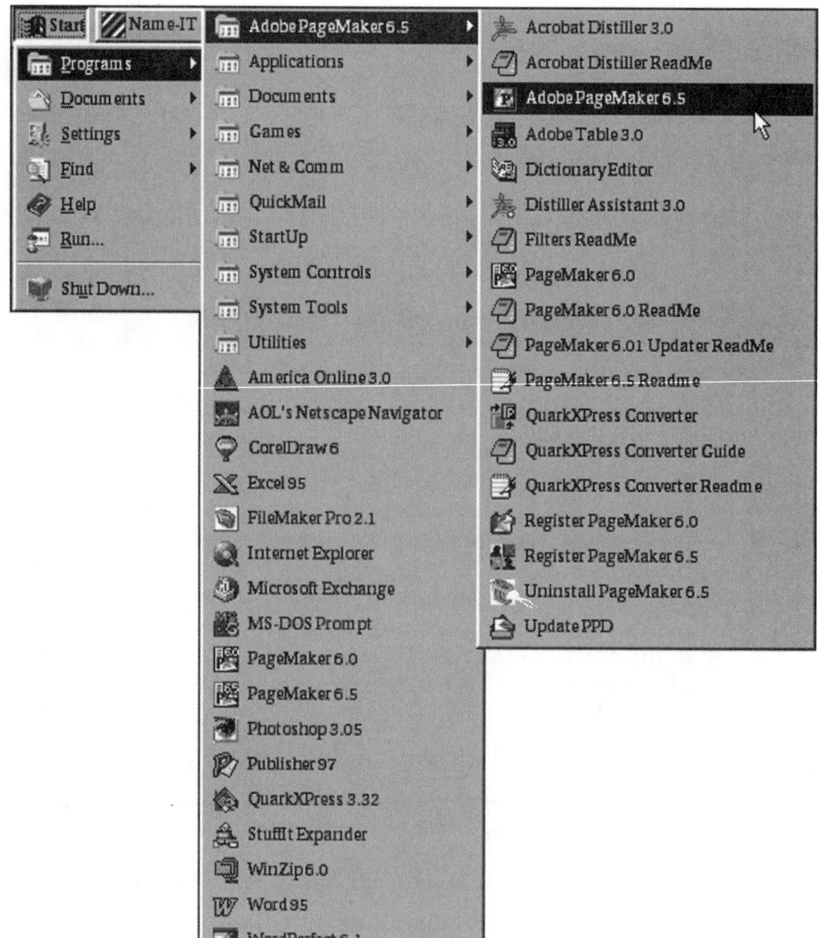

Figure 3-2: These menus appear when you launch PageMaker 6.5 under Windows 95.

The Mac requires you to click on a menu to open it — the menu can't open automatically for you as it can under Windows. Also, you have to keep the mouse button held down to keep the menu or submenu open — if you release your finger, the Mac assumes you're done and closes the menu. If you release your finger when the mouse pointer is hovering on a menu item, the Mac assumes you want to open that item. You can get your Mac's menus to work like Windows menus by using the shareware program AutoMenus Pro, available from Macworld Online's software collection (`http://www.macworld.com` on the Internet, or through America Online at the keyword Macworld); the cost is just $15 to register AutoMenus.

The Mac screens throughout this book may look a bit more "dimensional" (three-dimensional, to be precise) than those on your Mac. That's because I'm using a little program called Aaron that gives the Macintosh interface a 3-D look that's just right for the 1990s. (In fact, it's similar to the look of the new Mac operating system scheduled to be introduced in 1997.) You can get this shareware program from Macworld Online's shareware collection for an inexpensive registration fee. But if you like the Mac's natural look, don't worry. Everything I show you works exactly the same on your Mac; only the appearance is a little different.

The Shortcut to Launching PageMaker

You don't have to go through all the rigmarole of using the Start menu to power up PageMaker in Windows 95 or NT 4.0, or of wading through your hard disk and folders to find the icon for PageMaker on the Macintosh. You can create a *shortcut icon* (in Windows terminology) or an *alias* (in Mac terms) for the program.

In Windows 95 or NT 4.0, the steps are as follows:

1. **Double-click on the My Computer icon.**

   In other words, place the cursor over the icon and give the left mouse button two swift clicks in a row. You can find the icon in the upper-left corner of the Windows *desktop* (that's the fancy name for the main Windows screen), although because the icons can be moved, your My Computer icon may be elsewhere on your screen. (You can also rename My Computer, so the name may be different on your system as well.) A little window labeled My Computer appears.

2. **Double-click on the icon that represents your hard drive.**

   If you installed PageMaker on your C drive, for example, double-click on the C drive icon. A window showing a list of all the folders and files on your hard drive appears.

3. **Double-click on the Pm65 folder (or whichever folder you put PageMaker in during installation).**

   A new window appears, this time showing a bunch of different icons associated with PageMaker 6.5. (You may have placed PageMaker inside a folder, so if you don't see it at first, open the folders you do see to find out whether the PageMaker folder is inside another folder.)

4. **Drag the icon labeled Pm65 out of the window and onto the Windows desktop.**

That is, place your cursor over the icon until the icon becomes highlighted. (The correct icon is spotlighted in Figure 3-3.) Then press and hold the left mouse button down as you move the mouse. The icon follows along as you drag. After you move the icon onto the Windows desktop, release the mouse button. The icon appears on the desktop with the label *Shortcut to Pm65.* If you want to rename it, click on the shortcut with the right mouse button and select the Rename menu item. Then just type in the name you like (such as *PageMaker 6.5* rather than the default *Shortcut to Pm65*).

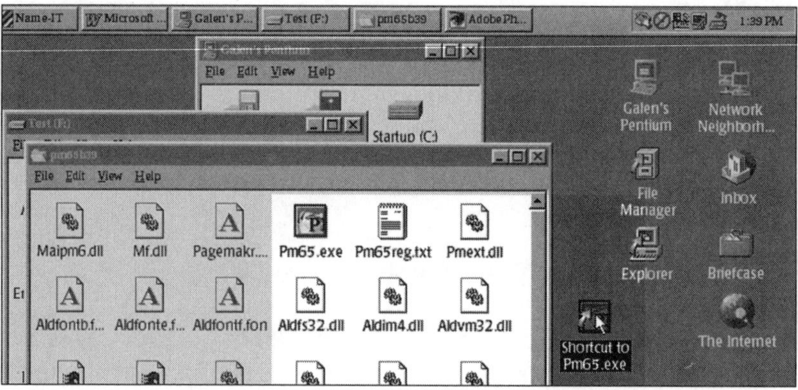

Figure 3-3: By dragging the PageMaker icon from its folder onto the Windows desktop, you create a shortcut that's easily accessible.

Now, anytime you want to start PageMaker, all you need to do is double-click on that shortcut icon. No more digging through the Start menu and all its submenus to find what you want.

If you want the PageMaker shortcut to appear in your Start menu's main list (so you don't have to go through several menus to find it) rather than on your desktop, just drag the shortcut onto the Start button instead of onto the desktop.

For more information about starting programs, creating shortcut items, and other Windows 95 topics, get yourself a copy of *Windows 95 For Dummies* by Andy Rathbone (published by IDG Books Worldwide, Inc.). Andy's book offers a wealth of great Windows tips and ideas that I simply don't have room to cover here.

On the Macintosh, the steps to creating an alias are as follows:

1. **Double-click on the Macintosh HD icon (or whatever the drive that contains the PageMaker program is called).**

   You can find the icon in the upper-right corner of the Macintosh *desktop* (that's the fancy name for the main Mac screen). Because the icons can be moved, your HD icon may be elsewhere on your screen. (You can also rename the Macintosh HD icon, so its name may be different on your system as well.) Place the pointer over the icon and give the mouse button two swift clicks in a row. A window showing a list of all the folders and files on your hard drive appears.

2. **Double-click on the Adobe PageMaker 6.5 folder (or whichever folder you put PageMaker in during installation).**

A new window appears, this time showing a bunch of different icons associated with PageMaker 6.5. (You may have placed PageMaker inside a folder, so if you don't see the PageMaker 6.5 folder at first, open the other folders that you do see to find out whether the PageMaker folder is inside another folder.)

3. **Click on the icon labeled PageMaker 6.5 to select it and then press ⌘+M.**

That is, place your pointer over the icon and then click on the mouse button once so the Mac knows that you want to work on that icon. The keyboard command ⌘+M runs a built-in Mac program that creates an alias, and you see a new icon on the screen called *PageMaker 6.5 alias*. (The correct icon is spotlighted in Figure 3-4.)

4. **Drag the alias icon to your desktop.**

Click once more on the alias icon and keep the mouse button depressed. Next, move the mouse pointer to a spot on the desktop where you want the PageMaker alias to be. When you release the mouse button, the alias icon is deposited at its new location. If you want to rename the alias, click on it with the mouse button and leave the pointer over the name. In a second, the name is highlighted, and you can type in a new name. If the name does not automatically get highlighted, click on the name once; then type in the name you want (such as *PageMaker 6.5* rather than the default *Adobe PageMaker 6.5 alias*).

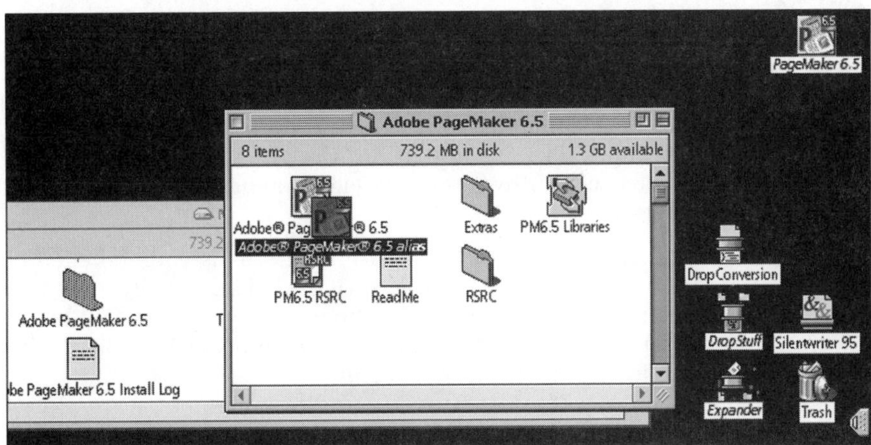

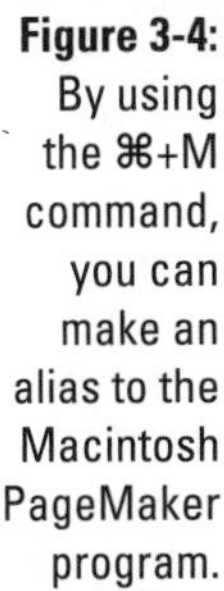

Figure 3-4: By using the ⌘+M command, you can make an alias to the Macintosh PageMaker program.

Now, when you want to start PageMaker, just double-click on that shortcut icon. No need to sift through your folders to find what you want.

If you want the PageMaker shortcut to appear in your Apple menu (the menu in the upper-left corner of the Mac desktop), rather than on your desktop, open up the System Folder and then drag the *PageMaker 6.5 alias* icon into the folder called Apple Items (this folder is inside the System Folder). The Apple menu is a convenient place to put alias icons for frequently used programs.

For more information about starting programs, creating alias items, and other Macintosh topics, get *Macs For Dummies* by David Pogue (published by IDG Books Worldwide, Inc.). His book gives you more great Mac tips and ideas than I can cover in this book.

Clicking Your Way to Happiness

You probably didn't notice, but you've already made great strides on your road to computer geekdom — well, you did if you read the preceding section, which introduces you to *dragging, clicking,* and *double-clicking.* Right off the bat, you discovered three important mouse-related terms and, except for that slight tic you acquired in your right eye, you didn't suffer any ill effects at all.

If by now you're convinced of how painless it is to become one with your computer, here's a rundown of other mouse terms you need to understand, along with a recap of terms presented in the preceding sections of this chapter:

- *Move* the mouse cursor by simply gliding your mouse across your desk or mouse pad. No button pressing required.

  On Windows, people use the term *cursor* for the little icon that represents where the mouse position is. On the Mac, people use the term *pointer.* They're the same thing.

- To *click* is to press the left mouse button once and then release it. For example, if you're advised to "Click on the PageMaker icon," place your mouse cursor over the icon and then press and release the left mouse button.
- To *right-click* is to click the right button instead of the left button. In most Windows 95 programs, right-clicking usually brings up special menus of commands and options. In PageMaker, right-clicking offers fast access to common commands for a specific object through what's called a *context-sensitive menu.*

Normally, the left mouse button is the primary button — you use it to perform most actions in most Windows programs. But if you're left-handed, you can switch the mouse buttons so that your right button does the primary tasks and the left button serves as the secondary mouse button. The instructions I give here and in future chapters assume that you're using the standard right-handed mouse setup and haven't changed your buttons.

- To *double-click* is to click the left mouse button twice in rapid succession without moving the mouse.
- To *drag* means to press the left mouse button, hold the button down as you move the mouse, and then release the button.
- If I ask you to *Shift+drag* or *Shift+click,* just hold down the Shift key as you drag or click. Likewise, for Windows users, when you see the terms *Ctrl+drag* or *Ctrl+click,* hold down the Ctrl key while you drag or click. And likewise, for Macintosh users, when you see the terms *⌘+drag* or *⌘+click,* hold down the ⌘ key while you drag or click. Finally, if you see Alt (for Windows) or Option (for Mac) combined with a drag or a click, just combine the specified key with a drag or click action. Some keyboard shortcuts use several of these key combinations, such as Shift+Alt or Option+⌘. Also, your keyboard likely has two each of the Alt, Shift, Ctrl, Option, and ⌘ keys — it doesn't matter which you use.

Macintosh mice typically have only one button, so if you use a Mac just ignore the words *left* and *right* when following mouse instructions. If you want to do the equivalent of the Windows 95 right-clicking within PageMaker, you can't. No PageMaker keyboard/mouse combination exists on the Mac to simulate the right Windows 95 mouse button. Even if you have a multiple-button mouse for the Mac, PageMaker doesn't support right-clicking on the Mac platform. Fortunately, the program rarely uses this feature even under Windows 95. When PageMaker does use the right-click features, the program provides menu or keyboard alternatives, so Mac owners lose no capabilities.

Chapter 4

Windowing, Scrolling, and More Vital Stuff

In This Chapter

- Working with program and document windows
- Mucking about in dialog boxes and menus
- Wielding tools and palettes
- Moving around the screen
- Saving your work and exiting PageMaker

You're seated at your workstation with your computer whirring away and PageMaker glowing on the screen. Palming the mouse, you're ready to pounce. The keyboard beckons. You're itching to let it fly. But, before you shift into overdrive, take a look around the cockpit and familiarize yourself with the controls.

This chapter tells you about the stuff you see on the screen when you fire up PageMaker and what all of it actually does. If you're a veteran PageMaker user, you probably already have the gist of the PageMaker components. In that case, I recommend zeroing in on the information highlighted with the Version 6.5 icon to find out what's different in this version. If you're new to computing, first check out Chapter 3 for the basics on getting PageMaker up and running.

Making Friends with the PageMaker Interface

For those of you who weren't born into a family of chipheads, the term *interface* refers to the collection of buttons, icons, scroll bars, and other on-screen stuff that lets you communicate with PageMaker. You might think of them as being similar to the instrument panel in a car's cockpit.

If you're familiar with older versions of PageMaker and Windows, the Version 6.5 interface shouldn't look terribly different. But a few new elements exist, particularly those related to Web publishing and the new layers feature (see Chapter 11 for more information on layers). Adobe is making all of its mainstay programs — Illustrator, Photoshop, and PageMaker — share the same basic look and feel. If you use any of these programs, you may already recognize some of the new elements in PageMaker 6.5.

The dull and boring program window

When you first start PageMaker 6.5 in Windows, you see the understated opening screen shown in Figure 4-1. Exciting, it ain't. But don't let appearances fool you — behind this simple facade await all kinds of powerful functions and commands. Figure 4-2 shows you the equally understated Mac opening screen.

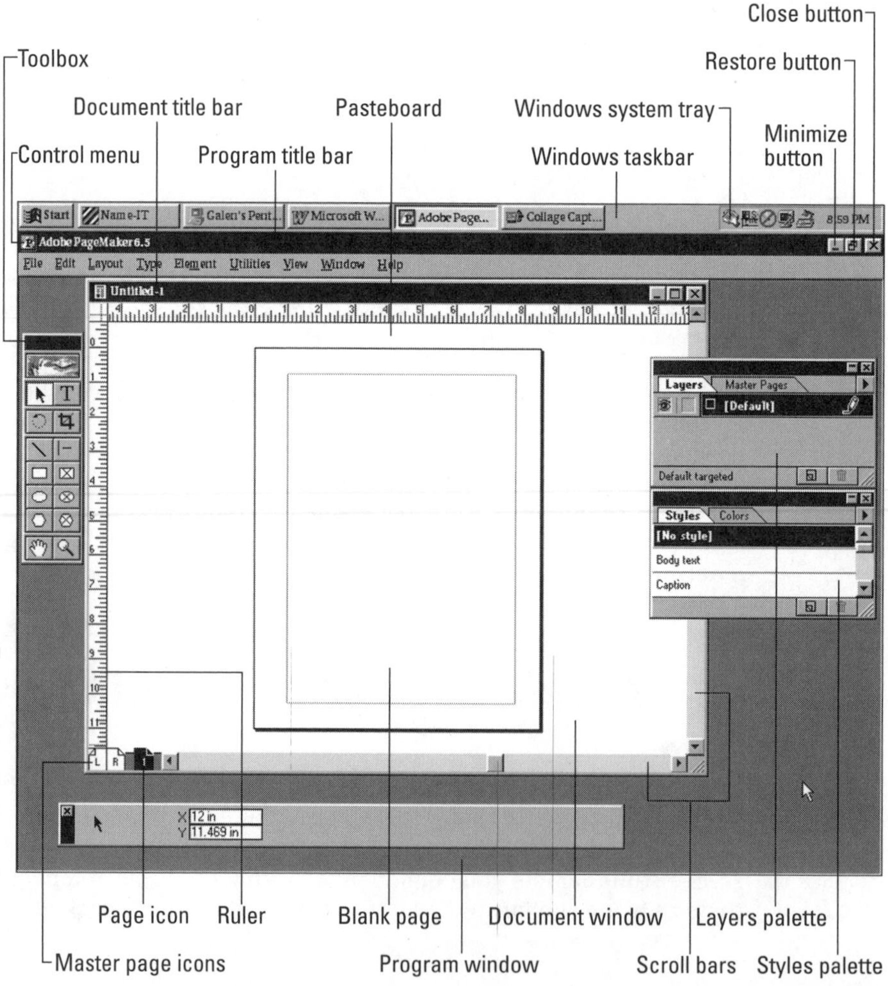

Figure 4-1: The basic PageMaker 6.5 window in Windows.

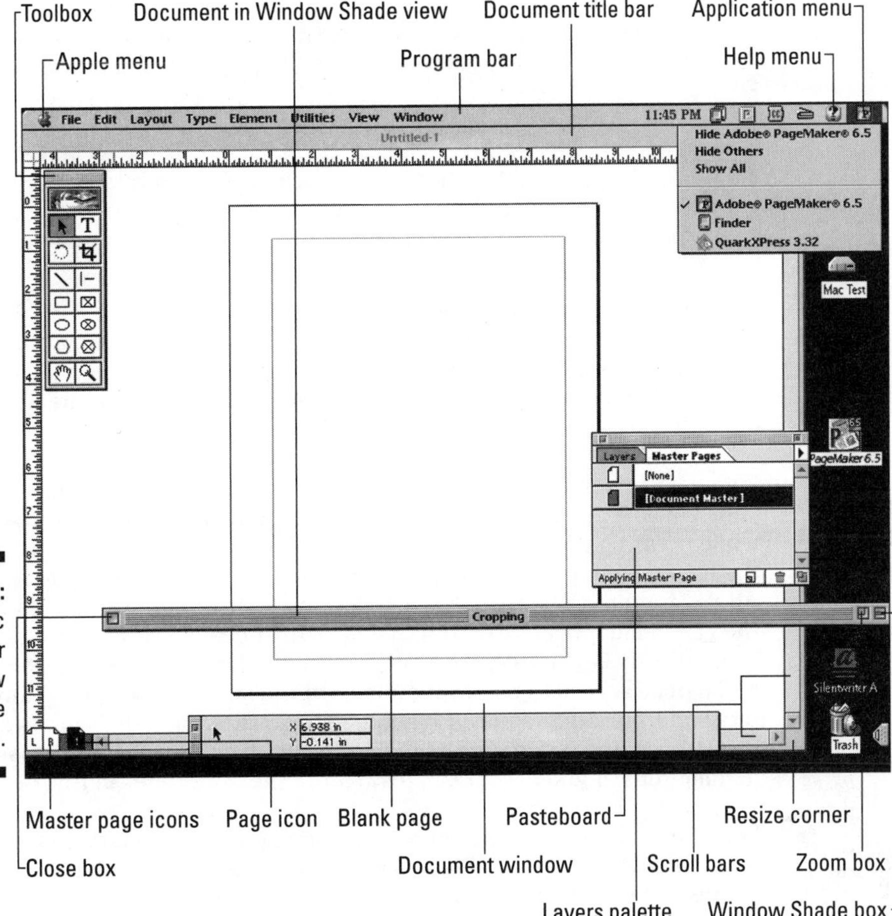

Figure 4-2: The basic PageMaker 6.5 window on the Macintosh.

The PageMaker interface in Windows and the Mac is practically identical. The few differences are due to the basic differences between Mac and Windows programs themselves. Throughout this section, I supply comparisons between the two platforms (or hardware foundations, to you non-geeks) when there are differences.

The following is a handy guide to the most basic of windows, known as the *program window.* These are its components:

- On the Mac, a *document window* (the window that contains your work, such as a layout in PageMaker) can be anywhere on-screen, while in Windows it has to be within the PageMaker program window. (A Mac program usually doesn't have a program window — just the document windows.)

- The *title bar* is that strip across the top of the window that tells you what program you're using. If the title bar doesn't say PageMaker 6.5, you missed a beat somewhere. See Chapter 3 for guidance in this area.
- To move a window around on screen, just drag its title bar.
- Directly beneath the title bar is the *menu bar.* The PageMaker 6.5 menu bar offers nine different *menus,* which are lists of related commands. The File menu, for example, contains commands that you use to open, close, save, and print files. Click on any word in the menu bar to display the corresponding menu.
- When you choose some menu items, you're presented with a *submenu.* (The arrow to the right of a command name indicates that the command has a submenu.) The submenu contains subcommands related to the first command item you chose. Again, just click on the option you want to select.

If you see underlined characters (for example, File), that signals a keyboard shortcut to an item in Windows: To get to a menu, hold down the Alt key while pressing the letter that's underlined in the menu name. After you have the menu open, press the underlined letter of the command you want — no Alt key required this time. For example, to choose the Print command from the File menu, press Alt+F and then press P. Because Windows evolved from a completely keyboard-based system called DOS, it allows both keyboard and mouse access to most functions. On the Mac, you won't see any characters underlined in menus and in dialog boxes as you do in Windows. Because the Mac started out mouse-based, it doesn't have keyboard access to all of its functions. If you use a Mac, just ignore the underlines in this book.

For an even quicker way to choose a command, use the command's *keyboard shortcut.* The available shortcuts are listed to the right of the commands in the menus. If you make the effort to memorize the keyboard shortcuts for at least the most commonly used commands, you can save yourself plenty of time. My favorites are listed in Chapter 20; plus, this book features a "cheat sheet" with the most useful shortcuts, which you can tear out and place next to your computer.

- The shortcut for the Print command, for example, is ^P on Windows. That little caret before the P stands for the Ctrl key. You press Ctrl+P to send your document to the printer. On the Mac, you see the ⌘ symbol, telling you to press the ⌘ key plus the P key (⌘+P) to send the document to the printer. Shortcut listings in Windows PageMaker also use the abbreviation *Sh* to indicate the Shift key, as well as *Alt* to indicate the Alt key. (On the Mac, you may occasionally see the symbol ⇧ to indicate the Shift key, and the symbol ⌥ to indicate the Option key.)

- In Windows, click on the *Minimize button,* labeled in Figure 4-1, to hide the PageMaker program. When you hide the PageMaker program in Windows, a PageMaker button appears on the *taskbar* at the bottom of the Windows desktop. To bring PageMaker back into Windows, just click on the Windows taskbar button. To hide the PageMaker program on the Mac, use the Hide command in the Applications menu (the rightmost menu on the Mac). The Mac displays an icon for the currently active program and lets you switch among all currently loaded programs, as shown in Figure 4-2. To unhide PageMaker, go to the Application menu and click on the PageMaker menu option.

In Windows, press Alt+Tab to switch among active programs. Each time you use this shortcut, the next program in line appears. You can keep doing this until you're dizzy.

- You can also hide the document windows that contain your layouts, while keeping PageMaker active. (You want to do this, for example, if you are working on several layouts and want to switch back and forth.) In Windows, you can also use a Minimize button for each open document window. On the Mac, use the *Window Shade box* (which looks like a horizontal bar cutting through a square), shown in Figure 4-2. Both methods hide all of a document window except the title bar; click on the title bar again to open the window back up. (The Window Shade feature comes with Mac System 7.5 and later, so it may not show up on your Mac.)

- To the right of the Minimize button in Windows is either the *Restore* button (a button with two little boxes on it) or the *Maximize* button (a button with just one box on it). When you first start PageMaker, the program window fills the entire screen. To shrink the window so that you can see other program windows or the Windows desktop, click on the Restore button. To make PageMaker or a document window fill the entire screen again, click on either the PageMaker or document Maximize button. To do the same thing for a document window, the Mac has a *Zoom* box at the window's upper-right corner (it appears as a small rectangle within a larger one). Zooming makes a window fill the full screen; if you click on the zoom box again, your Macintosh returns the window to its original size. (Remember, you have to use the Application menu to hide and unhide a program on the Mac.)

- In Windows, the button on the far right — the one with the X in it — is the *Close* button for PageMaker. A single click on this button shuts down PageMaker. Again, you can close a document window (but not PageMaker) by clicking on the document window's Close button instead of the PageMaker Close button. On the Mac, the *Close* box (the square at upper-left) closes a window (but not PageMaker). On both Windows and the Mac, if any window content is unsaved when you click on the Close button or Close box, PageMaker asks if you want to save it.

- To enlarge or reduce a minimized window in Windows, place the cursor over a corner or side of the window until the cursor changes into a two-headed arrow. Then drag until the window is the size you want it to be. On the Mac, move the pointer to the window's lower-right corner, and drag that corner to resize the window.

- In Windows, if you click on the PageMaker icon on the far left side of the title bar, you see a short menu known as the *Control menu.* But, because you can access all but one of these options by either dragging a window or clicking on a button, you almost never need to use this menu. The exception is the Clipboard command. Choose this command to see what's currently on the Windows *clipboard,* which is where Windows stores stuff that you've copied or cut from a document or graphic element. To do the same thing on the Mac, access the clipboard through the Edit menu's Show Clipboard option.

The more exciting document window

To start uncovering the real goodies in PageMaker, you need to open a document (also known as a *publication* in PageMaker lingo). To open a new document, choose the New command from the File menu (or just press Ctrl+N on Windows or ⌘+N on the Mac). You're immediately confronted by a dialog box full of frightening options. For now, ignore them and press Enter or click on OK (you find out all about this dialog box in Chapter 5). The dialog box disappears, and you see something that looks a lot like Figures 4-1 or 4-2.

The document window has almost the same elements as the program window described earlier, with some differences:

- In the Windows Control menu from the document window, there is no Clipboard menu option — that exists only in the PageMaker Control menu. Otherwise, a document's Control menu works just like the overall PageMaker Control menu.
- Beneath the title bar is the *horizontal ruler.* Along the left edge of the document window is the *vertical ruler.* You use the rulers to precisely position elements on a page, as discussed in Chapter 5.
- Along the right edge of the publication window is a scroll bar. Click on the up-pointing *scroll arrow* or the down-pointing scroll arrow to move the on-screen display up or down to reveal more of your document. To move in bigger increments, drag the *scroll box* up or down. You can also click in the scroll bar on either side of the scroll box to jump from one spot to another in your document.

- Another scroll bar sits along the bottom of the window. Click on the right- or left-pointing arrows to shift the view of your document to the right or left, respectively. Drag the scroll box to move in a more dramatic fashion. You can also click into it to jump around.
- An even quicker way to move around the screen is to use the hand cursor, known in some regions as the *grabber* cursor. Just press and hold down the Alt key (on Windows) or Option key (on the Mac) while dragging up or down with any tool but the Zoom tool (the one that looks like a magnifying glass). A little hand appears while you drag. When you release the Alt or Option key, the cursor changes back to the cursor for the tool you were using.
- That big rectangle in the center of your screen represents your new *page.* The blue and pink lines inside the page represent the left, right, top, and bottom page *margins.*
- The area outside the page boundary is called the *pasteboard.* The pasteboard is sort of like the electronic version of a drafting table — it's a handy holding area for graphics or other elements that you may want to place on your pages at a later time. Stuff on the pasteboard doesn't print when you print the document.
- The little icons in the bottom-left corner of the window — called *page icons* — represent the pages of your document. You click on these icons to move from page to page. (Figures 4-1 and 4-2 show a single-page document, so you see only one page icon. If you create a multiple-page document, you see an icon for every page.) The L and R icons represent the document's master pages, discussed in Chapter 12.
- Last but not least is the toolbox, located in the upper-left corner of the window. The toolbox is essential to creating, placing, and manipulating text and graphics in PageMaker, which is why it's discussed in glorious detail in the next section.

Tinkering with the toolbox

The PageMaker *toolbox,* also referred to as the *Tool palette,* is the digital version of a layout artist's tool chest. The tools are the instruments that you use to do your layout work. In Version 6.5, you get 14 tools, which is four more than in Version 6. To select a tool, click on the respective icon in the toolbox. The mouse cursor (*pointer,* in Mac-speak) changes to indicate what tool you've selected. Figure 4-3 shows the tools and their respective cursors.

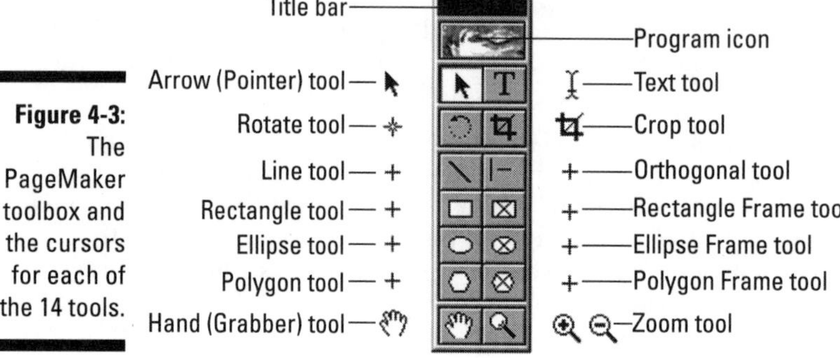

Figure 4-3: The PageMaker toolbox and the cursors for each of the 14 tools.

The following is what you find if you poke around the contents of the toolbox:

- The *Arrow tool* is the workhorse of PageMaker. Use it to select, move, and resize text blocks and graphics. Upcoming chapters explain everything you need to know. (PageMaker calls this tool the *Pointer tool.* I think that the Arrow tool is easier to remember, given the icon's shape, so that's the term I use.)
- The new and improved *Hand tool* does two things: Move the Hand tool with the mouse to slide around the pasteboard — no need to use the scroll bars — and use the tool to highlight all hypertext links to Web pages and other PageMaker pages (the subject of hypertext links is covered in Chapter 16).

- New to Version 6.5 are frame tool versions of the *Rectangle, Ellipse,* and *Polygon tools.* (The Polygon tool has also been reshaped; it now has six sides rather than five.) They're the three shapes with an X inside them. *Frames* are a new feature to PageMaker that give you the ability to create empty boxes that can hold text or graphics. Frames let you create a blank layout format that someone else can fill with text or graphics without worrying about misplacing each element. In previous versions of PageMaker, you had to place every element manually, in a free-form way, without these new framing placeholder boxes. The non-frame versions of these tools draw the indicated shapes as earlier PageMaker versions have done.
- Use the *Line* and *Orthogonal Line tools* to draw lines; these tools are covered in Chapter 13. (Orthogonal lines can be completely horizontal, completely vertical, or drawn at a 45-degree angle.)
- Use the *Text tool* to create and edit text, as described in depth in Part III.

- The *Rotate tool* lets you spin an object to any angle. Be aware that rotation is ignored when you create your Web documents, so don't bother with this tool unless you're creating printed publications.
- The *Crop tool* lets you cut away unwanted portions of graphics, as described in Chapter 14.

In case you ever forget which program you're working in (I admit it, I've done it myself), just click on the little PageMaker icon that appears on top of the toolbox. It's there to remind you that you're in PageMaker. Yes, it's odd — but true. Each Adobe program has its own graphic in that spot. If you look at the graphic carefully, you can see it's a piece of the picture on the box the program comes in. Click on the graphic to get a display of the program name and version number, and just click on the display to get rid of it.

To move the toolbox to a new location, drag its title bar. Version 6.5 no longer has a Close box or button on the toolbox, so you have to use Window⇨Hide Tools to hide the toolbox, and Window⇨Show Tools to redisplay the toolbox.

Sorting through the other palettes

In addition to the Tool palette, you can display eight other palettes. The palettes give you a convenient way to access some of the most commonly used PageMaker functions and commands. Figure 4-4 shows the palettes on screen together.

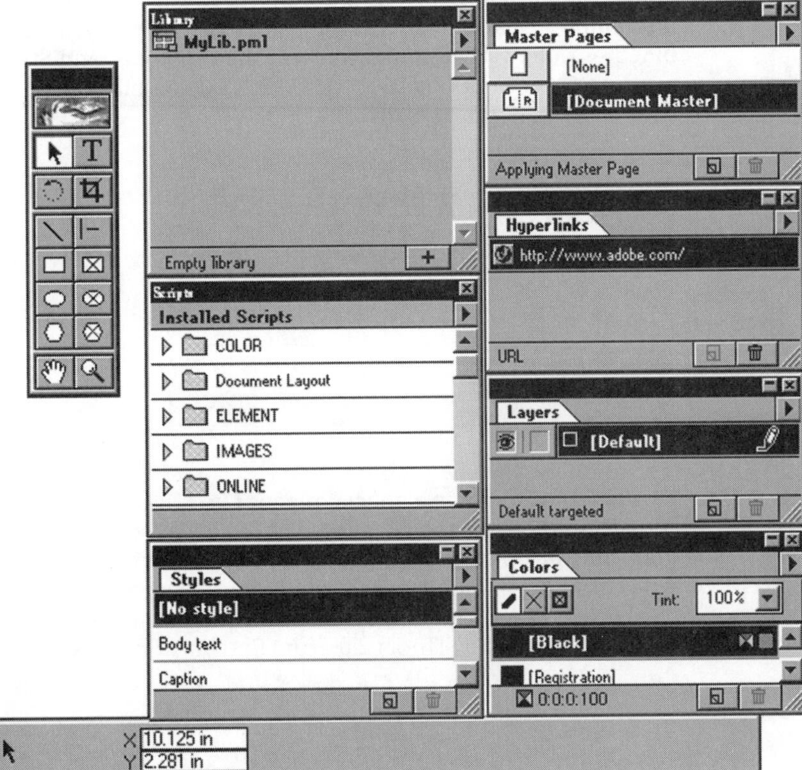

Figure 4-4: PageMaker provides palettes for quick access to program features. (The Tool palette is at left and the Control palette is at the bottom.)

To open, close, or move palettes, do the following:

- To display a palette, click on its name in the Windows menu. A check mark next to the palette name means that it's turned on.
- Click on a palette's Close button or box to remove it from view.
- Drag a palette's title bar to move it to a new on-screen location. Drag the palette's side or corners to resize it.

If you clutter your screen with too many palettes, you can't see what you're working on. As a thoughtful measure, PageMaker lets you combine up to five of them into one palette, and lets you resize all but the Control palette to whatever size makes sense for you. You can also hide palettes you're not using.

To combine palettes, just drag the title of one into the window of another. The dragged palette becomes part of the other palette's window. To switch among the grouped palettes, click on the tab for the palette you want. (Users of Microsoft's latest products recognize this tabbed palette technique and know that Microsoft programs don't let you decide which palettes you want to group together. The newest version of Photoshop also uses this technique.) To separate palettes, drag them out of a window; PageMaker creates a new palette window automatically. Or you can move palettes from one window to another. Figure 4-5 shows all five palettes that can be combined — Colors, Hyperlinks, Layers, Master Pages, and Styles — in one window. (You can't combine the Tool, Control, Library, or Scripts palettes with other palettes or each other.)

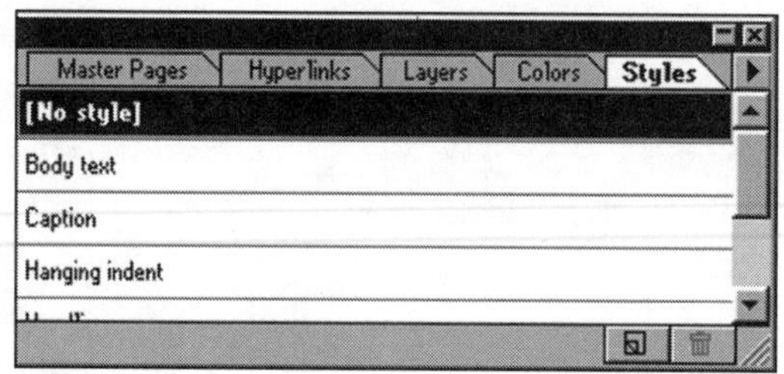

Figure 4-5: Five palettes combined into one window.

Two palettes reside in a special place. The Library and Script palettes are actually add-on programs called *plug-ins* because they are small programs that "plug in" to the PageMaker program. To activate or deactivate them, use Window⇨Plug-in Palettes. You can buy other programs that also appear as palettes and are hidden or displayed through this menu. The most popular set of plug-ins is PageTools 2.0, from Extensis Corp., which has 19 functions.

Here's a rundown of what each palette does:

- The *Colors palette* lets you quickly apply colors to various elements.
- The *Control palette* lets you change the formatting of text with a click of the mouse instead of wading through several levels of menus and submenus. Control palette options change based on what is selected, giving just the relevant options.

- The new *Hyperlinks palette* is where you define and apply hypertext links, both within your PageMaker document and to World Wide Web addresses (called *Uniform Resource Locators* or *URLs* for short). For example, `www.adobe.com` takes you to Adobe's Internet site. See Chapter 23 for examples of Web sites whose layouts I particularly like.

- The new *Layers palette* manages layers in your PageMaker document. With this new palette you can group elements and then hide, lock, or delete them all as a group. Unlike regular groups, a layer exists throughout your document. For example, you can have all English text on an English layer and all French text on a French layer, and then hide the French layer when printing the English version of the document.
- The *Master Pages palette* lets you create and use templates within your documents so you don't have to create common elements over and over. For example, if you are making a Web site for a company that sells car accessories, you can have a master page for your product-description pages, a second master page for directory pages, and a third master page for price-list pages.
- The *Library palette* provides access to *libraries,* where you can store text and graphics that you use frequently. The first time you click on the Library item you get a dialog box, in which you create your first library. From then on, the palette itself displays when you click on the Library item in the Window menu. Libraries are explained in Chapter 12.

- The *Scripts palette* offers access to *scripts,* which are miniprograms designed to automate certain tasks. (They're similar to the macros used by some word-processing programs, if that helps.) Because scripts are an advanced function, I don't cover them in this book.
- The *Styles palette* lets you apply a predefined combination of text formatting to a paragraph. For example, you can create a style called *Headline* to make sure that all the headlines have the right specs. You probably use a similar feature in your word processor.
- The *Tool palette* is the toolbox you met earlier in this section. This palette provides the mouse tools you use the most in PageMaker.

Talking Back to Dialog Boxes

When you choose a command from one of the PageMaker menus, you're likely to be greeted by a *dialog box.* A dialog box is the way PageMaker tells you it needs more information before it can carry out your wishes. The following list explains the different elements found in dialog boxes and what to do with these elements. The various bits and pieces are labeled in Figure 4-6:

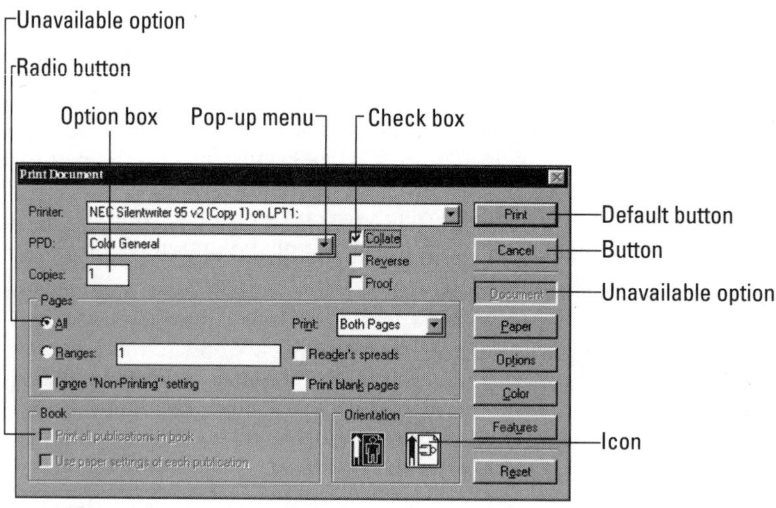

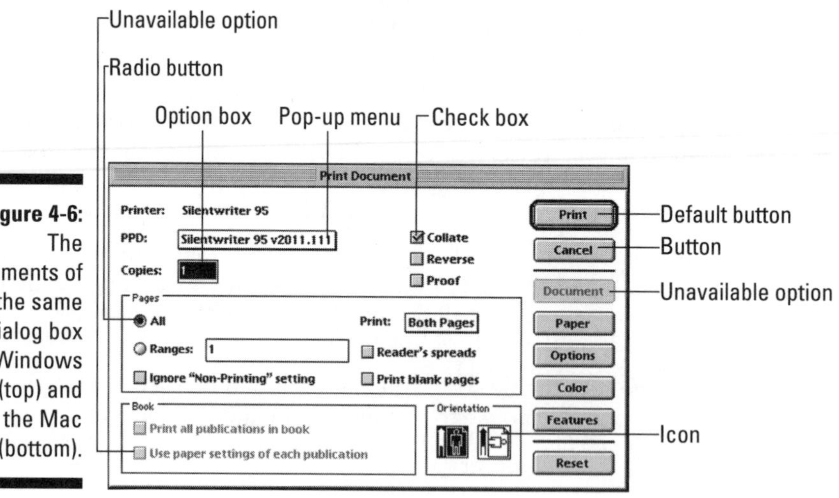

Figure 4-6: The elements of the same dialog box in Windows (top) and the Mac (bottom).

- A box in which you can enter numbers or text is called an *option box.* Double-click on an option box to highlight its contents. Then enter the correct information from the keyboard.
- *Pop-up menus* (distinguishable from other types of menus by its drop shadow) — also called *drop-down lists* by some folks — contain lists of options. In Windows, click on the down-pointing arrow to display the list. On the Mac or in Windows, just click anywhere in the menu. Then click on the option you want to use.
- You turn some options on or off by clicking on the corresponding *radio button.* When the option is turned on, a black dot appears in the center of the radio button. You can turn on only one radio button at a time in a group of radio buttons.
- Click on a *check box* to turn the corresponding option on or off. A check mark in the box indicates that the option is turned on. You can turn on as many check boxes in a group as you want. (The check mark may appear as an X on the Mac; that's fine.)
- The normal, rectangular *buttons* in a dialog box let you initiate a command or open other dialog boxes to access more options. In the dialog boxes shown in Figure 4-6, for example, you can click on the Print button to begin printing or click on the Options button to open a second dialog box containing printer options.
- The default button can be activated by pressing the Enter key rather than by using the mouse. In Windows, the default button is indicated by having a thicker rule around it; on the Mac, the default button has two lines around it.

- In Windows, instead of clicking on a button, you can select a button or option by pressing Alt plus the underlined letter of the button name.
- To move from option to option without using the mouse, press Tab. On the Mac, this usually moves you just from one option box to the next.

Getting Around

Okay, now it's time to understand how to maneuver through your workspace.

Use the scroll bars to move within your PageMaker layout, or use the Hand tool and simply move around the document by holding down the mouse button and then moving your mouse — PageMaker moves the layout just like you'd move a sheet of paper.

Changing your view

Although moving around is easy, you may find moving around to be even easier if you're seeing the document at a different scale. Standing back or moving in close are natural actions to take when working on physical paper, so PageMaker provides the electronic equivalents.

When you first open a new document, PageMaker displays your page in Fit in Window view. In this display mode, you can see your entire page in the publication window. If you want to take a closer look at your work — or, alternatively, step back farther for a long-range view — you can choose commands from either the View menu or use the Zoom tool.

In the previous version of PageMaker, page-view commands were chosen from the Layout menu. Although the Layout menu remains, these page-view options are now in the new View menu.

You can view your work in several ways:

- Choose View to display a submenu containing several preset page magnifications.
- Choose Actual Size to see your text and graphics at their approximate print size. Or use the shortcut Ctrl+1 (Windows) or ⌘+1 (Mac).
- Choose Entire Pasteboard to zoom out so that you can see all objects on your pasteboard. Or use the shortcut Ctrl+Shift+0 (zero) or Shift+⌘+0 (zero).

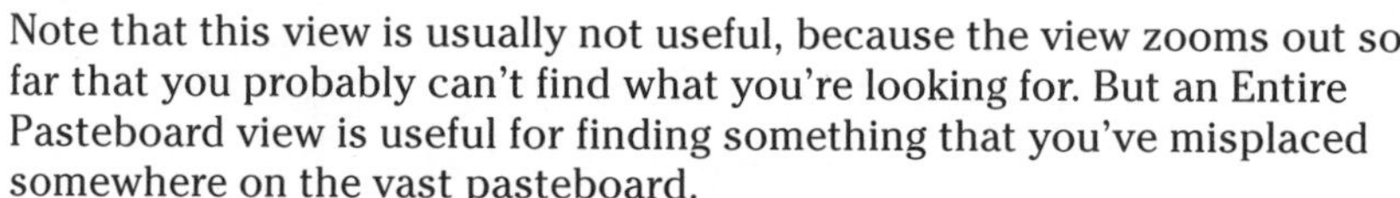

  Note that this view is usually not useful, because the view zooms out so far that you probably can't find what you're looking for. But an Entire Pasteboard view is useful for finding something that you've misplaced somewhere on the vast pasteboard.

- Choose Fit in Window to see the current page in your window. The degree of magnification depends on your page size and your monitor size. The keyboard shortcut is Ctrl+0 (zero) or ⌘+0 (zero).

- In Windows, shift+right-click to toggle between the Fit in Window and Actual Size views. The place you click on appears at the center of the document window. Ctrl+shift+right-click to toggle between Actual Size and 200% Size.
- An even quicker way to zoom in and out is to use the Zoom tool, labeled in Figure 4-3. To zoom in, click on the Zoom tool to select it. Then click on the area you want to magnify. (The plus sign in the magnifying glass cursor indicates that you're zooming in.) The spot you click on becomes centered in the PageMaker window. If you don't like to use the mouse, you can use the keyboard: Use Ctrl+plus-sign to zoom in. (Use the plus sign on the keyboard next to the Backspace key — the one on the numeric keypad won't work for this.)

- To zoom out, press and hold the Ctrl key (in Windows) or Option key (on the Mac) as you click with the Zoom tool. The cursor changes to a magnifying glass with a minus sign in it to indicate that you're zooming out. To avoid the mouse here, too, use Ctrl+hyphen (think of the hyphen as a minus sign). (Again, use the keyboard key, not the keypad key.)

- Note that zooming out is one of the few instances in PageMaker where the Ctrl key is used on Windows and the ⌘ key on the Mac is *not* its counterpart.
- Keep clicking with the Zoom tool to further magnify or reduce your view. The center of the magnifying glass cursor appears blank when you're zoomed all the way in or out. Using this technique, you can magnify your view by as much as 400 percent and reduce it to 25 percent.
- If you use the Fit Entire Pasteboard view, you can zoom out more than 400 percent, depending on the pasteboard size. On Windows only, you can zoom in more than 400 percent or reduce your view to less than 25 percent by right-clicking on the pasteboard and choosing the Other View option on the menu that appears and then entering your desired zoom percentage.
- You can also drag with the Zoom tool to surround a portion of your page with a dotted rectangle, known in desktop publishing circles as a *marquee.* When you release the mouse button, the area you surrounded is magnified so that it fills the screen, up to a maximum magnification of 400 percent.
- To temporarily access the Zoom tool while you're working with another tool, press and hold Ctrl+spacebar or ⌘+spacebar. When the cursor changes to the zoom in cursor, click to zoom in or drag to marquee the area you want to zoom in on. To zoom out using this technique, hold the Alt key (Windows) or Option key (Mac)+spacebar.

Dealing with multiple windows

You can open as many documents at a time as your computer's memory allows. To see two or more open documents side by side, choose Window⇨Tile. To display your open windows so that they're layered on top of each other, with only the title bars sticking out, choose Window⇨Cascade. To switch from one open document to another, click on the inactive document's title bar or choose its name from the bottom of the Window menu. On both the Mac and Windows, you can also press Ctrl+F6 to cycle through the open windows.

You can also resize and reposition document windows with the mouse. To resize, drag the lower-right corner. (In Windows, you can also drag any side or corner, not just the lower-right corner.) To reposition, just drag the document window's title bar. Remember that on the Mac, a document window can be anywhere on screen, while in Windows a document window has to stay inside the program window.

To switch from PageMaker to another running program, just click on that program's button on the taskbar if you're in Windows, or use the Applications menu if you're on a Mac. Use the taskbar (in Windows) or Applications menu (on the Mac) to get back to PageMaker when you're done with the other program. (In Windows, you can also use Alt+Tab to go from one program to the next, or use a very inexpensive, nifty utility for the Mac called Program Switcher that does the same thing; you can download it from Macworld Online on the Internet at `http://www.macworld.com` or on America Online at the keyword `Macworld`.)

Shutting Down and Saving Your Work

When you decide that you've had enough of PageMaker for the day, you need to do three things: Close your document, close PageMaker, and shut down your computer.

To close a document and save it for the first time

1. **Click on the Close button or box in the document window.**

   Or press Ctrl+W or choose File⇨Close. PageMaker responds by displaying a dialog box asking whether you want to save any changes you've made to your publication. In Windows, you can also Ctrl+F4 to close the window or double-click on the Control menu's icon.

2. **To save your changes, click on Yes or press Enter.**

   The Save Publication dialog box, shown in Figure 4-7, is displayed. If you don't want to save your changes, click on No instead and skip to Step 8. Click on Cancel if you decide that you're not ready to close the document after all.

3. **Select a file destination from the Save in pop-up menu.**

   In Windows, tell PageMaker where you want the file to be stored by selecting a folder from the Save in pop-up menu. On the Mac, use the pop-up menu above the file list to change folders. Figure 4-7 shows some other useful features in the Save dialog box.

4. **Give your publication a name.**

   Double-click on the File Name option box (in Windows) or the Save publication as option box (on the Mac) and then type in a name.

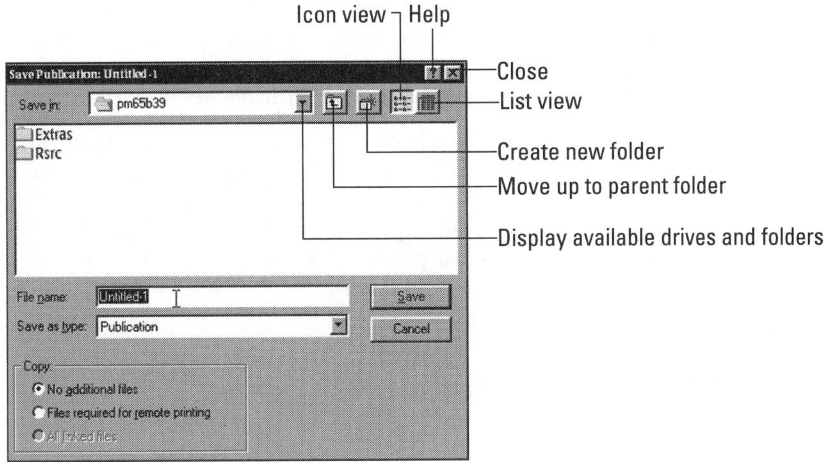

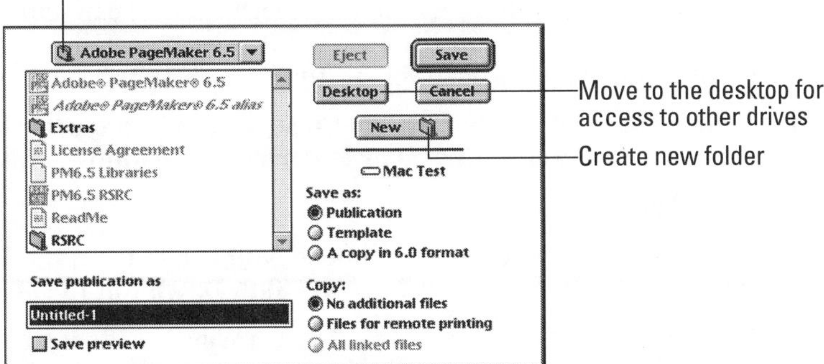

Figure 4-7: The Save Publication dialog box for Windows (top) and Macintosh (bottom).

5. **Choose a file type.**

   The Save as Type pop-up menu in Windows offers three choices. On the Mac, the three choices are displayed as radio buttons under the Save as option. The Publication option saves your document as a PageMaker 6.5 document. Choose Template to save your publication as a template, as explained in Chapter 12. And if you want to be able to open your publication in PageMaker 6.0, choose the A Copy in 6.0 Format option.

   If you choose the A Copy in 6.0 Format option, some features of your publication may be modified. You lose some of your hypertext links for your Web pages, for example, and any layers you've created (layers are discussed in Chapter 11).

6. **Choose a Copy radio button.**

   In most cases, you want to choose the No Additional Files option. The All Linked Files option copies linked text and graphics files, but not the special printing files to the same folder as the publication. (Those special printing files include hyphenation lists and kerning lists, which are of no use for Web documents and can be ignored.) You may want to use this option if you're passing off the documents to a colleague who is going to do additional layout or editing work on the document.

You rarely use the Files Required for Remote Printing option. This option is designed for sending files to a service bureau or commercial printer for printing, which is something you would never do with a Web document. This option copies all linked files and graphics plus other special files needed for printing to the same folder. You can then quickly copy the files to a floppy disk or SyQuest cartridge for your service bureau (this only applies, of course, to your print publications work and not to pages for the Web).

7. **Click on the Save button.**

   PageMaker saves your file.

   On the Mac, an extra option is included in the Save Publications dialog box: Save Preview. If you check this box, the Mac-based image catalog program Adobe Fetch (now sold as Extensis Fetch) can import a thumbnail preview of your PageMaker file into its catalog. (Chances are rare that you will ever need this feature.)

8. **To close PageMaker, click on the Close button in the program window. You can also use Ctrl+Q or ⌘+Q, and on Windows, Alt+F4.**

   PageMaker shuts down.

9. **To shut down your computer, choose Shut Down from the Windows Start menu (in Windows) or Special⇨Shut Down (on the Mac).**

   In Windows, when you see the Shut Down Windows dialog box, choose the Shut Down the Computer? radio button. Windows displays a message telling you to be patient for a minute and then displays a message saying that it's safe to turn off your computer. Give the computer's on/off button a press and go see what's been happening in the real world while you've had your nose to the computer screen.

   On the Mac, the system shuts off the power by itself, with a few exceptions (such as the Centris 610, Quadra 610, and some Performa models), for which you need to press the power button yourself after the message appears on screen saying that it's okay to turn off the Mac.

The next time you work on a saved document, PageMaker doesn't display the Save Publication dialog box after you click on Yes in Step 2 described earlier. It just resaves your document by using the same settings you chose the first time you saved. If you want to save the document under a new name or make other changes to the save options, choose File⇨Save As to open the Save Publication dialog box. Choose the options you want and then click on the Save button.

To ensure that you won't lose hours of work if your computer crashes while you're toiling in PageMaker, save your publication early and often. After you've saved a publication for the first time, you can just press Ctrl+S or ⌘+S to save the publication again. To save all open publications in one fell swoop, press Ctrl+Shift+S or Shift+⌘+S. Get in the habit of pressing Ctrl+S or ⌘+S frequently — you save yourself loads of grief when your computer decides to freak out on you (notice that I said *when*, not *if*).

Every time you switch from one page in your document to another, PageMaker saves the page you switched from, giving you some extra crash protection. When you restart your computer and PageMaker, the program uses that interim version, called a *mini-save*. If you're working on a layout and don't like what you've done, you can go back to the last minisave by holding down the Shift key as you choose File⇨Revert. (If you don't hold down the Shift key, it opens up the last version of the file you saved with the Save command, with Ctrl+S or ⌘+S, or by selecting Yes to the prompt after closing an unsaved document.)

Now that you've become acquainted with the PageMaker screens, dialog boxes, and so forth, you're ready to actually *do* something with the program.

With all this new computer wisdom under your belt, you are no doubt going to receive that invitation to lunch with the Webmaster crowd very soon. Remember to have some Zip disks sticking out of your shirt pocket — just to look extra cool.

Chapter 5

Filling in the Blanks

In This Chapter

- Opening new and existing documents
- Setting up margins
- Dividing your page into columns
- Establishing rulers and guides (and figuring out what to do with them)
- Using the Guide Manager

PageMaker 6.5 is sort of like Arnold ("Ahnüld") Schwarzenegger. No doubt you're thinking, "Oh, sure, and WordPerfect reminds *me* of Benji," but bear with me for a second. If you're like most people, the first time you saw Ahnüld on TV or whatever, you probably thought, "Get a load of this muscle-bound troglodyte. Is he a dim bulb or what?" But, unlike dozens of other celebrity Neanderthals who made millions and then promptly squandered every cent before they turned 35, Ahnüld invests his money shrewdly. Reputedly, nearly every business deal that the guy makes turns to gold.

So as you may imagine, an existing school of thought says maybe Ahnüld's not nearly as dumb as he looks. Maybe he acts dumb so that his audience won't feel threatened by the true Ahnüld, who is a thinker of brainiac proportions.

The same is true for PageMaker. After you start the program, all you see are a few pull-down menus at the top of the screen. Nothing fancy. Nothing at all, in fact, to lead you to believe that you haven't wasted some perfectly good money on another hopelessly rinky-dink piece of software. But, as you can discover in Chapter 4, the simple PageMaker facade is only that — a facade.

You see, PageMaker *pretends* to be dumb at first so that you don't feel insecure. Then, as you warm up to the program, it reveals more and more of its power, until pretty soon, you're feeling like you're hot stuff. It's a stealth program just as surely as Ahnüld is a stealth intellectual.

In this chapter, you get a glimpse beyond the unassuming exterior of PageMaker and start discovering its inner strengths. You find out how to take the first step in the page layout process — which is to set up columns and margins — and how to use tools such as ruler guides and the Guide Manager to make placing text and graphics easier.

Opening a New (Or Used) Document

In the old days, the first step in page layout was to grab a *layout board* — a thin piece of white cardboard that sported light blue vertical and horizontal gridlines. Layout artists pasted text and graphics on the board, using the gridlines to align elements on the page.

Now, in the PageMaker era, whether you are starting a new layout or reworking an existing one, you must grab the electronic equivalent of a layout board (a document, which is referred to as a *publication* in the official PageMaker dictionary) to start the layout process. Even though you're producing pages for the Web, you're still using this old-fashioned print metaphor. Remember, PageMaker is in the business of helping you create layouts — it doesn't care whether they end up on paper or online.

Starting from scratch

To open a new document, choose File⇨New or press Ctrl+N (in Windows) or ⌘+N (on the Mac). PageMaker responds by showing you the Document Setup dialog box, which lets you establish certain settings for your publication, such as page margins. To get a detailed explanation of the options in this dialog box, skip to the "Setting Up Your Pages" section in this chapter. If you just want to go to a blank page in PageMaker and leave the setup chores for later, press Enter or click on OK to accept the default settings already existing in the program.

Working on an existing document

To open an existing document, choose File⇨Open or press Ctrl+O or ⌘+O to display the Open Publication dialog box, as shown in Figure 5-1. Choose the folder that contains the document you want to open from the Look in pop-up menu (on the Mac, the pop-up menu has no name and appears above the file list box). Then, double-click on the filename in the file list box.

Details button (for list view)

Icon button (for icon view)

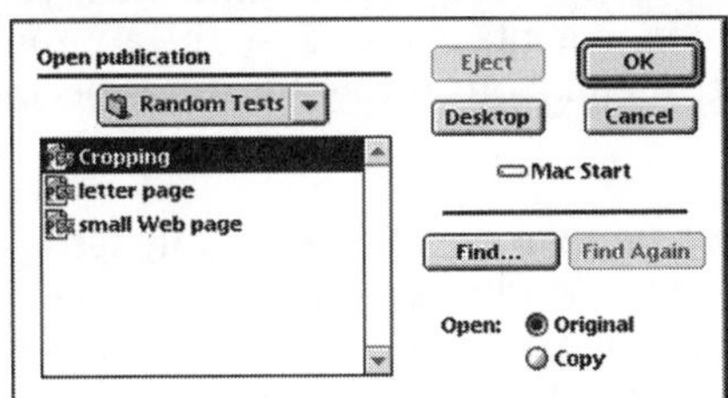

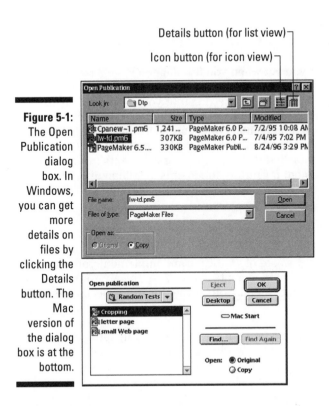

Figure 5-1: The Open Publication dialog box. In Windows, you can get more details on files by clicking the Details button. The Mac version of the dialog box is at the bottom.

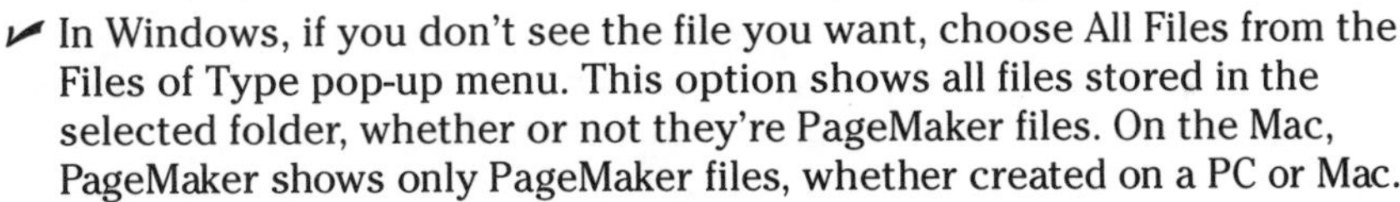

- In Windows, if you don't see the file you want, choose All Files from the Files of Type pop-up menu. This option shows all files stored in the selected folder, whether or not they're PageMaker files. On the Mac, PageMaker shows only PageMaker files, whether created on a PC or Mac.

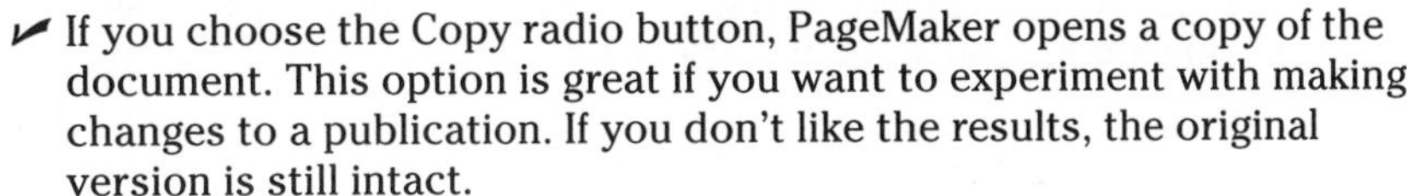

- If you choose the Copy radio button, PageMaker opens a copy of the document. This option is great if you want to experiment with making changes to a publication. If you don't like the results, the original version is still intact.

  Note: The Original button is grayed out unless you have selected a Version 6.5 PageMaker file — PageMaker automatically makes a copy of earlier-version files.

- In Windows, to get more information about a document, such as the size of the file and the date the document was last modified, click on the Details button, labeled in Figure 5-1. No such Mac equivalent exists.
- If you want to open a publication that you recently worked on, you don't have to mess with the Open Publication dialog box. To open the pre-existing publication, choose File➪Recent Publications and then click on the document name in the submenu.

Making Changes to Your Defaults

The simple interface that you get when you first launch PageMaker has an additional purpose (other than allowing you to think that you're smarter than the program). As it turns out, any setting that you choose in any of dozens of menus and dialog boxes when no document is open becomes a *default setting* for all future documents. For example, if you define colors, these colors are part of all future documents. If you create styles, they are part of all future documents. If you change the measurements from inches to millimeters, the measurement for future documents is millimeters. This is the handy-dandy way PageMaker enables you to adjust settings so that all new documents use them.

As you discover how to use the various options described in this and other chapters, you may find that you keep changing certain settings over and over. To eliminate this utter waste of your time and implement your changes once and for all, close all open documents and choose the appropriate command from the appropriate menu. Your revised settings become the new defaults.

You may be surprised when you find out how many default settings you can change. Don't worry if you don't know what even half of the following items mean; they're just presented here to plant a few subliminal flags in your brain. When you come across comprehensive descriptions of one setting or another in other chapters, the flag goes up, and you think, "You know, to change the default for this option, all I need to do is close the current document and choose this command." That's the idea, anyway. Whether it works is a matter for historians to discuss. Those historians who don't have anything better to do with their time, that is.

Before creating your Web pages, cruise through the following options to select your own default settings:

- Options in the Preferences dialog box (File⇨Preferences⇨General, or Ctrl+K or ⌘+K), which include ruler measurement units, guide settings, the Story Editor font, and save options

  The Preferences dialog box has been moved down a level in PageMaker 6.5 to accommodate the three new preferences dialog boxes (Online, Layout Adjustment, and Trapping) inside of it. So, the new Ctrl+K or ⌘+K shortcut will definitely save you a few steps.

- Document setup options such as page size, orientation, and numbering
- Multiple paste repeating values and offset amounts
- Number of columns, ruler display, and guide snap
- Automatic text flow

- Typestyle, font, size, tab, indentation, and other text settings
- Style sheets
- Link settings (so your layout picks up the latest version of any imported graphics)
- Hyperlinks display settings
- Color definitions
- Palette positioning

To establish default settings, choose either a command from the menu bar or choose File⇨Preferences and make your selections in the Preferences dialog box. (Most of these settings *don't* reside in the Preferences dialog box, but are on separate submenus, so it may help to make note of them.) Remember, you need to close any open documents to establish new default settings, but you don't need to restart your computer to make these settings stick.

Setting Up Your Pages

When you choose File⇨New or choose Ctrl+N or ⌘+N to create a new document, the Document Setup dialog box appears, as shown in Figure 5-2. This dialog box is where you give PageMaker basic instructions on how to set up your document, as the rest of this section describes. But nothing's set in stone. After you create your document, choose File⇨Document Setup to change these settings at any time.

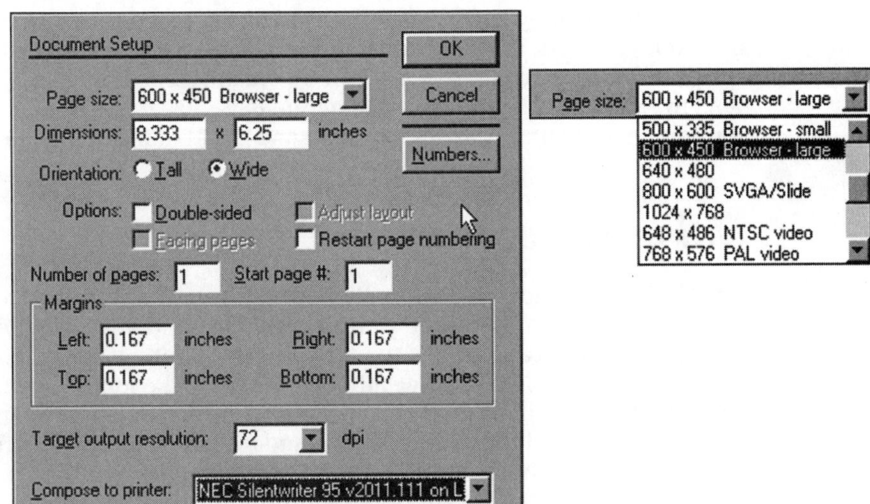

Figure 5-2: The Document Setup dialog box. The various Web-page sizes are shown at right.

At the beginning of this chapter, I said that PageMaker doesn't like to overwhelm you. Well, that's not *always* true. The Document Setup dialog box is a prime example of PageMaker doing its absolute best to frighten you into an apoplectic fit. To prevent you from entering some kind of computer-induced seizure, the next few sections examine each of the document setup options one at a time.

Before you can tell PageMaker how to set up your pages, you need to have an idea of how you want your finished publication to look. You don't need to have your entire layout planned, and you can always alter elements after you've worked on your publication for a while, but your job is easier if you already have answers to the basic layout questions. For example, do you want your Web page to have three or four columns of text per page? Do you want your pages to fit in a monitor screen, or do you want to use traditional paper sizes for your Web pages? (If you don't have the faintest idea how you want your pages to look, browse through Chapter 23, which shows some examples of effective layouts.)

Page-size settings

Select your page size from the Page Size pop-up menu. (See Figure 5-2.) Chances are that you want to select one of the new page dimensions designed for the Web, such as a 600 × 450 Browser – large, or 640 × 480. These measurements are in *pixels* — those tiny dots on the screen. (See the sidebar "Sizing up Web page measurements" in this chapter.)

You also can use one of the standard print sizes, such as Letter ($8^1/_2 \times 11$ inches), Legal ($8^1/_2 \times 14$ inches), or Tabloid (11 × 17 inches). You can even make up your own size. To do so, activate the Custom option in the Page Size pop-up menu by entering the measurements you desire into the Dimensions option boxes. Entering nonstandard numbers in the Dimensions option boxes tells PageMaker that you're creating a custom size. (You don't need to select the Custom option from the Page Size pop-up menu, although you can if you want to waste some time and avoid doing the dishes.)

Tall or wide?

For Orientation, select the Tall radio button if you want the page to have the long side of the page go from top to bottom. This option is called *portrait* in some programs because that's the way portrait paintings are generally oriented. Select Wide if you want the page to have the long dimension go from side to side (called *landscape* because landscape paintings are generally oriented from side to side). Most standard publications — letters and magazines, for example — use the Tall orientation.

Because Web-specific sizes are set to landscape by default, you don't need to worry about the tall versus wide issue. If you click on a Web page size (one of those listed earlier), the Wide orientation is selected because the "page" (that is, the screen) is wider than it is tall. For print publications, if you click on a paper size that is taller than it is wide, the Tall orientation is automatically selected. If you want to change the orientation — rotate the page 90 degrees — you do so by clicking on a new orientation for the current page size.

Note that all pages in a PageMaker document must be oriented the same way. Therefore, if you want both tall and wide pages in your layout (maybe you have a chart that you want to print in wide orientation because its rows are really long), put your wide pages in a PageMaker document separate from your tall pages. (Of course, you can keep everything in one document and just rotate that really wide chart 90 degrees, so that it appears horizontal when it prints, but you have to tilt your head to the side in order to read or edit the text on-screen. And although Ahnüld no doubt would recommend this type of aerobic workout, moving your mouse along one plane while your head is tilted on another requires a degree of hand-eye coordination that most non-21st-century cyborgs lack.)

Margins and side settings

An important consideration for the Web is the amount of the page margin. PageMaker chooses thin margins — only about $^{1}/_{6}$ inch (or, one pica in layout-speak) — as the default for its Web-oriented page sizes. On paper, you'd want a significantly wider margin, anywhere from $^{1}/_{2}$ to $1^{1}/_{4}$ inches. In print, wide margins help big sheets of paper look less intimidating (consider your reaction to a large page crammed with text — you'd probably ignore it). On computer screens, people don't seem to like big margins. The window borders already keep things separate, plus the monitor screen can't display nearly as much content as a full-size printed page. Making a screen look crowded is a hard thing to do (although you can if you want to!).

Given that monitor screens always seem to have insufficient room, your readers wouldn't want oversize margins on their Web pages. If you gave them big margins, they'd probably scroll up or down the window to chop off the margins anyhow. Therefore, be conservative on your Web page margins. A sixth of an inch is just fine.

On the other hand, don't make your margins much less than $^{1}/_{6}$ inch. You need some amount of margin so the text on your Web page doesn't touch the browser window's borders. Also, if you want to output your Web pages to a printer (maybe for proofing or to get approvals from the design and production honchos), you need the $^{1}/_{6}$-inch margin to print the pages correctly. Most printers need that much clearance around the edge of the page to give the printer rollers something to grab onto.

Whatever margins you set, keep in mind you can still put text or graphics anywhere on the page — the margins don't prevent that. They merely provide a visual guide to where additional text and graphics should go. PageMaker also works to keep text within the margins when you bring in text from your word processor, as covered in Chapter 7.

If you pick a print-oriented page size, PageMaker assumes that you are reproducing your finished documents on two-sided pages. That's what the Double-Sided check box refers to. If you're printing only on one side, uncheck the option. For Web pages, it doesn't matter whether your document specifies single- or double-sided pages. PageMaker knows a Web page isn't printed like a publication, so it automatically unchecks that box for Web-oriented page sizes.

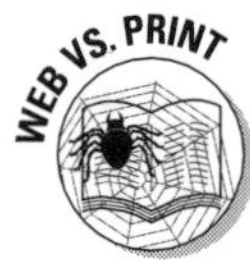

A good reason exists to select the double-sided pages option for print documents. Think about a ring-binder report — the kind with three holes on the inside of each sheet of paper. When you're setting up such a document, you want to leave enough space on the inside of the sheet to account for the holes. So you make the left margin a little wider than the right margin to leave enough room. That's great for the right-hand pages but, if you're printing double-sided, the left-hand pages are in trouble. Their right margins aren't wider, yet their right side is the side that's near the holes. (Whoops.) By having a double-sided option, PageMaker can track the pages' *inside* and *outside* margins rather than their left and right. The inside margin for a right-hand page is the left margin, but for a left-hand page, it is the right margin. In this example, you would set a wide inside margin to accommodate the holes. PageMaker figures out which way to shift the text on each page for you.

The Facing Pages check box is dimmed (unavailable) unless Double-Sided is checked. The Facing Pages option lets you position text or graphics to straddle the gap between pages. In other words, a large page element extends to the inside edge of the left-hand page and continues onto the right-hand page. On the Web, of course, pages don't do that, so this option is irrelevant to Web publishers.

Number of pages and page numbers

To tell PageMaker how many pages you want in your document, enter a number in the Number of Pages option box (now there's a shocker!).

If you decide after working on your layout for a while that you want to add pages to your document, you can do so in either one of two ways: You can change the Number of Pages value in the Document Setup dialog box (PageMaker then adds all the new pages to the end of the document), or

Sizing up Web page measurements

When you select a page size, its measurements appear in the Dimensions fields. (Web pages report their dimensions in inches.) This feature is handy because it gives you a feel for how a print-oriented page size appears on the Web. For example, the dimensions of a letter-size page are 8½ inches × 11 inches, while the dimensions of an 800 × 600 (SVGA) screen measure approximately 11.11 × 8.33 inches. That tells you a reader with a 17-inch monitor would have to scroll down to see the entire contents of a letter-size Web page. The depth of that monitor is about 8 inches, but a letter-size page would have a depth of 11 inches. But, there'd be plenty of room to the side of the reader's browser window to keep other things in view, such as drive icons or folders, because a 17-inch monitor screen is the equivalent of an 11-inch wide page and the letter-size page takes up only 8½ inches of it.

How do you decide on a size that's best for your Web page? First, you need to consider who you think is going to be viewing your Web pages. Then you need to decide how you want them to navigate through your pages.

For example, if you're producing pages for a corporate intranet and you know that everyone is viewing with 17-inch monitors, you can pick a size such as 800 × 600 VGA/Slide, which is the size of a 17-inch monitor's screen. The key measurement is the page width — don't select a page size wider than what you expect most people to be able to display. You don't want readers having to scroll from side to side.

Once you've figured out the maximum width for your page, you need to decide whether you want your pages to fit depthwise on the screen or whether you want your readers to scroll down. I can't give you a magic answer — it really depends on the kind of information you're presenting. Fortunately, whatever depth you choose won't mean too much, because if you have several pages of information in your PageMaker document, you can have PageMaker string them together to become one deep Web page that the reader would scroll down to read. Or you can export pages to the Web one at a time, in which case your readers would jump from one page to the other in sequence. You can even mix and match, exporting some pages individually and others strung together as a group.

If you're posting your pages to the Web, I recommend that you pick the 600 × 450 Browser – large setting or the 500 × 335 Browser – small setting. The large browser size assumes the reader runs the Web browser in full-screen mode on a 14-inch or 15-inch monitor, while the small browser size assumes the reader runs the Web browser in a smaller window on a 14-inch or 15-inch monitor.

The more business-oriented your target readers, the more I suggest you use the larger size. Most new business monitors measure 17 inches, which leaves plenty of room to view full pages and as well as other stuff on the screen.

you can choose Layout⇨Insert Pages. You then get the option of inserting the new pages before, after, or between the currently selected page or two-page spread. You can also specify which Master Page you want to apply to the new page.

Similarly, if you want to delete pages from the end of the publication, just alter the number of pages in the Document Setup dialog box. But if you want to remove pages from the interior of your document, choose Layout➪Remove Pages and specify which pages you want to delete.

The Start Page # option is set to 1 by default, which makes sense for most print documents; the first page in the document is numbered as page 1. If you choose a different number, the first page in the document is assigned that number, and each page thereafter is numbered accordingly. So, if you use 2 as the Start Page #, the first page is numbered page 2, the second page is page 3, and so on.

Why would you do this? Perhaps the first page of your print document is laid out vertically while the rest of the publication is oriented horizontally. You would create a single-page portrait (tall) document for the cover, and a second landscape (wide) document that begins at page 2 for the rest of the publication.

For the Web, page numbering doesn't matter, so don't worry about the Start Page # option or the Restart Page Numbering option, which comes into play if you use PageMaker's book feature to number pages across a series of printed documents.

Printer Settings

In most cases, the Target Printer Resolution setting shown in the Document Setup dialog box corresponds to the resolution of the printer selected from the Compose to Printer pop-up menu. The Compose to Printer setting should match the final printer for the page, not the intermediate printers you may use for proofing (for example, you would compose to an imagesetter or other high-resolution device that creates the final output, even if you intend to proof on a low- or mid-resolution color inkjet printer).

The Web, of course, has no target printer (you're "printing" to a screen). You don't need to worry about a target printer when creating Web pages, but do be concerned about the Target output resolution. The resolution should be set to 72 dpi (dots per inch), which is the resolution on a computer monitor. If you set the resolution higher than that, you create bigger images — because they have more dots composing each inch — that take longer for your reader to download (and aren't any better because a monitor is stuck at 72 dpi). When you export your PageMaker pages to HTML format, you can ask PageMaker to automatically export all graphics to 72 dpi.

Defining DPI

What is *dpi?* It's not pronounced *dippy,* by the way, but *dee pee eye,* and it stands for *dots per inch.* When you print to a laser printer, a dot-matrix printer, an imagesetter, an inkjet printer, a monitor screen, or anything more advanced than two cans tied to a string, everything is converted to a series of dots. For a black-and-white document, the pattern of black dots on the white paper simulates the shades of gray that you see. But if you use a magnifying glass, you can see the dots. (Computer screens have three sets of dots per image: one red, one green, and one blue; that's where the acronym *RGB* comes from.)

A printer's or monitor's dpi number tells you the size of the dots. The smaller the dots, the finer the image. Small dots fool your eye into thinking that it's seeing true shades of gray or color hues. On a monitor, the dots are set to a standard 72 dpi, although you can change that by increasing the resolution of your screen, which crams in more information. For example, a 17-inch monitor normally displays 800 pixels (dots) horizontally and 600 vertically. But in Windows PCs and in recent Macs, you can change this resolution to, say, 1,024 × 768 pixels, which happens to be the standard dimensions for a 19- or 20-inch monitor. By cramming those extra pixels on the 17-inch monitor, the dpi has to increase from the normal 72 dpi to 92 dpi. Of course, most people don't think to do this. They just regard a monitor as a 72-dpi "printer."

Take a look at Figure 5-3. It shows an image with a resolution of 1,270 dpi, which is what a high-density print imagesetter can achieve, and the same image reproduced at smaller dpi sizes (and labeled the size of the image files). The original image was enlarged to magnify the differences due to dpi — that's why the 72-dpi portion has so little detail — but the relative amount of detail from image to image is accurate.

On the Web, dpi is less important than it is for printed pages. If you place a 1,270-dpi image in PageMaker, you see it on screen at 72 dpi — the monitor resolution. Your 72-dpi images look fine on screen — until you put them next to photographs of the same subject from a magazine. We're just used to seeing less detail on screen than on paper.

Dividing Your Document into Columns

One of the advantages of using PageMaker instead of a word processor or HTML editor to create Web pages is that you can easily place text and graphics in columns. (The relative advantages of each of these tools is covered in Chapter 12.) Whether you're setting up a new document for the

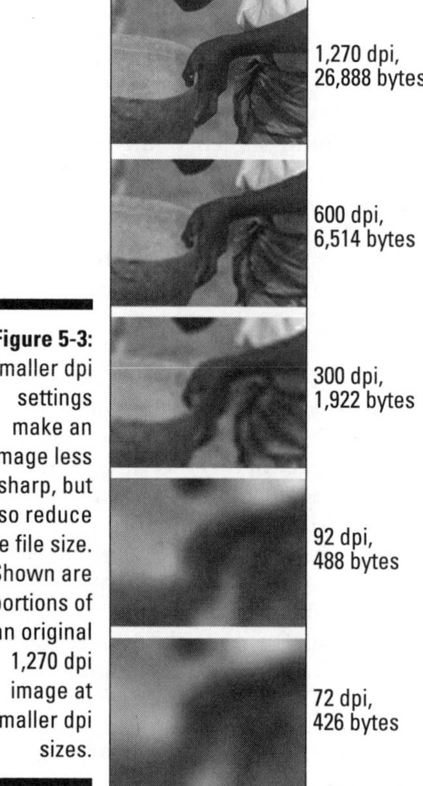

Figure 5-3: Smaller dpi settings make an image less sharp, but also reduce the file size. Shown are portions of an original 1,270 dpi image at smaller dpi sizes.

first time or making adjustments to an existing document, you establish column settings by choosing Layout⇨Column Guides. The Column Guides dialog box shown in Figure 5-4 leaps to the screen.

Here, you can set up the number of columns and the amount of space between them (called a *gutter* by publishing types). Figure 5-4 shows the dialog box with sample settings and the effects of those settings on the pages behind the dialog box.

The dialog box you see may be slightly different, depending on the following:

- If you're working on a multipage document and selected both Double-Sided and Facing Pages in the Document Setup dialog box, you can establish different column settings for left and right pages. To do so, select the Set Left and Right Pages Separately check box at the bottom of the Column Guides dialog box. But, as with some other settings options in PageMaker, you don't need to bother with this setting for Web publications.
- If you deselected the Double-Sided checkbox in the Document Setup dialog box, you won't get separate fields for left and right pages.

The Number of Columns setting merely establishes the base number of columns that PageMaker uses when you bring in text from a word-processor file. You can resize the columns by hand for individual text blocks at any time, and you can make your pictures any size and place them anywhere you want on the page.

Notice the Adjust Layout check box at the bottom of Figure 5-4. This new feature reflows any text within the page's previous column margins to match the new column settings. It's a nice touch that saves you some work if you happen to change your column settings.

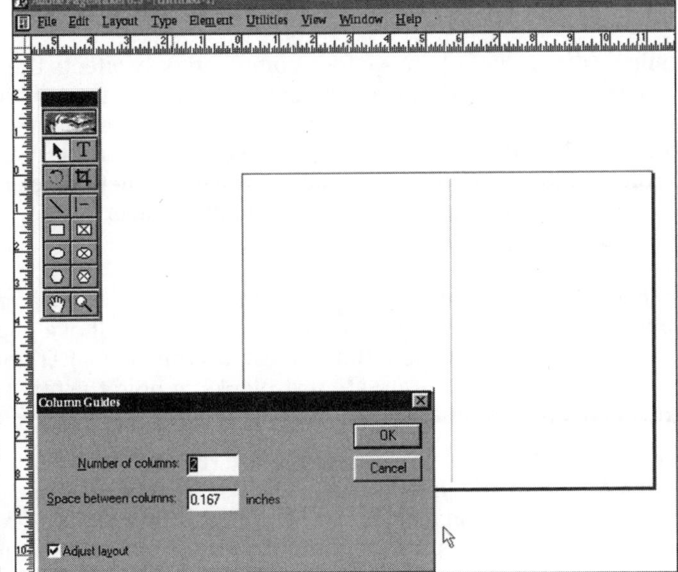

Figure 5-4: The Column Guides dialog box lets you set the number of columns per page.

Working with column guides

After you make your selections and press Enter, PageMaker displays dotted lines — called *column guides* — on your page. When you place text into your document (as explained in Part III), it falls within the column guides. Guides don't print when you print your document. You can adjust the columns after you've set them up.

- By default, PageMaker creates columns of equal size and spaces them evenly across your page. But you can change the width of any column by dragging its column guide. The gutter distance between columns stays the same.

- If you want to lock your column guides into place so that you don't inadvertently move them, turn on the Lock Guides command (choose View⇨Lock Guides, or use the shortcut Ctrl+Alt+; [semi-colon] or Option+⌘+; [semi-colon]). Note that this command used to be in the Layout menu in the previous version of PageMaker.

Suppose that you have a three-page document, and you set the margins and columns for page 2. But if you move to page 3 by clicking on the page icons in the bottom-left corner of the PageMaker window, you discover that no columns are set for that page. What gives? You told PageMaker what you wanted to do, and now it's ignoring you, just like your kids when you tell them to turn off that stupid Barney show and watch something that provides a realistic portrayal of dinosaurs, like *The Flintstones.*

The problem is that the Column Guides command only affects the pages you're currently viewing. That may be okay when you're working in a small document, but what if you're creating a 112-page Web site? Choosing Column Guides 112 times is bound to get you a little aggravated. Luckily, you can set columns for your entire document by using something called *master pages,* as discussed in Chapter 12, or by using PageMaker's Guides Manager feature, explained later in this chapter.

- You can create different numbers of columns on the same page — for example, you may want three columns on the top half of a page and two columns on the bottom half. But you can do this only after you place some text in your page or create text blocks to hold the text (placing text is explained in Chapter 7).

- If you turn on the Snap to Guides function (choose View⇨Snap to Guides or press Ctrl+Shift+; [semi-colon] or Shift+⌘+; [semi-colon]), the column guides take on a magnetic personality. Any text or graphics that you place near a column guide snap into alignment with the guide. (When you have the command turned on, elements also snap to ruler guides, as explained in the upcoming "Making page elements snap to it" section.) Note that the Snap to Guides function has moved from the Layout menu and the keyboard shortcut is new in Version 6.5.

- To make sure that you don't grab a column guide while you're trying to select a neighboring graphic or other element on the page with the Arrow tool, press Ctrl or ⌘ as you select.

Playing peek-a-boo with guides

The last thing you should know about column guides is that you can control how PageMaker displays them. The View⇨Bring Guides to Front command makes the guides overprint anything else on screen (of course, guides don't print when you print to paper or export to the Web). The next time you go to the View menu, the option is renamed Send Guides to Back. If you select this option again, the guides move so that they're behind everything. You can toggle the guide position from front to back with this pair of commands. Similarly, you can hide or show guides with the alternating menu options View⇨Show Guides and View⇨Hide Guides, or with Ctrl+; [semi-colon] or ⌘+; [semi-colon].

The Preferences dialog box (File⇨Preferences⇨General, or Ctrl+K or ⌘+K) lets you change the default guides setting for all new documents you create to Send to Front or Send to Back.

Setting Rulers and Ruler Guides

The rulers you see at the top of each publication window aren't ordinary rulers. They have hidden capabilities, all designed to make it easier for you to correctly position text and graphics on your pages.

If the rulers aren't visible on-screen, press Ctrl+R or ⌘+R to display them. If you want to hide the rulers and free up some screen space, press Ctrl+R or ⌘+R again.

Choosing a unit of measurement

By default, the rulers use inches as the unit of measurement. But you can change to another measurement unit by opening the Preferences dialog box (File⇨Preferences⇨General, or Ctrl+K or ⌘+K), as shown in Figure 5-5. This dialog box also lets you establish other preferences that affect the way PageMaker implements certain options and commands, as discussed earlier in the section "Making Changes to Your Defaults."

To get quick access to the Preferences dialog box, double-click on the Arrow tool icon in the toolbox.

To set ruler preferences, you use two pop-up menus: Measurements In and Vertical Ruler. The Measurements In option determines what unit of measurement is used throughout your layout — not only in the rulers, but also in dialog boxes, the Control palette, and so on. The inch is the basic measurement unit in the U.S., and the pica is the preferred system of measurement in U.S. publishing. You can also choose Millimeters (the unit used in Canada and most of the rest of the world) and Ciceros (the unit used in European publishing). If you choose Inches Decimal, you get 10 major tick marks ($^{1}/_{10}$ of an inch) per ruler inch rather than the standard 32 ($^{1}/_{32}$ of an inch). Use whatever measurement system you're comfortable with.

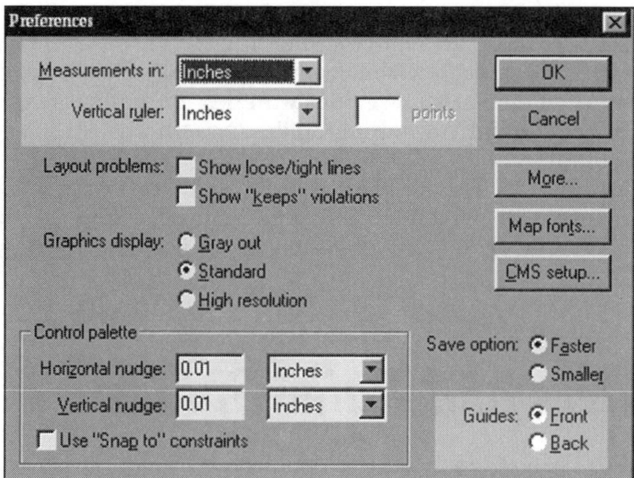

Figure 5-5: The Preferences dialog box where you can set your ruler and guide defaults.

The Vertical Ruler setting lets you choose a different measurement system for the vertical ruler. It doesn't affect other parts of the PageMaker interface. Why does PageMaker give you this second measurement option? The answer is based on a publishing tradition that you probably won't ever care about. But here goes anyhow: In traditional publishing, layout artists measured text width in picas and length in inches. The text's column width was usually narrow, so using a finer measurement system made sense. But the text length could be tens or even hundreds of inches for a magazine or newspaper article — maybe thousands of picas. Thus the two measurements. You still hear the occasional reference *column inches* at some crusty old newspapers, but you should avoid using the term in polite company.

Another alternative is to use the Custom option and define your own vertical ruler measurement units. You may want to use this option to establish a measurement unit that represents lines of text. Of course, the height of a line depends on the text's *leading* (the amount of space between lines), which changes from document to document and even within a single document. So no single measurement unit can accurately reflect all lines of text throughout a publication. But you can set the Vertical Ruler measurement unit to the number of points used for the basic body text's leading. Then you can easily count lines or, if the text in your text blocks aligns to the vertical ruler's increments, you can make sure that graphics and other elements line up with the text.

You rarely need to use the ruler setting Zero Lock command, which is found in the View menu. It's easier to show you this setting than explain it, so look at the ruler at the left in Figure 5-6 and compare it with the ruler at the right. At the upper-left corner of the rulers is an icon that looks sort of like a cross. This icon is the *ruler origin box.* By dragging the box, you can move the *zero points* (where the ruler measures zero) as demonstrated in Figure 5-6.

Choosing Zero Lock prevents you from making this change. If you do somehow move your zero points and want to put them back in their default positions, just double-click on that cross-like part of the ruler in the upper-left corner.

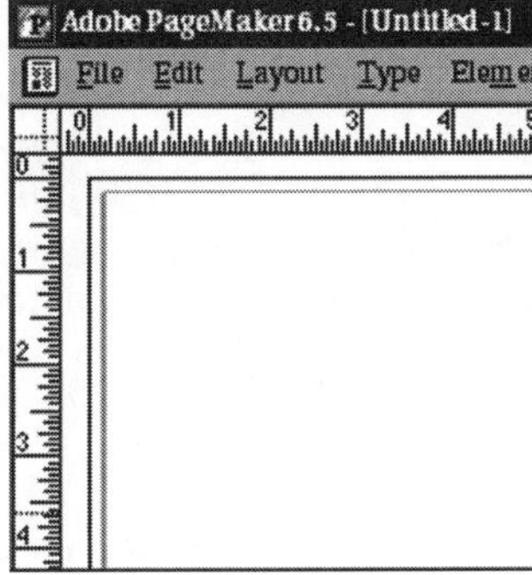

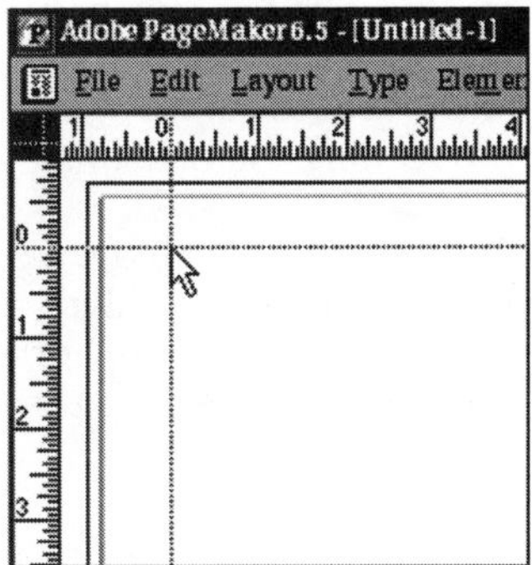

Figure 5-6: You can change the location of the zero points on the rulers (shown on the left).

Why would you want to change the zero point on your ruler? Well, doing so can come in handy when you're trying to measure distances between two elements, especially if you're not a math whiz. For example, if you want to find out how much space you've put between graphic A and graphic B, you can drag the zero point to line up with graphic A and move the cursor to Graphic B and read the ruler. Then you can quickly see the exact distance between the two elements with no messy addition or subtraction involved.

Making page elements snap to it

You can set up PageMaker so that page elements *snap* to ruler positions. When the snapping function is turned on, PageMaker aligns anything that you draw or place on the page along one of the tick marks on the ruler (whether or not the ruler is displayed). If you drag a graphic near a ruler increment, for example, the graphic jumps into alignment with the increment. It's a great way to make sure that elements aren't positioned all cockeyed from one another, creating those slight disparities in alignment that make folks bug-eyed as their brains notice that something is amiss though they can't quite figure out what it is.

- To turn on the ruler snap function, choose View⇨Snap to Rulers or use Ctrl+Alt+R or Option+⌘+R. A check mark next to the option name means that the function is turned on. Note that this is a new placement for the menu (it used to be in the Layout menu) as well as a new keyboard shortcut.
- If you select inches as your measurement unit, as explained earlier, elements snap to the nearest $^{1}/_{32}$ of an inch; if you select picas, they snap to the nearest point.

Creating ruler guides

Rulers are great as general positioning aids. But what if you want to line an element up to something more specific? That's where *ruler guides* come in handy. Look at Figure 5-7 and notice the lines that extend along the bottom and sides of the rectangle. These lines are ruler guides. Look above the rectangle for a similar line and a double-arrow cursor. That's a ruler guide in the process of being created. The ruler guides make properly positioning the rectangle and aligning future elements with its edges an easier task.

To create a ruler guide, move the cursor to a ruler, hold down the left mouse button, and drag a ruler guide out to where you want it to be. (You can drag from either ruler: The horizontal ruler at the top of the screen gives you horizontal guides, and the vertical ruler along the left side gives you vertical guides.)

- When you're positioning elements with your mouse, you can use guides to ensure alignment, not just as a general target. If you select Snap to Guides from the View menu — Ctrl+Shift+; [semi-colon] or Shift+⌘+; [semi-colon] — any text or graphic you place near a ruler guide jumps into alignment with that guide. You get instant, accurate alignment.
- When the Snap to Guides command is turned on, elements snap to column guides as well as ruler guides, as explained earlier in the section "Dividing Your Document into Columns."
- To move a guide, just drag it with the mouse. If you don't want guides — whether column guides or ruler guides — to be movable, select View➪Lock Guides or use Ctrl+Alt+; [semi-colon] or Option+⌘+; [semi-colon].

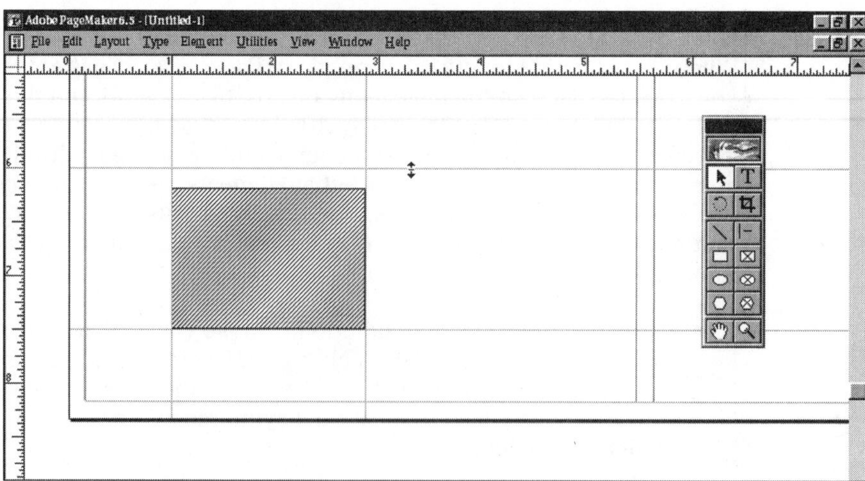

Figure 5-7: Drag ruler guides from the rulers to align objects easily.

- To remove a guide, drag it back to the ruler. To remove all guides, choose View⇨Clear Ruler Guides (you can't use this command when Lock Guides is active).
- If you're trying to select a graphic or text object with the Arrow tool but you keep selecting a guide instead, press Ctrl or ⌘ while you select the object.
- As you can with column guides, you can specify whether ruler guides appear in front of or behind other page elements. Just choose Bring Guides to Front or Send Guides to Back from the View menu. Or, to change the default setting, double-click on the Arrow tool icon in the toolbox to open the Preferences dialog box and then choose the appropriate Guides radio button.

Making Your Own Prefab Layout Grids

If you find yourself using the same arrangement of margins, columns, and ruler guides in lots of different documents, you may want to create a custom *layout grid* using the PageMaker 6.5 revised Grid Manager plug-in. When you open up a new document, you just tell PageMaker to apply your grid, and voilà — all your guidelines appear on the page. No more of that backbreaking business of dragging lines from rulers and choosing options in dialog boxes.

The Grid Manager is a significantly revamped version of what was called the Guide Manager in PageMaker 6.0. You now have more control over the grid settings, plus the Grid Manager's interface is more complex; it provides previews of your grids, for example.

You can create a grid by choosing Utilities⇨Plug-ins⇨Grid Manager and entering values into the Grid Manager dialog box, shown in Figure 5-8. As you choose the number of column, ruler, and baseline guides that you want to use, the page preview in the top of the dialog box updates to reflect your decisions.

Whoa! This is the first time I've used the phrase *baseline guide.* You know what a column grid is, and what a ruler guide is. So what the heck's a baseline guide? The baseline is the bottom edge of the lines of body copy. The baseline measurement is determined by the text's leading. Say you were doing a fancy brochure, and you wanted all the subheads and graphics to align with the bottoms of the lines of adjacent body text. The Baseline option in the Grid Manager shows you where all those bottoms (which you now know are called baselines) should be. Specify the leading amount for the body copy and the Grid Manager figures out where to draw the baselines. On the Web, you won't need to worry about this, because that fine a level of placement just doesn't happen in HTML documents. Each browser can have its own font and size settings and therefore will place elements a bit differently than another one would.

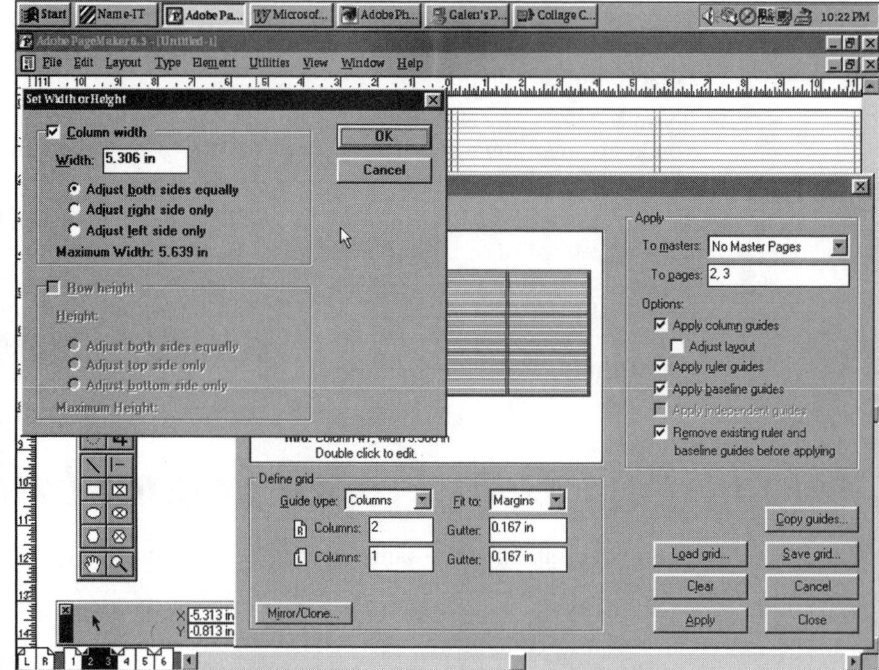

Figure 5-8: The complicated but extremely useful Grid Manager lets you set up your baseline guides, rulers, and column grids.

Mastering the somewhat intimidating Grid Manager is a matter of knowing some of its tricks:

- To use guides you've already set up, use the Copy Guides button. You're then asked for the location and name of a PageMaker document whose guides you want copied into the current publication.
- You can select the pages you want the grids applied to by filling in their numbers in the To pages option box. Separate page numbers with commas, such as 1, 4, 5, and page ranges with a hyphen, such as 1-4. You can also use the word "all" instead of numbers to apply the guides to all pages in the layout.
- You can fine-tune your grids in the page preview box by moving them with the mouse, or you can double-click into the desired location (look for a message to pop up at the bottom of the page preview). You get a dialog box that lets you enter specific grid values (also shown in Figure 5-8, at upper left).
- You can also apply grid settings to master pages via the To Masters options pop-up menu.

- After you define your grid settings, you can copy them to other pages with the Mirror/Clone button. That button brings up a dialog box that, if you are using facing pages, lets you copy settings from a left page to a right page or vice versa. (The left-hand outside settings become the right-hand inside settings, for example.) You can also mirror settings, which flips the left page's outside settings over to the right page's outside settings. Because facing pages don't really apply to the Web, you won't have to worry much about the difference between copying and mirroring.
- If you don't like the grid you've set and want to start over, click the Clear button. Then start over!
- Finally, you can save your grid with the Save Grid button. A saved grid can be imported into another PageMaker layout by using the Load Grid button.

Part III
Putting Words in Print and Online

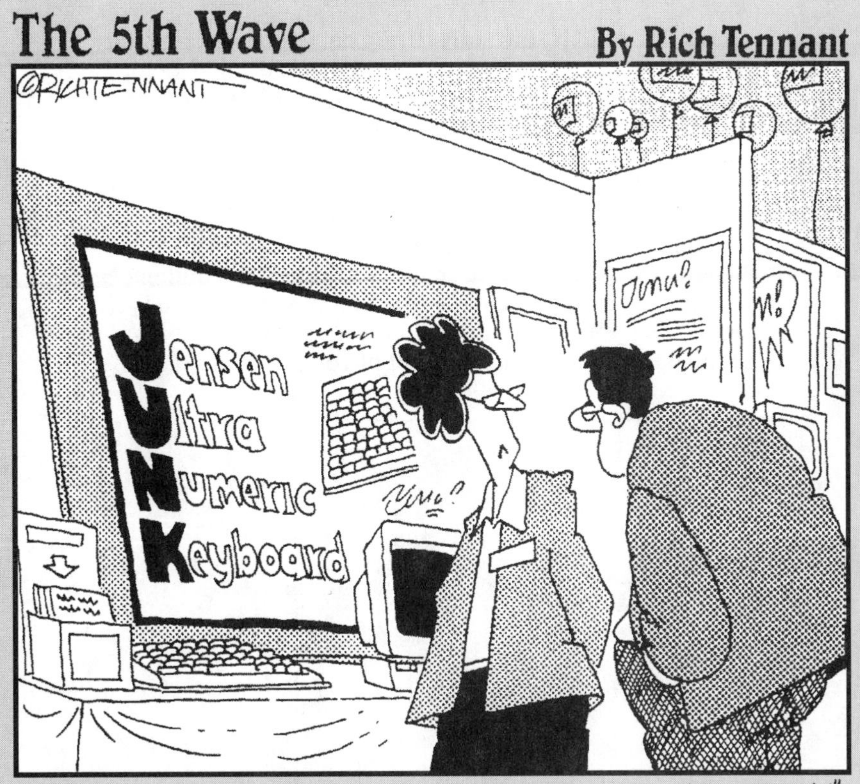

"FOR OBVIOUS REASONS WE DECIDED NOT TO USE AN ACRONYM."

In this part . . .

To some people, the subject of placing, formatting, and editing text is as about as dry as a mouthful of sand. Well, if that's your take on the topic, you're in for a surprise. For one thing, it's a cinch to change type styles, fonts, text spacing, and alignment — you know, all the ordinary stuff folks do when laying out text. And because it's so easy to change basic formatting features, you can experiment with different type treatments until you find the look that's right for your subject matter and audience. PageMaker lets you create interesting type effects that not only let you to add visual interest to your document, but also hammer home the point of your Web site display.

Chapter 6

All I Need to Know about Fonts and Type

In This Chapter

- A basic primer on typography
- Character formatting options for Web documents
- Paragraph formatting options for Web documents
- Special type characters that work on the Web

If you've spent the last several years honing your electronic layout talents, dazzling the world with fabulous publications rivaling the look of *Architectural Digest* (if it were published by the firm of Laser & Photocopier, Ltd.), you may very well flip your drop cap when you start publishing on the Web. All those typographical tricks you've taken for granted — kerning, tracking, em dashes, typographer's quotes, and all those fancy fonts you've had so much fun with — disappear from your PageMaker document once they hit the Web.

Type formatting on the Web is, in a word, *primitive* when compared with what you may have been used to. The Web was designed on the UNIX computer platform, in which words all look pretty much alike, and issues like typography just weren't a concern. The content was everything, esthetics just weren't in the picture. But, think of it as a small price to pay for the thrill of publishing to the World Wide Web. (And, if you really want fancy type, you can cheat and use graphics that include designer type, or use the Acrobat format covered in Chapter 19 — but be aware that both techniques make for larger files and longer downloading times for computer users viewing your pages on the Web.)

The vocabulary of desktop and Web publishing is based on traditional typesetting, which has its roots in the fifteenth century when one Johannes Gutenberg invented movable type. Thanks to its links with history, PageMaker offers the occasional obscure term, such as *font, leading,* and *kerning.* Long-dead geezers such as Aldus Manutius and Claude Garamond knew these terms right off the bat, but they may be foreign to you. Suffice to say, if you want to be type-wise, read this chapter.

A Basic Guide to Type Terminology

Typographic formatting is somewhat limited on the Web. This has to do mostly with *HTML* (the programming language used to turn PageMaker layouts into Web documents) and *browsers* (the software used to view HTML documents). (For more on HTML, what it is, and how it works, see Chapter 2. You can find information on browsers in Chapter 1.)

Because you have less to work with as far as text formatting goes, you need to use the few type tricks available as effectively as possible to make your Web pages stand out from the crowd. If you also work on print publications (and you probably do), understanding the following terms is vital. I give just the basic definitions here; for the full details, you want a print-oriented book such as *PageMaker 6 For Macs For Dummies* or *PageMaker 6 For Windows For Dummies* (both from IDG Books Worldwide, Inc.).

- **Font or Typeface:** The term *font* is frequently used as a synonym for *typeface* — a distinct set of alphabetical and special characters. In traditional publishing, a font is a variant of a typeface — **bold,** *italics,* and so on — at a certain type size, but in computerdom, the term *font* is now interchangeable with *typeface*.

  The most common typefaces available to personal computer users are Helvetica (same as Arial) and Times (and variants such as New Times Roman), or generic equivalents for these two fonts, such as Swiss and Dutch, respectively.

- **Serif and Sans serif:** A *serif* is one of the wedge-like doohickeys that stick out from some letters, such as on the bottom and upper left of the letter *p*. Using serifs is a way that type designers add a certain character to their typefaces. Typefaces that use these serifs are called *serif typefaces.* A *sans serif* typeface doesn't uses serifs (*sans* is French for "without"). Sans serif faces tend to have a more modern look.

- **Typeface or Type style:** A *face* is a typeface's specific style, such as boldface or italics. In the computer's deep recesses are the files that create the fonts and, in those recesses, a separate file exists for each face. You'll hear the terms *face* and *font* used interchangeably. Many programs, including PageMaker, use the phrase *type style* to mean *typeface*.

- **Bold, Italic, Oblique, Roman, Medium, and Book:** Different type styles emphasize text in different ways. Plain text — sometimes called *roman,* meaning upright with serifs — is by far the most common variety. Roman style is used to display *body copy,* which comprises the large blocks or columns of text that represent the heart and soul of information contained on a page. The sans-serif version of roman is called *medium* or *book*. The *italic* (cursive, for serif typefaces) or *oblique* (slanted, usually for sans serif typefaces) style may be used within body copy to highlight a foreign or unfamiliar phrase or simply to stress a word. The **bold** (darker) style is relegated to special text, such as captions and headlines. The italic style may also be applied to special text; you may even italicize bold text to create a ***bold italic*** style.

- **Baseline, Leading, and Line Spacing:** The *baseline* is the imaginary line on which the bottom of a line of characters rests. *Leading* is the amount of vertical space between the baselines in a paragraph of text — leading is often also called *line spacing.*
- **Point, Point Size, and Type Size:** The size of a character — known predictably as a character's *type size* — is measured from the topmost point of the tallest part (the *ascender*) of the typeface's tallest character to the very lowest point (the *descender*) of the deepest character. Type size is calculated in a unit of measure called *points,* in which one point equals $^1/_{72}$ of an inch (just over $^1/_3$ millimeter). That's why you frequently see type size called *point size.* So a character that measures 0.167 inch from tip to tail becomes 12-point type, the equivalent of pica type on a conventional typewriter — remember those? (It just so happens 12 points equals 1 pica.)

Text Formatting You Can Use for the Web

If you read the beginning of this chapter, don't be scared off by what I said about formatting limitations on the Web. You *can* do interesting things with type in Web documents, just not all of the text styling that you may be used to doing for the printed word.

When you export your layouts from PageMaker to HTML (the language used to create Web pages), you have two options to choose from that affect what typographic effects are preserved after exporting, as shown in the Options dialog box in in Figure 6-1:

- *Approximate Layout,* which keeps as much as possible of your layout formatting, including multiple columns within pages (selected with the top check box in the dialog box)
- *Preserve Character Attributes,* which ensures that the maximum amount of character formatting is retained during exporting to the Web (selected with the bottom check box in the dialog box)

If you compare Figure 6-2 with Figures 6-3 through 6-5, you get an overall impression of what survives in HTML (for example, that drop-cap *A* turned into body text). The rest of this section and Tables 6-1, 6-2, and 6-3 list exactly what formatting is preserved with each export option.

Select this option to preserve character formatting

Select this option to approximate layout

Options

☑ Approximate layout using HTML tables when exporting pages

Exported page width: 612 pixels

OK

Cancel

Style Assignments

PageMaker Style	HTML Style
[No style]	Body Text
Body text	Body Text
Caption	Heading 6
Hanging indent	Unordered List
Headline	Heading 1
Subhead 1	Heading 2
Subhead 2	Heading 3

☑ Preserve character attributes

Graphics

Export as: ○ All to GIF ○ All to JPEG ◉ PageMaker chooses

File Names: ○ Use long name ◉ Use short name (8.3)

☑ Downsample to 72 dpi

Figure 6-1: The Options dialog box determines what layout and character attributes are preserved during HTML export.

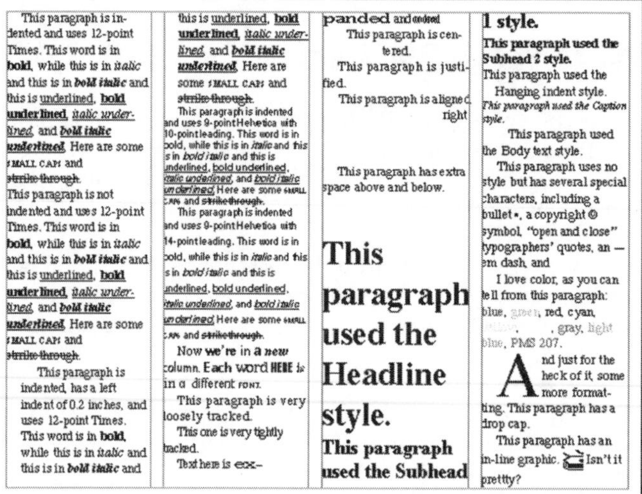
This paragraph is indented and uses 12-point Times. This word is in bold, while this is in italic and this is in bold italic and this is underlined, bold underlined, italic underlined, and bold italic underlined. Here are some SMALL CAPS and strike-through.
This paragraph is not indented and uses 12-point Times. This word is in bold, while this is in italic and this is in bold italic and this is underlined, bold underlined, italic underlined, and bold italic underlined. Here are some SMALL CAPS and strike-through.
This paragraph is indented, has a left indent of 0.2 inches, and uses 12-point Times. This word is in bold, while this is in italic and this is in bold italic and this is underlined, bold underlined, italic underlined, and bold italic underlined. Here are some SMALL CAPS and strike-through.
This paragraph is indented and uses 9-point Helvetica with 10-point leading. This word is in bold, while this is in italic and this is in bold italic and this is underlined, bold underlined, italic underlined, and bold italic underlined. Here are some SMALL CAPS and strike-through.
This paragraph is indented and uses 9-point Helvetica with 14-point leading. This word is in bold, while this is in italic and this is in bold italic and this is underlined, bold underlined, italic underlined, and bold italic underlined. Here are some SMALL CAPS and strike-through.
Now we're in a new column. Each word HERE is in a different FONT.
This paragraph is very loosely tracked.
This one is very tightly tracked.
Text here is expanded and condensed.
This paragraph is centered.
This paragraph is justified.
This paragraph is aligned right.
This paragraph has extra space above and below.
This paragraph used the Headline style.
This paragraph used the Subhead 1 style.
This paragraph used the Subhead 2 style.
This paragraph used the Hanging indent style.
This paragraph used the Caption style.
This paragraph used the Body text style.
This paragraph uses no style but has several special characters, including a bullet •, a copyright © symbol, "open and close" typographers' quotes, an — em dash, and
I love color, as you can tell from this paragraph: blue, green, red, cyan, , gray, light blue, PMS 207.
And just for the heck of it, some more formatting. This paragraph has a drop cap.
This paragraph has an in-line graphic. Isn't it prettty?

Figure 6-2: An original PageMaker layout, with various text and paragraph formatting applied.

WEB VS. PRINT

One way does exist to preserve on the Web all the fancy type formatting you learned for print publishing: You must create Acrobat Portable Document Format (PDF) documents instead of HTML documents. (Chapter 19 fills you in on the PDF format and how it works.)

PDF files take longer than HTML files to download from the Web to someone's computer, and also require either a browser plug-in or a reader program (both available from the Adobe Web site at `http://www.adobe.com/acrobat/`).

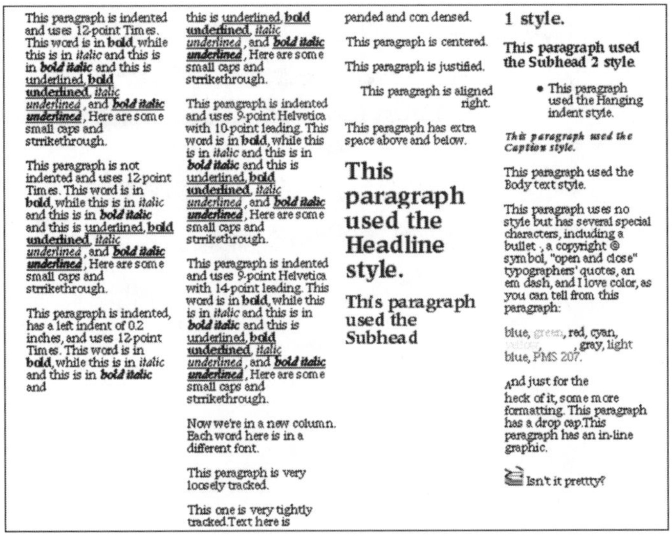

Figure 6-3: The HTML version of Figure 6-2 with layout approximated and character attributes preserved.

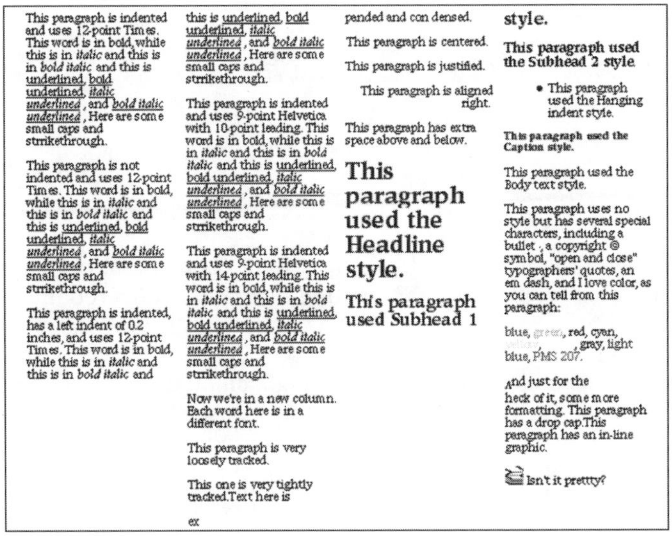

Figure 6-4: The HTML version of Figure 6-2 with layout approximated but character attributes not preserved. (Notice in particular that the boldface disappeared.)

Character formatting

HTML performs best with basic character formatting. You retain boldface, italics, and underlining no matter how you export your PageMaker document to HTML.

This paragraph is indented and uses 12-point Times. This word is in **bold**, while this is in *italic* and this is in ***bold italic*** and this is underlined, **bold underlined**, *italic underlined*, and ***bold italic underlined***, Here are some small caps and strikethrough.

This paragraph is not indented and uses 12-point Times. This word is in **bold**, while this is in *italic* and this is in ***bold italic*** and this is underlined, **bold underlined**, *italic underlined*, and ***bold italic underlined***, Here are some small caps and strikethrough.

This paragraph is indented, has a left indent of 0.2 inches, and uses 12-point Times. This word is in **bold**, while this is in *italic* and this is in ***bold italic*** and
this is underlined, **bold underlined**, *italic underlined*, and ***bold italic underlined***, Here are some small caps and strikethrough.

This paragraph is indented and uses 9-point Helvetica with 10-point leading. This word is in **bold**, while this is in *italic* and this is in ***bold italic*** and this is underlined, **bold underlined**, *italic underlined*, and ***bold italic underlined***, Here are some small caps and strikethrough.

This paragraph is indented and uses 9-point Helvetica with 14-point leading. This word is in **bold**, while this is in *italic* and this is in ***bold italic*** and this is underlined, **bold underlined**, *italic underlined*, and ***bold italic underlined***, Here are some small caps and strikethrough.

Now we're in a new column. Each word here is in a different font.

This paragraph is very loosely tracked.

This one is very tightly tracked.Text here is

ex
pended and con densed.

This paragraph is centered.

This paragraph is justified.

This paragraph is aligned right.

This paragraph has extra space above and below.

This paragraph used the Headline style.

Subhead 1 style.

This paragraph used the Subhead 2 style

- This paragraph used the Hanging indent style.

This paragraph used the Caption style.

This paragraph used the Body text style.

This paragraph uses no style but has several special characters, including a bullet -, a copyright © symbol, "open and close" typographers' quotes, an em dash, and I love color, as you can tell from this paragraph:

blue, green, red, cyan, , , gray, light blue, PMS 207.

And just for the
heck of it, some more formatting. This paragraph has a drop cap.This paragraph has an in-line graphic.

Isn't it prettty?

Figure 6-5: The HTML version of Figure 6-2 with character attributes preserved but layout not approximated.

Any boldface specification is lost if you don't check Preserve Character Attributes when you export. (Exporting to HTML is covered in detail in Chapter 17.)

Fancy text attributes such as strikethrough, small caps (in which lowercase letters are set as smaller uppercase letters), superscripts, subscripts, outlines, condensed (narrowed) type, expanded (widened) type, and shadows (available only in the Mac version of PageMaker) can't survive the trip through HTML — you simply end up with regular text.

Don't spend extra time formatting text at various different sizes — any such formatting is ignored. If you want specific sizes of text in your HTML document (that is, your PageMaker document in its Web incarnation), you need to use style sheets, which are explained in Chapter 9. You also lose any font specifications — as Chapter 1 explains. Your browser, not your HTML document, determines which fonts are seen online.

If you want to play it safe with a choice of font and type size, you can't go wrong with Times or a variant such as Times New Roman — the default font on Windows and Mac — set at 10 or 12 points. These Windows and Mac default settings are the typical default settings for browsers, too. If you use these font settings in PageMaker for your text when creating your Web pages, you have a better chance of designing something that your readers can actually see when browsing that looks the way it did when you created it.

Browsers support two typefaces, a *proportional* font (which is used most often and is typically set with Times) and a *fixed-width* font (which has a few specific uses and is typically set with Courier). Because most fonts don't survive the export to HTML, you really can't indicate in your text where you want the proportional font and where you want the fixed-width font to appear. The only way to specify a typeface and make it stick is by using a paragraph *style,* as explained in Chapter 9. This gives you an HTML style that is set for one font or the other; however, you can't mix and match two fonts within a paragraph.

Table 6-1 shows what text formatting is preserved when you export your PageMaker document to HTML.

Table 6-1 Text Formatting That Exports to HTML

Formatting	*Survives HTML Exporting*
Boldface	Yes*
Colors	Yes
Condensed Type	No
Expanded Type	No
Fonts	No
Italics	Yes
Kerning	No
Outlines	No
Point sizes	No
Shading	No
Shadows	No
Small caps	No
Strikethrough	No
Subscript	No
Superscript	No
Underlines	Yes

** Preserve Character Attributes export option must also be checked.*

Paragraph formatting

HTML operates best with basic paragraph formatting. Left, right, and centered text alignment make it to the Web if you click the Approximate Layout check box when exporting (as shown in Figure 6-1), but justified text exported to HTML comes out left-aligned. If you don't select Approximate Layout, you also lose right and center alignment during export.

Paragraphs in HTML Web pages are always separated with an extra space between them (typically a no-no in professional print layouts). A space between paragraphs serves the same purpose as indenting the first line in a multicolumn layout. It gives the reader a visual clue that a new paragraph is beginning.

All but the simplest formatting just doesn't survive the journey to HTML. Indentation, specified space above and below text blocks, leading (line spacing), and tracking (the amount of space between letters) all evaporate during HTML export. Drop caps (large capital letters with text wrapped around them) don't make the transition either, because they're created by sizing type and indenting lines, neither of which survives the trip to HTML. Table 6-2 shows you what kind of paragraph formatting makes it and what doesn't.

Table 6-2 Paragraph Formatting That Exports to HTML

Formatting	*Survives HTML Exporting*
Alignment	
Left	Yes
Right	Yes*
Centered	Yes*
Justified	No
Indentation	No
Leading	No
Paragraph styles	Partially (HTML styles are substituted for them)
Space above/below	No
Tracking	No

**Approximate Layout export option must be checked.*

Special character symbols

Thanks to laser printers and the gazillion (well, okay, tens of thousands) of fonts available today, special type symbols aren't so special anymore. On the Web, however, special type characters, such as the degree symbol, cent sign, and copyright symbol, remain special simply because most of them don't survive the trek over to the Web.

Symbols based on certain specific fonts (called *pi fonts* or *symbol fonts,* examples of which are the popular Symbol, Zapf Dingbats, and Wingdings) aren't displayed properly on a Web page because HTML doesn't recognize any fonts, including these pi fonts.

Not all browsers support all special symbols, even if the Mac or Windows does. This lack of symbol support is especially true of characters with diacritic marks (such as accent marks or tildes), because many older browsers aren't written with international text in mind (even through the Web is supposed to be World Wide). To find out what your foreign language readers are actually going to see, it's a good idea to preview your Web pages by using the browsers that the majority of your readers use.

Both Windows and the Mac let you create *bullets* (the little round or square shapes that begin some indented paragraphs), but HTML doesn't preserve the bullets you put in your PageMaker document. Bullets are a popular symbol, so the fact that they don't survive exporting into HTML is disappointing. But that doesn't mean you can't use bullets in your Web pages.

To add bullets to your document, you need to use a paragraph style that can be converted to one of the HTML *list styles*, in which numbers and bullets are automatically generated when a style *tag* (or code) is inserted into the text. These list styles can generate bullets automatically at the beginning of a paragraph (as you can find out in Chapter 9). Look closely at Figures 6-3 through 6-5 and you can see a bulleted paragraph in each. The bullet was created using PageMaker Hanging indents style, which the HTML export converted to the HTML Bullet List style (the code `<LI>` in HTML, if you want to get really geeky). This list style stuff is covered in Chapter 22.

The two HTML export options that affect text and paragraph formatting — Approximate Layout and Preserve Character Attributes — have no effect on whether symbols survive exporting. That's because HTML determines which special characters work on the Web, and the browser determines which of the HTML-supported symbols it can display.

Another element that's often used to represent a symbol is the *in-line graphic,* or *embedded graphic,* which is often used as a special symbol. Such graphics are pictures that are inserted into a line of text, as you can see at the bottom of the far-right column in Figure 6-2. These inserts survive export to HTML but are placed at the beginning of a paragraph, no matter where the graphic is inserted in the original publication. In fact, if you place an in-line graphic in the middle of a sentence, the graphic causes the paragraph to break at that point, as you can see in Figures 6-3 through 6-5.

A number of common symbols do survive exporting to HTML. You can pretty much guarantee that if a symbol exists on your keyboard (such as a dollar sign or percent sign) — and isn't created by using a Ctrl, Alt, Option, or ⌘ key combination, or isn't created with special utilities — that symbol is going to show up on your Web page.

You have to experiment, as well as rely on Table 6-3, to determine which of the more popular symbols in Windows or on the Mac survive the trip to the Web.

Table 6-3 Special Type Characters That Export to HTML

Character	*Windows 95*	*Macintosh*
Accented characters (Ä À Â Á Ã Â ä à â á ã å Ä À Ç ç Ë È Ê É ë è ê é Ï Ì Î Í ï ì î í Ñ ñ Ö Ò Ô Ó Õ Ø ö ò ô ó õ ø Ü Ù Û Ú ü ù û ú Š š Ý ý ÿ)	All but Š š Ÿ Ý ý	All but Š š Ÿ Ý ý
Diphthongs (Æ æ Œ œ)	None	Only Æ æ
International Punctuation (¿ ¡ « » £ ¥)	¿ ¡ « » £ ¥	¿ ¡ « » £ ¥
Legal Symbols (© ® ™)	Only © ®	Only © ®
Ligatures (ﬁ ﬂ)	None	None
Mathematical Symbols (± × ÷ ≠ ≈ ∞ √ ¼ ½ ¾)	Only × ÷ ± ¼ ½ ¾	Only ÷ ±
Miscellaneous Symbols (¢ °)	¢ °	¢ °
Text Symbols († ‡ § ¶)	Only § ¶	Only § ¶
Typographic Characters (· – — … ’ ‘ ” “)	Only ’ ‘ ” “ (but replaced with keyboard equivalents " ')	Only ’ ‘ ” “ (but replaced with keyboard equivalents " ')

Chapter 7

The Joy of Text

In This Chapter

- Entering text directly in PageMaker
- Importing text from a word-processing program
- Creating text blocks the new frames way
- Working with text blocks and frames

Remember back in the fourth grade, when the world's most evil teacher, Mrs. Sneets, made you write a letter to a senator in cursive writing? You had to use one of those cartridge pen thingies — the ones that leave big old blobs of ink on your paper if you're not careful. On the whole, creating a document that pleased The Evil One took about a zillion hours (including a few that you should have been able to spend at recess, playing murder ball). And then the stupid senator didn't even write you a real letter back — he just had his secretary send you some lame form letter that didn't even *mention* your request to have the FBI do some checking up on one Mrs. Harriet M. Sneets.

Happily, those days are behind you forever. Now that you have PageMaker, you can generate a document full of fabulous-looking words with hardly any trouble at all. Why, you're almost certain to get the job done way before recess time.

If you've used a word processor before, you already know much of what you need to know to create text in PageMaker. The process that you use to delete or add a word, for example, is pretty much the same as in Microsoft Word or WordPerfect. But in PageMaker, you put text in *text blocks,* which are like storage containers for all your well-thought-out words (and your not-so-well-thought-out ones, too). This chapter explains the basics of getting your thoughts down on screen and also gives you the lowdown on importing text, creating text blocks, and working with the new frames feature.

Importing Text versus Entering Text Directly

You can put text into your PageMaker document in two ways: You can *import* text (PageMaker calls this process *placing* text) or enter text directly.

To *import* text simply means to copy the contents of a word processor document into PageMaker. As an alternative, you can use the PageMaker text-editing tools to compose your text in PageMaker. These tools aren't either/or options — you are probably going to import some of your text and enter some directly.

- Compose your main text — the stories and the like that make up the bulk of your publication — in a word processor and import the document into PageMaker. Why? Because a word processor is designed just for this kind of work. And almost everyone has a word processor, so a group of people can exchange drafts of stories for editing and approval purposes if necessary. Also, if different people are working on different stories for the publication, to have each person enter his or her text into the main PageMaker document is pretty hard (not to mention downright chaotic and time consuming). Instead, you can have different writers and editors create and refine the stories in their separate word processors and then turn the whole batch over to the PageMaker layout person.
- Create the embellishments and adjustments — such as titles and corrections — in PageMaker. Writing a headline in your word processor and then importing the text into PageMaker doesn't make a lot of sense. In the first case, more work is involved in importing such a small piece of text than in creating the text in PageMaker. Of course, you can write the title with the rest of the story in your word processor but, even then, you are going to find yourself needing to add text to your publication as you refine your layout. For example, you are often going to end up creating a series of Web pages to keep information in manageable chunks and, when you do, you are likely to need to add new titles or short indexes (lists of topics off to the side of the main text) within PageMaker.

Entering text directly in your PageMaker document

If you want to create text right in your PageMaker document, just follow these steps:

1. **Click on the Text tool.**

   Figure 7-1 shows the Text tool. When you choose the tool, the cursor (or pointer, in Mac or Windows-speak) changes from an arrow to the text cursor, also labeled in the figure.

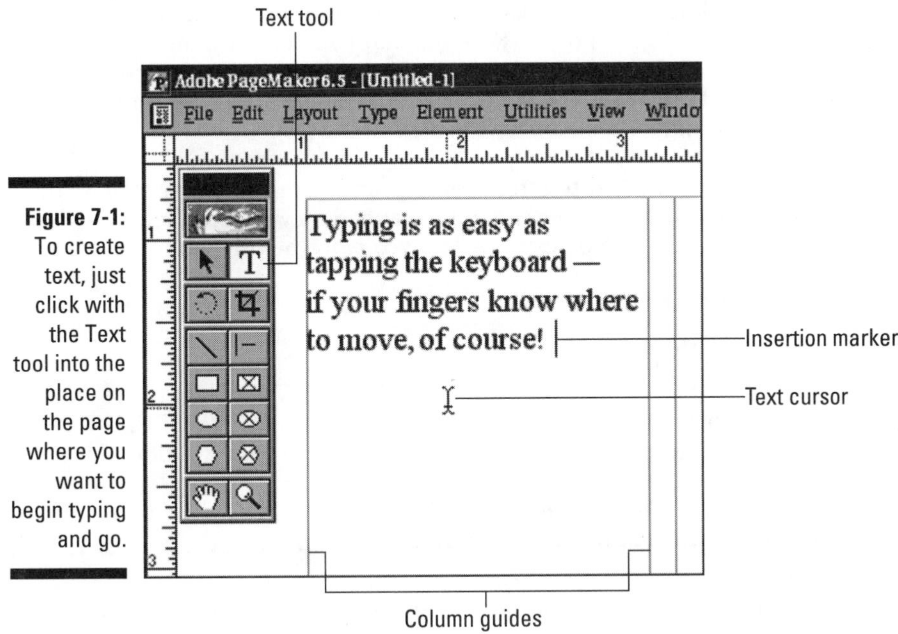

Figure 7-1: To create text, just click with the Text tool into the place on the page where you want to begin typing and go.

2. **Click at the spot where you want to enter the text.**

   After you click, a blinking insertion marker appears to indicate where the first letter that you type will appear. If you click within a set of column guides, PageMaker automatically moves the insertion marker to the left edge of the column. If you don't have any columns set up, the cursor jumps to the left margin of the page. (When you don't specify that you want two or more columns, PageMaker views your document as having one big column that stretches from the left margin to the right margin. So in this case, the margin guides really serve as column guides.)

3. **Start typing.**

   PageMaker places the text you type within the column (or margin) guidelines.

When you're zoomed out on the page (for example, if you're in fit-in-window or 50 percent view) and enter text in a small type size, PageMaker displays your text as just a bunch of little *X*s — a feature known as *greeking text.* To zoom in on your document and see the actual characters you typed, choose a larger view size from the View menu or use the Zoom tool.

To control how PageMaker greeks text, choose File➪Preferences➪General (or use Ctrl+K in Windows or ⌘ +K on the Mac) and click on the More button. Then change the Greek Text Below Value in the More Preferences dialog box. For example, if you set the value at 5 pixels, PageMaker greeks any characters smaller than 5 pixels in size.

If you don't want your text to stretch across an entire column or stay within the confines of a column — for example, maybe you want to place a headline across three columns — you can create a *text block* before you begin typing:

1. **Select the Text tool.**
2. **Drag to create a text block.**

   Click at the place where you want text to begin. Then drag to create a rectangle big enough to hold your text, as shown in Figure 7-2. You can drag in any direction, starting in any corner. Don't worry about drawing the text block perfectly; you can always resize and reshape your text block later, as explained in the section at the end of the Chapter, "Working with Text Blocks and Frames."

   When you release the mouse button to end your drag, the lines that indicate the boundaries of the text block disappear. Don't panic — the text block is still there; you just can't see it.

3. **Start typing.**

   The text stays inside your new text block.

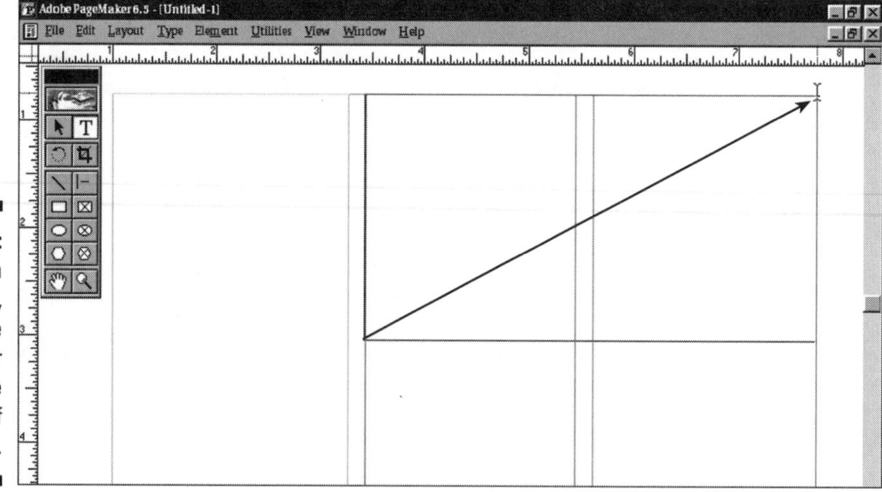

Figure 7-2: To create a text block, drag the Text cursor to define the area of the block.

The technique for dragging to create a text block does have one odd catch. If you draw a text block across several columns, the block sometimes ends up being the width of the first column, not the width of what you drew.

Creating text blocks the new frames way

A happenin' new way to create text blocks has been introduced with PageMaker 6.5. The *frames* feature lets you define a text block by the usual dragging method, except that the block stays put, even with no text inserted into it. A frame essentially creates a container for your text that you can fill later. Text frames can be created independent of text, so they come in handy as standing elements or as placeholders for your later work.

Text frames can be created with the Rectangle, Ellipse, or Polygon frame tools. These tools look like the regular ones except they have an X drawn through them. Figure 7-3 shows the new PageMaker 6.5 tool palette with the new frame tools and a text block created with the Rectangle Frame tool.

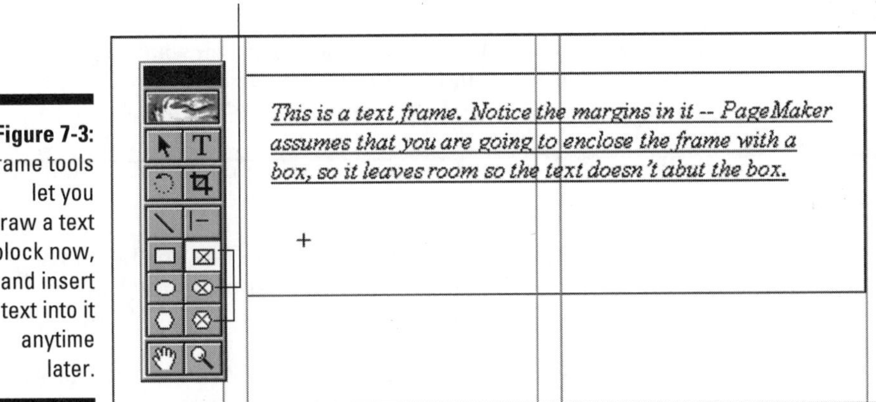

Frame tools
This is a text frame. Notice the margins in it -- PageMaker assumes that you are going to enclose the frame with a box, so it leaves room so the text doesn't abut the box.

Figure 7-3: Frame tools let you draw a text block now, and insert text into it anytime later.

Frames can hold either text or graphics, so you can also use them as placeholders in which to place elements later. Chapter 13 covers graphics placement.

Text frames can be linked together (PageMaker likes to say *threaded*) like regular text blocks so that the text flows from frame to frame. (However, text cannot be linked from a text frame to a regular text block, or vice versa.) You can also import a word-processed document into PageMaker and place it directly within a text frame (importing text is covered in the next section).

A text frame differs from a regular text block in several ways:

- After a text frame is created, you can go back and add its contents any time you want — even days later. With a text block, you have to start typing text immediately after creating it.
- A frame can contain either text or graphics (but not both), but a text block contains only text.
- A frame can be boxed with a line, have a shaded or patterned background, or both (extras your standard text block doesn't offer). These graphical elements don't export to HTML (the language used to create Web pages), however, so save them for your print publication projects.

- You can align text with the top or bottom of the frame, or center the text vertically within the frame. This alignment disappears during export to the Web so, once again, save this feature for your print publications.

If you have used a frame and want to get rid of it without getting rid of the text or image inside the frame, use Ctrl+F or ⌘+F, or Element⇨Frame⇨Separate Content. This option separates the frame from its content; you can then delete the unwanted frame.

PageMaker automatically puts a box around frames. If you want to get rid of this box, use Element⇨Stroke⇨None. To prevent unwanted boxes, make sure that no frame or line is selected, and use Element⇨Stroke⇨None to reset the publication's default stroke weight to none. If no publication is open when you do this, the new setting becomes the default for all future publications.

You can use the Ellipse and Polygon frame tools (as well as the Rectangle tool) to create text blocks, but those shapes don't export to the Web. Instead, they are converted to rectangles.

After you create a frame, you'll see that the text is surrounded by a margin of space. That's because PageMaker assumes that you want to put a box around the type, so it automatically includes a margin to keep the type from butting against the box. To change those margins, use the Frame Options dialog box, which you access via Ctrl+Alt+F or Option+⌘+F, or via Element⇨Frame⇨Frame Options. Be sure to have the frame selected with the arrow tool before you try to open the Frame Options dialog box, which is shown in Figure 7-4.

To avoid always having to get rid of frame margins, change the Rectangle Frame tool default to zero margins. To do so, double-click on the Rectangle Frame tool (shown in Figure 7-3). You get the Frame Options dialog box. Enter your preferred margins (use zeroes for none) and close the dialog box. From that point on, any frame created with that tool in that publication uses the new margin settings. If no publication was open, all publications created in the future use these new settings.

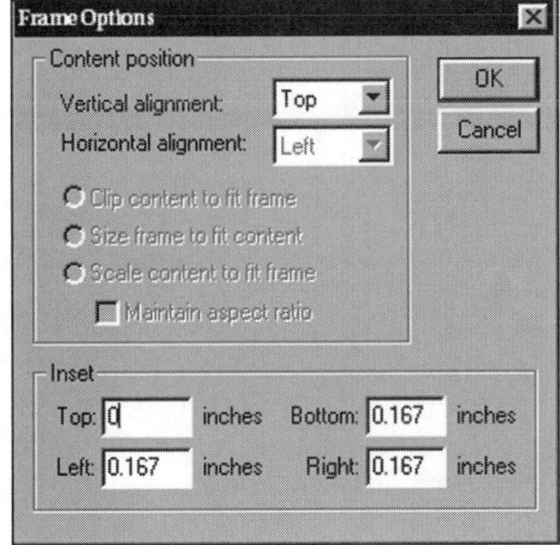

Figure 7-4: Use the Frame Options dialog box to change the margins and text alignment in a text frame.

Importing text

To import (*place,* in PageMaker lingo) text from a word processor document (or other program) into a PageMaker document, follow these steps. (If you're importing text into a frame, select the frame first by clicking on it with the Arrow or Text pointer.)

1. **Choose File⇨Place or press the keyboard shortcut, Ctrl+D or ⌘+D.**

   PageMaker gives you the Place or Place Document dialog box, shown in Figure 7-5.

2. **Navigate through the directories on your disk in the normal Windows or Macintosh fashion.**

   Double-click on a directory or folder to open it. Then scroll through the text files and click on the one you want.

3. **Choose placement and formatting options.**

   First, the placement options: The three choices are pretty straightforward. Choice 1: As New Story brings the text in as a new, separate story, in addition to whatever you may have in your publication already. Choice 2: If you're inserting text in a text block or text frame (and have clicked in the text with the Text tool or selected the text block with the Text or Arrow tool), the options Replacing Entire Story or Replacing Frame's Content will substitute the text for the text in the text block or frame that's currently selected. Choice 3: Selecting the Inserting Text option adds the text into the currently selected text, placing the imported text at the location of the text cursor. This option appears only if you have planted your cursor in the page where the text is to be inserted.

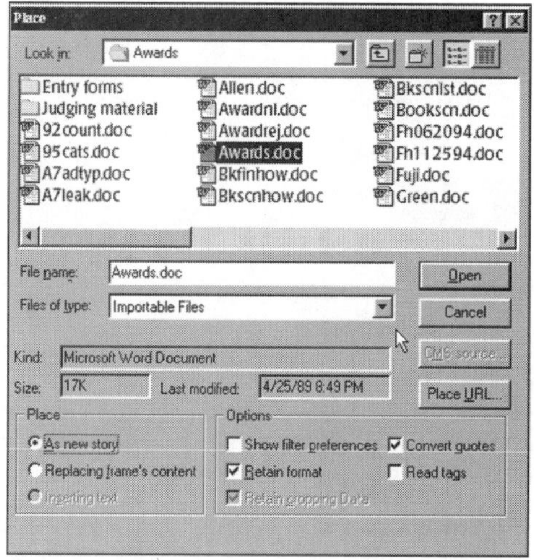

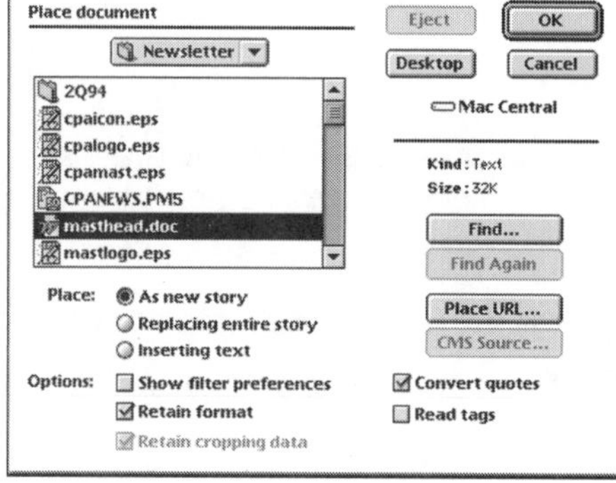

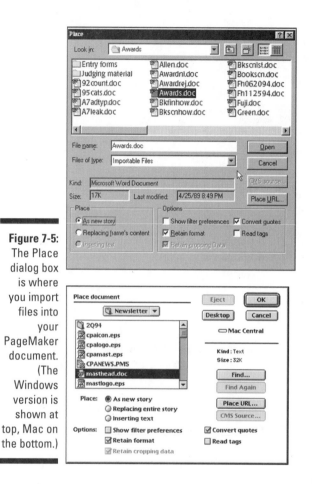

Figure 7-5: The Place dialog box is where you import files into your PageMaker document. (The Windows version is shown at top, Mac on the bottom.)

Story is the PageMaker term for an article or other chunk of text. A story comprises all the text in a single text block or frame or in a group of linked text blocks or frames. (Linked blocks and frames are explained in the section "Working with Text Blocks and Frames" later in this chapter.)

Second, the text formatting options: Retain Format, Convert Quotes, and Read Tags. You should be familiar with the text you're importing before selecting any of these options — you may look at the text first in a word processor to see, for example, whether it uses style sheets or includes character formatting. If it does, you must decide whether you want to retain the styles and formatting. (This issue is covered in more detail in Chapter 9.)

Because most Web browsers do not support typographic (curly) quotes and dashes, you have no reason to enable the Convert Quotes option. You probably should enable Retain Format, however, because you want to

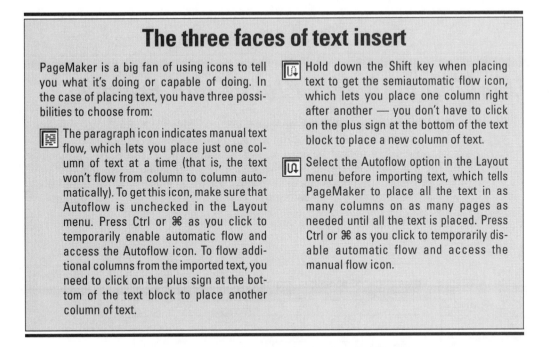

The three faces of text insert

PageMaker is a big fan of using icons to tell you what it's doing or capable of doing. In the case of placing text, you have three possibilities to choose from:

- The paragraph icon indicates manual text flow, which lets you place just one column of text at a time (that is, the text won't flow from column to column automatically). To get this icon, make sure that Autoflow is unchecked in the Layout menu. Press Ctrl or ⌘ as you click to temporarily enable automatic flow and access the Autoflow icon. To flow additional columns from the imported text, you need to click on the plus sign at the bottom of the text block to place another column of text.

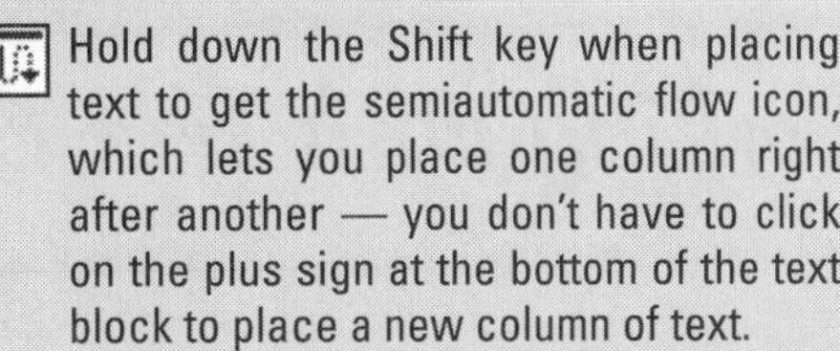

- Hold down the Shift key when placing text to get the semiautomatic flow icon, which lets you place one column right after another — you don't have to click on the plus sign at the bottom of the text block to place a new column of text.

- Select the Autoflow option in the Layout menu before importing text, which tells PageMaker to place all the text in as many columns on as many pages as needed until all the text is placed. Press Ctrl or ⌘ as you click to temporarily disable automatic flow and access the manual flow icon.

preserve boldface and italics. The Read Tags option applies only if you have a document coded with the PageMaker paragraph tags, something rarely used in this era of word processors that have real style tag capabilities.

4. **Click on Open.**

   PageMaker redisplays the current page and shows you a status box indicating that it's importing the text as you requested. When PageMaker finishes importing the text file, and you move the cursor onto the page or pasteboard, the cursor changes to a paragraph shape or a snake shape.

   Note that when you choose the File⇨Place command to begin the importing process, you don't have to be at the page where you want the text to be placed. You can switch pages after importing the text but before clicking at a location at which the text is to be placed (as described in the next step). But it's easier to be at the desired page before you import the text.

5. **Click at the spot where you want PageMaker to place the text.**

   Depending on the setting of the Autoflow option in the Layout menu, the text flows across the page, within the current column, or through several pages (which PageMaker creates if needed), as described in the nearby sidebar, "The three faces of text insert."

6. Select the Autoflow option you want before clicking into the spot where you want the text to go.

Working with Text Blocks and Frames

After you create a text block or frame, you can move it around the page and change its size or shape by using the Arrow tool. Before you can do any of that, however, you first have to *select* the text block or frame. To do so, click on the text block or frame with the Arrow tool. PageMaker displays the boundaries of the text block or frame, as shown in Figure 7-6. Note that the official PageMaker manual refers to a text block's top and bottom boundaries as the *windowshade.*

Windowshade

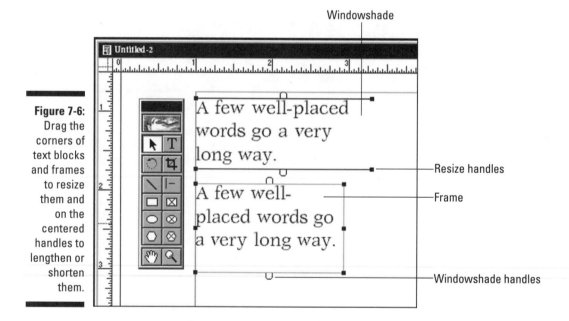

Resize handles

Frame

Windowshade handles

Figure 7-6: Drag the corners of text blocks and frames to resize them and on the centered handles to lengthen or shorten them.

- To move a text block or frame, place the Arrow tool inside the block, and press and hold the mouse button until the cursor changes to a four-way arrow. Then drag the text block or frame to a new position. (You can move the block or frame before you see the four-way arrow but, if you do, PageMaker displays only the text block or frame and not the text, during the move.)
- To move a selected text block or frame, press the arrow keys on your keyboard — a great technique for nudging a text block or frame a short distance.

- To resize a text block or frame, drag one of the windowshade or resize handles, labeled in Figure 7-6. You can drag vertically, horizontally, or diagonally.

- If you see a dashed box extending from the bottom of a text block or frame, it means that the text block or frame isn't long enough to accommodate the current line of text. If you drag the windowshade handle to the bottom of that dashed box or frame (or past the bottom), the remaining text will appear on the screen.
- The little tabs on the top and bottom of the text block or frame — called *text placement handles* — give you information about the text inside the text block or frame. Figure 7-7 shows the three different text placement handles you may encounter. A down-pointing arrow in the bottom tab means that you don't have enough room in the text block or frame for all the text in the story and there's more to be placed. To enlarge either the text block or frame, drag its bottom handles or click on the text placement tab. When you click on the tab, PageMaker displays the paragraph placement icon. Click at the spot where you want to put the overflow text. An empty bottom tab means that no more text needs to be placed.

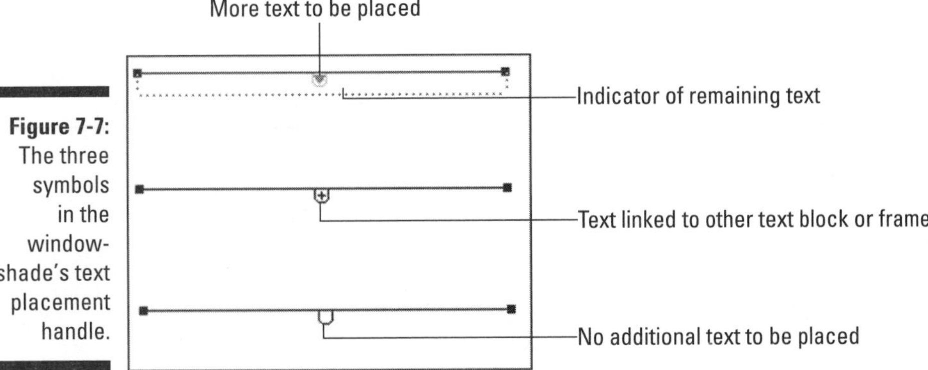

Figure 7-7: The three symbols in the window-shade's text placement handle.

- After you place overflow text, you see a plus sign in the bottom tab of the initial text block or frame. You also see a plus sign in the top tab of the overflow text block or frame. The plus signs indicate that the text blocks are *linked*. For more information about working with linked text blocks and frames, see Chapter 11.
- To delete a text block or frame, select the text block or frame with the Arrow tool and then press Backspace (in Windows, you can also press the Delete key). PageMaker zaps both the text block or frame and the text inside the section into electronic oblivion. If you want to delete the contents of a frame while retaining the frame itself, choose Element⇨Frame⇨Delete Content.

Chapter 8

More Joy of Text

In This Chapter

- Making quick text changes
- Editing text in the Story Editor
- Using and customizing the spell checker
- Understanding search-and-replace
- Undoing bad moves

Nobody gets everything right the first time. Fortunately, fixing mistakes in PageMaker is a fairly easy task. Correcting most of your minor goofs, and some of your bigger ones, can take almost no time at all, unlike growing out that chop job your hair stylist promised would give you a fresh new look (okay, so maybe the Elvis sideburns weren't so *GQ* after all).

If you've done something undesirable (or just flat out wrong), or if you've simply changed your mind and want to do it differently, don't panic. PageMaker understands the fickle human mind and is well prepared with its arsenal of commands, tools, shortcuts, and other remedies to help make you look infallible (which is a whole lot better than covering up your work with a baseball cap and trying to convince everyone of how much cooler it looks that way).

Editing Text

If you need to make substantial changes — or if you want to check the spelling of your text — use the PageMaker built-in word processor, the Story Editor, described later in this chapter in the section "Using the Story Editor." But if you need to make only a few small changes, you can simply select the offending text with the Text tool and make your edits as follows:

- To insert text, click at the spot where you want to add text. Then start typing. PageMaker shoves all the text that falls after the insertion marker to the right to make room for the new characters.

- To delete text, drag over the characters to highlight them. (The highlight means that the characters are selected.) Then press Delete or Backspace.
- Alternatively, you can click with the Text tool to the left of the first character you want to banish from your page. Then keep pressing Delete (to delete to the right) or Backspace (to delete to the left) until you've wiped off all the text you don't like.
- To move text from one place to another, select the text you want to move and then choose Edit⇨Cut or press Ctrl+X (in Windows) or ⌘+X. (on the Mac). PageMaker whisks the selected text out of the text block and into a temporary holding tank known as the Clipboard. Place your cursor at the spot in your PageMaker layout where you want to place the text and choose Edit⇨Paste or press Ctrl+V or ⌘+V. PageMaker puts the text into its new home.
- You can also use the Clipboard to make a copy of a piece of text and then place the copy in a new location. Select the text, choose Edit⇨Copy or press Ctrl+C or ⌘+C, place the cursor at the spot where you want to place the copied text, and use Edit⇨Paste or press Ctrl+V or ⌘+V.

Just for good measure, here are a few selection tips to keep in mind:

- In addition to dragging over text to select it, you can click at the start of the text you want to select, press Shift, and click at the end of the text.
- To quickly select a word, double-click on the word. Triple-click (that is, click the left mouse button three times rapidly) to select a paragraph.
- To select all the text in a story — which means all the text in a text block or frame plus the text in any linked text blocks — choose Edit⇨Select All or press Ctrl+A or ⌘+A.

Using the Story Editor

If you're making a lot of changes to your text, you are likely to find the editing process easier in the Story Editor than in the normal layout view. For one thing, PageMaker can process your edits in the Story Editor faster than in the layout view. In addition, the Story Editor offers such word-processing features as a search-and-replace function and a spell checker.

To open the Story Editor, select the Text or Arrow tool, click inside the story you want to edit, and then choose Edit⇨Edit Story or press Ctrl+E or ⌘+E. Another method is to triple-click on the text block with the Arrow tool selected. The Story Editor appears, as shown in Figure 8-1.

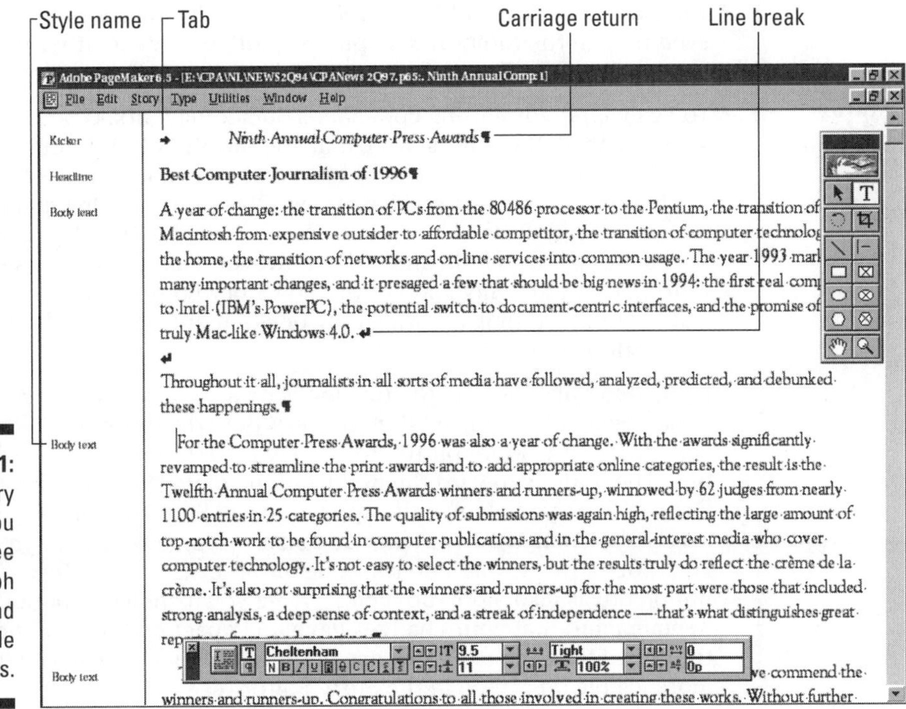

Figure 8-1: In the Story Editor you can see paragraph styles and invisible characters.

You can also create an entirely new story in the Story Editor and then place this new story into PageMaker. Make sure that your cursor is outside of all text blocks and press Ctrl+E or ⌘+E. After you enter your text and close the Story Editor, PageMaker shows you a dialog box that asks whether you want to place the text. Click on the Place button to get the text placement cursor. Then place your text as you normally do.

Before I go any further, you need to know a few things about the Story Editor window:

- The Story Editor displays all text in the selected story. Whether the story continues across 70 pages or is only a single word long, all text in the story is available in the window. Just use the arrow keys and scroll bar to scroll to the portion of the story that you want to edit.
- When you open the Story Editor, several menus change. The Layout menu is replaced by the Story menu, the Element and View menus disappear, and a few commands that were previously dimmed in the Utilities menu become available.

- You can't access any of the PageMaker tools inside the Story Editor, even though the toolbox is displayed (notice how the other tools are grayed out). The Text tool appears to be perpetually selected.

- You can apply formatting commands, including fonts, type sizes, style sheets, and all the others, to text inside the Story Editor, but you can't see the results of your changes. (Formatting commands are the subject of Chapter 6.) The Story Editor shows all text in a single typeface and type size, regardless of any given text's real formatting. You can still see type styles such as bold and italic, however. This setup may seem weird, but it's actually good news. The Story Editor is designed especially for text editing; showing only one font and type size helps the Story Editor run faster.

- If you don't like the way the text looks on-screen, you can change the appearance. Choose File➪Preferences➪General, or use Ctrl+K or ⌘+K, and click on the More button to display the More Preferences dialog box. The options toward the middle of the dialog box, spotlighted in Figure 8-2, let you change the appearance of Story Editor elements on-screen. To change the typeface and size, select new options from the Font pop-up menu and enter a value into the Size option box. (The Size option box is also a pop-up menu, giving you a choice of popular sizes.) Keep in mind that your changes have no impact on the font and size of the actual text; the only purpose of these options is to make your text more legible on-screen in the Story Editor.

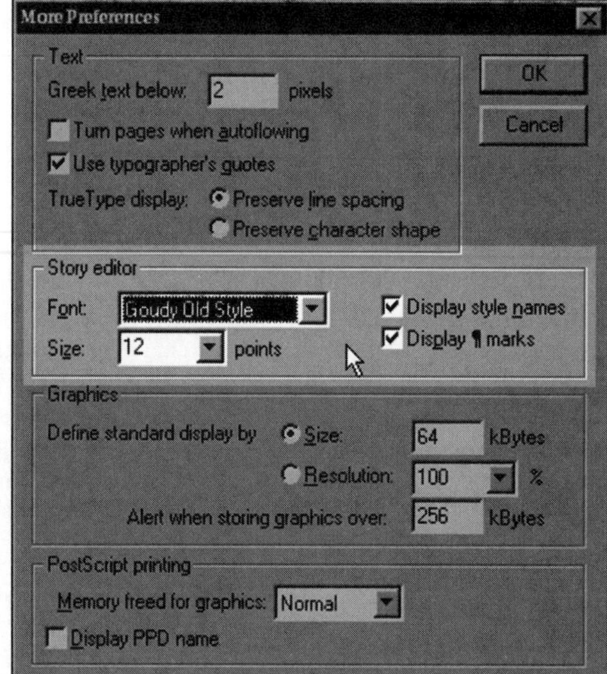

Figure 8-2: In the More Preferences dialog box, you can decide how text is displayed in the Story Editor.

- The left column of the Story Editor window shows the style applied to each paragraph (styles are explained in Chapter 9). If no style sheet name appears in the column, no style sheet is applied to the text. If you don't want to see the style name column, deselect the Display Style Names option in the More Preferences dialog box or uncheck the Display Style Names command in the Story menu.
- In the Story Editor, you can view invisible characters such as tabs, line breaks, and carriage returns, as seen in Figure 8-1. Spaces appear as small dots. Being able to see these characters can be very useful; these characters are normally invisible, so losing track of them can be easy. But if you want your invisible characters to stay invisible, uncheck the Display ¶ Marks option in the Story menu or deselect the Display ¶ Marks check box in the More Preferences dialog box.
- All selection techniques work the same way in the Story Editor as they do in the standard layout view. Double-click on a word to select it, triple-click to select a paragraph, and so on.
- Changes made inside the story window are automatically applied to your document, just as if you had edited the text in the standard layout view.
- To close the Story Editor and return to the layout view, click on the Close box of the Story Editor window, press Ctrl+W or ⌘+W, or choose Story⇨Close Story.
- You can also return to the layout view without closing the Story Editor, which makes accessing the editor faster next time around. Either press Ctrl+E or ⌘+E, choose Edit⇨Edit Layout, or click in the layout window in the background. When not in use, the Story Editor remains on-screen but appears gray. Click on the title bar to make the window active again.

Checking Your Spelling

Another benefit to editing your text in the Story Editor instead of standard layout view is that you gain access to a spell checker and a search-and-replace function.

To spell check your text, choose Utilities⇨Spelling or press Ctrl+L or ⌘+L to display the Spelling dialog box, shown in Figure 8-3. Click on the Start button to instruct PageMaker to begin looking for misspelled words. (After you start the spell checker, the Start button becomes the Ignore button.) When PageMaker finds a word that doesn't match any of the spellings in its dictionary, the unknown word is displayed at the top of the dialog box. Provided that the Alternate Spellings check box is checked, PageMaker also offers a list of alternates below the Change To option box.

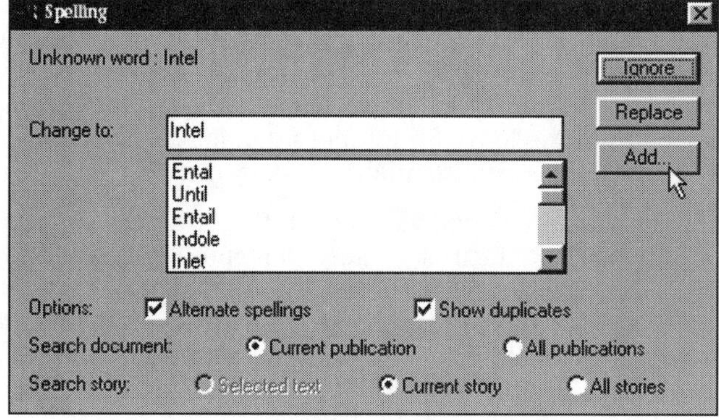

Figure 8-3: The Spelling dialog box lists misspelled words and offers alternate spellings.

At this point, you have three options:

- **Select an alternate:** Click on an Alternate Spellings to make this altered form appear in the Change To option box. Then click on Replace to change the word in your document and search for the next misspelling. Or just double-click on the correct word to do the same thing in a single action.
- **Correct the word manually:** If no correct alternates appear, you have to locate the correct spelling the old-fashioned way: by looking up the word in the dictionary. So much for progress, eh? When you find the right spelling, enter it into the Change To option box and click on Replace.
- **Ignore the word or add it to the dictionary:** If the word is spelled correctly — not even PageMaker knows every word on the planet — you have two choices. Either click on the Ignore button to continue on to the next misspelling or add the word to the PageMaker dictionary, as explained in the next section.

Here's how the remaining options in the Spelling dialog box work:

- **Show Duplicates:** Selected by default, this check box instructs PageMaker to search for any repeated words. The makers of the B-movie *Attack of the the Eye People* — that's how the title reads on-screen — needed to use this option. Unfortunately, they didn't have spell checkers back then. Leave this option turned on.

WEB VS. PRINT

- **Search Document:** You can check the spelling of words in more than one PageMaker document at a time. If you select the All Publications radio button, PageMaker checks all documents belonging to the same book as the current document. (A *book* is a collection of publications that can be jointly indexed or have a common table of contents. For Web publishing, this feature is not applicable; it really only applies to your print publications.) Keep in mind that checking multiple documents at the same time may take a lot of time. Choose Current Publication to check the current document only.

- **Search Story:** These radio buttons let you check only the selected text in the Story Editor; all text in the story, whether selected or not; or all stories throughout the entire PageMaker document. Select the All Stories option at least once before saving the final version of your document so that no text block is left unchecked. The Selected Text option is grayed out (unavailable) unless you select some text before opening the spell checker.

Teaching PageMaker to spell

PageMaker can be a little irritating in its zeal to find misspelled words. You can't tell the program to ignore words that contain only a single letter, abbreviations composed entirely of capital letters, or words with special punctuation (as in *PageMaker's* versus *PageMaker*). To get PageMaker to stop bugging you about a specific spelling, you have to add the spelling to the dictionary.

To add lots of new words to the dictionary — for example, if you want to add a list of employee names or technical terms — use the separate Dictionary Editor program, as described later in this chapter. But if you just want to add a word or two, just click on the Add button in the Spelling dialog box. The dialog box shown in Figure 8-4 appears.

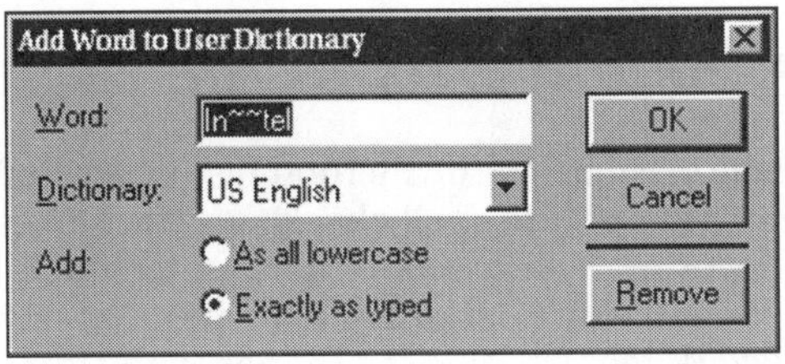

Figure 8-4: Use this dialog box to add a word to the PageMaker spelling dictionary.

- The Word option box contains the word as it's spelled in your document. Tilde (~) symbols divide the word into syllables. Each tilde represents the location of a possible hyphen. The number of tildes indicates precedent. In other words, PageMaker is more likely to break the word at a two-tilde point than a one-tilde point.

  The original tildes represent the best guess PageMaker can make. If you don't like the location of a tilde or the precedent applied to a specific hyphenation point, delete a few tildes, add a few more elsewhere, and so on. For example, if you prefer that PageMaker hyphenate *trichologist*

as *tri-chologist*, rather than *trichol-ogist*, position more tildes between the *i* and *c*, as in *tri~~~chol~~o~gist*. You can enter up to three tildes in a row to represent a very high level of preference. If you never want the word to hyphenate, delete all tildes from the word.

- A trichologist, by the way, is the scientific term for hairdresser. Isn't it amazing how much information you can pack into one $19.99 book?
- If the misspelled word begins with an uppercase character because of an appearance at the beginning of a sentence, but you want PageMaker to save the word using only lowercase characters, select the As All Lowercase radio button near the bottom of the dialog box. If the word is a special term — such as PageMaker — that always needs to be capitalized exactly as it appears in the Word option box, leave the Exactly As Typed radio button selected.

Click on OK to add the word to the PageMaker dictionary. After the program adds the word, you are returned to the Spelling dialog box.

In case you're wondering about the Remove button, this button lets you remove words from the dictionary. Say you accidentally add the word *tricologist* instead of *trichologist*. To get rid of this word, click on the Add button in the Spelling dialog box (it doesn't matter what word appears in the Change To option box). Then enter *tricologist* into the Word option box — with or without tildes, again it doesn't matter — and click on the Remove button. The misspelled word is out of there.

Adding lots of new words to the dictionary

Adding words to your dictionary using the method just described is fine if you want to add a few words as you're spell-checking a document. But if you need to add a long list of words — for example, a list of technical or scientific terms used in your industry or a list of brand names that have odd capitalization (such as *PageMaker*) — give the Dictionary Editor utility a whirl. The Dictionary Editor, a separate program that comes bundled with PageMaker, lets you import a list of words that you create in a word processor and add all the words to the dictionary in one fell swoop.

To add a list of words using the Dictionary Editor:

1. **Create a list of the words you want to add to the dictionary.**

   You can type your list in a word processor or any other program that can save files in the text-only (indicated by the .TXT extension in Windows) format. Put a carriage return, space, or tab between each word you want to add to the dictionary.

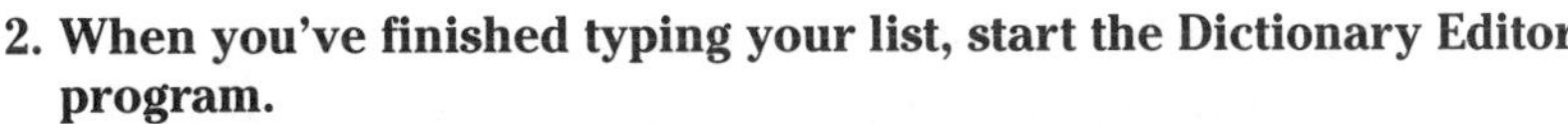

2. **When you've finished typing your list, start the Dictionary Editor program.**

On the Mac, you have to do some sleuthing to find the program. First go to the folder that contains the PageMaker 6.5 program. Now open the Extras folder. Now open the Typography folder. Then you find the Dictionary Editor. In Windows, follow the same path described earlier for the Mac, but note that on Windows the directory containing the Dictionary Editor (named Deapp in the directory) is called Text, not Typography.

3. **Choose File➪Open, select the dictionary you want to edit, and click on OK.**

The main PageMaker dictionary is named Aldusnc.UNC in Windows and AldUsn.udc on the Mac.

In Windows, you can find the dictionary inside the Usenglsh folder (assuming you installed the US English dictionary). The Usenglsh folder is stored inside the Prx folder, which is inside the Linguist folder, which is inside the Rsrc folder, which is inside your main PageMaker folder. (Whew!) Don't be fooled by the Usenglsh folder that's in the Rsrc folder — it's a different, separate Usenglsh.

On the Mac, the dictionary is in a similar location: From the PageMaker folder, go first to the RSRC folder, then to the Linguists folder, then to the Proximity folder, and finally to the US English folder (or whatever folder has your language's dictionary).

After you click on OK, you see a dialog box that contains a list of words, a Word option box, and buttons that enable you to add, replace, and remove words from the dictionary. But you're going to import your list, not add words one at a time, so you can ignore the dialog box.

4. **Choose File➪Import.**

The Import From Text File dialog box appears. In the scrolling file list, select the file containing the list you want to import. The dialog box also offers two other options: Hyphenate On Import Using Algorithm (say *that* three times fast) and Import Words Already in Dictionary. If you choose the former option, the Dictionary Editor hyphenates your words according to how it thinks the words need to be hyphenated. If you don't choose this option, the Dictionary Editor doesn't hyphenate your words at all (you can add hyphenation information later if you want).

If you choose the second option, the Dictionary Editor replaces any word that has the same spelling as a word you import with the new word. For example, you could overwrite *Pagemaker* with *PageMaker.*

5. **Click on Open or press Enter.**

Your new words appear in the Dictionary Editor word list.

6. **Adjust the hyphenation of your new words.**

   If you choose the Hyphenate On Import Using Algorithm radio button in Step 4, the hyphenation marks for your new word display in the scrolling list. To change the hyphenation of a word, double-click on the word to place it in the Word option box and add or delete tildes, as explained in the earlier section "Teaching PageMaker to spell."

   If you didn't choose the Hyphenate On Import Using Algorithm option, double-click on the word to place it in the Word option box and then choose Edit⇨Hyphenate to see the suggested hyphenation from the Dictionary Editor. Add or delete tildes to change the hyphenation. Click on Replace to make the Dictionary Editor accept your changes.

7. **Choose File⇨Save to save your amended dictionary and click on the Close box to quit the Dictionary Editor program.**

Finding that Special Word

The Spelling command searches your text for spelling errors. But what if you have something more specific in mind? Suppose, for example, that you're pretty sure that you mentioned Vice President Muckimuck in your document, but you're not positive, and now he's moved on to lusher pastures. You decide that you'd better double-check than risk Web-wide embarrassment for your company. The question is, how?

The answer is, Utilities⇨Change. When you choose this command (or press Ctrl+H or ⌘+H) when working in the Story Editor, PageMaker displays the Change dialog box, found at the bottom of Figure 8-5.

PageMaker actually offers two commands for finding text, Utilities⇨Change and Utilities⇨Find. The Find command is specifically designed for finding text that you don't want to change. But what's the point? As Figure 8-5 demonstrates, the Find dialog box merely offers fewer options than the Change dialog box; the Find dialog box has no unique aspects, so there's no point in using it. Furthermore, by sticking with Utilities⇨Change for all your searching needs, you have to memorize only one keyboard equivalent, Ctrl+H or ⌘+H.

Hunting down some text

After you display the Change dialog box, enter the characters that you want to find in the Find What option box. Then press Enter (or click on the Find button, which becomes the Find Next button after you click it). If the first instance of the text isn't the one you were looking for, press Enter again (or click on the Find Next button). That's all there is to it.

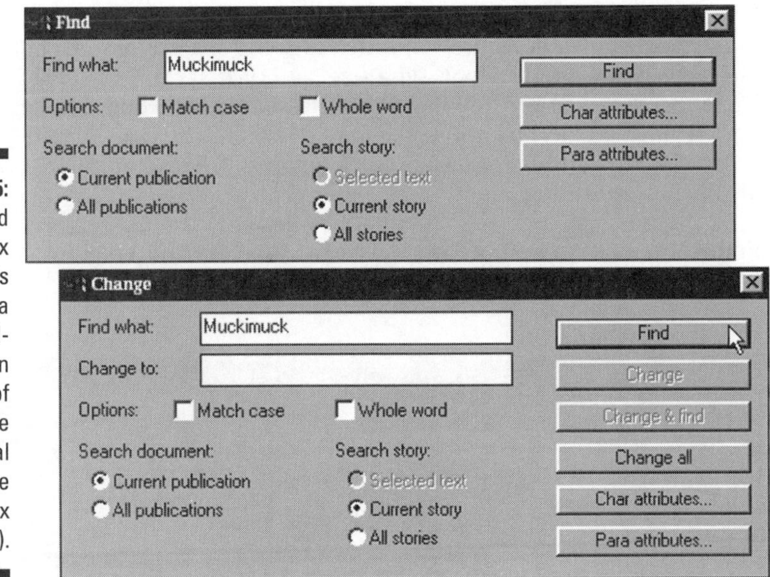

Figure 8-5: The Find dialog box (top) is merely a stripped-down version of the more functional Change dialog box (bottom).

To modify your search, select either of the two check boxes below the Change To option box:

- **Match Case:** If you select this option, PageMaker finds only those instances of a word that match the capitalization of the text entered into the Find What option box. For example, when searching for *Muckimuck,* PageMaker ignores the colloquial use of *muckimuck* and searches for the word exclusively in a proper noun form.
- **Whole Word:** When selected, this option searches for whole words and not just partial words. For example, if you search for *hang,* you may also find *hang*er, c*hang*e, and *shanghai.* To eliminate all words but *hang* from your search, select the Whole Word option.

You also have access to the same Search document and Search story options that are present in the Spelling dialog box. To find out how these work, back up a page or two and read the descriptions in the section "Checking Your Spelling."

Searching by format

You can also search for text that's formatted in a certain way. For example, you may want to find only italicized references to Muckimuck's Luck with Bucks. To search your text in this fashion, click on either the Char Attributes or Para Attributes button.

If you choose Char Attributes, you get the Change Character Attributes dialog box, shown in Figure 8-6, which lets you search for certain formatting characteristics, such as font, type size, and type style. The settings shown in Figure 8-6, for example, tell PageMaker to search for 9-point, italic, New Baskerville text. If you choose the Para Attributes button instead, you can search for three different paragraph formatting characteristics: style, alignment, or leading.

In the previous version of PageMaker, the Char Attributes button used to be labeled Text Attributes. Shifty, huh?

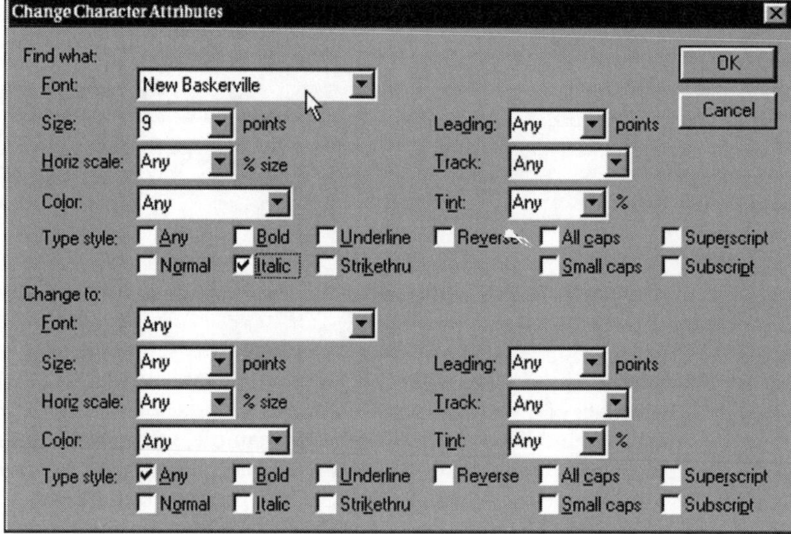

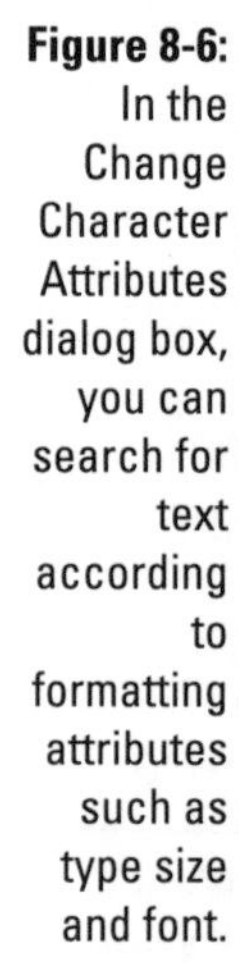
Figure 8-6: In the Change Character Attributes dialog box, you can search for text according to formatting attributes such as type size and font.

In either dialog box, select the formatting you want to locate from the options in the top half of the dialog box — those in the Find What section. (The options in the bottom half of the dialog box control the formatting of replacement text, a subject discussed later in this chapter.)

Press Enter or click on the OK button to exit the Change Character Attributes dialog box and return to the Change dialog box.

Searching for special characters

In addition to checking for plain old everyday text, you can search for the PageMaker special characters (em spaces, discretionary hyphens) and even invisible characters (carriage returns, tabs). To do so, enter special codes into the Find What option box. All codes include the caret (^) character. To create this character, press Shift+6. Most of these codes are the same as they are in WordPerfect or Microsoft Word. Table 8-1 lists the most common codes.

Capitalization of code characters doesn't matter. For example, both ^t and ^T find tabs.

Table 8-1 Character Search Codes

Character	*Search Code*	*Note*
Carriage return	^p	*p* for paragraph
Line break (Shift+Enter)	^n	*n* as in new line
Tab	^t	*t* for tab
Automatic hyphen	^5	Doesn't work in Change To box
Discretionary hyphen	^-	
Nonbreaking hyphen	^~	
En dash	^=	
Em dash	^+	
Standard space	^w	*w* for white space
Em space	^m	
En space	^>	> because it's thicker
Thin space	^<	< because it's so thin
Nonbreaking space	^s	
Nonbreaking slash	^/	

PageMaker provides one other special character code, ^?. This so-called *wild card character* searches for absolutely any character of text. So if you enter *spr^?ng*, you find *spring, sprang,* and *sprung*. You can even use more than one wildcard character in a row. If you enter *spr^?^?^?*, you also find *sprint, sprite, sprout,* and *spruce*.

But wait. With all these caret codes, how do you manage to find a regular old caret? The answer is to enter two carets in a row (^^).

Replacing found text with new text

Now suppose that former mailroom worker Upstart has risen to take Muckimuck's old job. Your latest company news is due on your Web site tomorrow and you need to replace every instance of *Muckimuck* with *Upstart*.

Again, the Change dialog box is your key to success. Enter *Muckimuck* in the Find What option box and *Upstart* in the Change To option box. Then use one of the following combinations of buttons:

- To change every instance of *Muckimuck* to *Upstart,* click on the Change All button. PageMaker automatically changes every occurrence of the text.
- To check each occurrence of *Muckimuck* before changing it — perhaps a couple of Muckimuck's duties are being transferred to Department L's VP Rapier — click on the Find button. When PageMaker finds an occurrence of *Muckimuck,* you have the option of changing the word to *Upstart.* To do so, click on the Change & Find button, which changes the text and searches for the next occurrence. Alternatively, you can enter *Rapier* into the Change To option box and then click on Change & Find. Or, finally, you can click on the Find Next button to leave this occurrence of *Muckimuck* intact and search for the next one.
- The Change button just changes the selected text without searching for the next occurrence. Most likely, the only time you want to use this button is when searching for a single occurrence of a word.
- Use the Para Attributes and Char Attributes buttons to access the text-formatting options discussed earlier. The options in the Change To Sections control formatting of your placement text.

  All the special character codes in Table 8-1 also work in the Change To box, except the automatic hyphenation code.

To this day, PageMaker doesn't offer an option to undo changes made from the Change dialog box, as do Microsoft Word and other word processors. So make sure that you really want to change your text — and that you've entered the correct characters in the Find What and Change To option boxes — *before* you initiate this command. (Try to press Shift and choose File⇨Revert to revert to the last minisaved version of your document, as explained in the next section, but the odds aren't great that this maneuver will work.)

Undoing Bad Moves

PageMaker offers a couple of other ways to correct your mistakes: the Undo command and the Revert command. Memorize these two commands — you are likely to use them a lot.

- Edit⇨Undo (Ctrl+Z or ⌘+Z) reverses your last action. For example, if you delete a paragraph of text and then think better of your correction, you can choose Undo to get your paragraph back. Whew, that was a close one!

- PageMaker only remembers the last action you took, so you have to choose Undo immediately after you goof up. If you click the mouse button or do anything else before choosing Undo, the command doesn't work.
- If you change your mind about undoing something, you can choose Edit➪Redo to undo your undo. But you have to choose Redo before you do anything else, including clicking the mouse. How's that for a fine how-do-you-do?

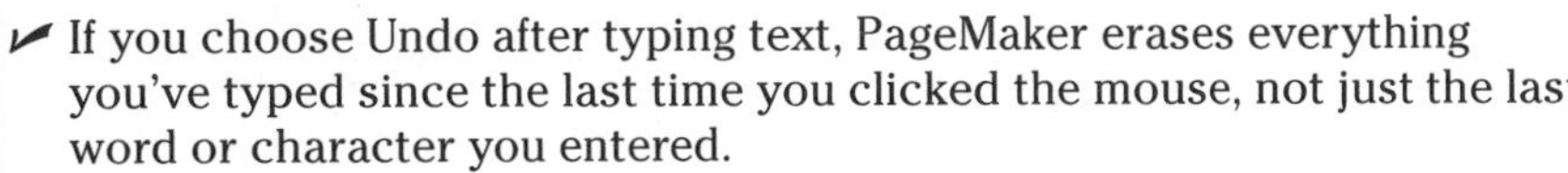

- If you choose Undo after typing text, PageMaker erases everything you've typed since the last time you clicked the mouse, not just the last word or character you entered.
- File➪Revert gets rid of all the edits you made since the last time you saved your document. Using this command is like getting a fresh start on the day's work.

- PageMaker automatically performs what it calls minisaves when you take certain actions, such as moving to a new page, switching between layout and Story Editor view, and printing a document. To revert to the last minisaved version of your document, hold down the Shift key as you choose File➪Revert.

- Undo can't undo everything. The command can't undo most File menu commands (Print, Save, and so on); Type menu commands (font and type style settings, for example); or changes you make using the Style and Colors palettes. This is yet another good reason for remembering the cardinal rule of computerdom: *Save early and save often.* That way, if you really mess up your document and need to use the Revert command to get rid of the evidence, you don't lose a whole day's work.

You now know the basics of placing text into your PageMaker document — but the fun's only just beginning. In the next chapter, you find out how to do even more with text, from setting up styles to save gobs of time and make your pages even more perfect, to doing some stylish effects for your well-groomed Web pages.

Chapter 9

Staying in Style

In This Chapter

- Creating styles to automate paragraph formatting
- Importing styles from other documents
- Applying styles
- Creating HTML-equivalent styles in PageMaker
- Translating PageMaker styles to HTML styles

PageMaker has been able to create styles since its beginning, and creating styles remains one of the most indispensable functions the program offers. When I say *create styles,* I'm not thinking of the wardrobe sense of a Jackie Onassis (whose *fake* pearls sold for a quarter million bucks) or the cool panache of a Cary Grant (who was probably born with style but no sweat glands). *Styling,* in the land of electronic page layout, is what you do to quickly fashion text the way you want it.

Styles — also called *style sheets* — give you the ability to apply a bunch of different formatting options (type size, typeface, paragraph indents, leading, and so forth) with just a keystroke or two. Styles have become commonplace — any desktop publishing program worth its silicon uses them, as does every major word processor. Using styles is a real time-saver, and learning how to apply them is well worth the effort.

For example, if you decide that you want all your headlines to appear in a particular typeface and size, with a certain amount of spacing before and after them, you can create a style called *Headlines.* Then, instead of formatting each headline one by one, first setting the typeface, then the size, and then the paragraph spacing, you just apply the Headline style to the appropriate heads. PageMaker automatically does all your formatting for you in one fell swoop.

On the Web, such elaborate formatting just doesn't hold up because it isn't supported in HTML (the language that PageMaker uses to translate its pages into Web pages). That doesn't mean that styles can't help you. They can, if you use them to help you prepare your text for the kind of formatting HTML can support.

You may create one style for your first-level headlines, one for second-level heads, one for body text, and one for an index. Styles not only give you more time to work on more important matters than formatting, they also ensure consistency. You don't have to remember from one day to the next what formatting you're supposed to use for a particular text element. On the Web, this consistency is critical, given that you have so few ways to differentiate the look of one paragraph from another — you must use the styles appropriately or risk confusing (or losing) your readers.

Creating and Editing Text Styles

Here's what you do to define a new style:

1. **Choose Type⇨Define Styles or use the shortcut, Ctrl+3 (Windows) or ⌘+3 (Mac).**

   PageMaker displays the Define Styles dialog box shown in Figure 9-1. If you selected text before opening up the dialog box, the [Selection] option is highlighted, which means that PageMaker has collected all formatting information for the selected text and will base the new style's characteristics on it. If no text is selected, the new style is based on the characteristics of a style called No Style, which all PageMaker documents have.

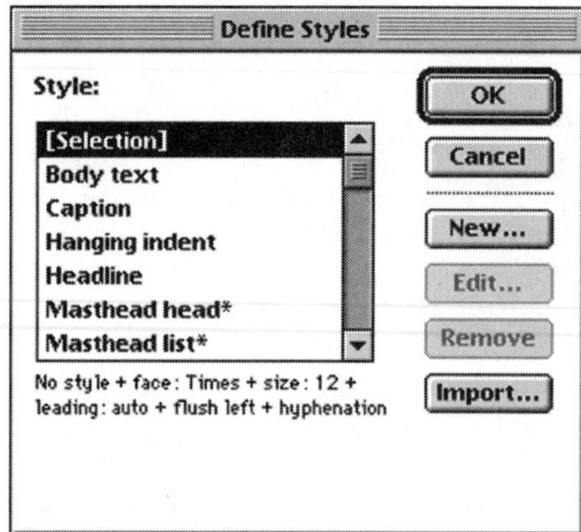

Figure 9-1: You can create new styles or edit existing ones in this dialog box.

2. **Click on the New button.**

   You get the Edit Style dialog box, shown in Figure 9-2. Enter the name of the new style in the Name field. Notice that the Based On and Next Style fields are already filled in, either with No Style or whatever style was applied to the text that was selected when you entered the Define Styles dialog box. If you want to base the new style on a different, previously defined style, select that style from the Based On pop-up menu.

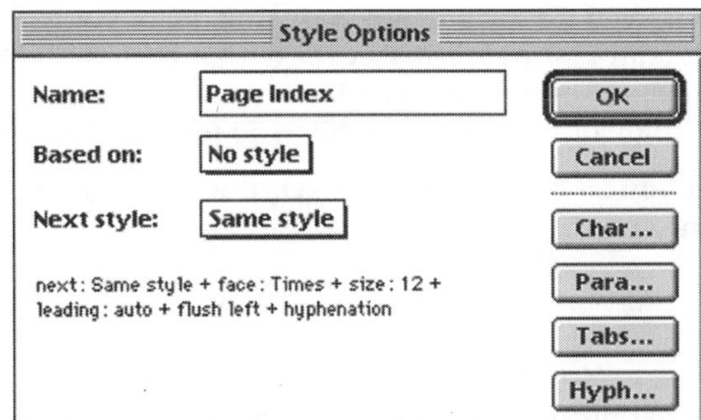

Figure 9-2: You can define the settings for a new style or change settings for an existing style in this dialog box.

Microsoft Word defines a default style called Normal, and chances are that the text you create in Word has this style applied (it is, after all, the default). If you create a style in PageMaker called Normal, Word text using the Normal style will be redefined to use the PageMaker Normal style. Going this route saves you from having to apply your basic body style — the style used for the bulk of your text — in PageMaker. It's especially handy because no way exists to edit the settings for No Style, so you can't really use that as your body style. (The chances that the No Style formatting will match your body style's settings are close to zero.)

3. **Choose the Next Style.**

   Some text elements are always followed by text that has a different style. For example, a byline may always be followed by text that uses the Normal style. In cases such as this, you should set the Next Style option box to that other style (use the pop-up menu to select any existing style). Otherwise, select Same Style.

4. **Use the Char, Para, Tabs, and Hyph buttons to access the Type Specifications, Paragraph Specifications, Indents/Tabs, and Hyphenation dialog boxes.**

   You have to go through them one at a time. For Web documents, only the first two are relevant.

   At this point, you specify how you want to format any text to which you apply the style. Set the options in the various dialog boxes just as you do to format text normally. All three dialog boxes have buttons that open other dialog boxes.

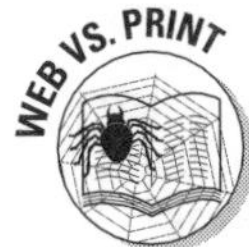

If you check the Include in Table of Contents check box in the Paragraph Specifications dialog box, the style that you're creating or editing is included in any table of contents generated by PageMaker for the document. This option can be useful for Web publishing to generate a menu of pages; however, chances are your Web pages won't be complex enough to warrant the effort of creating a table of contents in

PageMaker. And even if they are, any reorganizing of your Web site later on in an HTML editor would probably make that table of contents outdated. In most cases, I recommend you create your own Web page menus, rather than allow PageMaker to do so for you.

5. **Click OK until you're back in the Style Options dialog box, and then click OK again.**

Congratulations! You have a new style! And, now for a few final thoughts on creating styles:

- To modify an existing style, use the Define Styles dialog box just as if you were creating a new style, but click on the Edit button instead of the New button. You can delete a style by clicking on the Remove button.

- If you want to use styles that were defined in another PageMaker document, click on the Copy button and find the document through the dialog box. After you select the document, click on OK. You may get a prompt asking whether copying over existing styles is okay. If you give PageMaker the go-ahead, any style in your current document whose name is the same as in the other document is replaced by the other document's style. So be careful when using this feature.
- You can define styles based on the formatting of existing text. One way is to select some formatted text and go to the Define Styles dialog box as described earlier; the formatting of the selected text becomes part of the new style. Or you can use the Control palette instead. To use this method, click with the Text tool inside the paragraph whose formatting you want to turn into a style. Make sure that the Control palette is in paragraph mode (that's what the ¶ button does), highlight the style name, enter a new name, and press Enter. The result is a new style.
- A similar technique is to highlight the text, hold down the Ctrl or ⌘ key, and click on No Style in the Styles palette. Doing so takes you to the Edit Style dialog box, in which you can enter the new style name and make changes. This method isn't as fast as the Control palette method, but it does let you make further changes to the style more easily.

- You may notice that a paragraph's style name sometimes has a plus sign (+) after it. The plus sign means that the selected paragraph's formatting has been modified from the style's settings. Perhaps, for example, you italicized some text or changed the margin for that paragraph. Note that the text cursor (or *pointer* in Mac-speak) has to be on the modified portion of the paragraph; the plus sign appears only if the current selected text in the paragraph is different from the style settings.
- To make the styles you define available to all future documents, close all open documents and then define or edit your styles. To be safe, quit PageMaker after you finish defining your default styles. PageMaker saves the default settings to disk when you quit the program. This way, if your machine crashes or you encounter a system error, you don't lose all your work.

Importing Styles

When you import text and check the Retain Format check box (in the Place dialog box), PageMaker loads in any styles and text formatting defined in the word processor document. PageMaker adds many default formatting settings for options that the word processor doesn't offer, such as tracking. But the basics — such as font, size, indents, and alignment — are all brought into PageMaker along with the text.

The Place dialog box offers an option called Read Tags. You may think that you need to check this box to import your styles — especially if you're familiar with programs that use the term "style tags" instead of "styles." But if you select the option, you actually are turning off the automatic style-import feature. You use the Read Tags option to import text that was formatted to work with earlier versions of PageMaker, in which you placed the style name, enclosed in angle brackets, at the beginning of a paragraph to indicate what style you wanted PageMaker to apply to the text. If you wanted PageMaker to give a paragraph the Body Text style, for example, you placed the code `<Body Text>` at the beginning of the paragraph. The option that you *do* want to have checked is Retain Format; that brings in the word processor file's style (and other) formatting.

Sometimes, the text that you're importing has a style name not already defined in PageMaker. When this happens, PageMaker creates a new style (based on No Style). In the Control palette and in the Define Styles dialog box, an asterisk (*) is added to the style name so that you can tell that the style is undefined in PageMaker. If you don't have a Credit style in PageMaker but a Credit style is in an imported Word document, for example, PageMaker applies a style called *Credit** to the paragraphs coded in Word with its Credit style. Simply edit the style settings the normal way and change the name back to *Credit*. Similarly, PageMaker marks such new styles by placing a disk icon to the right of the style name in the Styles palette.

Applying Styles to Text

To apply a style to a paragraph, just select the paragraph with the Text tool, click on a style name in the Control palette, and then click on the Apply button or press Enter. You can apply styles in Story Editor view and in layout (normal) view.

For another way to choose styles, display the Styles palette by choosing Window⇨Show Styles or pressing Ctrl+B or ⌘+B. Click on a style name to apply it to the selected text. If your document uses lots of styles, you may find using the Styles palette easier than using the Control palette to choose styles, because you can resize the palette as needed to display all your style names at once.

The shortcut for showing the Styles palette changed with this version. It used to be Ctrl+Y or ⌘+Y; now it's Ctrl+B or ⌘+B. That's just PageMaker trying to keep you alert.

To view all styles applied to your document, switch to Story Editor view (via Ctrl+E or ⌘+E) and choose Story➪Display Style Names. (For more information about the Story Editor, see Chapter 8.)

Exploring HTML Styles

HTML (HyperText Markup Language) uses about a dozen text styles that most browsers can understand. (*HTML* is the language that makes up Web pages and allows you to create links to other places in your site or any other page on the Web; *browsers* are the programs that display HTML documents, better known as Web pages.) You should know what these styles are and keep them in mind when you define your PageMaker styles and design your Web pages. The most common HTML styles fall into three basic groups: text, headlines, and lists. When you export your PageMaker document to HTML, your PageMaker styles are translated to these HTML styles.

Before I go any further, let me warn you that some pretty geeky stuff crops up in the rest of this section. After I describe each of the HTML type styles, I provide some information on the actual HTML coding used to create the style. You can completely avoid the whole business of coding by never opening your HTML files in a word processor or HTML editor. Nevertheless, I'm providing this basic information in case you want to tweak your pages after exporting them from PageMaker to HTML — something I expect many of you will do. If this kind of coding makes you want to close this book and fire up a game of Solitaire for relief, just jump to the next paragraph when you see the HTML coding — each one starts with a bracket character that looks like this: <, so it's easy to spot.

You never see the actual HyperText Markup Language codes when you're working in PageMaker. The program creates the code for you automatically — based on the styles used in your layout — when it exports your PageMaker layout to HTML Web pages. You can see this hidden code only if you edit those Web pages in an HTML editor or text editor. Although PageMaker automatically generates the HTML codes, you do have some control over which HTML styles your PageMaker styles are translated to, as described in the "Converting Styles: PageMaker to HTML" section later in this chapter. In the lists of styles that follow in this section, I indicate the standard HTML translations (also called *mappings*) in documents that use the default PageMaker styles.

One other thing to keep in mind: The names of HTML styles are not editable — these style names are part of the standard HTML codes. Web browsers know how to handle only these predefined styles and only with these particular names. In PageMaker, of course, you can name or rename a style any way you want to.

The following list of HTML styles includes some that are unknown to PageMaker. If you want to include these styles in your Web pages, you need to do some work in an HTML editor after exporting your document from PageMaker.

Text styles

You can export four different HTML text-oriented styles from PageMaker:

- **Body Text:** This is a standard paragraph style that makes up most of your Web text. Body Text paragraphs are not indented, and they have an added line of space between them. If you want to force a break in a line, but want no additional space between the lines, use the new-line command (Shift+Enter) to generate the HTML break command (`<BR>`). It works just like a new line command in PageMaker. In fact, using Shift+Enter in PageMaker produces a new line break in HTML. PageMaker's Normal and No Style styles are automatically translated to this HTML style during export. If you look at the actual HTML code generated by PageMaker, you see the code `<P>` indicating this style.
- **Blockquote:** This paragraph style is very much like Body Text except that each paragraph block is indented from the left — just like long quotes are in books. (I realize that *Blockquote* is spelled here as one word; that's truly how the HTML style is spelled.) No PageMaker style is automatically translated to Blockquote. In HTML, you see the code `<BLOCKQUOTE>` for this style.
- **Address:** Think of this as Body Text in italics. It's typically used to indicate a Web address, as in "For more details, go to such-and-such Web address." However, it makes a great style for captions, too. No PageMaker style is automatically translated to Address. In HTML, you see the code `<ADDRESS>` for this style.
- **Preformatted:** Sometimes you *don't* want the browser to format text (that is, make it fit in whatever width the browser window happens to be). That's when the Preformatted style comes in handy. It makes the browser use a fixed-width font (such as Courier), and it prevents the browser from restyling the text to fit the window. You can use this style to align lists properly and call attention to commands and file and directory names. No PageMaker style is automatically translated to Preformatted. In HTML, you see the code `<PRE>` for this style.

Because this style prevents the browser from formatting, you need to ensure that your line breaks won't disappear. PageMaker doesn't insert breaks at line endings (for any text) of a column or text frame when exporting to HTML, even with Approximate Layout checked. This means you have to indicate page breaks yourself — with Shift+Enter for a forced line break or by using Enter to create a new paragraph. (See Chapter 6 for an explanation of how the Approximate Layout option affects text formatting.)

Figure 9-3 shows how these four styles typically look in an HTML document when viewed in an Internet browser. Bear in mind that one browser may display the same text style differently than another browser.

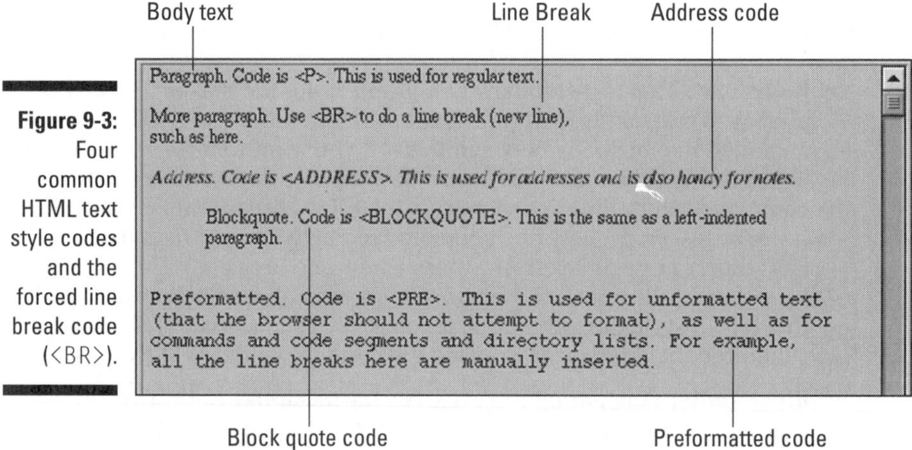

Body text
Line Break
Address code
Paragraph. Code is <P>. This is used for regular text.
More paragraph. Use <BR> to do a line break (new line),
such as here.
Address. Code is <ADDRESS>. This is used for addresses and is also handy for notes.
Blockquote. Code is <BLOCKQUOTE>. This is the same as a left-indented
paragraph.
Preformatted. Code is <PRE>. This is used for unformatted text
(that the browser should not attempt to format), as well as for
commands and code segments and directory lists. For example,
all the line breaks here are manually inserted.
Block quote code
Preformatted code

Figure 9-3: Four common HTML text style codes and the forced line break code (<BR>).

Headline styles

You can export six different headline styles from PageMaker to HTML. The catch is, in every case you end up with boldface text. The only way you can differentiate headline styles is by their size — each one can be different. (Be aware: The headline size that ends up in your Web page is determined by the individual browser. Because of this, headline sizes are described in relative terms and not with actual point sizes.) Figure 9-4 shows how the sizes of the various heading styles compare.

- **Heading 1:** This is the biggest headline style available. Use it as the equivalent of a book chapter title, such as for the title of your home page. PageMaker automatically assigns any text tagged with its Headline style to the Heading 1 style during HTML export. If you look at the actual HTML code, you see it coded as <H1>.

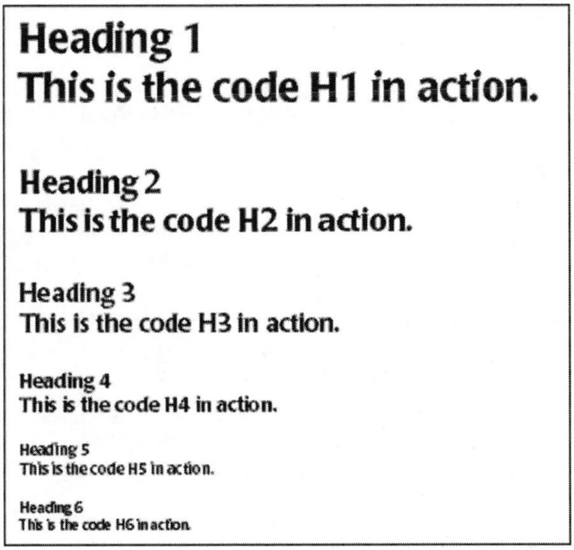

Heading 1
This is the code H1 in action.

Heading 2
This is the code H2 in action.

Heading 3
This is the code H3 in action.

Heading 4
This is the code H4 in action.

Heading 5
This is the code H5 in action.

Heading 6
This is the code H6 in action.

Figure 9-4: The six heading styles available in HTML. (You can see that size is about the only thing that distinguishes them.)

- **Heading 2:** This is the next largest headline style. Use it for section titles and subheads within a story or page. PageMaker automatically assigns any text tagged with its Subhead 1 style to the Heading 2 style during HTML export. In HTML, you see this style coded as `<H2>`.
- **Heading 3:** This is the third-largest headline style. Use it for secondary subheads within a story or a page, or for labels. PageMaker automatically assigns any text tagged with its Subhead 2 style to the Heading 3 style during HTML export. In HTML, you see it tagged as `<H3>`.
- **Heading 4:** Now you're getting into fairly small headings. This size is just a bit bigger than boldface body text. It can be used for captions, although I prefer the Address tag for that use. It's your decision. You can choose which HTML style a PageMaker style is translated to, as described in the section "Converting Styles: PageMaker to HTML" later in this chapter. PageMaker automatically assigns any text tagged with its Caption style to the Heading 4 style during export. In HTML, you see it coded as `<H4>`.
- **Heading 5:** This style is even smaller than Heading 4. It's basically the same size as body text, so you have to decide if you really want something this small as a heading. No PageMaker style is automatically translated to Heading 5. In HTML, you see the code `<H5>` for this style.
- **Heading 6:** What can I say? This is a *really* small headline size. Maybe you can do something creative with a heading this size. No PageMaker style is automatically translated to Heading 6. In HTML, you see the code `<H6>` for this style.

List styles

You can export five list styles from PageMaker to HTML. Each list style looks pretty much the same from browser to browser (more or less like bulleted lists) except for the Ordered style, which produces a numbered list.

- **Unordered List:** This is your basic bulleted list. In Chapter 6, I bemoan the inability to set a bullet character in PageMaker and have it survive during HTML export. The actual bullet character may not survive, but you can still have bulleted paragraphs through this list style. PageMaker automatically assigns any text tagged with its Hanging Indent style to the Unordered List style during export. In HTML, you see it coded as <UL>, and you see the code <LI> in front of each paragraph, courtesy of PageMaker's HTML export. That code is what generates the bullets — for example, if you change <LI> to the code <P> (the code for body text), which you could do in an HTML editor, you keep the list but lose the bullets.
- **Ordered List:** This is your basic numbered list. As with the bullets in an unordered list, the numbers are automatically generated. PageMaker has no automatic translation of a PageMaker style to the Ordered List HTML style. HTML aficionados (and you know who you are) should note that the code for this style is <OL> and that HTML uses the same code (<LI>) in front of each paragraph to generate the numbers as it does to generate bullets for paragraphs using the Unordered List HTML style. *Remember:* PageMaker automatically adds the coding for numbers to this style when exporting to HTML.
- **Menu List:** Although PageMaker treats the Menu List style like an ordered list, it assumes that each item in the list is fewer than 20 characters long. The use of this style tells the browser to pack columns closer together than it would with the Ordered List style (as usual, the style's appearance is largely determined by the browser). PageMaker has no automatic translation of a PageMaker style to the Menu List HTML style. In HTML, the code for this style is <MENU> and HTML uses the same code (<LI>) in front of each paragraph to generate bullets as it does in a paragraph using the Unordered List style. PageMaker automatically adds the coding for bullets to this style when exporting to HTML.
- **Directory List:** This style is similar to the Menu List in that the code tells the browser to compactly format the list entries. The difference is that browsers that understand this style don't assume the list items are fewer than 20 characters long. PageMaker has no automatic translation of a PageMaker style to the Directory List HTML style. In HTML, the code for this style is <DIR> and HTML uses the same code (<LI>) in front of each paragraph to generate the bullets as it does for the Unordered List style. PageMaker automatically adds the coding for bullets to this style when exporting to HTML.

- **Term List and Definition List:** These two HTML styles are very similar. Both produce unindented list items, such as the first word in a glossary definition or the first-level index entries in this book. No extra line space follows a Term List paragraph, while a standard line space follows a Definition List paragraph. The effect is like that of a glossary definition or second-level index entry — which is reflected in the style name. Each paragraph after the first in a Term List or Definition List begins with the code <DD>, which tells the browser to indent that paragraph. Any paragraph that doesn't begin with <DD> is not indented.

  PageMaker has no automatic translation of a PageMaker style to the Definition List HTML style and can't translate PageMaker styles to the Term List HTML style (that would have to be done in an HTML editor). In HTML, the codes for these styles are <DT> for Term List and <DL> for Definition List. (Each item in a Definition List should start with the tag <DD> but PageMaker uses the <LI> tag instead, which results in bullets in front of each item. If you want to get rid of the bullets, you have to edit the HTML file yourself.)

The left half of Figure 9-5 shows the five list styles as they should appear when coded in an HTML editor, and the right half of the figure shows the lists as they would appear if created by PageMaker and exported to HTML. Clearly, PageMaker isn't 100 percent in control of HTML list styles.

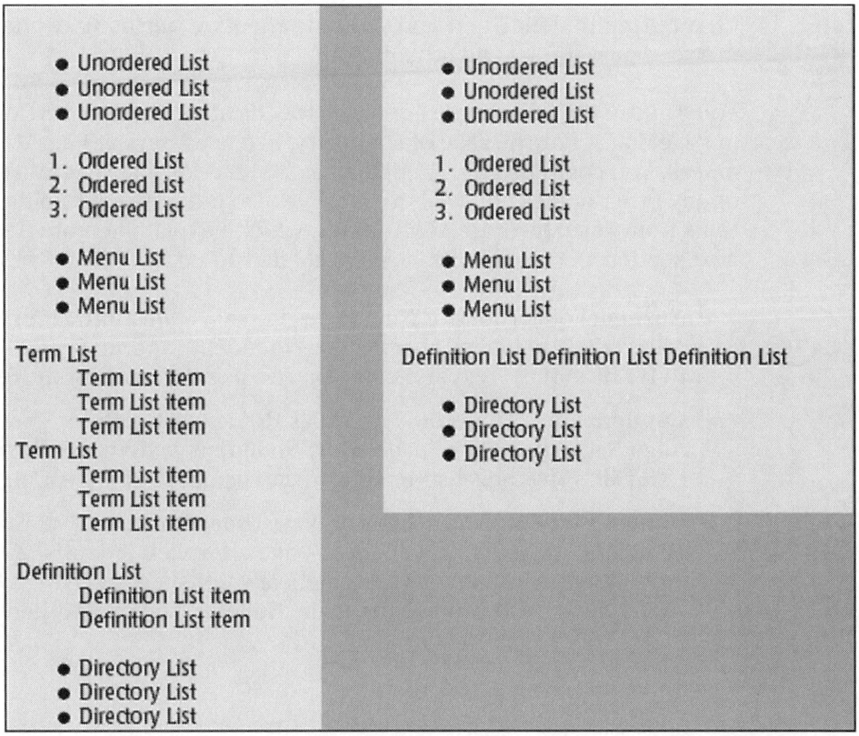

Figure 9-5: HTML list styles properly formatted in an HTML editor (at left) compared with the HTML formatting PageMaker generates during HTML export.

PageMaker Styles That Work in HTML

If you've read the previous three chapters of Part III, what I'm about to tell you may be obvious, but I'll say it anyhow: Don't spend time creating complex formatting styles in PageMaker for use in Web documents. They'll probably evaporate once they're exported to HTML. Instead, create PageMaker styles that approximate what you actually see on the Web.

Whatever you name your styles, create and edit them in a new PageMaker document and save it as a template for use in future Web documents — or, if you produce nothing but Web documents, do this editing with no publication open. These revised styles then become the default styles for all future PageMaker documents.

A handy PageMaker feature is the template — a publication that can't be saved again to the same name; instead, it forces you to choose a new name so you still have the original template for use later. To save a document as a template, use File⇨Save As (or Ctrl+Shift+S or Shift+⌘+S). Enter any name you prefer for the template in the File Name option box. But before you click the Save button, go to the Save As Type pop-up list and change the type from Publication to Template. The Save option in the File menu is now grayed out for this document, forcing you to use Save As.

Use the Define Styles dialog box (Ctrl+3 or ⌘+3) to add and edit styles, the Char button to define font and size, and the Para button to define spacing between paragraphs and indentation.

You can use the following list of basic specifications to create HTML-like styles in PageMaker. For the sake of simplicity, I've used default PageMaker style names. You could use the HTML names instead for your PageMaker styles — or any other names you wish to use. I've also indicated automatic translations from PageMaker to HTML styles, which I explain in more detail in the next section, "Converting Styles: PageMaker to HTML."

- **Normal:** Font: Times or New Times Roman; Style: Normal; Size: 12 points Align left; 0.16 inches Space after; No indent (automatically translates to HTML's Body Text style; or, you can use the name Body Text)
- **Caption:** Font: Times or New Times Roman; Style: Bold; Size: 12 points; Align left; 0.16 inches Space after; No indent (automatically translates to HTML's Heading 4 style; or, you can use the name Heading 4)
- **Hanging indent:** Font: Times or New Times Roman; Style: Normal; Size: 12 points; Align left; 0.16 inches Space after; Left indent: 0.25 inches; First indent: –0.25 inches (automatically translates to HTML's Unordered List style; or, you can use the name Bulleted List or Unordered List)

- **Numbered list:** Font: Helvetica, Geneva, or Arial; Style: Normal; Size: 12 points; Align left; 0.16 inches Space after; Left indent: 0.25 inches; First indent: –0.25 inches (set to translate to HTML's Ordered List style; or, you can use the name Ordered List)
- **Address:** Font: Times or New Times Roman; Style: Italic; Size: 12 points; Align left; 0.16 inches Space after; No indent (set to translate to HTML's Address style)
- **Quote:** Font: Times or Times New Roman; Style: Normal; Size: 12 points; Align left; 0.16 inches Space after; 0.25 inches; Left indent (set to translate to HTML's Blockquote style; or, you can use the name Blockquote)
- **Literal:** Font: Courier or Courier New; Style: Normal; Size: 12 points; Align left; 0.16 inches Space after; No indent; All word spacing options: 100 percent; All letter spacing options: 5 percent; Pair kerning unchecked — use the Spacing button in the Paragraph Specifications dialog box to get these spacing and kerning controls. (Set to translate to HTML's Preformatted style; or, you can use the name Preformatted.)
- **Headline:** Font: Times or New Times Roman; Style: Bold; Size: 30 points; Align left; 0.16 inches Space after; No indent (automatically translates to HTML's Heading 1 style; or, you can use the name Heading 1)
- **Subhead 1:** Font: Times or New Times Roman Style: Bold; Size: 24 points; Align left; 0.16 inches Space after; No indent (automatically translates to HTML's Heading 2 style; or, you can use the name Heading 2)
- **Subhead 2:** Font: Times or New Times Roman; Style: Bold; Size: 16 points; Align left; 0.16 inches Space after; No indent (automatically translates to HTML's Heading 3 style; or, you can use the name Heading 3)
- **Menu:** Font: Helvetica, Geneva, or Arial; Style: Normal; Size: 12 points; Align left; 0.0 inches Space after; 0.25 inches; Left indent: –0.25 inches first indent. (Set to translate to HTML's Menu List style; or, you could use the name Menu List. Note the use of a sans serif font to distinguish the Menu style from Unordered List style.)
- **Definition:** Font: Helvetica, Geneva, or Arial; Style: Normal; Size: 12 points; Align left; 0.16 inches space after; 0.25 inches; Left indent. (Set to translate to HTML's Definition List style; or, you could use the name Definition List. Note use of a sans serif font to distinguish this style from the Quote style.)

Converting Styles: PageMaker to HTML

Unless you started out by reading this part of the chapter (it's hard to resist skipping to the end to find out if the cat burglar really is a thief or a detective trying to bust a ring of criminals), you probably have a basic grasp of how to create styles in PageMaker and the common HTML styles that work on the Web. It makes sense at this point to create a template that has PageMaker styles with the same names as the HTML styles.

In the previous section, "PageMaker Styles That Work in HTML," I used existing PageMaker style names wherever possible. But I could have used names that match the HTML names, or names completely of my own invention. Figure 9-6 shows the Options dialog box that lets you assign PageMaker styles to corresponding HTML styles. Text tagged with a specific PageMaker style uses the HTML style name of your choosing. (The figure shows only the default name assignments; any PageMaker styles you define would also be shown, and any PageMaker styles you remove would not be shown.)

When you start creating your PageMaker document, take a look at the available PageMaker paragraph styles and decide if you have enough. If not, you can add styles as needed (the previous section of this chapter describes several possibilities). Decide if you want to use the default PageMaker style names, or create styles with names that match the HTML style names, or use some other naming convention that makes sense to you. Then follow the steps described later in this section when you export your PageMaker file to HTML format. (Chapter 17 shows you the complete HTML export process; I concentrate just on styles here.)

You can change the default translation of PageMaker styles to match the HTML styles with the following steps:

1. **Select File⇨Export⇨HTML in the PageMaker document where you're changing the settings to open the Export HTML dialog box.**

   A publication must be open to get this dialog box.

2. **Click on the Options button to open the Options dialog box (shown in Figure 9-6).**

3. **Find the PageMaker style or styles that have HTML translations that need to be changed to more appropriate style names.**

   A list of all PageMaker styles that you defined in the document is in the Style Assignments box on the left, while the name of the HTML style that each PageMaker style is translated to is on the right. If the PageMaker style you want to reassign is not visible, scroll through the Style Assignments box until you find it.

4. **Click on the HTML style name you want to change.**

   Here's where you get to override PageMaker's HTML-style export translations. Make sure that you click on the HTML style name that is to the immediate right of the PageMaker style whose HTML-style translation you want to change. A pop-up list appears (see Figure 9-7), showing all available HTML styles. Select a new style.

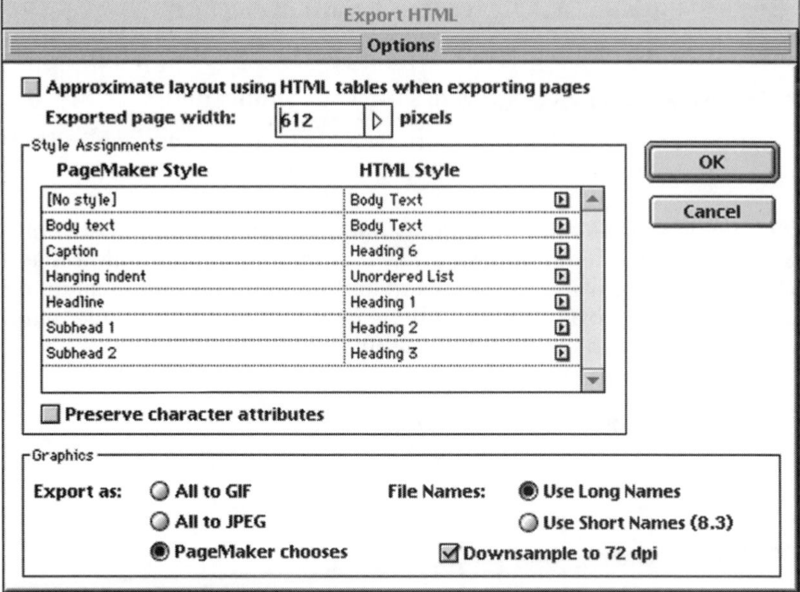

Figure 9-6: The Options dialog box is where you assign PageMaker styles to a corresponding HTML style (just default assignments are shown).

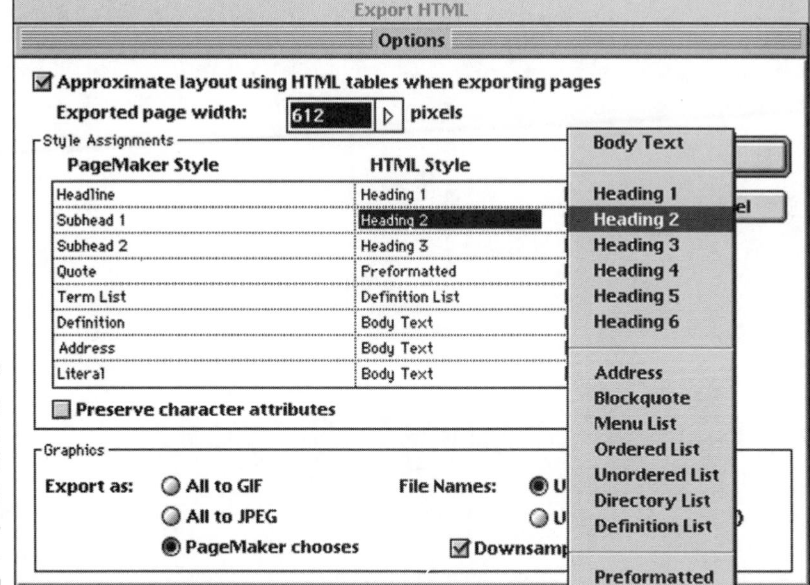

Figure 9-7: The pop-up list of available HTML styles.

5. **Click on OK to leave the Options dialog box.**
6. **Click on Done to leave the Export HTML dialog box.**
7. **Select File⇨Save As to save your publication.**

   These HTML export options are stored with the publication and affect only that publication and any others created from it.

If you want to create a style mapping for use in multiple documents, create a template as described earlier in this chapter in the section "PageMaker Styles That Work in HTML" and do this style-translation mapping in the template. Then, when you create new documents from this template, these style translations are immediately available.

That's it! Now you're stylin'.

Part IV
Pumping Up Your Layout Power

"Would you like Web or non-Web?"

In this part . . .

Once you've acquired the basic PageMaker skills, it's time to really work those layout muscles. After all, layout is what makes PageMaker more than just a fancy way to cut and paste. In this part, you learn how to set up a Web page, how to deal with element placement and page length, how to manage graphics and text, and how to use the built-in automation and labor-saving features of PageMaker. Once you've got these techniques under your belt, all those pumped-up, steroid-popping designers who used to sneer at you with wet towels in the locker room will look at you with newfound respect. They'll probably even ask if they can carry your notebook computer for you.

Chapter 10

The Layout Shuffle

In This Chapter

- Planning your layout
- Laying out Web page text
- Aligning columns
- Adding, deleting, and moving columns
- Locking and grouping elements
- Adjusting a print-page layout for the Web

Layout is not something that happens right the first time. After all, you're working with a whole bunch of pieces, trying to make them fit together and look nice at the same time. It's sort of like assembling a jigsaw puzzle, but you don't have a picture on a box top to tell you what the end results should be.

Even if you have a basic design in mind — such as a three-column format with a couple graphics on each page — inevitably you'll end up moving your text and graphics after you place them, and then moving them again, and modifying some of your selections as you add new elements and begin to see how everything takes shape.

Chapter 7 shows you how to place text into PageMaker and Chapter 13 shows you how to place graphics. But simply inserting these elements into your document doesn't mean they're laid out for you. Why not? PageMaker is not a mind-reader, and it has no idea what layout you have in mind. You wouldn't want PageMaker to automate your job out of existence, would you? You would? Well, give it time. Machines will take over all our jobs one day, and then they'll round us up and put us in zoos, and our pain and suffering will be over. But in the meantime, you still have to tell PageMaker what to do with your text and graphics.

Starting a Layout

The best way to explain the layout process is to provide you with some examples. With that in mind, this chapter covers the steps in creating a simple, mostly one-column format Web site.

The first thing you should do is make a list of all the stories and all the graphics you want to include. Prioritize those elements: Which should get prominent attention and appear on the main home page or early in your Web site? Which can be broken into several pages if the material starts to overcrowd the layout or make the page too long for easy scrolling up and down a screen? Which stories include graphics — a chart, a scanned photo, or maybe an illustration?

Next, sketch out your ideas for placing page elements before you start the layout. Do a rough sketch with paper and pencil — much less work than doing it on a computer, even with PageMaker. Figure 10-1 shows such a sketch for the *home page* (the first page that readers sees when they access a Web site) and a couple sketches for section pages that I use as examples in this chapter.

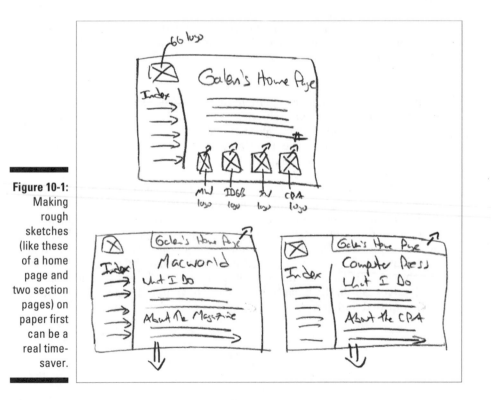

Figure 10-1: Making rough sketches (like these of a home page and two section pages) on paper first can be a real time-saver.

This list should help decipher the symbols written in the sketches:

- The # symbol is a layout convention for "end of story."
- The single-line arrow is a convention for "text continues," meaning the page links to another page. I also use this symbol for graphics that have links to other Web pages.
- The double-line arrow indicates that the page will scroll beyond what fits in one screen.
- A shape with an *X* through it represents a graphic.

Many Web site designers may not think to use these written symbols that originated from print conventions, but these marks adapt well to planning Web layouts. They can help those of you experienced with print to make the transition to online layouts.

Putting Your Text in Place

Before laying out your Web site, you need to create a blank copy of the site's pages (called a *template*) that has all the stuff that you're going to use every time on your site — a logo, title, column formatting, and so on. Figure 10-2 shows the template for a home page with graphic elements in place and before text is added. You can see that column guides (covered in Chapter 5) are part of the template. They work wonders to keep everything in its proper place.

Don't panic if you don't know about templates yet. If you're curious, you can skip ahead to Chapter 12 to find out all about them. Or, if you want to know how those graphics at the bottom of the template in Figure 10-2 got there, skip way ahead to Chapter 13. All you really need to know for now is that templates help you to automate the placement of items in your page. The point of this chapter is to show you how to approach the layout process, not to show you how to create the specific Web pages used as examples in this chapter. If some of the information being presented seems a little fuzzy to you, rest assured that everything will eventually fall into place.

Planning the home page

Assume that you've compiled your list of stories and graphics and have decided which ones should appear where. The next thing to do is to place the home page lead story, such as I've done in Figure 10-3.

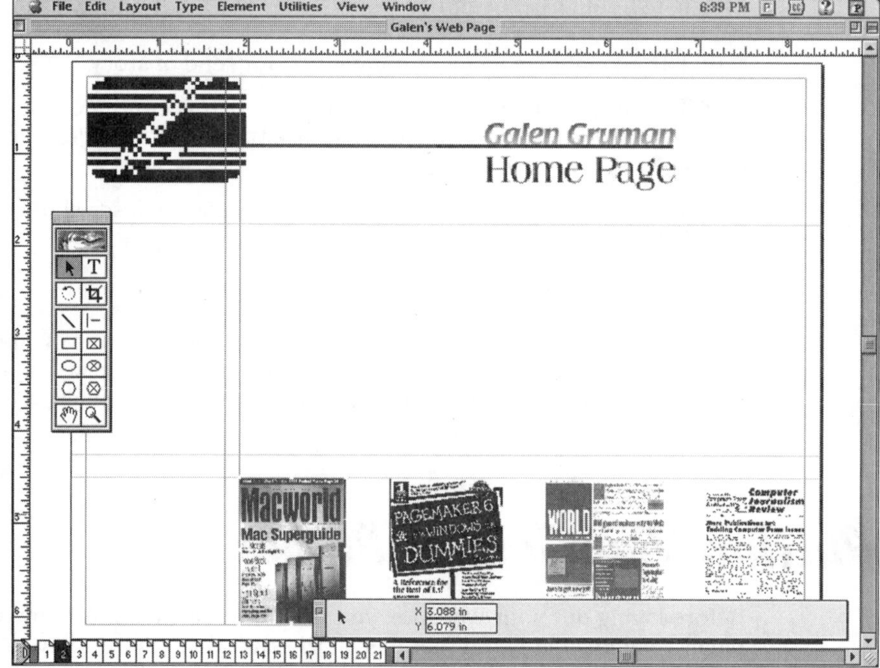

Figure 10-2: The template for the author's Web site's home page, with graphics in place and before text is added.

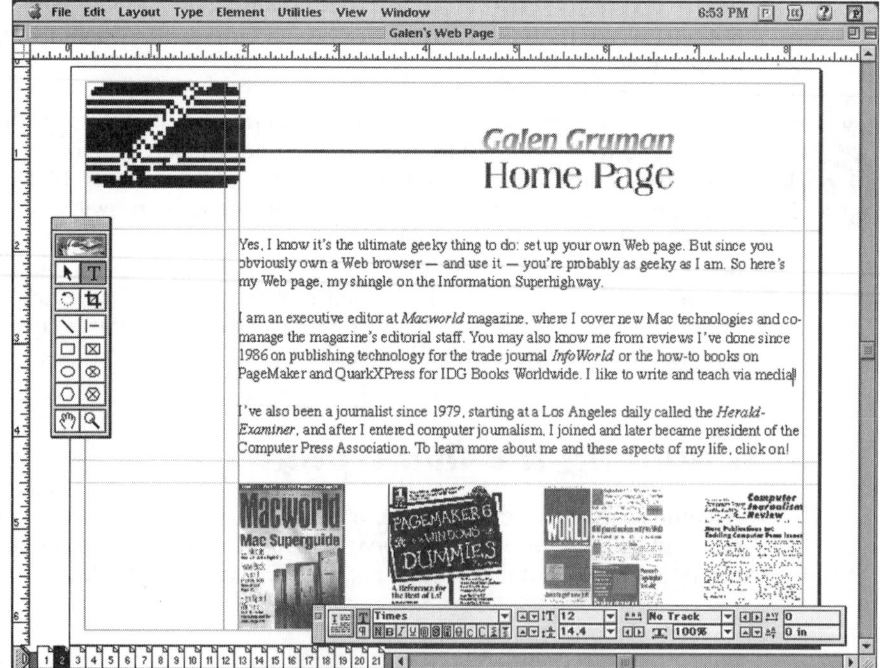

Figure 10-3: The home page as it looks after the first story is entered.

You may notice that the entire home page fits in the publication window, which is set at 600 × 450 Browser – large page size, for those of you who thrill to these kinds of techno specs. (Web page sizes are covered in Chapter 5.) I believe that a home page should require little or no scrolling to be viewed in its entirety. A home page is the summary of what your site offers, sort of like a magazine cover. You want to grab the attention of readers, not make them work to find out what you're all about. My advice: Push information details down to the next level of pages that make up each section of your site.

The following explains some of the steps I used to create the first story that appears in my home page:

- The story (which I typed directly into PageMaker) starts a little less than two inches down from the top of the document page (to match what I sketched out in Figure 10-1). I used a ruler guide to set the text's top position (guides are covered in Chapter 5).
- If you turn on Snap to Guides through the View menu, or by using Ctrl+Shift+; [semicolon] or Shift+⌘+; [semicolon], imported text and graphics snap to the guides you have set up. You can then be assured that even if you don't position your story's paragraph cursor precisely on a column's left boundary, the text will still be accurately positioned. Without these guides, wherever you click is the text's left boundary, while the right boundary extends to the nearest column guide (with or without Snap to Guides).

  In Figure 10-4, you can see that I placed the column guides so that the index column on the left is narrower than the main text column. (To move a column guide, just drag it from its default position.) When I entered text with the PageMaker Text tool, the text cursor was automatically positioned along the column guide, ensuring that the text I was hammering out was in the correct position. (Chapter 5 tells you about column guides in more detail.)

- PageMaker doesn't always place text inside your column guides. If you click too far away from the column boundary when placing text into your page, PageMaker won't know that you want the text to be confined to the column. It makes the text as wide as it can — stretching out to the page's right margin or to the boundary of a nearby graphic. This feature can be a real nuisance, because you then have to resize the column by hand. The only way to reduce the chance of this problem happening is to work in an enlarged close-up view (such as 200 percent) and make sure that your cursor is near or on the correct column location to begin with. (More on placing text can be found in Chapter 7.)

I could have placed another story on the first page, or fine-tuned this story. One option isn't better than the other — it just depends on how certain you are of what you want to do.

For this example, the text that was entered fits well and everything aligns, which means I can now create my index text. I knew well in advance (back when I did my rough sketch of my home page) that I'd include an index of subjects covered in my site. The narrow column to the left of the main text block was set aside as the spot for the index. The result is shown in Figure 10-4.

You may want to know how I created the index using a couple of PageMaker tools:

- The index text also aligns against its margins, thanks to the use of guides and the Snap to Guides option.
- I used several text *styles* (the subject of styles is covered in Chapter 9):

  I labeled the index headline "On This Site" with the style Subhead 1, which translates to the HTML Heading 2 style.

  I labeled the index subheadings with Subhead 2 style, which translates to the HTML Heading 3 style.

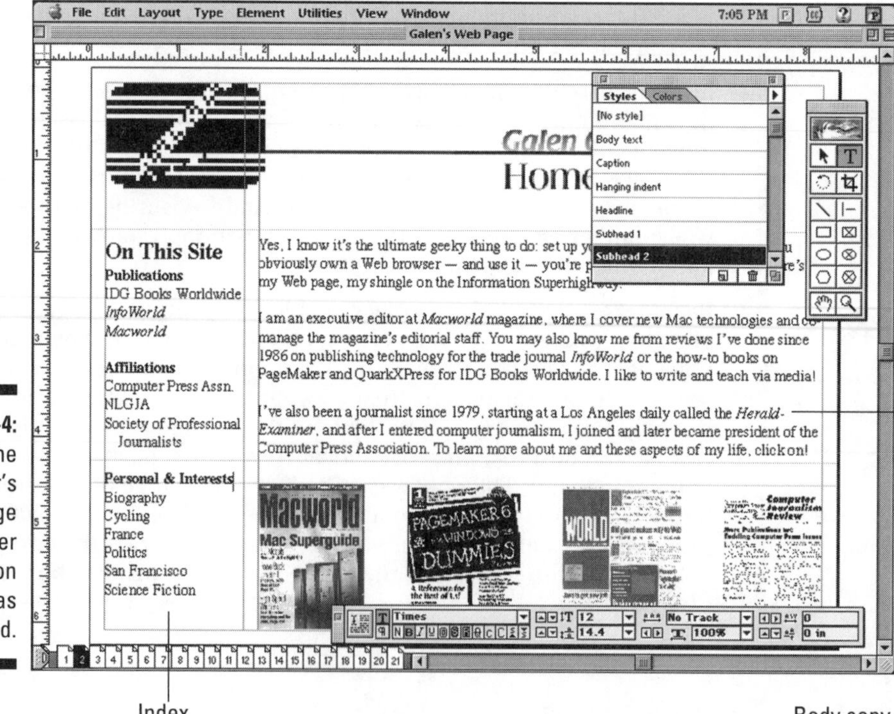

Figure 10-4: How the author's home page looks after the section index was added.

The index items use the Hanging Indent style, which translates to the Unordered List style (this HTML style adds bullets to these items).

The first story, by the way, uses the Body Text style, which translates to the Body Text HTML style.

HTML is the computer language that turns PageMaker pages into Web pages. You can read up on HTML in Chapter 2 (for the basic background on HTML), in Chapter 9 (which has information about HTML styles), and in Chapter 22 (which supplies technical details on HTML editing and codes).

With all the text for the home page laid out and the graphics in place, the home page is essentially done, and you're ready to tackle the rest.

Planning the section pages

The section pages that readers can link to through the home page index (see Figure 10-5) look a little different than the home page. I scaled down the header graphic and dropped the images that were at the bottom of the page. I made use of column guides in the same way (although with different settings) to ensure proper alignment of elements and used the same text styles as in the home page.

Because the section page items are used on every page of the site except the home page, they are set up in the document's master pages, a time-saving feature explained in Chapter 12.

The term *section page* refers to a Web page that begins a section or is part of a Web site section — somewhat like the opening page of a book chapter, or the first page of a magazine article (with the magazine cover being akin to a home page). Each of the sections in the index on the home page links to a section page. Section pages can also link to subsections, and so on.

I can add text to these section pages like any other in PageMaker: by typing the text in directly or by creating it in a word processor and importing it. The Body text style eventually translates to the HTML Body Text style. So far, this is the same process used to create the home page.

Dealing with text overflow

In the home page, everything fits neatly in a single document page on the screen. But not all of the text for the section page fits in a single page. If pulled down, the text block would stretch beyond the boundary of the document page, as Figure 10-5 shows. Plus, there's more text that hasn't been entered yet (the "About the Magazine" part from the sketch in Figure 10-1 has to be squeezed in).

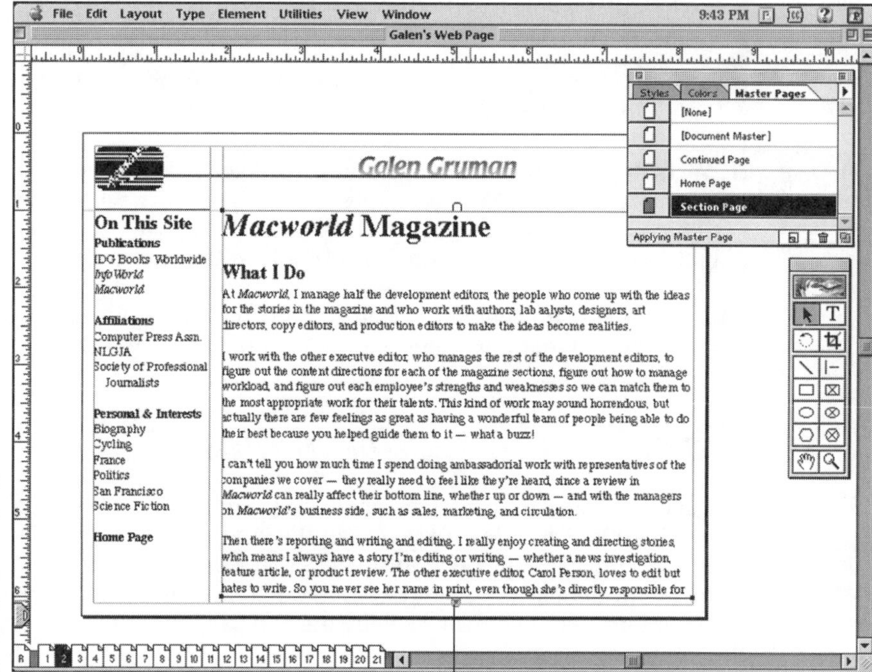

Figure 10-5: A section page from the author's Web site.

What should be done? Extend the text block below the PageMaker page boundary? Or jump the story to a new PageMaker page? The obvious answer is . . . jump to a new PageMaker page. (After all, that's what you do in print layouts.) But, the obvious response may not be the correct one.

Because we're talking about the Web, you need to extend the text block down past the page boundary. If you jumped the story to a new PageMaker page, you'd get a page break in the exported Web page where the jump occurred, which you definitely don't want (Figure 10-6 shows what happens when you do this). The basic rule is as follows: A page should contain everything that you want a reader to scroll through on screen — but no more. Just make sure that no text blocks start outside the PageMaker page boundary — the HTML export won't see them and they'll be missing from your Web page.

If you have loads of text, you may run out of room on the PageMaker pasteboard as you extend the story down, in which case your choices are to stop typing or reduce the text size to make it all fit. If you have that much text, you may be trying to cram too much on one page. Breaking the page up into several subtopics, with hyperlinks from one page to another, may be the

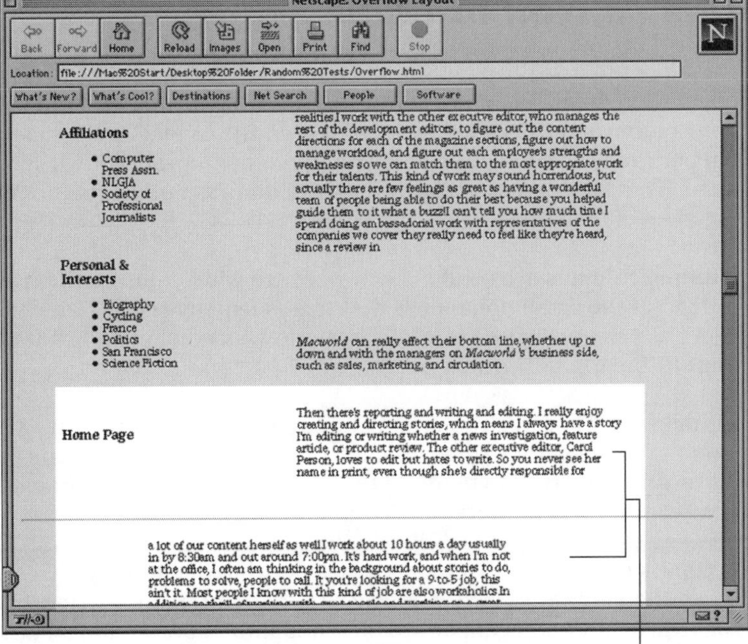

Figure 10-6: Jumping text from one PageMaker page to another in your layout may result in unaligned columns in the exported Web page.

better choice. For example, instead of 20 screens on your company's organization, have one page for Sales, one for Manufacturing, and so forth. Each page would be linked to a section page that explains the divisions in the company.

My rule of thumb is to limit Web pages to a depth of three screens of material; the less scrolling for the reader the better.

Working with Columns

Although you may be perfectly content with Web pages that have everything you want to say lumped into one column, chances are that you want to create multicolumn pages at least occasionally to add some variety to your layouts.

One column or two?

Laying out text in deep multiple columns on the Web falls into the territory of a design no-no — think about the reader having to scroll down to read one column and then way back up to read the other. Text columns that run deeper than the screen result in way too much up-and-down screen movement. That's one reason why Web pages don't generally feature multiple columns of long text.

Multiple columns are used in print because wide chunks of text are difficult to read at the small point sizes that text is usually set in. Readers of a single sheet of print material can easily scan down a column and shift their eyes back to the top of the next one.

Although HTML can now support multicolumn text formatting, you just won't see long side-by-side columns of text on a Web page. The grid (or pattern) of a Web page tends to be more horizontal than vertical, so the eye can scan the screen more quickly.

Column orientation in Web pages is somewhat like the organization of icons on your computer screen. Chances are that your icons are more horizontally than vertically arranged, or are bunched into short columns in the window. And that's kind of what a Web page is after all, an arrangement of elements on a computer screen.

Looking at Figure 10-7, which page would you rather read on-screen? I'd guess the layout on the left. (I'll admit these pages aren't the greatest attention-grabbers. But they do demonstrate that long side-by-side columns that run below the document screen mean lots of scrolling for the reader.)

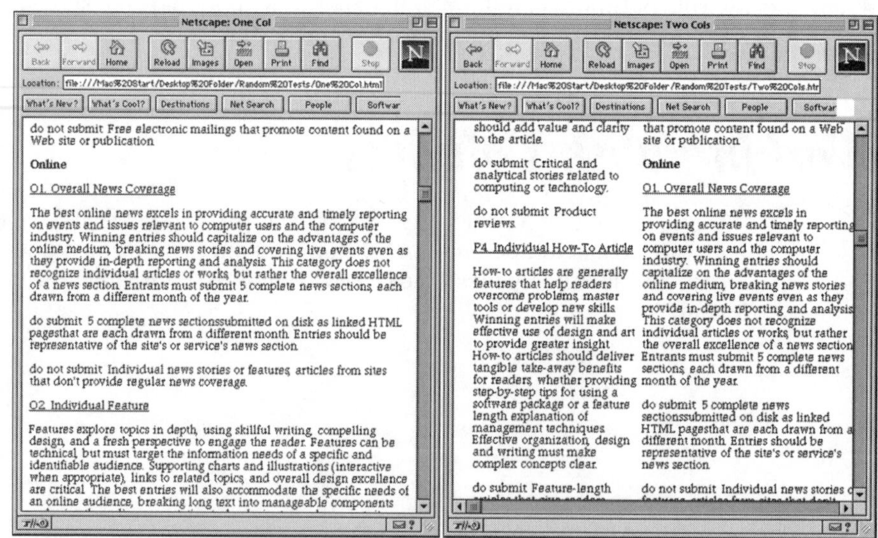

Figure 10-7: When a Web page layout runs off the screen, multiple-columns will require more scrolling than single columns.

Multiple columns have their place on the Web. Just make sure that your reader doesn't have to scroll for days to get through them. The reader may simply click off and away to another Web site.

Making text columns line up

Unless you use Snap to Guides, text columns may not align correctly. Even if you do use Snap to Guides, columns may not align exactly along the top or bottom of a *ruler guide*. To create a ruler guide, move the cursor to a ruler, hold down the mouse button and drag the ruler guide out to wherever you want it. Ruler guides come in handy to help you position specific elements on a page.

Misalignment of columns can be a nagging problem when you're creating a PageMaker layout. Fortunately, you can use the Control palette to fix off-balance columns by giving them the same upper coordinate. Here's how:

1. **Select the text block in the first column.**
2. **Select Window⇨Show Control Palette or press Ctrl+' (apostrophe) or ⌘+' (apostrophe) to get the Control palette.**
3. **Select an upper handle on the Control palette's Proxy button.**

   The *Proxy button* is that little square on the left of the palette; the handle that is thicker than the others is the selected one.
4. **Jot down the Y value.**

   The *Y value* in the Control palette reflects the vertical position of the text block.
5. **Select the next text block and look at its Y coordinate.**

   If you want the second text block's *Y coordinate* to match the first text block's, enter the first text block's Y coordinate in the Control palette and press Enter or click on the Apply button (at the far left of the Control palette).
6. **Repeat Step 5 for every column you want to align.**

Another way to align text blocks is by using the Balance Columns plug-in. Using this addition is much faster than changing each column's coordinates in the Control palette. To use this addition, select all the columns you want aligned (click on the first text block and Shift+click on the other text blocks). Then choose Utilities⇨Plug-ins⇨Balance Columns to get the Balance Columns dialog box (shown in Figure 10-8).

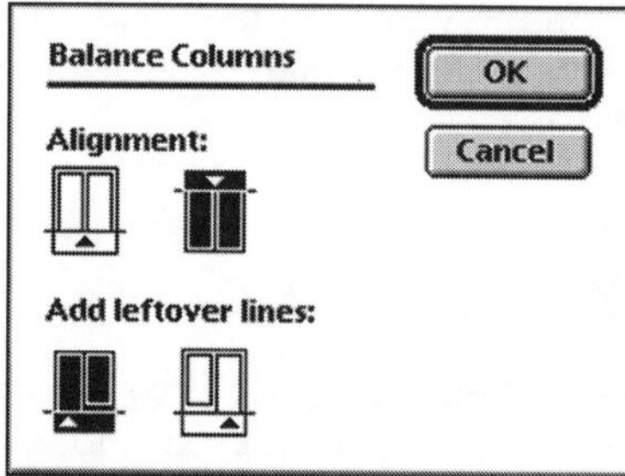

Figure 10-8: Use this dialog box to align columns.

Under Alignment, choose the left icon to have all selected columns begin at the Y position of the highest text block; click the right icon under Alignment to align the bottoms of all the columns with the bottom of the lowest text block. The bottom two icons in the dialog box let you choose where you want PageMaker to place any leftover lines; choose the left icon if you want them added to the left column, or choose the right icon if you want them added to the right column. Click on OK to close the dialog box and balance the columns.

So why would you ever align columns the long way described earlier? Because Balance Columns makes assumptions that may not be true: It aligns columns based on the position of the highest text block (or the lowest, if you're aligning the bottoms). Of course, you can still use this addition and then use the Control palette to change the Y coordinate for all of the text blocks simultaneously. If multiple elements are selected, any changes made to coordinates or other palette values are applied to all the selected elements. Any options that can't be applied to multiple elements don't appear in the Control palette.

By the way, while you're using the Control palette to align columns, you can also change the column width, height, and horizontal coordinate (via the settings in the W, H, and X option boxes, respectively).

Altering columns and text blocks

After you've laid out text in columns, you may decide that you want to change the number of columns or maybe move a column somewhere else. Be careful. This part of doing a PageMaker layout can really get you in trouble. Not that it's your fault — the blame lies in how PageMaker handles text blocks. If you're not careful, you can accidentally delete text, perhaps permanently. An example of how it works follows.

Changing the number of columns

Say you have a one-column story that you decide should be a two-column story to make it visually distinct from the rest of the text on the page. So all you need to do is select the text block holding the column of text and tell PageMaker to change the number of columns to two, right? Wrong — just try to find a command or option to do this.

What PageMaker has you do is create a whole new column, which isn't that hard. All you have to do is resize the existing one, making it skinnier, click on the more-text icon on the existing column's windowshade handle, and click again where you want to place the new column.

But if you wanted to go from two columns to one, you have to get rid of one column and resize the remaining ones. Deleting a column is where you can accidentally lose text.

Assume you have a three-column layout and you want to turn it into a two-column layout. Your first instinct may be to slice out one of the columns of text and paste it into another column. So you cut out the middle column (using Edit⇨Cut, or Ctrl+X or ⌘+X) and resize the other two columns, making them wider. That deleted text block is removed from the chain, or thread, of text blocks making up the story. Even if you paste the cut text block back in, it remains apart from the original story. When you select the pasted block, the linked-text icons are replaced by the no-text icon on its windowshade handles.

To reinstate the text from that cut block back into the story, you'd have to switch to the Text tool, select all text in that block (via Edit⇨Select All, or Ctrl+A or ⌘+A), place your text cursor at the end of the previous block or the beginning of the next block, and paste that text into the block. A royal pain. (And, if you used Edit⇨Clear or pressed the Delete key to delete the text block, you can't paste it back in — it's gone for good, unless you're very quick with the Ctrl+Z or ⌘+Z undo combo.)

You can recover deleted or cut text and relink it to the rest of the story in another way: Reimport the text via File⇨Place, or Ctrl+D or ⌘+D. When doing so, you click on a text block within the story, open the Place Document dialog box, select the text file, and — this is crucial — click on the Replacing Entire Story button before clicking on OK. However, this approach has several potential problems:

- If the text was created directly in PageMaker, obviously no text file exists to reimport.
- If the text was changed in PageMaker, those changes will be lost — unless you exported the changed text from PageMaker to the text file (via File⇨Export).

- If the source text file was modified in the word processor for another use after you imported it the first time, you'll be importing the new version, which may have significant changes.

However, you can avoid this whole mess and change the number of columns without having to delete a word. Instead of cutting the unwanted column, select one of the column's windowshade handles and roll it up (or down) until it touches the other handle. Figure 10-10 shows what this looks like. You don't even have to delete the empty windowshade — if you select any other element and then try to reselect it, you'll find that it's gone — kaput, dead. The text automatically reflows into the remaining columns. Now all you have to do is resize the text blocks to fit the new column arrangement.

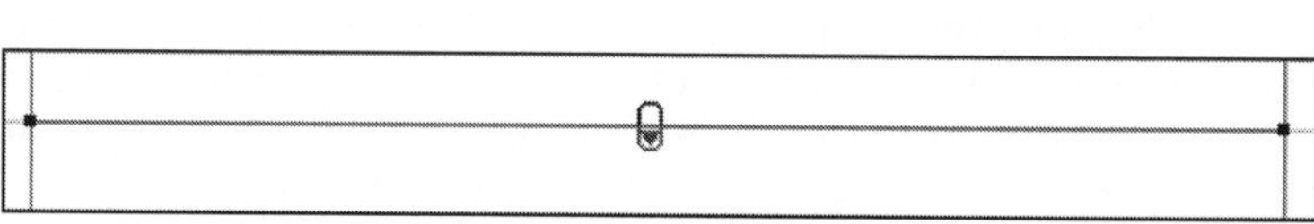

Figure 10-9: To delete a column without cutting text, roll up the windowshade until the handles touch.

Moving columns and text blocks

Problems can arise if you decide you want to move a column of text from one page to another by cutting and pasting.

Don't cut and paste linked text blocks. You lose the invisible thread that runs through copy blocks that makes it possible to flow text in order.

Instead, use the empty windowshade technique described in the previous section to remove a text block from a page. Click on the linked-text or more-text icon on the bottom of the last remaining text block on the page to get the paragraph icon, move to the new desired page, and click where you want the column to continue. (You get the linked-text icon if the text block you're adding somewhere else falls within a series of linked text blocks; you get the more-text icon if the text block to be deleted and added elsewhere is the last text block in the series.)

If you want to move a text block within the current page or within the current facing pages, just select it and drag it to its new location.

Inserting columns or text blocks

For Web publishing, this isn't a trick you do that often. Your documents probably won't be so long and complex that you'd need to insert a new column between existing columns of the same story. But I know you wanna know anyway, so how do you add a text block between two linked blocks so that the text flows through the new block?

Click on the bottom linked-text icon of the text block that will precede the new text block, or click on the top linked-text icon of the text block that will follow the new text block. Either way, you get the paragraph icon. Move to where the new text block should be inserted, position the paragraph icon where you want to place the new text block, and click the mouse button. A text block appears, and you should see that text flows properly through it from the previous text block and to the next one.

You can use this same technique to add columns or other text blocks on the same page, not just on different pages, or to start a story earlier in the layout — just click on the no-text icon on the top windowshade handle of the first text block in the story and move back and click where you want the column to start.

Locking and Grouping Elements

Once you have a text block positioned where you want it, you may want to secure it to that location. Here's how: Select the item or items (remember to Shift+click on items after the first one if you're selecting a group of text blocks). Then use the command Element⇨Lock Position (Ctrl+L or ⌘+L) to lock them in place. (To unlock them, use Element⇨Unlock, or Ctrl+Alt+L or Option+⌘+L.) This method also works for graphic elements that are part of your layout.

You may want to group several elements together so you can move them as a single unit. Select the items and then use Element⇨Group (Ctrl+G or ⌘+G). To ungroup elements, select any element in the group — notice the dashed line around the entire group — and use Element⇨Ungroup, or Ctrl+Shift+G or Shift+⌘+G).

Adjusting Print Layouts for the Web

PageMaker 6.5 has a new feature that simplifies the process of converting print-page layouts to Web-page layouts. This feature is called Adjust Layout, and it automatically realigns page elements when you change page dimensions from print size to screen size, making it easier to reuse your print material for Web pages.

Most print publications are vertically oriented — deeper than they are wide — because $8^1/_2$ by 11 inches is the paper size standard. But Web pages are horizontally oriented because a computer monitor is usually wider than it is high. (When you create Web layouts from scratch, as described in Chapter 5, you probably need to specify a horizontal page size, such as 600 × 450 – Browser large, or 484 × 335 Netscape – Mac.)

If you open up a document designed for print, with a page size of Letter (8.5 by 11 inches), how do you get it horizontally oriented? Just follow these steps:

1. **Open the Document Setup dialog box.**

   Select File⇨Document Setup, or use the shortcut Ctrl+Shift+P or ⌘+Shift+P.

2. **Pick the appropriate page size for the Web page version of your document.**

   Use the Page size pop-up menu in the Document Setup box to choose the new size.

3. **Click on the Adjust Layout checkbox.**

4. **Click OK.**

   Here comes the magic part: PageMaker moves the page elements around (but doesn't resize them exactly) to fit the new page size and orientation. Figures 10-10 and 10-11 show the before and after (print and screen layout versions).

Be sure to save the rearranged layout under a new name so you don't wipe out the original print version!

The adjusted layout obviously needs some fine-tuning. PageMaker merely moves the elements around to maintain the relationship among them given the boundaries of the new page size and orientation. But it's better than doing everything yourself.

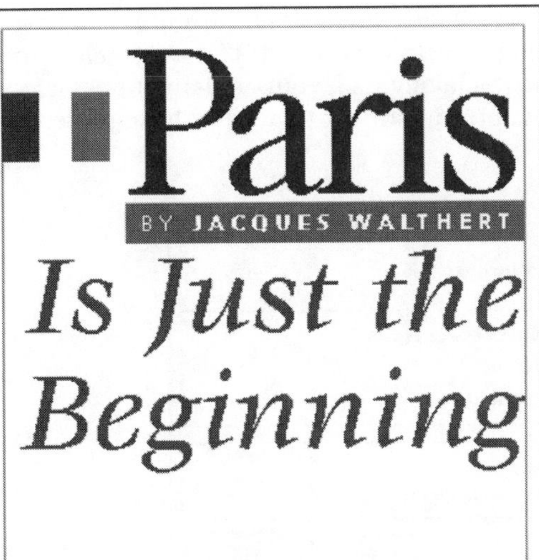

Figure 10-10: A PageMaker layout created for print publication.

Figure 10-11: The print-oriented page from Figure 10-10 after PageMaker adjusted the layout to fit a Web-page size. It's far from perfect, but it beats having to do all the rearranging yourself.

You can control how PageMaker moves items around. The Layout Adjustment Preferences dialog box (in Figure 10-12) lets you select the factors that PageMaker should use in making its layout-adjustment decisions. Select File⇨Preferences⇨Layout Adjustment to access these preferences.

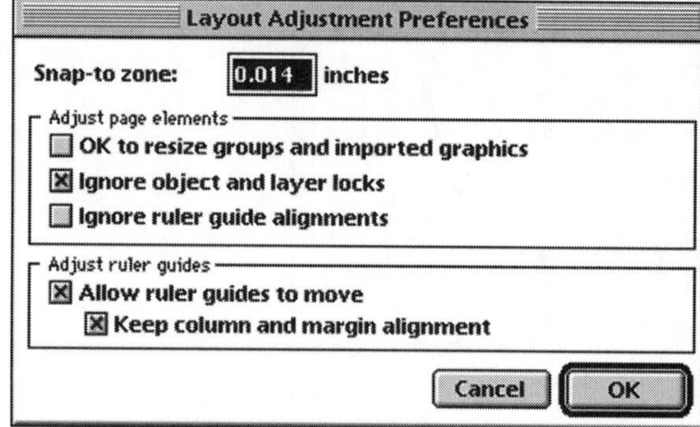

Figure 10-12: Use this dialog box to tell PageMaker how you want the layout adjusted.

As with all preferences, any changes you make to the Adjust Layout Preferences dialog box when no document is open becomes the default setting for all future documents. Otherwise, the preferences change for just that document.

Chapter 11

What Are Links and Layers — And Why Should You Care?

In This Chapter

- Connecting with links
- Updating graphics and text files automatically
- Editing source files from within PageMaker
- Deciding whether to store a copy of graphics or text in your layout
- Working with live links
- Using the new layers feature

When you place text or a graphic into your layout, a lot goes on behind the scenes. First, PageMaker checks the format of the file you're importing and then tries to import the file. For text, PageMaker translates the word-processor format into its own format. For graphics, PageMaker builds an image of the graphic that it will use to display the graphic on-screen (EPS drawings come with their own prebuilt screen images).

Second, PageMaker checks to see where the file resides — somewhere in the disk and directory (or folder, in Mac lingo) — and records that information along with the file name and the last modification date. Third, PageMaker lets you place the file in your layout.

The second step is where *links* come into play. Links are like little electronic homing devices that tell PageMaker where to find the original file. With links, PageMaker can tell whether a graphic or text file has been modified and, if you so specify, replace it with the newer version. PageMaker also needs links when printing graphics because, in many cases, it substitutes the original graphic for the on-screen display image to get the best-quality output.

The types of links discussed in this chapter are not to be confused with *hypertext links* used in creating Web pages, which are covered in Chapter 16.

All of this importing and linking stuff can happen automatically if you choose, which can be good and bad. It's good if you want PageMaker to always use the latest version of a graphic, bad if you don't. It's also bad if you think that PageMaker is automatically importing the latest version of a graphic but, in fact, the option that tells the program to do this is turned off, or vice versa. So get in the habit of checking the link settings, as explained in this chapter.

If you're working with multiple layers, a new feature introduced in this version, PageMaker also tracks where each object in your layout (either text or graphics) resides. This gives you control over which layers of objects are displayed or printed and which are eventually exported as part of your Web page.

Setting Link Defaults

The time to set your link options is when you first create a new document. To do so, use Element⇨Link Options with nothing selected. (If you establish link settings when no document is open, your settings become the defaults for all future documents.) Figure 11-1 shows the dialog box that appears. Note that there are two sets of options — one for text and one for graphics. Also note that the options are indented underneath each other — that's because in order for an option to be available, the one above it must be checked. This indentation is meant to remind you of that fact.

Although Figure 11-1 shows the dialog box for setting a document's defaults, you can also display a similar dialog box for a particular element and establish settings to control that element's behavior. (You won't get both the text and graphics options, just the setting appropriate for the selected element.) To do this, select the item whose link options you want to modify, and use Element⇨Link Options to open the dialog box.

An easy way to get the Link Options: Defaults dialog box on Windows is to select the element and click the right mouse button to get a list of available options.

There's no reason to have the same linking rules apply to all your elements — it would be silly, for example, to link a logo that's never going to change to its source file. And it would be equally silly not to link a graphic that changes every month (such as for a calendar) to its source file. That's why you can set link options individually.

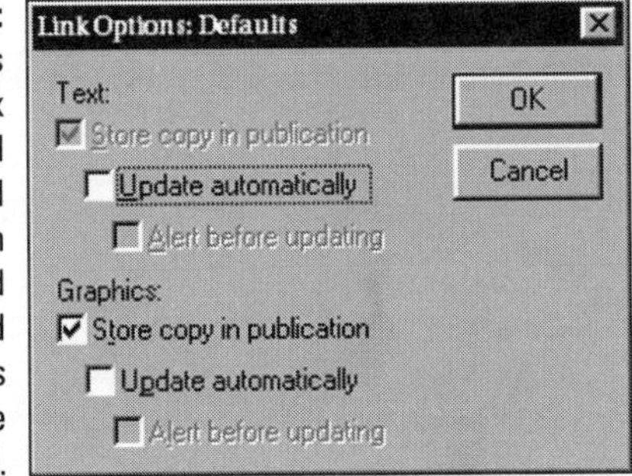

Figure 11-1: Use this dialog box to control how and when imported text and graphics are updated.

The Store Copy in Publication option

The first option in the Link Options: Defaults dialog box is Store Copy in Publication. This option, strangely enough, copies the text or graphic file into your PageMaker document. In other words, the text or graphic is actually inserted into the PageMaker file. You'll notice that this option is checked and dimmed for text — that's because text is always stored in the publication. PageMaker gives you no choice in the matter.

For graphics, checking this option doesn't lock you into copying a particular graphic into PageMaker. In the More Preferences dialog box (File➪Preferences➪General➪More, or Ctrl+K in Windows or ⌘+K on the Mac), you can tell PageMaker to alert you if the graphic you're importing is larger than a specified file size by entering that value in the Alert When Storing Graphics Over box. This option is spotlighted in Figure 11-2. The reason to set this threshold is to prevent the PageMaker document from getting too big; after all, if you're linked to the original graphic, you don't really need that graphic copied in PageMaker. I recommend setting the size threshold to a low number, such as 64K.

Here's how it works. Suppose that you set the Alert When Storing Graphics Over value at 64K, but you import a graphic at 167K. PageMaker displays a dialog box that lets you choose whether or not you want to copy the graphic file into PageMaker.

Should you check the Store Copy in Publication box for graphics? It depends. If you do, and the original files get lost, you still have a copy in your PageMaker layout that can be used for printing. If you don't, your PageMaker file stays smaller because the graphics won't have a duplicate inside the file. My advice is to check the item but set a fairly low threshold in the Alert When Storing Graphics Over amount — for example, 64K (the minimum allowable setting). Thus, small graphics are copied in while you retain the option to link just big ones.

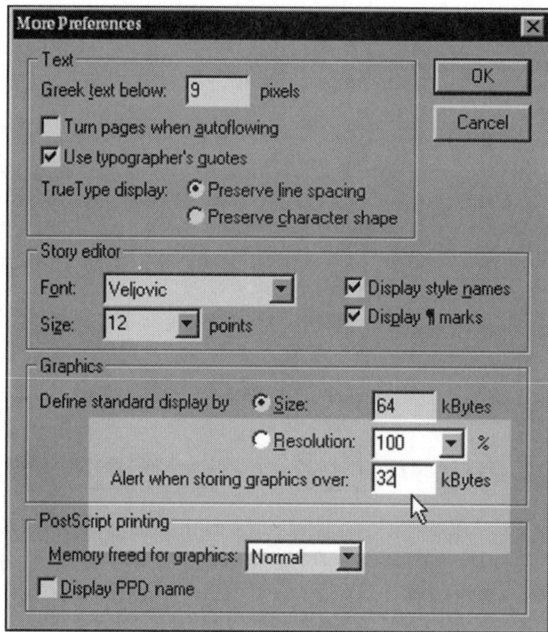

Figure 11-2: The Alert When Storing Graphics Over tells you when graphics over a certain size are being imported into your PageMaker files.

Files that are copied in are also linked — PageMaker still keeps a reference to the original file, for reasons that will soon become clear.

Should you ever lose the original file, remember that PageMaker keeps a low-resolution copy of the graphic in your document. For print publishing, this copy is not acceptable for publication but, because the Web displays graphics at a mere 72dpi — the same resolution as that of the low-resolution copy — you can actually safely use the copy as a substitute for the original graphic.

As I explain in Chapter 13, Kodak Photo CD images can't be stored in a publication — the image files are just too large. So you have to relink to the Photo CD every time you open the publication. Alternatively, you can open the Photo CD image in an image-editing program and save it in a format that can be stored in the publication, such as TIFF. Or you can choose the Save to CIELAB TIFF File option that PageMaker offers you when you first place a Photo CD image. Again, with the Web's low resolution, you don't need such a high-resolution version of images in your publications, so I recommend you save a copy of the original Photo CD image in TIFF format.

The Update Automatically option

The second option in the Link Options: Defaults dialog box's Text and Graphics sections, Update Automatically tells PageMaker that every time you open the publication it should check to see whether the source files have been changed or moved. That's why PageMaker records the file information when it first places the file. Even if PageMaker previously copied a graphic or text file into the PageMaker layout file, it checks to see whether the source file has changed. If so, it replaces the old version with the updated file in your layout.

Select this option if graphics and text change frequently and you want to make sure that the latest version is used in the layout. For example, if your Web site features a Q&A section that you update monthly with a guest columnist, you may want to save the columnist's photo under some generic filename like GUEST.TIF and simply substitute the latest photo each month. Then, when you open the document, PageMaker loads in the latest columnist's photo. Of course, for this option to work, you need to make sure that the source file is changed only when planned — it's embarrassing to have the wrong photo for a particular columnist simply because someone changed the photo early or the Web page was updated a little later than normal.

Note that if you decide not to copy graphics into the PageMaker file, the Update Automatically option is checked and grayed out. All such linked files are automatically updated because PageMaker must link to the source file each time you open the layout: There's no internal copy for PageMaker to use.

Disabling the Update Automatically option for text files is generally a good idea. If you have some text files that do change frequently, you can select this option, but understand that any editing or formatting that you did in PageMaker gets lost when the layout is updated with the new text file.

You can export your current text (via File⇨Export) to your word processor file to get around this loss. For Web-publishing purposes, however, it doesn't matter that the exporting process loses special formatting, such as tracking, kerning, drop caps, and other PageMaker-specific features not found in a word processor. Most of this formatting doesn't survive exporting to HTML anyway.

The Alert Before Updating option

The last option, Alert Before Updating, is available only if the other two options above it are selected. This option gives you a chance to override an automatic update as the PageMaker file is being opened. You know how smart it is to let something go off on its own without someone paying attention — the IRS, Congress, a high-school student. No, you insist that they check in with you before doing something that might affect you. That's what this option makes PageMaker do.

If you want automatic updating to catch any unplanned changes to your source files but you want to retain control over whether those updated files actually get used in PageMaker, check this option. If you are certain that you want elements to be updated automatically, with no notice to you, don't check the box.

Updating Individual Elements

After you establish your default link settings, you may want to change them for individual elements, as explained earlier. You can change the link settings for individual elements by selecting the elements and using the Link Options: Defaults dialog box to set their behavior, as previously described. But you can do more than that.

PageMaker offers a separate dialog box to manage the links themselves. The Link Options: Defaults dialog box controls the behavior of the linking feature; the Links Manager dialog box controls which element is linked to which source file. Figure 11-3 shows the Links Manager dialog box, which you access when you choose File⇨Links Manager or press Ctrl+Shift+D or Shift+⌘+D.

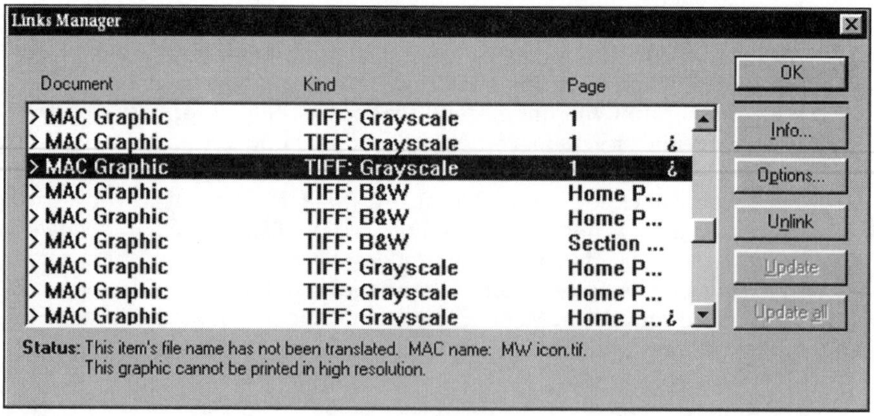

Links Manager

Document	Kind	Page
> MAC Graphic	TIFF: Grayscale	1
> MAC Graphic	TIFF: Grayscale	1 ¿
> MAC Graphic	TIFF: Grayscale	1 ¿
> MAC Graphic	TIFF: B&W	Home P...
> MAC Graphic	TIFF: B&W	Home P...
> MAC Graphic	TIFF: B&W	Section ...
> MAC Graphic	TIFF: Grayscale	Home P...
> MAC Graphic	TIFF: Grayscale	Home P...
> MAC Graphic	TIFF: Grayscale	Home P... ¿

OK | Info... | Options... | Unlink | Update | Update all

Status: This item's file name has not been translated. MAC name: MW icon.tif.
This graphic cannot be printed in high resolution.

Figure 11-3: The Links Manager dialog box shows you the status of each link and allows you to update links.

- Click on the Info button in the Links Manager dialog box to get information on a current link, including the file's physical location, the date it was placed in PageMaker, its size, and the date it was created. Figure 11-4 shows Mac and Windows dialog boxes with link information about an imported graphic.

- Via the Info button in the Links Manager dialog box, you also can change the source file for an element. If you select a new file and click on Open or press Enter, you can substitute the new file for the old source file. When would you want to use this option? Well, suppose that you're doing a story on Jane Fonda for a Web site on film legends. But the only picture you have of her is an old movie still from *Barbarella.* For lack of a better image, you go ahead and use it. The next day, a coworker comes in with a copy of *Jane Fonda's Best-Selling Workout for the Dead.* You rip it from said coworker's hands, throw it on the scanner — completely ignoring copyright laws — and use the Info button to link the imported *Barbarella* graphic to the new image. The old image is then replaced.
- Via the Options button, you can change the link behavior — this button accesses the same link options you find in the Link Options: Defaults dialog box described earlier in this chapter.

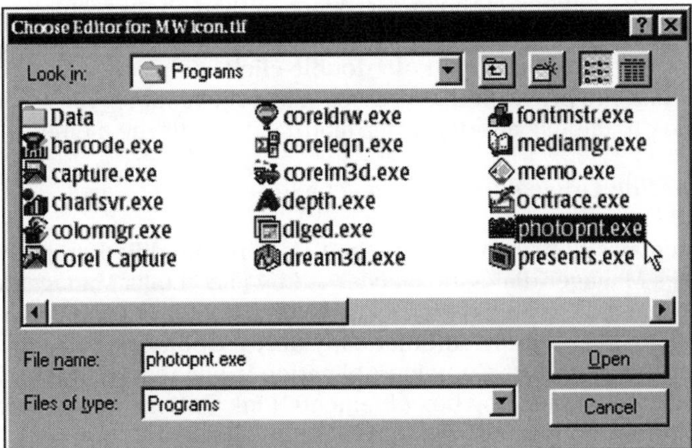

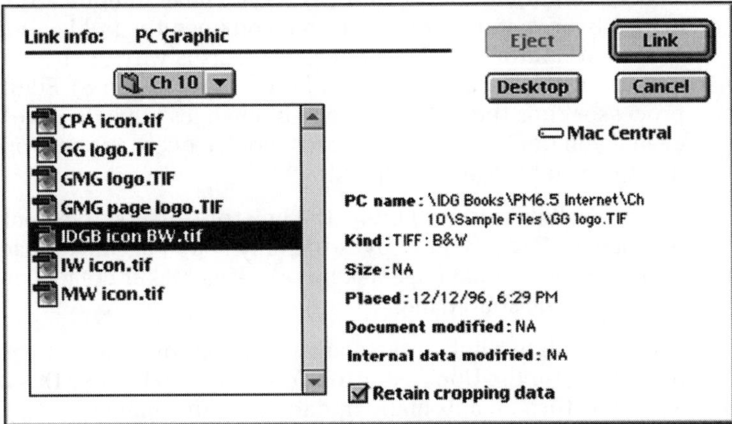

Figure 11-4: Use these dialog boxes to find missing files or to substitute a file. (At top is the Windows version; at bottom is the Mac version.)

Say that you're working in a layout and you notice that a graphic needs a touch-up. You know how to use Photoshop for this kind of work, so why not just fix the flaw yourself? Why not indeed. You can switch to Photoshop and load the image or, if you want to save some effort, select the image by clicking on it, and then press and hold the Alt or Option key while double-clicking on the image in PageMaker. Presto: PageMaker launches Photoshop and opens the source image file.

Another way to do the same thing is to select the graphic in PageMaker and choose Edit⇨Edit Original. (Of course, you need to have enough RAM to have both PageMaker and Photoshop running at once — which requires at least 16MB of system RAM on Windows and 40MB on the Mac.)

If you want to edit the element in a program other than the one that created it — for example, if you want to use Corel Photo-Paint or Fractal Design Painter to alter a TIFF image that was created in Photoshop — hold the Shift key when selecting Edit⇨Edit Original or press Alt+Shift or Shift+Option when double-clicking on the image. You can then choose which program you want to launch for your editing work. Figure 11-5 shows the dialog box. (You also get this dialog box if you Alt+double-click or Option+double-click an element and the program that created it is not available. You then use this dialog box to choose another program that can edit the element.)

Using the Edit Original feature can get a little tricky at times:

- You may still have to update the link to the modified graphic (via the Links Manager dialog box, accessed by File⇨Links Manager, or Ctrl+Shift+D or Shift+⌘+D) even if you use Edit Original. PageMaker updates the graphic automatically only if Update Automatically is checked and Store Copy in Publication is *un*checked in the Link Options: Defaults dialog box (Element⇨Link Options). Got that? If these options aren't exactly right, the graphic won't get updated.
- Text will not update automatically — you have to update the link manually or wait until the next time you open the publication (assuming Update Automatically is checked). This is why the best place to edit text in PageMaker is in the Story Editor (see Chapter 8). Editing in a word processor runs the risk of wiping out changes made in PageMaker — even if you don't change the words, you've likely applied formatting. So don't use Edit Original with text.
- Use the Unlink button to break the link to a selected element. That way, the internal PageMaker copy is the only copy PageMaker uses or tracks. If there is no internal PageMaker copy, PageMaker creates one when you unlink the source file.
- You can update a link for an element whose source has been modified by clicking on the Update button. You only need to use this option when you turn off automatic updating for an element.

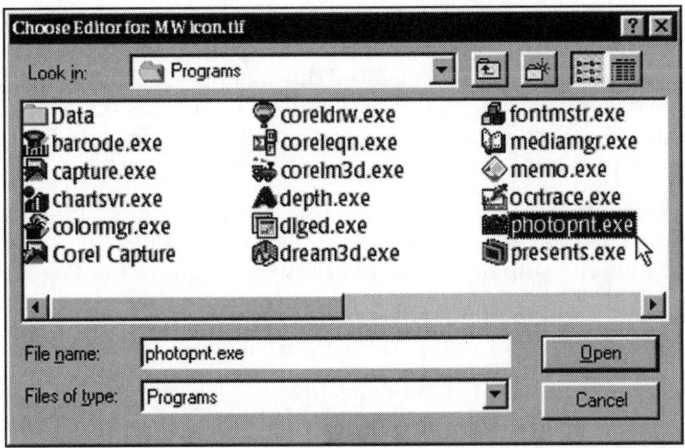

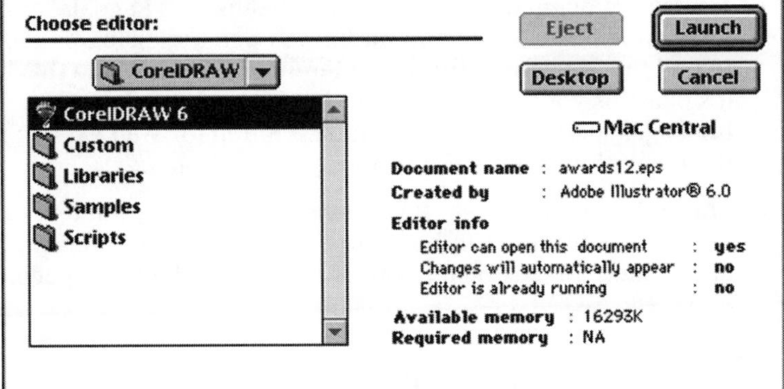

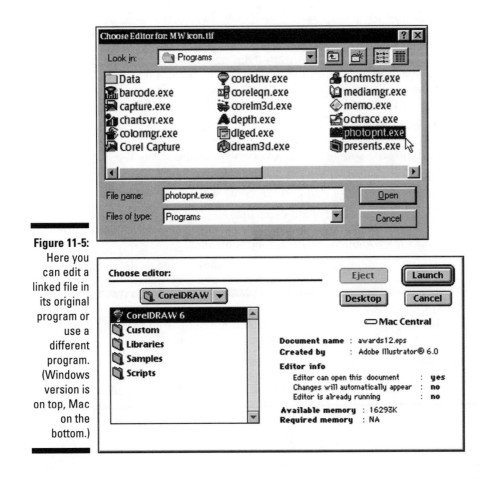

Figure 11-5: Here you can edit a linked file in its original program or use a different program. (Windows version is on top, Mac on the bottom.)

- If you click on Update All, PageMaker updates all links to source files that have been modified. Again, you only need to use this option if automatic updating is turned off.

Recognizing Symbols for Links Problems

You may have noticed a few wacky symbols that accompany element names in the Links Manager dialog box. (See Figure 11-3.) These symbols are shorthand for link problems; if you select a filename, you get a detailed description after the word *Status* at the bottom of the dialog box. Here's a rundown of what the symbols mean:

- The upside-down question mark (¿) means that the text or image may not print correctly.

- The greater-than sign (>) means that the file came from a different platform (a Mac file used in a Windows publication or vice versa) and did not have its name translated during import; that means that PageMaker can't check to see whether the file has been modified. Figure 11-6 shows the dialog box that lets you translate files when you open a PageMaker publication from a different platform.
- An exclamation point (!) means that both the source file and the copy inside PageMaker have been modified (this applies just to text), and updating the source file will overwrite changes in the PageMaker copy.
- The minus character (–) means that a source file has changed but PageMaker has not updated the internal copy.
- The plus character (+) indicates that an element's source file has changed and that the element is marked for automatic updating the next time you open the PageMaker document.

- The right-side-up question mark (?) means that PageMaker can't find the source file. Use the Info button to open the dialog box in Figure 11-4 to find the file or substitute a different file. If you leave this link broken, it's okay for your Web document because the preview image retained in the PageMaker file has sufficient resolution for Web export; however, the resolution is not sufficient for printing to paper.
- The code *NA* means that there is no source file — the text or graphics were pasted via the Clipboard (if text was entered directly in PageMaker, this text can't appear at all in the Links Manager list).

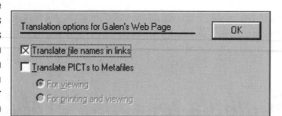

Translation options for Galen's Web Page
OK
Translate file names in links
Translate PICTs to Metafiles
For viewing
For printing and viewing

Figure 11-6: Select the Translate File Names in Links option when opening a PageMaker publication from another platform.

Working with Layers

An intriguing new feature in PageMaker is the *Layers palette,* which lets you group layout elements so you can choose to display or print only selected parts of your publication, depending on your current needs.

If you're familiar with traditional pasteup, you remember the transparent acetate sheets that layout artists used to tape on top of their layout boards. One layer was used to indicate which items would be printed in which color, another layer was used to indicate items to be "knocked out" of the background, and another layer would give nonprinting production instructions. Layers are the PageMaker version of the old overlays. Layers are like transparent electronic sheets. If you use Photoshop 3.0 or a later version, you're already familiar with the concept. If not, here goes!

First off, to use the layers feature, you must have the Layers palette visible. Use Window⇨Show Layer, or Ctrl+8 or ⌘+8. Figure 11-7 shows the palette with its pop-up menu active. This palette enables you to not only create layers, but also edit, rearrange, or delete them.

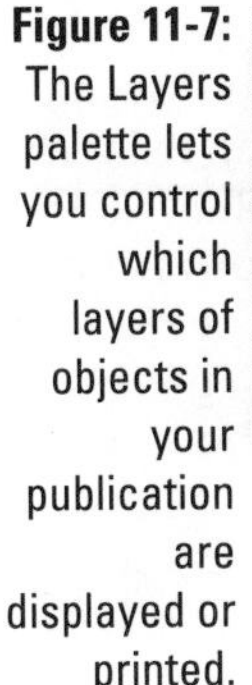

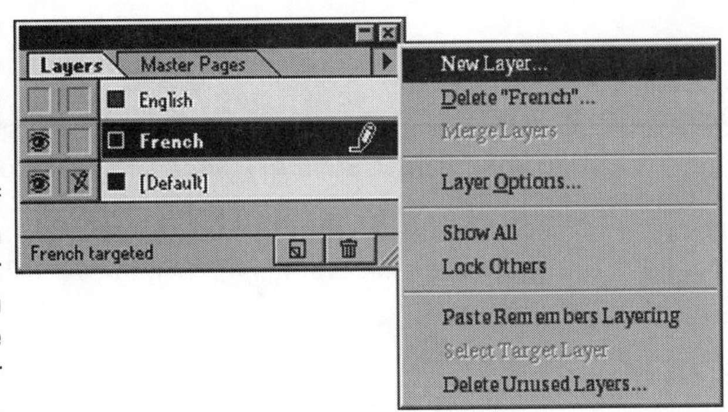

Figure 11-7: The Layers palette lets you control which layers of objects in your publication are displayed or printed.

Layers are a great way to organize objects across your publication because a layer is a publicationwide element. The layers affect the entire document, not just pieces of it.

For example, imagine you're producing a Web site for a Canadian organization. Canada is a bilingual country by law, so you need a French and an English version of each page. (I'm of French-American heritage, so I naturally picked this as my Web site example.) You could have two different publications, one in each language, but that's a production hassle. Every layout change, for example, would have to be laboriously cross-checked over both publications.

Layers offer you an easier way to accomplish this task. With layers, you can group all the common elements (essentially graphics, in this case) on one layer, have all English text on a second layer, and all French text on a third layer.

To create a new layer, use the New Layer menu option from the palette. You get the dialog box shown in Figure 11-8. Enter a name for the layer and, if you want to, assign the layer a color via the pop-up list of colors. This feature really comes in handy because the selection handles around an element appear in the color of the layer that the element is on, giving you an idea of which elements are on what layer. This is particularly important if several layers are visible.

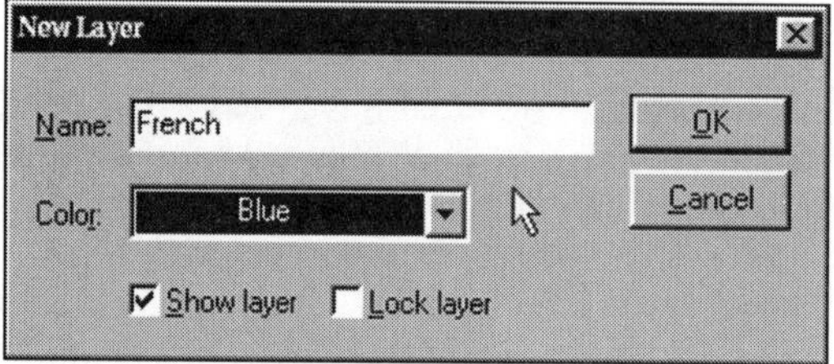

Figure 11-8: The New Layer dialog box.

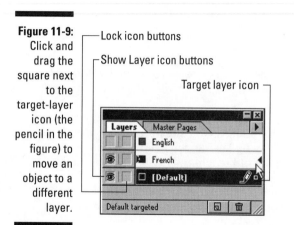

Any objects that you created before adding layers to your document reside on the [Default] layer, which you can see in Figure 11-9. To move an existing object to a different layer, select the object with the Arrow tool. Then go to the Layers palette. Notice how the pen symbol (the *target-layer* icon) is on the layer that contains that object. Click-drag the little square to the right of the pen to the layer where you want the object to reside. You get a guide pointer as you move the square to a different layer. (Figure 11-9 shows the pointer on the French layer.)

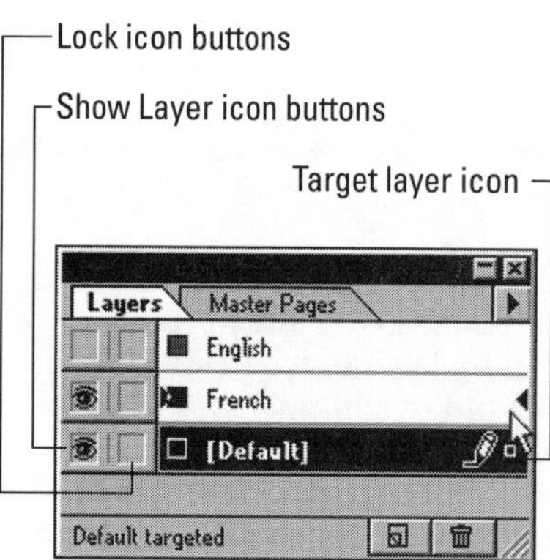

Figure 11-9: Click and drag the square next to the target-layer icon (the pencil in the figure) to move an object to a different layer.

That's all there is to moving objects from layer to layer!

The icons and two columns of boxes on the Layers palette's left side help you to manage working with multiple layers. Any layer with the Show Layer icon (👁) is visible — and will print out or export to HTML. Any layer with the Lock icon (✗) cannot be modified. These options are a big help if you want to work on, say, just the French text without disturbing the underlying graphics. In this case, just make the English layer invisible and lock the [Default] layer. (If you had both the French and English layers visible, the French and English type would overlap.)

To tie this all together, look at Figures 11-10 and 11-11. They show the same document easily produced in two different languages — all thanks to layers. You might recognize these pages as part of my Web site from Chapter 10. *Vive la différence!*

How do you turn the Show Layer and Lock icons on and off? Just click on the square buttons in the Layers palette (see Figure 11-9). The left column displays the Show Layer icons and the right column of icons shows the Lock icons. You can also use the Layers palette menu options, as shown in Figure 11-7.

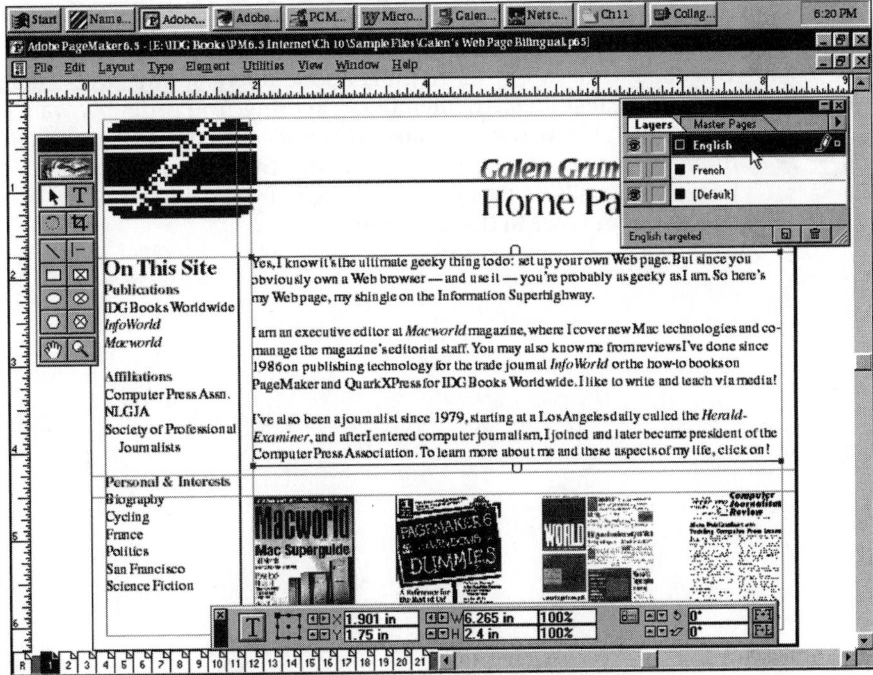

Figure 11-10: A multilayer document showing its English-language layer.

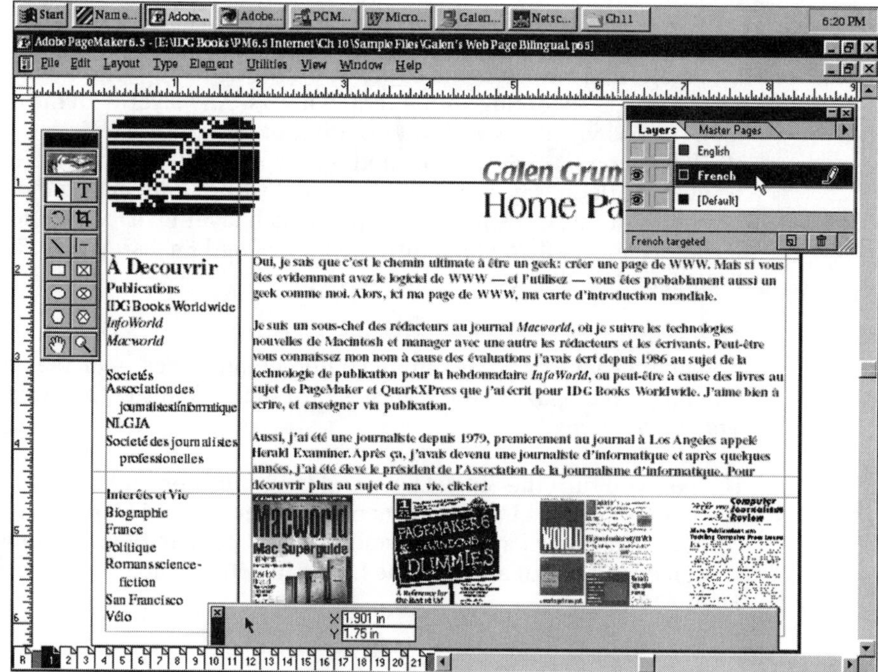

Figure 11-11: A multilayer document showing its French-language layer.

You need to know one more thing about layers: In the Layers palette menu is an option called Paste Remembers Layering. You probably want this selected most of the time, because this option ensures that objects you copy from a number of layers get pasted onto the same layer either on the current page or on a different page in your PageMaker layout — even if you change to a different layer in the meantime.

Chapter 12

Doing Less Work Next Time

In This Chapter

- Creating master pages to automate layout
- Using the multiple master pages feature
- Making a document template
- Storing frequently used items in libraries

One of the biggest benefits of using a program such as PageMaker is that it can automate many of your layout tasks. In Chapters 1 through 11, you can find out how to use some of the basic layout features of PageMaker, such as text styling, guides and rulers, and the new layers feature, to make your life easier. But to take full advantage of the PageMaker time- and energy-saving benefits, you need to become acquainted with the three features discussed in this chapter: master pages, templates, and libraries.

If you're unfamiliar with desktop publishing, these three concepts will probably seem pretty foreign to you at first — and not nearly so exciting as such topics as, say, specifying colors and creating hypertext links. But if you spend just a little time getting acquainted with these concepts, you'll be amazed at how many of your routine layout chores you can hoist off onto PageMaker. Why, you'll have so much free time on your hands that you'll finally be able to master that Minesweeper game those Microsoft folks so generously included with your copy of Windows 95 or the Jigsaw Puzzle those Apple folks so generously included with System 7.6. Hey, this may just be an exciting chapter after all!

Using Master Pages

You may have noticed that the far bottom left corner of the PageMaker window has two little page icons labeled *L* and *R*, or just one icon labeled *R* if the document doesn't use facing pages. (Publications for the Web typically don't use facing pages, as explained in Chapter 5.) Those icons represent master pages.

Master pages are sort of like the basic building blocks for your pages. By placing an element on a master page, you can have PageMaker automatically place that same element on any pages you specify. For example, if you want to put a company logo at the bottom of every page in an eight-page brochure, you can place it once on a master page and tell PageMaker to automatically add that logo to all other pages. You can use master pages not only to automate the placement of repeating elements, such as logos and page numbers, but also to establish column and margin settings for your pages. In Chapter 10, I used master pages to set up three kinds of pages in my Web site.

In addition to saving you the time and effort of placing repeating elements over and over again throughout your document, master pages help to ensure consistency. You don't have to worry about whether you're placing that logo in precisely the same spot on every page, for example — PageMaker handles that for you.

Creating your Document Master pages

PageMaker has two basic types of master pages: Document Master pages and regular master pages. Confused yet? Hang with me, because this subject is not as bad as it seems.

You see, every PageMaker document you create has two default Document Master pages (or just one if you're not using facing pages in your layout). Anything you place on these pages appears in all pages of your document unless you specify otherwise (which you learn how to do a little later). In addition to these Document Master pages, you can create other master pages. But these other master pages don't have any effect until or unless you apply them to selected pages.

For the sake of convenience, I refer to the default master pages as Document Master pages. If I'm referring to the other type of master pages — or if I'm referring to both kinds of master pages — I just use the plain, lowercased term, *master pages.* Yeesh!

To place items on a Document Master page, just click on either the L or R page icon, depending on whether you want to work on the left- or right-hand Document Master. Then establish columns, guides, margins, and other page settings as you normally would and place any elements that you want to appear throughout your document. To leave the Document Master page and return to your layout, just click on one of the standard page icons next to the master page icons.

Because Web documents typically have only R masters, I'll dispense with talking about both R and L master pages from now on and just use the letter R, unless there's something you need to know about L master pages for print documents.

After you create additional master pages, you must first select the Document Master item (as explained in the upcoming section "Editing a master page") before clicking on the R page icon. Otherwise, you open the master page applied to the current page — which may or may not be the Document Master.

Any settings you establish or elements you place on your L Document Master page appear on all left-hand pages in your document by default. Similarly, all the stuff you put on the R Document Master page appears on all the right-handed pages. If you're not using facing pages, anything you put on the R Document Master page appears on all pages in your document. However, if you apply a different master page to any page (as described in the next few sections), that master page overrides the Document Master. You also can override Document Master column and guide settings by choosing new ones from the Layout menu.

Creating additional master pages

You can create additional master pages in three ways: You can create them from scratch, base them on an existing master page, or base them on an existing page on your document. In all three cases, you use the Master Pages palette, shown in Figure 12-1. To display the palette, choose Window⇨Master Pages or press Ctrl+Shift+8 (Windows) or Shift+⌘+8 (Mac).

In previous versions of PageMaker, the keyboard shortcut for displaying the Master Pages palette was Ctrl+H or ⌘+H. That shortcut now brings up the Change dialog box in the Story Editor. Now you press Ctrl+Shift+8 (Windows) or Shift+⌘+8 (Mac). Keeps you on your toes, doesn't it?

To create a master page from scratch:

1. **Click on the right-pointing triangle in the top-right corner of the Master Pages palette.** Up pops the Master Pages palette menu, as shown in Figure 12-1.

2. **Choose New Master Page.**

   As an alternative to using the pop-up menu, you can Ctrl+click or ⌘-click on the [None] item in the palette. Plus, PageMaker 6.5 adds a third method: Click on the New button at the bottom of the palette.

   No matter which way you choose to create a new master page, the dialog box shown in Figure 12-2 appears. If you want to create a two-page master spread, select the Two Page radio button. If you want to create just a single master page, click on the One Page radio button. Then specify margin and column guide settings for your new master page or pages and enter a name in the Name option box. Note that the Two Page radio button is grayed out if the document doesn't have facing pages, which is typically the case with Web documents.

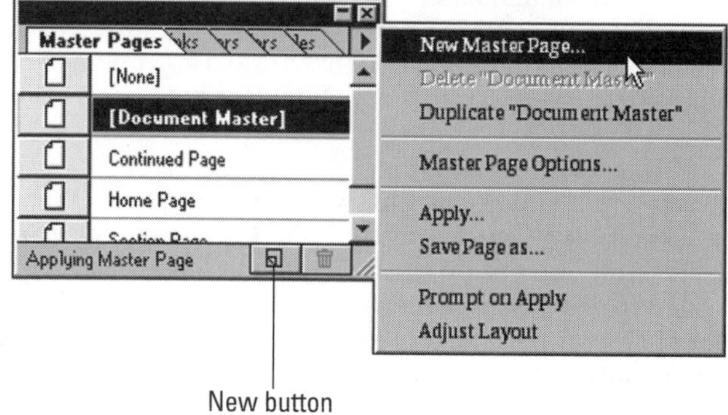

Figure 12-1: The Master Pages palette and pop-up menu let you create as many master pages as you want.

3. Click on OK.

Your new master page (or two-page spread) appears in the window, and its name appears on the Master Pages palette. You can now add whatever elements or layout guides you wish to your new master page(s). To return to a regular document page, just click on its page icon at the bottom of the document window.

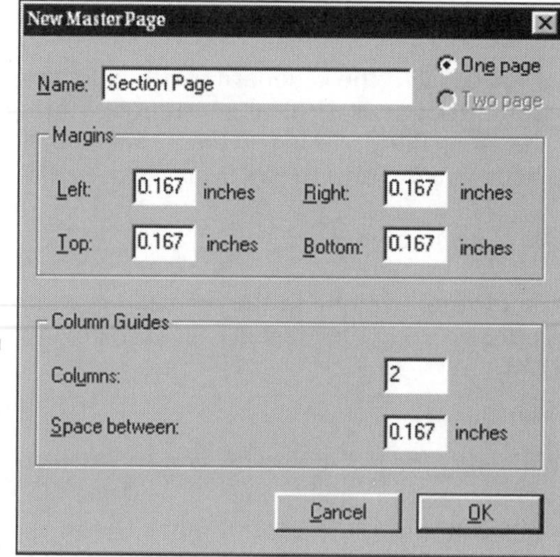

Figure 12-2: The New Master Page dialog box.

Creating new master pages from existing ones

If you want a new master page to use the same column settings, margins, or other elements that you've already established on another master page, you can save time by simply duplicating the first master page and then modifying it as necessary.

To do so, make sure that you are viewing the master page you want to duplicate — click on R and then use the Master Pages palette to select the master page you're duplicating (just click on the page's name). Now choose Duplicate from the Master Pages palette pop-up menu to display the Duplicate Master Page dialog box. Choose the name of the master you want to copy from the Duplicate pop-up menu, enter a name for the new master page in the Name of new Master option box, and click on the Duplicate button, as shown in Figure 12-3. Your new master page appears in the publication window, and you can then add new elements to the page or remove existing ones.

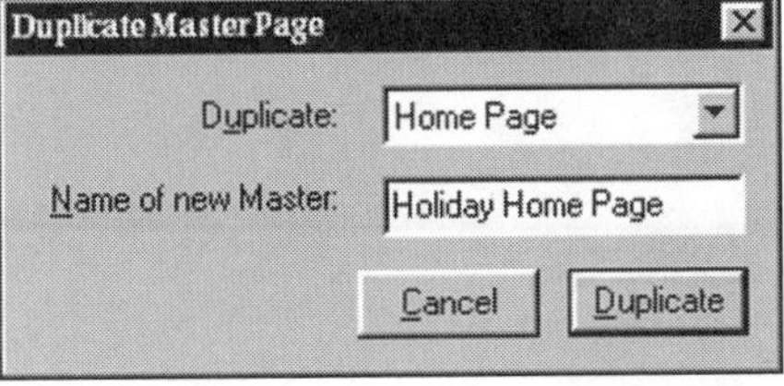

Figure 12-3: The Duplicate Master Page dialog box.

If you don't first move to the master page you want to duplicate, PageMaker thinks that you want to apply whatever master page you're duplicating to the current page. If you end up accidentally changing your current layout by applying a wrong master page, you can fix your goof with Ctrl+Z or ⌘+Z, or Edit⇨Undo.

To prevent a single click on a master-page name from accidentally reformatting the current page, select the Prompt on Apply option from the Master Page palette's pop-up menu. If that option is checked, you get a dialog box asking you to confirm whether you want a master page to be applied each time you click a master page's name from the palette.

You can also use an existing page in your layout as the basis for a new master page. Just click on the page icon for the existing page, choose Save Page as from the Master Pages palette menu, give the new master page a name, and then click on the Save button.

Applying master pages

PageMaker automatically applies your Document Master pages to all the pages in your document. If you want to use one of your other master pages on a particular page, you have to apply the master page to the page. Any Document Master page settings or elements are then overridden for that particular page. But any other existing text or objects on the page stay put (you may need to adjust text flow or graphic positioning to account for changes in margin or column settings, though).

A new checkbox item called Adjust Layout, which relates to master pages, appears in several PageMaker dialog boxes. Adjust Layout is also a menu item in the Master Pages palette pop-up menu (see Figure 12-1). What Adjust Layout does is move and even resize elements for the best fit with new master-page settings. Adjust Layout doesn't always get it exactly right, but this option does help with some of the adjustment work that applying new master pages (or page sizes) requires.

You can tell PageMaker how to "think" about adjusting layouts by setting the preferences in the Layout Adjustments Preferences dialog box, shown in Figure 12-4. To get this dialog box, use File⇨Preferences⇨Layout Adjustment. (Chapter 10 covers the layout-adjustment feature in more detail.)

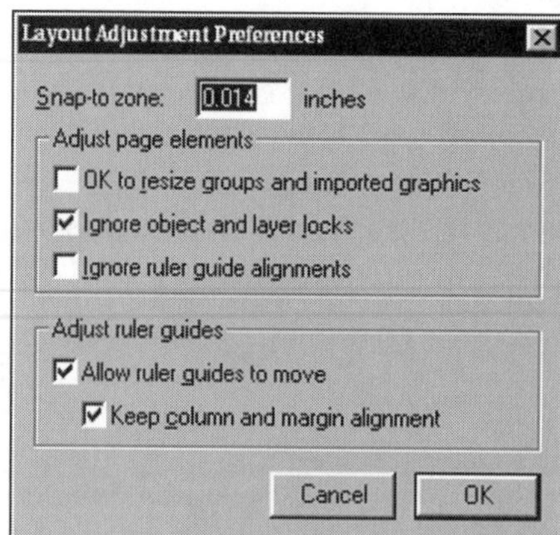

Figure 12-4: Almost artificial intelligence: You can tell PageMaker how you want it to adjust layouts when master pages and page sizes change.

- To apply a master page to the page you're currently working on, just click on the master page's name in the Master Pages palette.
- To determine which master page is applied to a page, turn to the page and look at the Master Pages palette. The name of the master page being used is highlighted.

- To apply a master page to several pages at once, choose Apply from the Master Pages palette pop-up menu to display the Apply Master dialog box, shown in Figure 12-5. Choose the name of the master page you want to apply from the Master Page list box. Click on the Page Range radio button and enter the desired page numbers or range of pages. Click on the All radio button to apply the master page to all pages. Note that you can use commas for nonsequential page selection and hyphens to indicate page ranges. Click on the Apply button to close the dialog box and apply the master page.

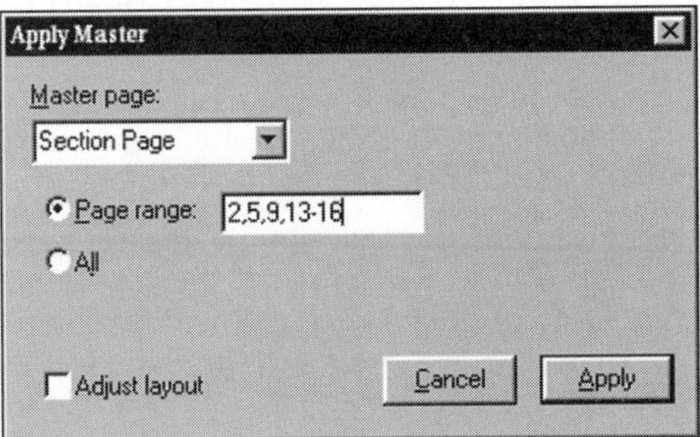

Figure 12-5: The Apply Master dialog box lets you apply a master page to multiple pages all at once.

- If you're working on facing pages, select the Set Left and Right Pages Separately check box if you want to apply one master page to the selected left-hand pages and another master page to the right-hand pages. (This check box appears between the All and Adjust Layout check boxes *only* if you're working on facing pages.) The dialog box then displays two pop-up menus, one for selecting the left-hand master page and another for selecting the right-hand master page.
- You can hide the master page elements on a page by turning to that page and choosing View⇨Display Master Items. Choose the command again to redisplay the master page items. Again, the column and ruler guides from the master page remain displayed.

The Display Master Items menu option has moved in PageMaker 6.5 to the View menu. Also, this command no longer has the shortcut Ctrl+J or ⌘+J, as the previous PageMaker version did. (That shortcut now displays the Colors palette.)

Removing master pages and their elements

To delete master pages, or selected master-page elements from a page, use these techniques:

- To remove master page elements from a page, apply the None master to the page, either by clicking on None in the Master Pages palette or choosing None from the pop-up menu in the Apply Master dialog box. The column and ruler guides from the master page remain. To remove elements and all guides, press Shift as you choose None in the Master Pages palette.
- You can override master page column and margin settings on a particular page by simply choosing new settings from the Layout menu or Document Setup dialog box (File⇨Document Setup).
- To delete a master page altogether, click on the master page name in the Master Pages palette, choose Delete from the pop-up menu (shown grayed-out in Figure 12-1), and then click on the Delete button in the dialog box that appears. PageMaker applies the None master to all pages that had used the deleted master page. As before, column and margin guides remain, but you can override them by establishing new column and margin settings.

Anything on a master page appears underneath anything created on a standard page. For example, if you place an image on a master page, any text or image placed on a standard page in that same location appears on top of the image rectangle (assuming that text wrap is turned off for the rectangle). But you can change the stacking order of the master page and standard page elements if you want; just use the Element⇨Arrange⇨Send to Back (Ctrl+[or ⌘+[) or Bring to Front (Ctrl+] or ⌘+]) commands. If you want to move items one level at a time through the stacking order, use Element⇨Arrange⇨Send Backward (Ctrl+Shift+[or Shift+⌘+[) or Element⇨Arrange⇨Send Forward (Ctrl+Shift+] or Shift+⌘+]).

Editing a master page

If you want to change the margins or column setup on a master page, make sure that you have opened the master page and then select its name from the Master Pages palette and choose the Master Pages Options command from the palette menu. Or just Ctrl+click (or double click) on the master page name in the palette (you won't need to switch from a regular page to the master page to use this shortcut). PageMaker displays the Master Page Options dialog box, which offers the same margin and column guide settings as the New Master Page dialog box shown back in Figure 12-2. You can also change the name of the master page in this dialog box if you want.

You can also change guidelines in the master page itself by click-dragging column and ruler guides to their new positions and adding or deleting ruler guides, as described in Chapter 5. Changing column guides in the master page itself is a must if you want columns to be of different widths.

If you want to add or remove elements from a master page, you have to make the master page active in the publication window. You can do this in two ways:

- To display the master page applied to the current page of your document, double-click on the master page icon at the bottom of the document window. If you're currently working on a spread (this applies to your print publications only — you won't have facing pages on the Web), and you have different master pages applied to the left- and right-hand pages, PageMaker displays the right-hand page master. If you select a name from this pop-up list, that master page will appear, and you then can edit it.
- Choose Layout⇨Go to Page or Ctrl+Alt+G and select the master page from the pop-up menu in the Go to Page dialog box.

Building a Template

Although master pages go a long way toward automating the layout process, you can go even one step further by creating templates for those documents you produce on a regular basis — say, for example, a new-product notice that you update monthly. A template lets you save all the master pages, styles, HTML export settings, and other elements that you need each month as you lay out your Web site's pages. (See Chapter 17 for information on HTML settings.) Then, you just modify the template as needed for each update.

What do you want your template to contain? Here are some ideas:

- The correct number of pages for the document
- Styles (body text, caption, headline, and so on), as discussed in Chapter 9
- Master pages containing repeating elements and margin and column settings
- Standing text — such as "How to Get More Information," that may appear in almost every Web page or site
- The HTML export document titles that define story and page ranges for export from PageMaker to HTML (see Chapter 17)

You can build a template in either one of two ways: You can construct a template from scratch or you can convert an existing layout into a template. For example, after you've laid out the first notice of your monthly product update, you can save the document as a template.

Building a template from scratch is the easy way, but it assumes that you know in advance what the template needs to contain — which means that you have to know the requirements and look of the layouts that will be based on it. Converting an existing layout into a template is harder because you have to remove any elements that can't be used in all or most of your future Web pages. But this method can also be the best way because it lets you figure out what the layout needs to look like by using a real example before finalizing the template.

Whichever method you choose, you lay out a template document the same way you lay out a regular document. To turn the document into a template, choose File➪Save As (or Ctrl+Shift+S or Shift+⌘+S) to display the Save Publication dialog box. Select Template from the Save As Type pop-up menu and give your template a name that you'll be able to distinguish easily. Click on OK, and PageMaker saves your document as a template.

In Windows, PageMaker 6.5 gives your custom template filenames the extension T65, while regular PageMaker 6.5 documents get the extension P65.

On both the Mac and in Windows, the template page icon shows the lower right corner of the page turned up, while the publication icon shows the upper right corner of the page turned down.

Creating a layout from a template

To start a new document based on a custom template that you've created, choose File➪Open (or Ctrl+O or ⌘+O) and choose the template from the list. PageMaker opens a copy of the template. You can then add new elements to, or delete existing elements from, the document.

Templates may contain mocked-up or previous text and graphics as placeholders for your real text and graphics. You can delete or replace them as you would any graphic or text block. For example, to replace a graphic placeholder with your own graphic, select the placeholder and then choose Replacing Entire Graphic in the Place dialog box when you import your graphic. To replace a placeholder story, choose Replacing Entire Story.

You can also use frames, a new feature in PageMaker 6.5, as placeholders for text and graphics. Frames are a kind of box that you can place text or graphics in. Chapter 7 covers frames in more detail (the frames tools are the ones with an X through them in the toolbox).

When you're finished creating your document, save it as a regular document by choosing File⇨Save (or Ctrl+S or ⌘+S), entering a document name in the Save Publication dialog box, and choosing the Publication option from the Save File As Type pop-up menu.

Editing a template

Over time, you'll probably need to update your templates to incorporate new design elements or other changes. To edit a custom template, choose File⇨Open and select the template. Select the Original radio button if you want to edit your original template. If you want to keep that template intact and work on a copy of the template instead, select the Copy radio button.

When you finish updating your template, choose File⇨Save As, give the template a new name if you wish, select Template from the Save File as Type pop-up menu, and click on OK. Remember: Because it is a template, you can't just use the regular Save command.

Getting Your Library Card

If you produce a lot of documents for the same client or company, you'll find that you use certain elements, such as logos, in almost every piece you create. You can keep these elements on the pasteboard — the portion of the PageMaker screen outside the page boundaries — but that can get real cluttered real fast, and it doesn't let someone else easily access those elements for another layout, either. A better answer is to put these elements in a library.

A *library* is simply a holding tank for frequently used items. You can access the elements in a library — and put new elements into a library — by using the Library palette. You just drag stuff into and out of the palette, as explained a little later. Libraries are quick, convenient, and they keep your desktop all neat and tidy-like.

You can create as many libraries as you need. You may want to keep all your public Web site's logos and boilerplate text (the standardized material used in multiple publications) in one library, and keep elements that you use in your company's internal Web site reports in another library.

PageMaker 6.5 thoroughly changed the process of creating libraries, so if you're used to PageMaker 6.0 libraries, read through this section carefully. The functions are essentially the same, but the way you use it is more like PageMaker palettes.

PageMaker 6.0 libraries cannot be read by PageMaker 6.5. To retain them for use in PageMaker 6.5, put them into a PageMaker document (using PageMaker 6.0), then open that document in PageMaker 6.5 and move the libraries to a new Version 6.5 library.

Creating libraries

To create your first library, choose Window⇨Plug-in Palettes⇨Show Library. The Library palette appears. Access the pop-up menu by clicking on the arrow in the palette's upper right corner. Then click on the New Library option. Type in a name for your library in the File name box and choose the folder you want to store the library in. Figure 12-6 shows the Library palette with a newly created, empty library.

- To open an existing library, click on Open Library in the palette menu. You can have only one library open at a time.
- When you close the library palette and reopen it — even if you're in a different document — the last library you had open becomes active. This is because libraries are not associated with specific documents but are available instead to all documents.

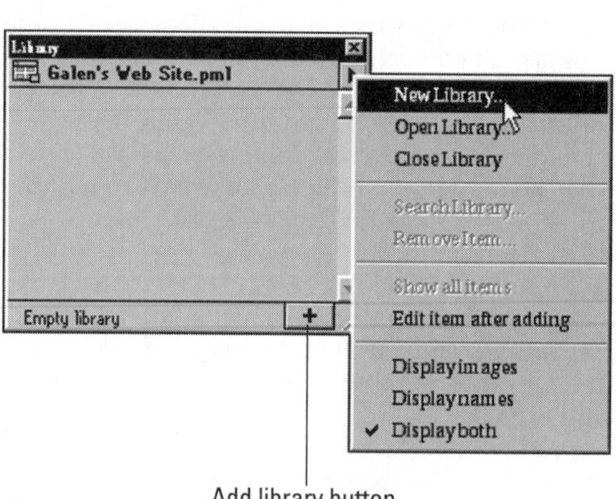

Figure 12-6: The Library palette, shown with pop-up menu unfurled, is the place to create and manage your libraries.

Adding and deleting library elements

To add an object or text element to a library, select it with the Arrow tool and then click on the Add button (shown with a + sign) at the bottom right of the Library palette (which you can see in Figure 12-6). To add several items at once, click on the first object, Shift+click on the rest, and then click on the Add button.

- Note that if you copy a text block into a library, it retains its text formatting but not its style name. Thus, when you place the text in another layout, it will have the No Style style. You can, of course, apply a style to it once you've used it in an actual document.
- When you paste an element into a library, PageMaker gives it the name *Untitled* followed by a dash and a number. Because libraries are searchable — that is, you can enter the name of a library element and instruct PageMaker to hunt down that element for you — a good idea is to give the element a name you can search, especially if you'll be creating fairly large libraries.
- To name an element, double-click on it in the Library palette. PageMaker displays the Item Information dialog box shown in Figure 12-7. You can add keywords and a description into the dialog box to make it easier to find the element in the future.

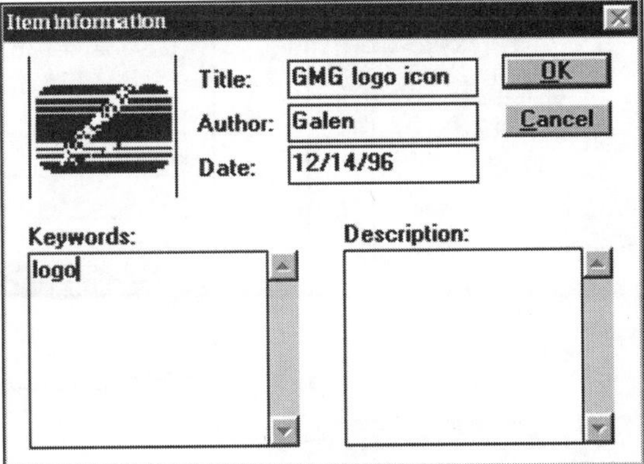

Figure 12-7: The Item Information dialog box lets you enter information that helps you track down library items in the future.

- If you always want to fill in keyword and title information, check the Edit Item After Adding option in the Library palette pop-up menu.
- To delete an item from a library, select the item in the Library palette and choose Remove Item from the Library palette pop-up menu. Click on OK to confirm your decision to toss the item into the abyss.

Note that you cannot use Ctrl+X or ⌘+X, or File➪Cut, to delete a library element. In fact, trying to do so deletes whatever is selected in your layout, not the element selected in the library. So be careful!

Deleting the library element does not delete it from your layout nor does it delete the original element's file from your drive.

Setting library displays

After the Library palette is displayed, you can resize the palette to make it wider or deeper, which lets you see more of its contents. Use the scroll bar to move through the library.

Figure 12-8 shows a library palette with several items, in both the default view (which shows an icon and a name) and in a name-only view. There's also an icon-only view, which looks almost exactly like the icon-and-name view. You determine the view in the Library palette's pop-up menu through the Display images, Display names, and Display both options.

In Windows only, you can change the Library palette view with a pop-up menu that appears when you right-click inside the Library palette, as shown to the right in Figure 12-8.

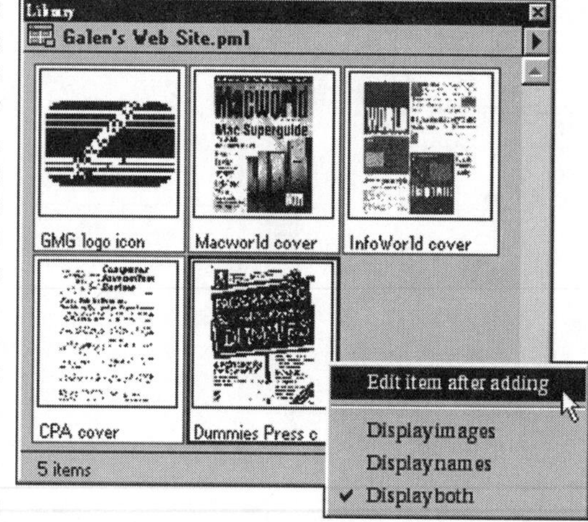

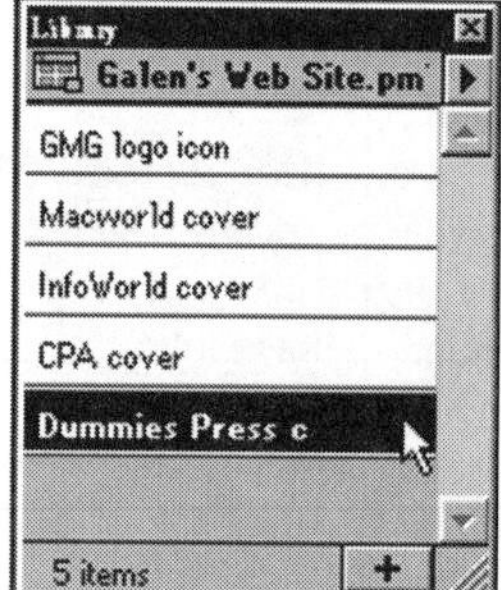

Figure 12-8: Two views of the Library palette, with icons and names (left) and with names only (right). (The pop-up menu at right is in Windows only.)

Finding library elements

As noted earlier, you can just scroll through the palette to find a particular element. But if the library has many elements, to search for an element by its keyword, author, or name (title) is easier. To do this, choose Search Library from the Library palette pop-up menu. The Search Library dialog box, shown in Figure 12-9, then appears.

- To search by a keyword, just enter it into the Search by keyword option box. If you want to search by two or more keywords, separate them with spaces.

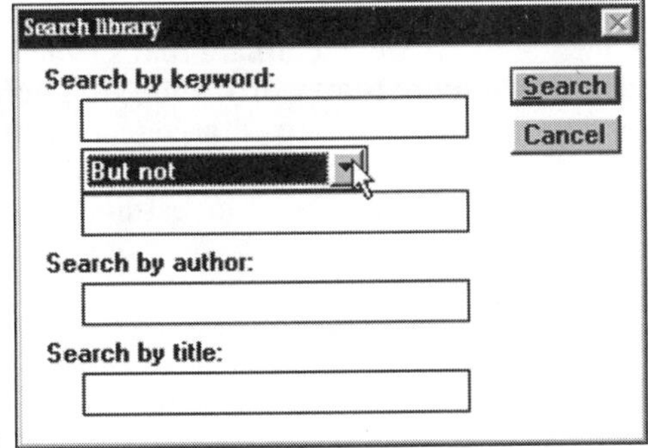

Figure 12-9: You can use this dialog box to search by keywords for items in your Library.

- The search option is smart enough that it doesn't require exact matches. For example, if the author's name is *Alexander* and you enter *Alex* as the name to search, PageMaker finds any author whose name includes the characters *a, l, e,* and *x,* in that order.
- Notice that there's a pop-up menu in the Search by Keyword section. The default setting is One keyword only. If you choose this option, PageMaker searches for the single word (or words) in the top option box. The other options are And, Or, and But Not. If you choose And, the element must use both keywords in order for PageMaker to find it. If you choose Or, the element must use at least one of the two keywords. If you choose But Not, the element must use the first keyword but not the second keyword (that's why it's called *But Not*!).

After PageMaker finishes its search, it displays only those items that met the search criteria in the palette. (If it didn't find any elements that match your search request, it notifies you with a polite dialog box. Click on OK and go back to the drawing board.) To redisplay all the items in the Library palette, choose Show All Items from the palette pop-up menu.

Using library elements

This is the easiest part: To use a library element, just click on the element (the square border gets thicker) and drag it from the palette to anywhere in your PageMaker document. PageMaker places the element wherever you release the mouse button. Note also that it places the element at its original size, not the preview size shown in the palette. After you place the element, you can modify it just like any other element.

When you drag an element from the library into a document, the preview stays in the library — you're copying the element from the library, not actually removing it from the library.

Setting up libraries, master pages, and templates requires some up-front time and energy. It takes a while to create a template that's exactly right. But the payoff down the road makes it more than worthwhile. You not only save yourself lots of time in the long run, you end up with Web sites and print publications that are more consistent and professional looking — in short, you get a heck of a lot more from your PageMaker investment.

Part V
Say It with Pictures

In this part . . .

Admit it: It's the pictures that get you. Consider the Internet. It would probably still be inhabited solely by university eggheads and Defense Department geeks were it not for its ability to support eye-catching graphics, both naughty and nice (this is the G-rated version of *PageMaker 6.5 For Dummies, Internet Edition* in case you're interested).

You might not have realized it, but in addition to being a powerful page layout program, PageMaker is also a mini-graphics studio. PageMaker doesn't have the high-powered drawing and image editing capabilities of a full-fledged graphics program such as Photoshop or CorelDraw, but it does have the basic set of features you need to create simple graphics and enhance the images, drawings, and photographs that you import from other programs. In this part, you find out how to bring pictures into your Web documents, how to manipulate them for the special look you want, and how to ensure they look Web-worthy on computer screens from Los Angeles to Lisbon. By the time you're finished with these three chapters, you'll be so full of the artistic spirit that you'll probably feel the urge to cut off an ear (or maybe just go shopping for a beret).

Chapter 13

Adding Pretty Pictures

In This Chapter

- Preparing graphics files for import
- Using PageMaker graphics formats
- Placing graphics
- Recognizing the Web's favorite graphics
- Copying images for export to the Web
- Adding lines to your document

This chapter is about graphics, the one thing you can't create in PageMaker. Oh sure, you can draw lines, rectangles, polygons, and ellipses, but unless you intend to limit yourself to crude drawings of stick figures and smiley faces, you need more sophisticated tools.

That's why PageMaker lets you import graphics. You can create a picture in just about any graphics program you choose, save the artwork to disk using one of several different file formats, and insert it into your PageMaker publication. Inside PageMaker, you can stretch the graphic, label it with text, crop it so only a part appears, or apply special filters to alter images.

Preparing Graphics for PageMaker

Just as you need to prepare text in your word processor for use in PageMaker, you need to prepare your graphics for importing. And, naturally, the preparation you need to do depends on the program you used to create the graphic and the type of graphic you created.

Graphics come in two basic types: *bitmap* and *vector*. Bitmap graphics are made up of square dots called *pixels,* and vector graphics are made up of lines. For example, everything printed by your laser printer becomes a bitmap graphic on the page because the entire page is composed of a series of black dots on the white paper — take a magnifying glass and check!

Some programs create their images the same way, using a pattern of colored or black dots to render an image. Paint programs, scanners, and photo editors generally create bitmaps. Adobe Photoshop, Corel Photo-Paint, and Fractal Design Painter are probably the most popular paint and photo-editing programs, but another dozen or so programs are in use.

Bitmap images are good for representing continuous ranges of colors with soft edges, such as impressionist paintings and photographs. But, because they are made up of patterns of dots, enlarging or reducing them too much can make the dots ungainly or too fine to reproduce well.

Vector drawings, on the other hand, are great for high-contrast art, such as weather maps, architectural plans, logos, charts, informational graphics, and all kinds of other bright, colorful artwork you may see in *USA Today*. A vector drawing is composed of lines, circles, and other shapes that can be stretched, combined, and otherwise manipulated, all without appearing the least bit jagged. Eventually, when they're printed to paper or displayed on screen, these drawings are converted to bitmaps; but in the computer, they are vectors, which means that they can be resized without any loss in quality. CorelDRAW!, Adobe Illustrator, and Macromedia FreeHand are the best-known drawing programs but, again, other programs provide the same capabilities.

Keep in mind that most vector programs can export a bitmap version of their drawings, and some programs let you combine bitmap and vector images in one file. The words *bitmap* and *vector* are techie terms, and many people are now using the terms *image* and *drawing* to refer to these types of formats. This book calls them *image* and *drawing* as well, and uses the term *graphic* to mean both. (Figure 13-1 shows examples of both bitmap and vector art.)

What formats can PageMaker import?

PageMaker can import many formats of graphics — as long as you have the right import filter installed. A list follows that explains the major formats that PageMaker supports; if you try to load a file in one of these formats and get a message saying that PageMaker doesn't know how to place it, get your install disks or CD, run the PageMaker Installer program, and perform a custom installation (as described in the Appendix) to install the missing filter.

PageMaker can import any of the following major formats, plus a few other more obscure formats. (All the formats listed here support color and grayscale graphics, unless otherwise noted.)

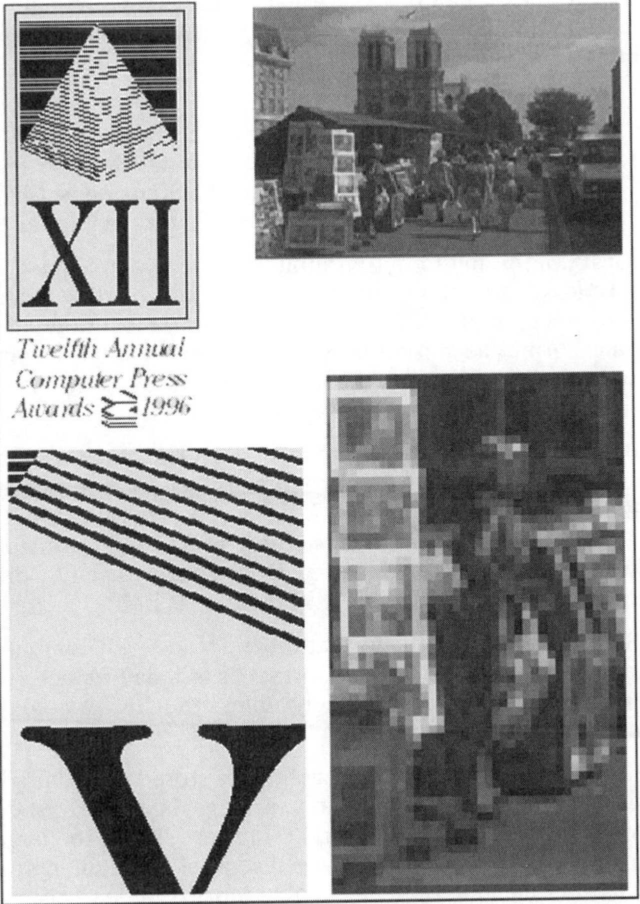

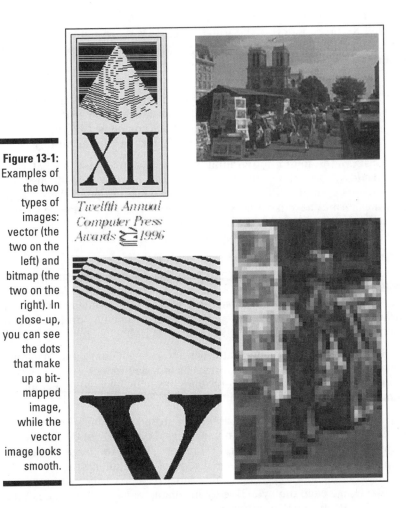

Figure 13-1: Examples of the two types of images: vector (the two on the left) and bitmap (the two on the right). In close-up, you can see the dots that make up a bit-mapped image, while the vector image looks smooth.

If you're moving graphics files from Mac to Windows or vice versa, your networking or disk-exchange software may need to know the exact PC extension or Mac file type. That information is included with each file description. Be aware that sometimes the capitalization for the Mac file types is a little bizarre. Capitalization is crucial, so enter your file types exactly as this book lists them.

Image formats

- **TIFF:** TIFF, the Tagged Image File Format, can be produced by most graphics programs. TIFF is the standard image format on most personal computers, including Windows PCs and Macintoshes. The PC extension is .TIF; the Mac file type is TIFF.

- **PCX:** PCX, the PC Paintbrush format, is a PC standard similar to TIFF. It's been around forever and was definitely the de facto standard on PCs before TIFF came along. The PC extension is .PCX; the Mac file type is PCX.

- **GIF:** Whether you pronounce it with a hard *g* or a soft *g* like the peanut-butter spread, you'll get to know this format for the Web — it's the standard format for Web graphics. The PC extension is .GIF; the Mac file type is GIFf (one example of some weird file format capitalization).

- **JPEG:** JPEG, the Joint Photographic Experts Group format, is what's called a *lossy* format. It strips out some details to allow graphic files to take up less memory. JPEG is now the second most popular Web graphics format because it makes images much smaller memory-wise, allowing the images to download and display faster on the Web. The PC extension is .JPG; the Mac file type is JPEG.
- **BMP:** BMP, the Windows bitmap format, is the format used by the Windows built-in screen shot program as well as that little Paint program found in the Windows Accessories program group. Most new programs support it, but because the TIFF and PCX formats came along earlier and are more standardized, BMP is rarely used by professionals. The PC extension is .BMP; the Mac file type is BMP.
- **MacPaint:** The first image format for the Macintosh computer, MacPaint remains a black-and-white-only format to this day. In fact, running into MacPaint images is highly unlikely, unless they're very old and come from the Mac. The PC extension is .MAC; the Mac file type is PNTG.
- **Photo CD:** PageMaker can import images stored in Kodak's Photo CD format, but it can't store them in your PageMaker file as it does other graphics formats because Photo CD files are simply too large. (Storing graphics inside your documents is discussed in detail in Chapter 11.) Because of this limitation, PageMaker must be able to access the original image each time you open your document — which means that if you share your file with other people or take it to a service bureau, you have to give them the image CD as well. The PC extension is .PCD; the Mac file type is PCDI.

  To get around this problem, you have two options. You can either open the image in an image editor such as Photoshop or Corel Photo-Paint and save it as a TIFF file (or in another acceptable image format) before bringing it into PageMaker. Or, you can take advantage of an option that PageMaker offers when you try to import a Photo CD image directly, which is to save the file in the CIE Lab TIFF format (a special variety of TIFF). Both options result in smaller file sizes, letting you either store the image file in your PageMaker document or save to a floppy disk or other removable storage media (such as a SyQuest or Zip cartridge).

Drawing formats

- **EPS:** The Encapsulated PostScript format is the standard drawing format for professionals. Almost every program that supports PostScript printers can create this format, and it's incredibly reliable. The only problem is that only PostScript printers can print EPS graphics. If you use a PCL or QuickDraw printer or some other non-PostScript device, don't use EPS unless you also have software such as Zenographics' SuperPrint for Windows or GDT Softworks' PowerPrint for Macintosh, which converts EPS Files so they can be output on a non-Postscript printer. Don't worry about the Web, though — PageMaker can handle them for HTML export. The PC extension is .EPS; the Mac file type is EPSF.

- **Illustrator:** Adobe has reintroduced support for its Illustrator format after removing it from PageMaker 6.0. The Illustrator format is supported by both Windows and Mac PageMaker for versions 5.0 and 6.0 of the popular Mac graphics program. The PC extension is .AI; the Mac file type is TEXT or EPSF.

- **CorelDRAW!:** The CorelDRAW! format is very popular on PCs, so more and more layout programs are starting to import it directly. PageMaker 6.5 for Windows supports this format, although PageMaker 6.5 for Mac does not. The CDR and CMX formats are the native formats used by CorelDRAW! and CorelDRAW! clip art, respectively. However, import support in PageMaker stops at CorelDRAW! version 5.0, even though CorelDRAW! is on version 7.0 for Windows 95 and version 6.0 for the Mac. The PC extension is .CDR (.CMX for clip art); the Mac file type is CDR3, CDR4, or CDR (CMX for clip art), depending on the version (CDR is for version 5.0).

- **DCS:** DCS, the Desktop Color Separation format, is another variant of EPS in which each of the four colors used in professional printing — cyan, magenta, yellow, and black — has its own file. These four files are then coordinated by a fifth file (the DCS file), which is what is actually imported into PageMaker. Don't worry about this format unless you want to print professional-quality, full-color graphics, which you won't do on the Web. The PC extension is .DCS; the Mac file type is EPSF.
- **Windows Metafile (WMF):** The Windows Metafile Format was the first Windows drawing format and is still common for low-end and midrange graphics programs. Note that WMF also supports photographic images. The PC extension is .WMF; the Mac file type is WMF.
- **PICT:** The Macintosh Picture format, PICT is the Macintosh equivalent of Windows Metafile. The PC extension is .PCT; the Mac file type is PICT.
- **DXF:** The AutoCAD Digital Exchange Format is used by CAD (computer-aided design) programs on PCs and workstations. The PC extension is .DXF; the Mac file type is TEXT or BINA.

- **CGM:** The Computer Graphics Metafile has some presence in the CAD (computer-aided design) market. The Mac version of PageMaker has more trouble dealing with this format than the Windows version, not recognizing as many varieties of the CGM format as the Windows version does. The PC extension is .CGM; the Mac file type is CGMF.

- **QuickTime Frame:** QuickTime is Apple's movie format, which has also become the top Windows movie format. PageMaker 6.5 can now import frames from movie files — you get to pick the frame during import. The PC extension is .MOV; the Mac file type is MooV.

Less-popular formats supported only in the Windows version of PageMaker include the GEM (Graphics Environment Manager) format that has been unused since the mid-1980s, the HPGL (Hewlett-Packard Graphics Language) format used on some plotting devices, the Lotus PIC format used to create charts in Lotus 1-2-3, and the WordPerfect Graphics format used within the WordPerfect word processor for charts and such.

If PageMaker doesn't support your graphics program's native file format (the one that's used by default), chances are that the graphics program allows you to save files in a format that PageMaker does support. For example, PageMaker cannot import the Photoshop format (PSD) but Photoshop can save images in TIFF, PCX, JPEG, EPS, and several other formats that PageMaker supports.

What to do before you import

In most cases, you can just import a graphic file as is, with no preparation. But in some cases, you need to do something special.

If you want to place files that were created on a Windows 95 PC into a Mac PageMaker document, you may need to rename the file first so that it does not exceed the Mac's 31-character file-name limit. And if you're moving files from Mac to PC, be sure to add the two- or three-character suffix (called an *extension*) to your Mac file names so the PC knows what kind of file it is. For example, a file called *New Web* on the Mac becomes *New Web.p65* on the PC. (The *.p65* part won't show up in the Windows 95 menus and windows — unless you override the Windows 95 View settings and tell Windows 95 to display them, as I prefer to do — but it's what Windows 95 uses to find the right icon for the file.) Use the file name extensions indicated earlier.

For images, the most important thing to do is to get rid of any extraneous information. For example, if the image area is 3 × 5 inches, and the bottom 2 inches are blank, crop out those bottom inches in your image-editing program before saving the file. Similarly, if you want only a portion of the image used in the PageMaker layout, crop out the parts you don't want (save the cropped file to a new name if you want to have a copy of the original file for use elsewhere).

Cropping is selecting the part of an image that you want to keep and getting rid of the rest — like clipping a photo from a magazine and throwing the rest of the page away. Most image-editing programs have cropping tools.

Cropping in PageMaker is easy, so you may be tempted to do the cropping there instead of in your image editor. But one good reason exists to crop the image in the original program: That 2 inches of blank space is actually a series of white dots. Those dots take up disk space and space inside the PageMaker file. When you crop in PageMaker, you're not changing the actual image file, just hiding part of it, and the hidden portion continues to consume disk space. Another advantage to cropping in the source program is that you are ensured that whoever does the layout has only the part of the image you want to be used.

Here are a few additional image preparation issues to keep in mind:

- **Color type:** If your source image is color and you will be displaying or printing your document in grayscale or black-and-white, convert the graphic to a grayscale or black-and-white image before importing it into PageMaker. (Again, save the altered file with a new name if you want to preserve the original.)

  You should convert the graphic before importing it for two reasons. First, the file will be smaller, which saves disk space and decreases print time. Second, while PageMaker can convert color images to grayscale or black-and-white images on its own, these transformations don't survive export to HTML (the language used to create Web pages), because the HTML export uses the original image, not the copy inside PageMaker.

- **Size and resolution:** For color and grayscale images, make sure that the image size is the same as it will be in your PageMaker layout. Enlarging or reducing an image can make it hard to read or just downright ugly. Enlarging more than 25 percent can result in very blocky images, while reducing more than 25 percent can cause distortions called *moirés*. When exporting to HTML, PageMaker converts your images to JPEG or GIF format, which can cause further distortion to the moirés.

- **Cross-platform TIFFs:** PC versions of TIFF are different from Mac versions of TIFF. Usually, PageMaker can detect whether the file was saved in a PC or Mac TIFF, and everything works fine. When PageMaker can't make this distinction, the symptoms are obvious: The image looks like a photographic negative. You can fix this problem by resaving the TIFF file in the final platform's format (Photoshop has this feature, for example) or by loading the TIFF file into another image-editing program and using its invert feature to make a negative of the negative, which changes the image back to normal. That version of the file can then be used in PageMaker.

- **Photo CD images:** When you import a Photo CD image, PageMaker displays a dialog box that lets you crop the image, change the image dimensions or resolution, sharpen the image, and rotate and flip the image. PageMaker also offers controls that let you adjust the brightness and contrast of 1-bit (black-and-white) and grayscale bitmap images (via Element⇨Image⇨Image Control), but these are ignored during HTML export. I strongly advise that you use an image-editing program such as Photoshop or Corel Photo-Paint to import, adjust, and export to TIFF format any Photo CD files you want to use.

The following information applies to drawings saved as EPS files, because those are the most complex. For other types of drawings, you really don't have to prepare anything ahead of time for import into PageMaker.

- **Colors:** If you defined colors in an EPS file created in, say, Illustrator or FreeHand, PageMaker imports those color definitions along with the file and adds them to the list of colors in the Colors palette (see Chapter 15 for more details).

  If a color already defined in your PageMaker file has the same name as a color in the imported EPS graphic, you'll see a dialog box asking whether you want to preserve the existing PageMaker color definitions or use the EPS file's definitions. Sometimes, neither answer is right — you want both. So make sure that you use unique names in PageMaker and in your drawing program. (For non-EPS drawings, this is not a problem because all colors in imported files are immediately translated to a mix of red, blue, and green and no longer have names.)

  Also, make sure that the color model used to create the color — RGB or CMYK — matches that of your output device. For the Web, that means RGB. See the sidebar "What's a color model, anyway?" in Chapter 15 for more information about CMYK and RGB.

- **Fonts:** EPS drawings that include text formatted with typefaces that are not built into your printer and installed and active in Windows or the Mac may not print correctly. The solution is to convert the text to curves in the drawing program before importing the file into PageMaker.

- **Previews:** EPS drawings from Macs may display as gray boxes or as a white box with the name of a file and creator at the top. This happens because an EPS file is actually a program that tells the printer how to draw the image. What you see on-screen is actually a bitmap preview, and the preview format created by a Mac program may not be PC-compatible or vice versa. Also, some older EPS files may not include a preview file at all. But not to worry, the file will print correctly.

Bringing Graphics into Your Layout

After you've prepared your image as described in the first part of this chapter, import it by taking the following steps.

PageMaker refers to the process of bringing a file into your layout and then positioning it on your page as *placing*. I tend to use the word *import* to refer to the process of bringing a graphic into your file and use the word *place* when referring to the PageMaker commands or when the focus is on the positioning of the graphic.

1. **Go to the page in your layout where you want to place the graphic.**

   Note that any graphic placed in a master page, described in Chapter 12, will appear on all pages in the document that use that master page.

2. **Change your view so that you can see the whole page or at least the area in which you want to place your graphic.**

3. **Select a text block or existing graphic, if desired.**

   If you want the new graphic to replace an existing graphic, click on the existing graphic with the Arrow tool to select it. If you want the new graphic to be an *in-line graphic* — one that moves with a particular piece of text — select the Text tool and click on the location in the text where you want the graphic to be inserted. (Think of an in-line graphic as a special character that happens to be a graphic.)

   Note that when you export to HTML, the in-line graphic will be separated from the text and placed either above or below it, depending on which end the graphic is closest to.

4. **Choose File⇨Place (Ctrl+D on Windows or ⌘+D on the Mac) to open the Place dialog box.**

   Figure 13-2 shows the dialog box. Sort through your drives and directories or folders to find the file you want to place and then click on the file name. Note that PageMaker displays only the files for which it recognizes the format *and* has the appropriate import filter installed.

5. **Choose a Place option.**

   The Place options in the lower-left corner of the dialog box change depending on whether you clicked inside a text block or selected a graphic in your layout in Step 3. If you selected a graphic with the Arrow tool, you can choose Replacing Entire Graphic in order to replace the selected graphic with the new one. If you don't want to replace the selected graphic, choose As Independent Graphic. If no graphic was selected when you began importing, As Independent Graphic is the only choice.

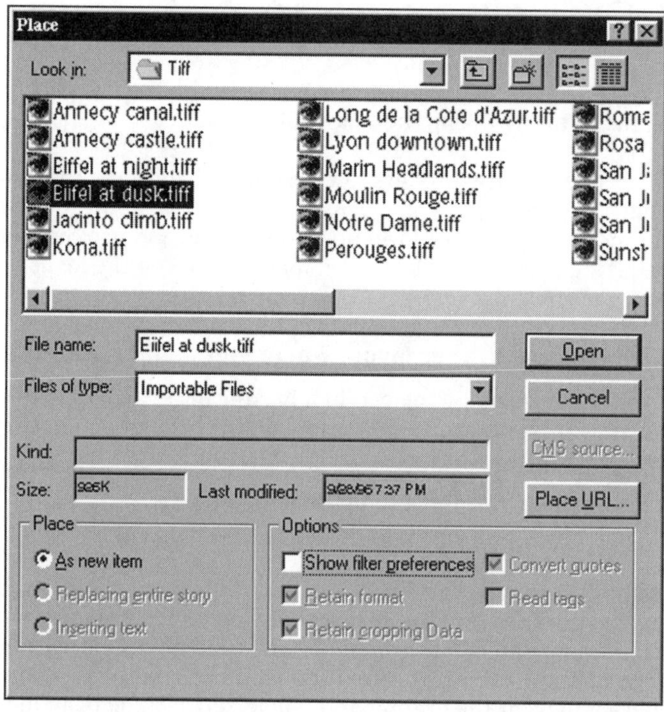

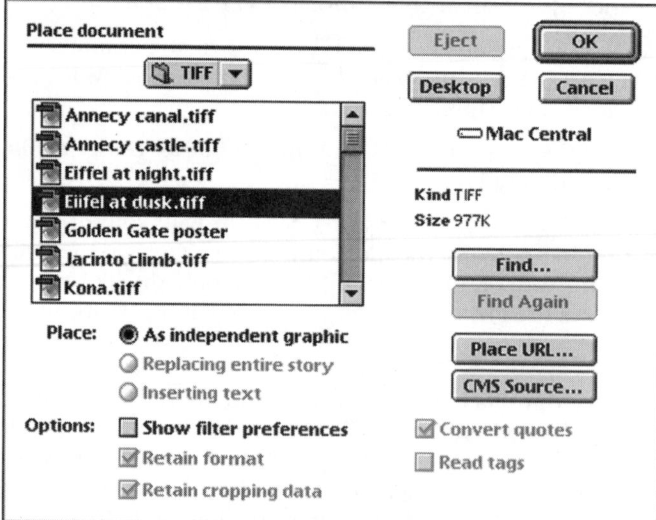

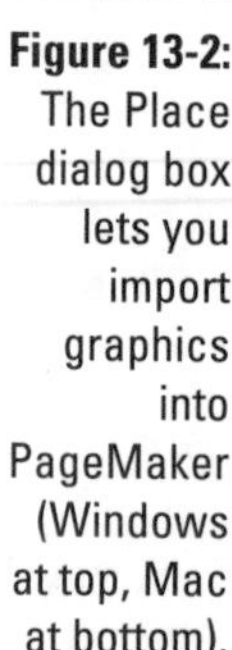
Figure 13-2: The Place dialog box lets you import graphics into PageMaker (Windows at top, Mac at bottom).

When you replace a graphic, any text wrap, sizing, or effects (such as rotation) that you applied to the old graphic are automatically applied to the replacement as well. Select the Retain Cropping Data check box if you want to apply any cropping you did to the current graphic to the replacement graphic. (Cropping is explained in more detail in Chapter 14.)

Remember that most special type formatting, such as text wrap and some sizes, don't survive HTML export, as Chapter 14 explains.

Note that all the Place options don't appear until after you click on the name of the file you want to import.

6. **Click on the Open button.**

   If PageMaker has trouble importing the graphic, it displays a dialog box telling you that the filter does not support the file format. Open the graphic in the program that created it to make sure the file is okay, and resave it before trying to import it again.

   You may also get a dialog box that says the file is very large and asks you to confirm whether to copy the graphic into PageMaker. Whether you answer yes or no, PageMaker places the graphic; by *copy*, it means bring a copy of the graphic file into the PageMaker file.

7. **Place the graphic if necessary.**

   If you choose the As Independent Graphic option, you see a small square icon that changes depending on the type of graphic you're importing. Figure 13-3 shows the various icons and the types of graphics they represent. The upper-left corner of the icon represents the upper-left corner of the graphic. Move the cursor to where you want to place the graphic and click the mouse button. Your graphic appears.

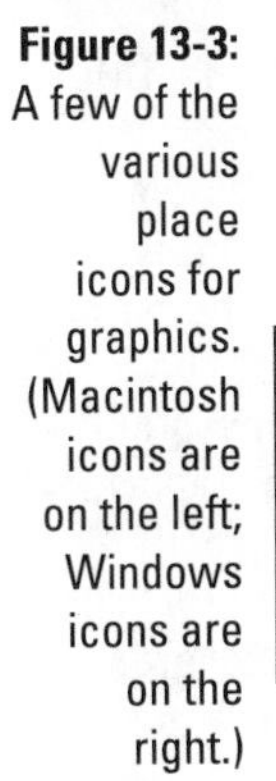

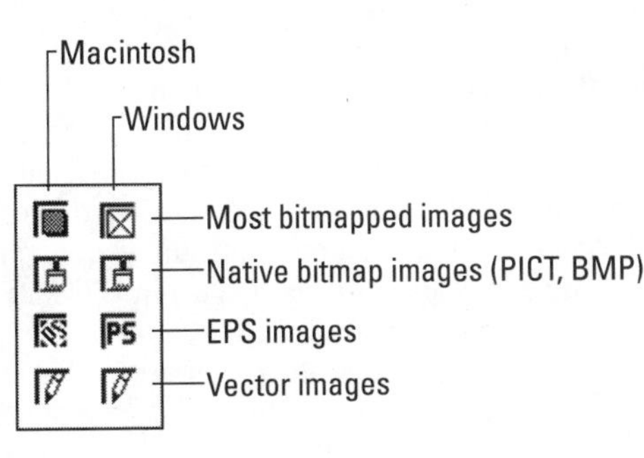

Figure 13-3: A few of the various place icons for graphics. (Macintosh icons are on the left; Windows icons are on the right.)

   If you chose As Inline Graphic or Replacing Entire Graphic, your graphic appeared at the spot you clicked with the Text tool or in the position of the graphic being replaced.

PageMaker has the ability to wrap text around graphics, so the text surrounds the graphics boundary, a pretty neat effect. In print, this can look terrific, but on the Web this effect is stripped out, leaving text to the side of, above, or below the graphic.

I recommend you set up PageMaker so text wrap is turned on as shown in Figure 13-4 (the two middle icons are selected). Doing so ensures that text falls above or below any graphic in its column, so what you see in PageMaker pretty much approximates how the page will look on the Web. To get the Text Wrap dialog box, use Element⇨Text Wrap, or Ctrl+Alt+E or Option+⌘+E. Make sure that no graphics are selected; that way the settings will apply to all future graphics.

Recognizing the Web's favorite graphics

No matter what kind of format an image is in when you import it into PageMaker, it is converted to one of the two standard Web graphics formats when you export your PageMaker document to HTML. Those formats are GIF and JPEG.

The GIF format is typically used for smaller images that don't have a lot of detail. The format is similar to PCX and TIFF in that it can be compressed, which is crucial for the Web. Because the Internet is getting clogged up and many modems are just plain slow, many computer users are getting increasingly impatient and don't want to wait a minute more than they have to for images to be displayed on their screens. Because GIF compresses well, it has become a Web standard. (Compression is built into the GIF format; you don't have to do anything special to make a GIF file compressed, unlike PCX and TIFF formats.)

Sometimes even a compressed GIF file is too large to work well on the Web. That's when the JPEG format is used. This file format is designed for maximum compression, which is achieved by eliminating some of the detail in your image. How much detail it tosses out depends on the image's complexity — sometimes you won't notice, and other times bluriness or blotchiness indicates where detail was removed. Because it's highly compressed, JPEG is the standard format for photographs and large images transmitted over the Web and embedded in Web pages.

When you export your PageMaker document (a process explained in Chapter 17) to HTML, PageMaker chooses whether to convert your document's graphics to GIF or JPEG automatically, so you don't need to worry about figuring out which of the two will display better or faster on the Web. During the conversion, PageMaker does not alter your original graphics files — it creates a new GIF or JPEG file for each image and links that file to the HTML page that's being exported. The PageMaker document continues to use the original graphics, in whichever format they were created.

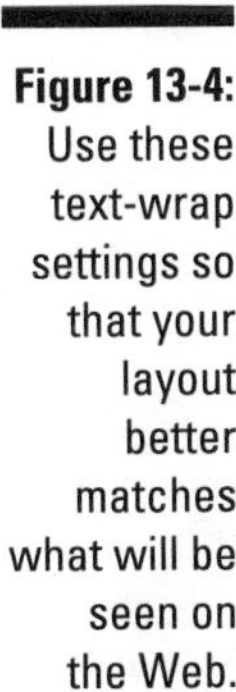

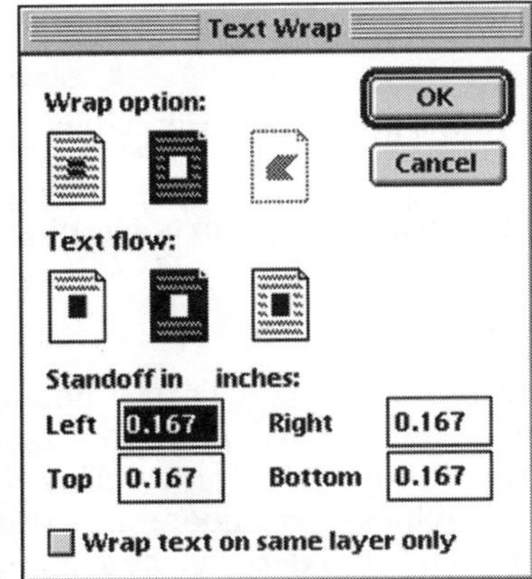

Figure 13-4: Use these text-wrap settings so that your layout better matches what will be seen on the Web.

Copying Graphics for Export

If you want to use an image in more than location in a Web document, you won't be able to copy the image with the standard copy and paste commands (Ctrl+C or ⌘+C and Ctrl+V and ⌘+V).

During HTML export, PageMaker exports only those graphics that have links unique to them (links are the tools that tell PageMaker where to find an original file during export). That means if you copy a graphic to be used several times in a document, only the original copy will be exported, in the location it was first imported into. (This happens only during HTML export. For print publications, you can copy and paste to your heart's content — each graphic copy prints properly. The same is true with Acrobat publications, which are described in Chapter 19.)

This export limitation has its exceptions:

- If you import a graphic that's relatively small in terms of memory from another program, and the entire graphic is copied into the PageMaker document, then multiple copies of that graphic can be exported to HTML. (Chapter 11 covers how to determine when an image should be copied in its entirety into your publication, rather than linked to an external file.)
- If the graphic appears on a master page, it is exported to each page that uses that master page.

You probably don't want to exit or minimize PageMaker to make copies of your graphic, each with its own file name, and then go back to PageMaker to import each one. Fortunately, you can do this task in an easier way:

1. **Place the graphic into your PageMaker layout as described in the section "Bringing Graphics into Your Layout."**

2. **Make copies and paste them wherever you want them to appear in your Web site's layout.**
3. **Do any fine-tuning and edits to the graphics as described in the next section and in Chapter 14.**
4. **Go to the first copy and select it; use File⇨Export⇨Graphic to export the image to a new file.**
5. **Be sure to give the file a new name. (*Untitled* is the default.)**

   Don't worry about changing the format (via the Format pop-up menu on the Mac and Save as Type pop-up menu in Windows) to something else, unless you want the image saved in a different format. This ability to save in a different format comes in handy as a poor man's translation utility, but is not needed for the purpose I describe here.
6. **Make sure that the Link to New Image option is checked, as shown in Figure 13-5.**

   If you check the Save Cropped Area option, only the part of the image displayed on screen is saved — this means anything that has been cropped out is removed from the export file. Of course, the original file is untouched.
7. **Click Save.**
8. **Repeat Steps 1 through 6 for each image that has been copied and pasted and was not copied wholly into the publication during import.**

This technique saves the copy as a new file and creates a link from PageMaker to that new file.

Creating Lines

PageMaker has a several graphics tools to create lines, polygons, ellipses, and rectangles. But only horizontal lines export to HTML, so put aside those other tools for your Web pages and save them for your printed publications.

Adding a line is easy: Click on the Orthogonal Line tool (|—)and then move your cursor to where you want to start the line. Click and drag until you've reached the point where you want the line to end and release the mouse button.

You can use the regular Line tool, (\ ) but unless the line is perfectly horizontal, it won't export to HTML. Hold down the Shift key when drawing a line to make it perfectly horizontal.

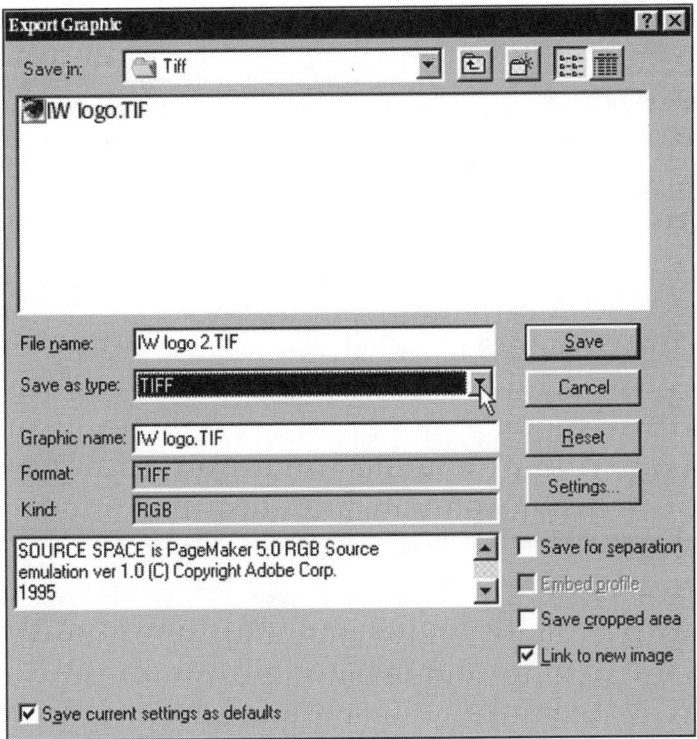

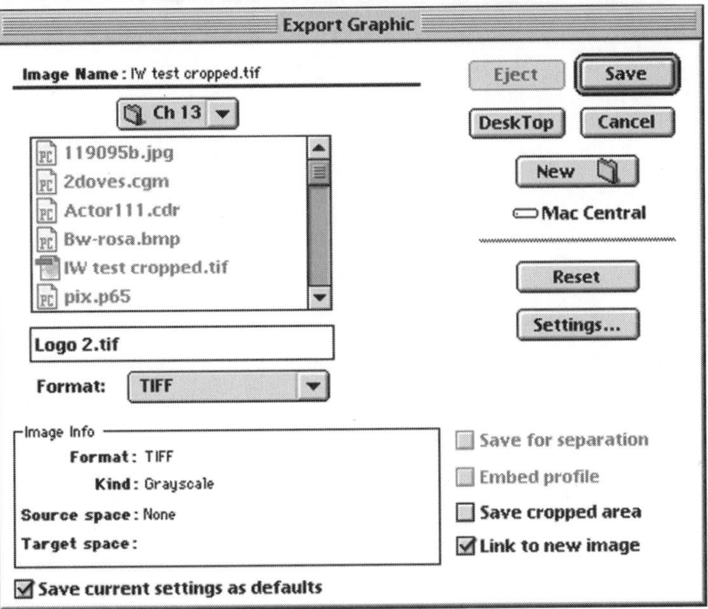

Figure 13-5: The Export Graphic dialog box is where you can export graphics to new files, a must for some graphics to survive HTML export. (The Windows version is at top, Macintosh on the bottom.)

For print publishing, you can draw lines in several different thicknesses (also called *weights*), but during HTML export all lines end up being the same weight (usually 1 or 2 points, although it depends on the browser). So don't worry about using Element⇨Stroke (or double-clicking the Orthogonal Line tool) to change your line weight. Just make sure that the stroke weight is set to 1 point, which you can easily see while doing your layout. If you set the stroke with no line selected, whatever weight you then pick will be the weight for all new lines in the document.

Chapter 14

Sizing, Shaping, and Other Final Touches

In This Chapter

- Resizing and cropping images
- Making elements align along a row or grid
- Discovering which graphics work for the Web
- Applying special effects
- Using Photoshop effects on TIFF images

Stop me before I use this cliché: A picture is worth a thousand words (oops, too late). Well, it's true, and it's also true that a picture can also make you want to *read* a thousand words — and whether you're publishing printed pieces or posting pages on the Web, that's at least as important as the visual message a picture conveys.

If you had a chance to wander through Chapter 13, you found out which graphics file formats you can use in PageMaker 6.5, how to import graphics into your layout, and how to copy images for export to HTML (the language that lets you develop pages for the Word Wide Web). In this chapter, you find out how to shape and size images to better fit your layout, plus you get a peek at the special effects PageMaker can apply to your images.

Sizing and Trimming a Graphic

When placed, a graphic is the same size as it was in the originating program. You may not like that size. Fortunately, you can change it. Notice the little black rectangles around the edges of the graphic. These rectangles are called *handles,* and you can use them to resize or crop a graphic. Figure 14-1 shows a selected graphic's handles.

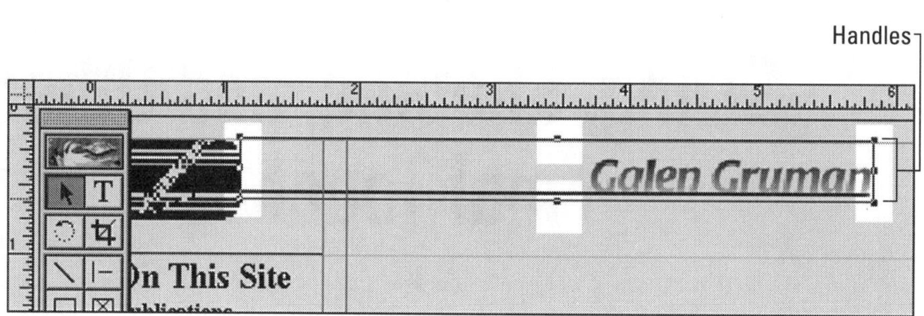

Figure 14-1: Resize or crop an image by using its handles, the square blocks displayed around a selected image.

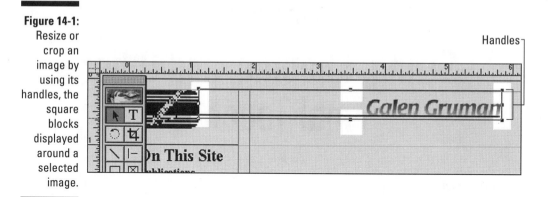

Resizing

To resize a graphic, select the Arrow tool, click on the graphic to select it, and then drag one of the graphic's handles. Dragging away from the graphic makes it bigger; dragging toward the graphic makes it smaller. Note that the handle you choose is significant. Choosing a center handle resizes the graphic in one dimension (the handles on the side change its width, while those on the top and bottom change its height). Choosing a corner handle resizes both dimensions.

Don't resize bitmap images more than 25 percent, or you may end up with moirés, or blocky images, when you print your document. Instead, resize your graphic in the program you used to create it or in an image-editing program.

You can easily distort a graphic by resizing it along one dimension or by dragging a corner handle at any angle but 45 degrees. Most mere mortals don't have the kind of coordination that's required to precisely calculate the angle that they're moving the mouse. Fortunately, a way exists to resize a graphic proportionally so that it does not become distorted: Hold down the Shift key while dragging. Be sure to release the mouse button *before* you release the Shift key.

Resizing by mouse makes a lot of sense when you're experimenting. But you can resize graphics more precisely by using the Control palette, as Figure 14-2 shows. If you know the degree of enlargement or reduction, you can specify it in the palette's W and H option boxes and have PageMaker apply it for you. Or you can enter the new dimensions or click on the Nudge arrows to the left of the W and H option boxes to change the values gradually, until the size looks right to you. A good technique is to use the mouse to do a rough resizing and then use the Control palette for fine-tuning.

Before entering resize values into the Control palette, you need to select a *reference point* by clicking or double-clicking on one of the handles (little black squares) on the Proxy button (circled in Figure 14-2). The handles on the button correspond to the points around the edge of your graphic. The center square corresponds to the center of your graphic. The selected proxy button handle appears larger than the others.

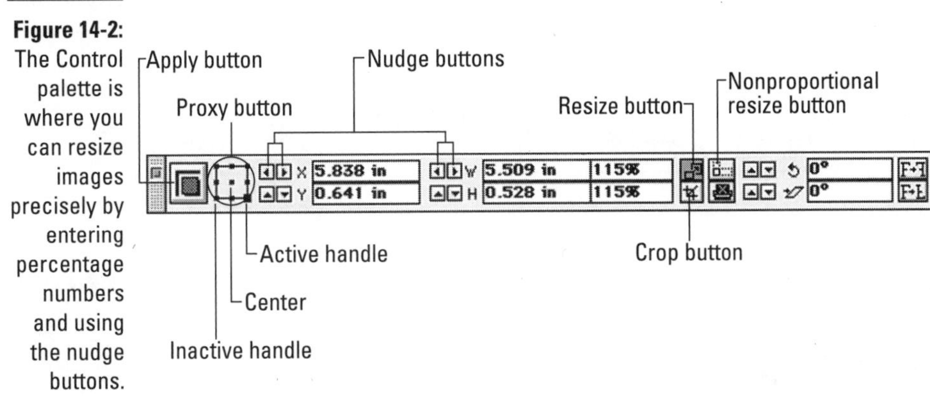

Figure 14-2: The Control palette is where you can resize images precisely by entering percentage numbers and using the nudge buttons.

- If you click on a handle in the Proxy button, the corresponding point on the graphic stays put as you resize the graphic.
- If you double-click on a handle in the Proxy button, it changes into a two-headed arrow, and the corresponding point on the graphic moves as you resize the graphic.

Try resizing an object by using both methods to get a feel for the way each works.

When you resize an image, the Resize button on the Control palette is automatically highlighted. But if you selected graphics with a tool other than the Arrow tool, it won't be. In this case, you can click the Resize button to change to the Arrow tool.

To the right of the Resize button is a button that indicates nonproportional resize (see Figure 14-2), which means that if you change one of the resize percentages (to the left of the Resize button), the percentage along the other dimension is unaffected. If you click on that Nonproportional Resize button, you get a different icon, a Proportional Resize button, that represents proportional sizing along the horizontal and vertical axes. Having this Proportional Resize button active is the same as holding the Shift key when resizing via the mouse.

Resizing lines is a process similar to resizing with other graphics. You can easily edit a line's length and position by using the mouse or Control palette. To resize by mouse, select the arrow tool, click on the line to select it, then drag one of its two handles. You can also use the Control palette, shown in Figure 14-3 to change line length (by entering a value in the box next to the L or you can use the "Nudge" arrows to the left of the L).

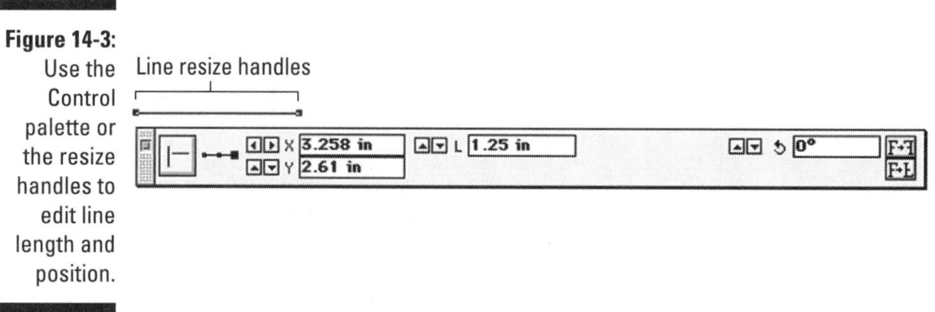

Figure 14-3: Use the Control palette or the resize handles to edit line length and position.

Cropping

Cropping eliminates part of a graphic that you don't want to print without affecting the original image file. To crop a graphic, select the Crop tool ( ) in the Toolbox, click on the graphic to select it, and drag one of the graphic's handles. Drag toward the center of the graphic to crop out part of the graphic; move away from the center to uncrop a previously cropped graphic.

If you don't crop the graphic exactly right the first time, don't panic. Remember, you're not actually deleting any of your graphic when you crop it in PageMaker; you're just hiding it from view.

Just as with resizing, the handle you pick determines whether the crop is along one dimension or two. Also, holding the Shift key while cropping ensures a proportional crop (although most crops are not proportional because you usually want to get rid of a particular portion).

If you like the size of your cropped image, but want to show a different portion of the graphic, place the Crop tool cursor in the center of the graphic, and press and hold the mouse button. When the hand cursor appears, drag to scroll around your image. When the portion you want to show is within the boundaries of the cropped graphic, release the mouse button.

If you prefer, you can use the Control palette to crop a graphic. Click on the Crop button in the palette (identified in Figure 14-2) and then click or double-click one of the handles on the Proxy button (also labeled in Figure 14-2) to set a reference point for your crop. Here is what you need to know about cropping via the Control palette:

- As with resizing, if you click on a Proxy button handle, the corresponding point in your graphic remains stationary during the crop. If you double-click on a Proxy button handle, the corresponding point moves during the crop.
- Click on the center reference point in the Proxy button to crop a graphic evenly from all sides. (In-line graphics can be cropped only from the center when you use the palette.)
- Note that when you use the palette for cropping, the percentage fields disappear — you can crop only by using the Nudge arrows or entering the crop values in the W and H (width and height) option boxes.

Working with Graphics as a Unit

Chapter 13 shows how to deal with graphics one-on-one. But you can also gang graphics together as a single unit, which really helps simplify your layout work.

Suppose that you've created a home-page *banner* (a standing element that runs along the top of a page) similar to the one in Figure 14-4 that is composed of more than one graphic. After getting all the objects arranged just so, you decide that you'd rather place the graphic at the bottom of your page instead of the top.

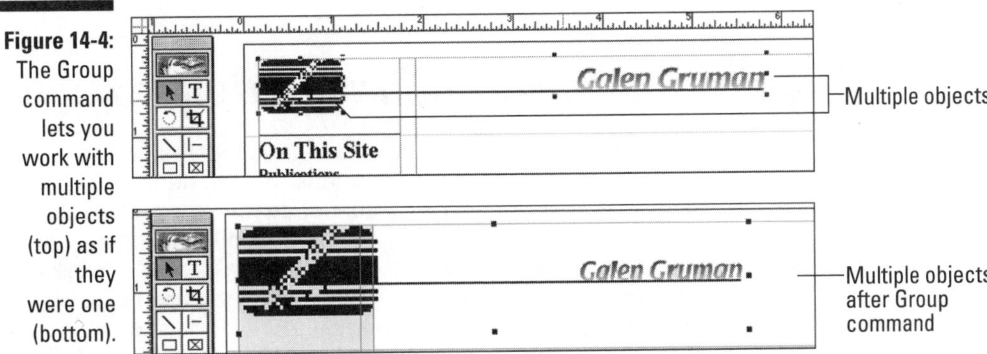

Figure 14-4: The Group command lets you work with multiple objects (top) as if they were one (bottom).

You can select all the components of the graphic by clicking on the first one and then Shift+clicking on all the other elements — or by dragging around them with the Arrow tool — and then dragging the whole kit and kaboodle down the page. But what if you change your mind later on in the day and decide that the thing looked better up at the top of the page instead? You'd have to go through the process of selecting all the individual elements again.

A better solution is to use the Group command. After you group all the elements in the graphic together, PageMaker treats them as a single entity. You can then easily move, copy, or apply special effects to a graphic without having to worry whether you've selected all of its components. One click on your graphic selects everything. You can group text blocks as well as graphics, or both.

To group elements, first select them by Shift+clicking on them with the Arrow tool or by dragging a marquee around them with the Arrow tool. Then choose Element⇨Group, or press Ctrl+G or ⌘+G. Notice how you have one set of handles for the entire group, no longer one per object. If you later want to ungroup the objects, select the graphic and choose Element⇨Ungroup, or press Ctrl+Shift+G or Shift+⌘+G.

In PageMaker 6.5, the Group and Ungroup commands are now part of the Elements menu (they had been in the now-defunct Arrange menu). The Ungroup command also has a new keyboard shortcut: Ctrl+Shft+G or Shift+⌘+G. (It used to be Ctrl+U or ⌘+U, which now opens the Fill and Stroke dialog box.)

- Just because your objects are grouped doesn't mean that you can no longer make changes to the individual components. You can select and edit an element in a grouped object by Ctrl+clicking or ⌘+clicking on it. Use the Arrow tool if you want to edit a graphic element and the Text tool if you want to edit text.
- If you resize a grouped object, press Shift during the resizing to ensure that the aspect ratio of all elements in the group remains the same.

Aligning and distributing multiple objects

Take a look at Figure 14-5. The page is part of a document trumpeting awards received by the outfit that just so happens to have published this book. What's so special about this page? Well, notice how the award logos align, as do the text blocks below them. To position elements like this, you can use the mouse and eyeball it — except that would take a lot of work and isn't usually accurate. Or you could use the Control palette and calculate the positions for each element — except that takes a lot of work, and few of us are that great at math anyhow. So what's left? The Multiple Paste command, that's what, which you get via Edit⇨Paste Multiple.

Here's a look at how this command works:

1. **Select and copy something.**

   To copy, just press Ctrl+C or ⌘+C. PageMaker sends the copy to the Clipboard.

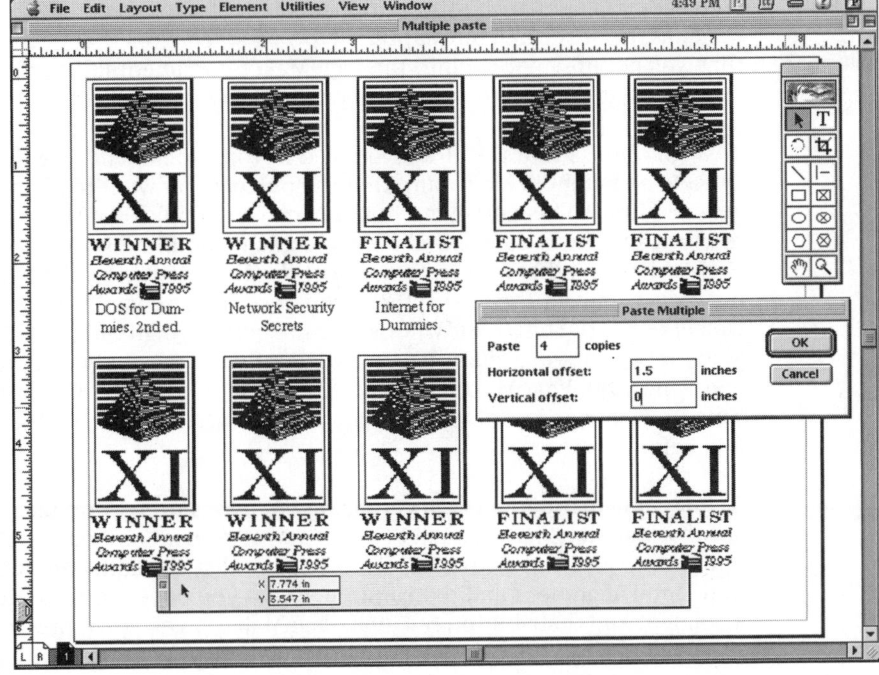

Figure 14-5: With the Multiple Paste dialog box, you can precisely position duplicates of text blocks or graphics.

2. **Choose Edit⇨Paste Multiple and specify how many copies you want pasted as well as the horizontal and vertical offsets.**

   The offset values tell PageMaker how far apart to space each copy. In the figure, the spacing is 1.5 inches horizontally but 0 inches vertically, which places the copies from left to right in a straight row.

3. **Click on OK, and the copies appear.**

Notice that in Figure 14-5 not all elements are the same. The text has been edited, of course, but also five of the images say "Winner" and five say "Finalist." How would that happen? Copy an image labelled Winner through the Multiple Paste dialog box and then select one of the images you want to replace with the Finalist logo. Use the Place dialog box (File⇨Place, or Ctrl+D or ⌘+D) to select the Finalist graphic and turn on the Replacing entire graphic option. PageMaker places the new graphic precisely where the old one was. Cool, huh?

You can use this technique any time you have a regular series of similar objects, even if they're different. One example is a stack of overlapping cards, where you may offset each card by, say, a quarter inch horizontally and vertically and then replace each of the copies with a different card — Queen, Jack, Ace, and so on. Keep in mind that on the Web any such overlapping is lost. The graphics would appear side by side or in a vertical series.

If you copy images with this multiple-paste technique, you need to update the links, as described in Chapter 13. Doing so ensures that each graphic that was not fully copied into the PageMaker document links to its own source image file and then exports properly to HTML.

To align objects that are already placed in your document, use the Align Objects command. (Make sure that the objects you want to align are selected first.) This command not only can align objects either horizontally or vertically, but it can also place a specified amount of space between each object — otherwise known as *distributing* objects. To align and distribute objects, select them with the Arrow tool and choose Elements➪Align Objects or Ctrl+Shift+E in Windows or Elements➪Align or Shift+⌘+E on the Mac (notice the rare difference in menu-option names between Macintosh and Windows). PageMaker displays the dialog box shown in Figure 14-6. Note how uneven the objects are on the page; that's why this command was invented!

At first glance, the Align Objects dialog box looks pretty complex, but it's not that bad. Basically, you get two sets of alignment and distribution options — one set for vertical alignment and distribution, and one set for horizontal alignment and distribution. When you click on the various alignment and distribution buttons, PageMaker gives you a preview to show you what each of the options does; just keep playing around with the icons until you get the look you're after and click on OK to apply your changes.

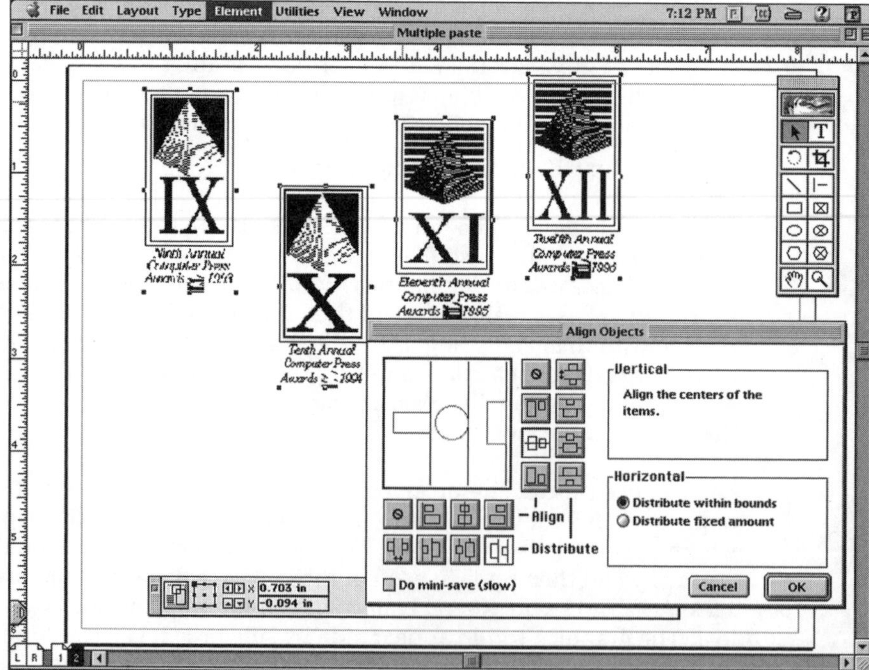

Figure 14-6: The Align Objects dialog box (in the lower right of the figure) lets you arrange multiple objects just about any way you wish.

You can choose *either* of the a horizontal alignment or distribution options for the selected objects, but not both. The same goes for the vertical alignment and distribution options. You can, however, choose both a horizontal alignment option and a vertical distribution option (or vice versa) for the selected objects.

If you choose a distribution icon, some additional options appear. If you choose the Distribute Fixed Amount radio button, you can specify how much space you want to place between each object. Just enter the value in the Space option box. If you choose Distribute Within Bounds, PageMaker places the objects an equal distance apart within the bounds of the selection. For example, if you're distributing objects horizontally, the leftmost and rightmost objects stay put, and the other objects are spaced out evenly between them.

An option called Do Mini-Save (Slow) is found at the bottom of the Align Objects dialog box. Check this option if you want to be able to undo the distribution or alignment changes you're about to make. (PageMaker's normal Undo command can't undo these changes.) If you don't like what you see after you align or distribute objects, immediately press and hold the Shift key as you choose File⇨Revert to restore your document to the way it looked before you opened the Arrange Objects dialog box. (By pressing the Shift key as you choose the Revert command, you tell PageMaker to revert to the last mini-saved version of your document, as explained in Chapter 8.)

Locking objects in place

It happens to the best of us: You spend an hour getting the various elements lined up on your page just so, and then you accidentally drag something out of place. Or worse, some editor or art director comes in and monkeys with your layout and wrecks the whole thing.

PageMaker has a feature to help prevent these ugly scenarios. After you get a graphic or text block positioned just so, select it and choose Element⇨Lock Position, or press Ctrl+L or ⌘+L. Your object is now stuck firmly to the page, just as surely as if you'd welded it there with Krazy Glue.

The Lock Position menu option was moved to the Element menu in PageMaker 6.5, now that the Arrange menu is history.

- To unlock an object, choose Element⇨Unlock, or use Ctrl+Alt+L or Option+⌘+L.
- When you select a locked object, its handles are gray instead of black. (The handle color may not be gray on some Windows PCs if the desktop color scheme uses a color instead of the normal gray.)

- You can't delete a locked object; you have to unlock it first.
- You can edit a locked object as long as your edits don't change the size or position of the object.

- To make sure that your locked objects stay locked, don't tell your editor or art director about the locking feature. Otherwise, they'll figure out that all they need to do to move your objects around is to choose the Unlock command.

Applying Special Effects

Up to this point, everything I've covered about graphics has been pretty basic stuff. Okay, enough of that. Here is where you find out how to create special graphic effects that will cause friends and coworkers to hang over your shoulder and wonder, "Just how was that done?"

But first, what doesn't work on the Web

PageMaker is chock full of special effects that let you flip, rotate, and slant graphics — effects known collectively as *transformations.* Before you get itching to try this stuff for your Web pages, I have to warn you that many transformations don't survive HTML export (but you can still use them to your heart's content for your print publications). The stuff that won't head over to the Web I won't explain in detail, but I can tell you which features to ignore so you don't waste your time on them for naught. These effects are covered in detail in the print-oriented *PageMaker 6.0 For Macs For Dummies* and *PageMaker 6.0 For Windows For Dummies* (both by IDG Books Worldwide, Inc.).

The following graphic effects evaporate during export to HTML and are best forgotten when designing your Web pages:

- Any graphics created with PageMaker graphics tools (rectangles, ellipses, polygons, and any lines except horizontal lines)
- Fills and patterns created in PageMaker
- Rotation
- Skewing (slanting)
- Mirroring and flipping
- Text wraps
- Masks, which are a way of cropping graphics behind irregular and elliptical shapes

- Tints (shading)
- Output screening (on gray-scale or one-color-tinted bitmap images)

What does that leave? A few neat ones, as you're about to see.

Distorting a graphic

By using the resizing techniques described earlier in the section "Sizing and Trimming a Graphic," you can distort an imported graphic by stretching it or contracting it nonproportionally. (The resized image can be exported to HTML sporting its new shape.)

As an example, look at Figure 14-7. The British flag at left has been copied and nonproportionally resized. It ends up in a stretched-out shape, which you could use as a banner to fill the top margin of a Web page about fish-and-chips joints or the lasting influence of Gilbert and Sullivan on musical theater.

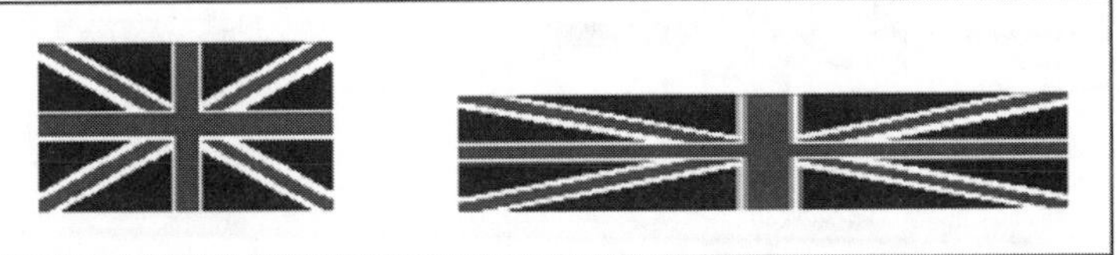

Figure 14-7: Example of a distorted graphic (at right).

Colors

If you import a black-and-white or gray-scale TIFF image or a black-and-white vector graphic image, you can apply a color to it: Just select the image and then click on the color you want it to be from the Colors palette. (Colors are covered in detail in Chapter 15.)

Photoshop filters

You can go way beyond colorizing your TIFF images. If you're working with an RGB, grayscale, or CMYK TIFF image, you can apply some of the same special-effects filters (also known as *plug-ins*) that you can apply in Photoshop, Adobe's popular image-editing program. *Filters* perform calculations that change how an image appears; they're called filters because they often remove certain kinds of data, such as colors or shades, or pixels aligned in certain directions.

Not all special-effects filters work with all three types of TIFF images. The one that's usually troublesome is the CMYK TIFF format, which you likely won't be using, because the Web uses RGB as its color model (and not CMYK as most professional printers do). Chapter 15 covers color models in more detail.

PageMaker comes with 47 special effects built in. To explore them, just do the following:

1. **Select your TIFF image and then choose Element⇨Image⇨Photoshop Effects.**

   The Photoshop Effects dialog box appears, as shown in Figure 14-8.

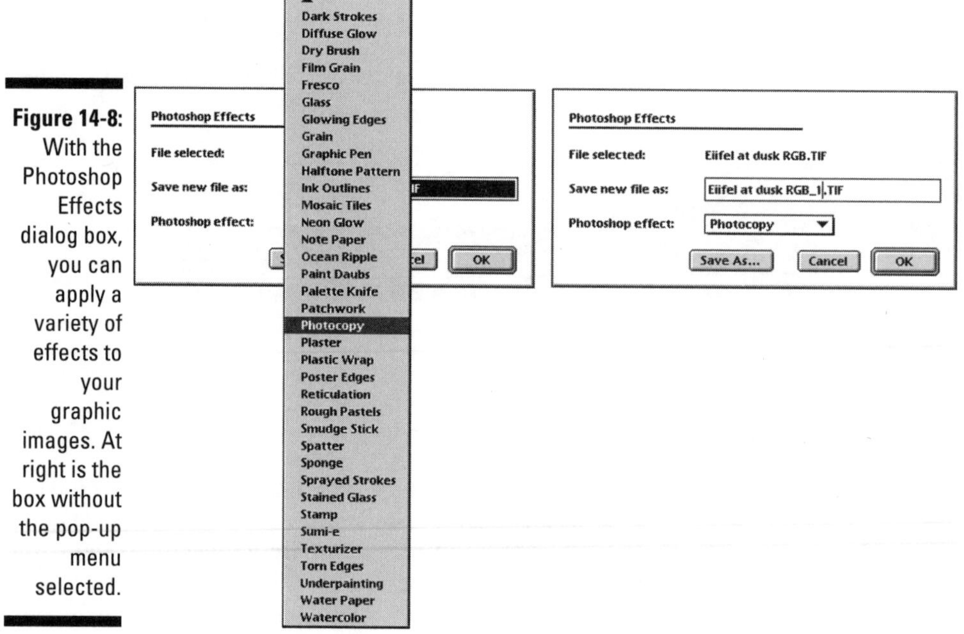

Figure 14-8: With the Photoshop Effects dialog box, you can apply a variety of effects to your graphic images. At right is the box without the pop-up menu selected.

2. **Create a copy of your original image.**

   You can't undo these special image effects. So applying the effect to a copy of your image rather than the original is best. To do so, just enter a new name in the Save New File As option box. (PageMaker automatically creates a new file name each time you apply a filter — the people behind the program clearly want you to leave your original as is. So if you don't like the effect, you can just import the original file back into your layout.) To store the image in a file other than where the original is stored, click on the Save As button, choose a folder, and click on OK.

3. **Choose an effect from the pop-up menu.**

   Experiment with the different filters and see what each one can do. But for now, just choose any effect at random. Then click on OK. PageMaker buzzes and whirs for a few seconds and then displays a dialog box similar to the one shown in Figure 14-9. Each Photoshop filter has its own dialog box with appropriate controls for that particular effect. The effect in Figure 14-9 was achieved through the Photocopy filter, which gives you Detail and Darkness *slider* options. A slider lets you control how strong the effect is.

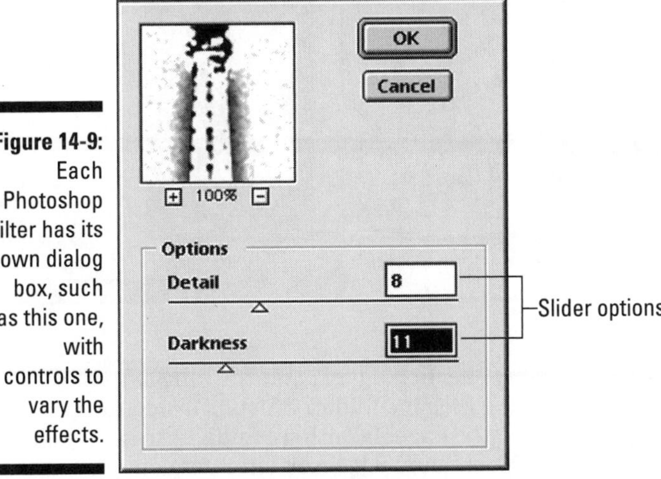

Figure 14-9: Each Photoshop filter has its own dialog box, such as this one, with controls to vary the effects.

   In the Photoshop filter dialog boxes, you can vary the range of the effects by adjusting the various slider bars and other controls. The dialog box and its options depend largely on what the filter is capable of doing. Most filters have a preview window that shows you what your image will look like if you apply the effect.

4. **Click on OK.**

   PageMaker makes some more gurgling noises and displays a progress bar and then finally displays your altered image. Figure 14-10 shows the results of two of the built-in effects, Photocopy (in the middle) and something called Craquelure, which applies an antiqued effect (on the right) to two TIFF images. (The originals are on the left.)

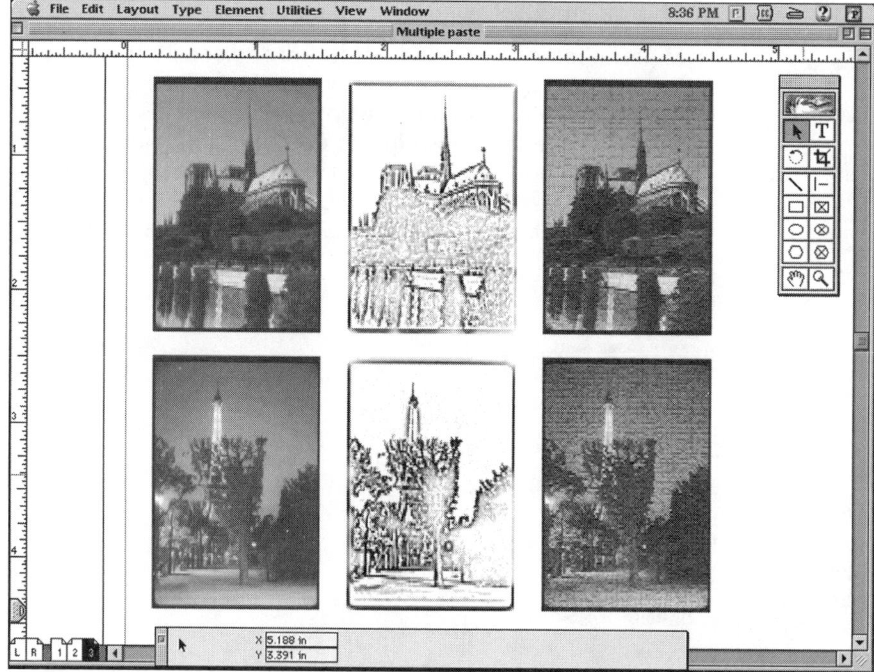

Figure 14-10: The original drawings are on the left. The others are Photoshop effects.

To install any additional special effects plug-ins, add the plug-in to the Effects folder, which is inside the Plug-ins folder, which is inside the Usenglsh folder, which is inside the PageMaker Rsrc folder. (Aren't treasure hunts a blast?) Or, if you own Photoshop 3.0.4 or a later version, you can create a shortcut — also known as an *alias* in Mac-speak — to the Photoshop Plug-ins folder. You can then access any of the filters in the Photoshop Filters folder. (If you need help creating an alias, see Chapter 3.)

Chapter 15

Let There Be Color!

In This Chapter

- Introducing color models
- Using the Colors palette to apply colors
- Defining your own custom colors
- Accessing libraries of colors
- Importing and deleting colors
- Using Web-safe colors

If you've ever had a printed document commercially reproduced in color, you know the process beats using crayons, but it's significantly more complicated and more expensive, what with color separations, film work, and press setup and running time. As much as you'd like to, you can't present your printer with a color printout and say, "There you go. Let me know when you've printed a thousand copies of that."

When you're publishing to the Internet, film, ink, paper, and presses simply don't figure into the publication equation. Color is still a big deal on the Web, but you don't need to worry about stuff like color separations, color matching, or color registration. You *do* need to know how to select and define colors for your Web publication, however. This chapter shows you how to use the colors available in PageMaker so that you can turn what would otherwise be a boring black-and-white document into a vivid Technicolor masterpiece.

A Primer on Color Models

You have loads and loads of individual colors at your disposal, but did you know that the entire Web and print spectrum comes from just a few colors? You may recall that in grade school you learned that you can make any color by mixing the so-called *primary* ones — red, blue, and yellow. For commercial printing, mixing these three colors doesn't produce such great results. Mixing blue and red ink, for instance, results in a blackish mud instead of purple.

So instead of using primary colors, commercial printers rely on four *process* colors: cyan (a greenish-blue), magenta (a deep purplish-pink), yellow, and black. This scheme of four colors is also known by the acronym *CMYK* (K is used for black so it won't be confused with B for blue). This four-color process allows printers to specify percentages of each color to cook up just about any shade you want (so says the theory behind this *color model).* This process involves color *separations,* in which pages are separated into their cyan, magenta, yellow, and black components. When the separations are combined during printing, you get the full-color effect.

Web publishing also employs a color model but, because instead of a printing press you have a browser and instead of paper you have a computer monitor, the color model isn't CMYK. Web publishing uses another model called *RGB.* The letters stand for red, blue, and green — the three colors of light that a monitor or TV uses to create all colors. With either the CMYK or RGB model, the color you want is produced by mixing the basic colors in the correct proportions.

Physics is a funny thing. Even when it comes to colors. Take the colors of printing ink. Light reflects off ink and the reflections combine to form colors. On a computer monitor (or your TV set), red, green, and blue light (the RGB color scheme) combine to form white light. A monitor "subtracts out" a percentage of these three colors to create all the colors you see. It's kind of like a prism. White light goes in one side, and a rainbow of colors comes out of the other.

When you select colors for your document, most programs (including PageMaker) ask you to choose the color model you want to base the colors on. Pick the one that your final output device uses to get the closest color match possible. If you're creating slides or preparing documents for distribution on the Internet, choose RGB. If you're printing on paper, pick CMYK. Be aware that the colors you see on your monitor and those you get on your printed piece may vary, because the monitor displays colors in the RGB model, while printers (except slide printers) use the CMYK model.

RGB and CMYK aren't the only color models. A company called Pantone is probably the best known supplier of premixed ink colors, which are called *spot colors.* (RGB colors are also considered spot colors, because once they're mixed they aren't separated at printing like CMYK colors are.) PageMaker provides access to the enormous Pantone Matching System (or PMS) color library. Spot colors often look very different on screen than they do in print, because monitors aren't particularly well-suited to displaying spot colors (a shade of blue, for example, may appear purple on-screen). PageMaker comes with a bunch of spot-color models, not just Pantone. Of course, for Web publishing what you see on screen is what counts, so this color-matching problem really isn't a big deal.

Defining color management

Computer monitors, printers, scanners, and other pieces of electronic publishing equipment all perceive and reproduce colors a little differently. Certain types of equipment can reproduce a broader range of colors than others. A color printer, for example, can produce fewer colors than a color monitor. Because of this fact, the colors you get when you print your document may not match the colors you see on your monitor.

A *color management system* — CMS, for short — compensates for the color discrepancies between the different pieces of equipment involved in publishing your document. A CMS keeps track of the range of colors that each piece can reproduce and makes sure that your on-screen image reflects the colors that your printer can actually produce. If your image contains any color that your printer can't handle, the CMS replaces it with the nearest equivalent color available from your printer.

PageMaker 6.5 is equipped with the Kodak Precision Color Management System, which is just one of several color-management programs available. If you choose File⇨Preferences⇨General, or use Ctrl+K or ⌘+K, and click on the CMS setup button, you can specify whether you want PageMaker to use the Kodak CMS, a CMS that you've bought from a different vendor, or no CMS. You can also specify what types of devices you'll be using to produce your documents, so the CMS knows how to adjust colors.

For Web publishing, your best bet is turn the CMS off. Even for print, it's best to turn off the color management option unless you're experienced with using color management software. You really need to worry about color management only if you're producing very high-end color graphics. If you work on both print and Web documents, and you encounter lots of problems because your on-screen colors and your printed colors don't jibe, ask a PageMaker guru or your service bureau representative for help in making adjustments to the CMS settings.

Dabbling with the Color Palette

Here comes the fun, hands-on part! PageMaker provides access to a few colors right off the bat. If you choose Window⇨Show Colors (or press Ctrl+J or ⌘+J), you display the Colors palette, shown in Figure 15-1.

The Colors palette in PageMaker 6.5 uses a new shortcut: Ctrl+J or ⌘+J, rather than Ctrl+K or ⌘+K as in previous versions. Ctrl+K or ⌘+K now opens the Preferences dialog box.

The palette initially offers ten color options, which work as follows:

- **[None]:** This first option removes any color that you've applied to an object in PageMaker. You can't use [None] as the setting for text if you want to get rid of the text color; you have to choose [Black] or [Paper]. If you apply [None] to an imported EPS graphic, the graphic's original colors are restored.

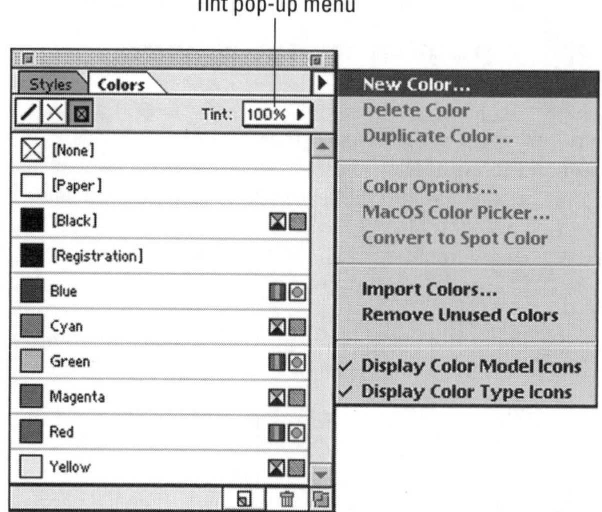

Figure 15-1: The Colors palette (shown in its default state) and its menu of options.

- **[Paper]:** This option represents the color of the paper. Essentially, this means white.
- **[Black]:** Black is the default ink. Use this color when creating black-and-white documents, spot-color documents, and process-color documents. In other words, you always need black.

- **[Registration]:** Text and graphics colored with Registration appear on all separations printed from PageMaker. This comes in handy for non-printing instructions or labels that appear on each color separation. For the Web, this is the same as [Black].
- **Blue, Cyan, Green, Magenta, Red, Yellow:** These colors are provided as samples of the kinds of colors you can create.

Incidentally, you may have noticed that some colors — [None], [Paper], [Black], and [Registration] — appear in brackets and others don't. The brackets indicate that the color is permanent and cannot be removed from the Colors palette. You can remove nonbracketed colors at whim.

Applying colors

To assign a color to a selected object, follow these simple steps:

1. **Select the element that you want to color.**

   Select text with the Text tool and objects with the Arrow tool.

2. **Specify how you want the color applied.**

   Generally, this means doing nothing.

For some of the objects that don't translate to HTML (the markup language that enables you to create documents for the Web), you can apply colors more discretely. For example if you drew a rectangle, you can have one color for the border and one for the fill. That's what the Line and Fill buttons, respectively, let you control before applying a color. (See Figure 15-1 for the buttons discussed here.) The Both button lets you apply one color simultaneously to both the line and fill. The PageMaker default is the Both button, which is fine for Web purposes.

If you want to apply a tint of color — for example, 20 percent red — to your selected text or object, select a tint percentage from the Tint pop-up menu. But remember that tints don't survive HTML export.

3. **Select the desired color.**

   Click on a color in the scrolling portion of the Colors palette. If you want to see more colors at a time, enlarge the palette by dragging down on its bottom edge. Of course, you won't have many colors to choose from until you add them as described in the next section.

Adding colors

Chances are you want to use more or different colors than the scanty basic set of default PageMaker colors. To add colors to your palette, choose Utilities⇨Define Colors, which gives you the dialog box shown in Figure 15-2. Then click on the New button. Or, try a faster method: Select New Color from the Colors palette menu (shown in Figure 15-1). Both techniques produce the same result: You get the dialog box shown in Figure 15-2.

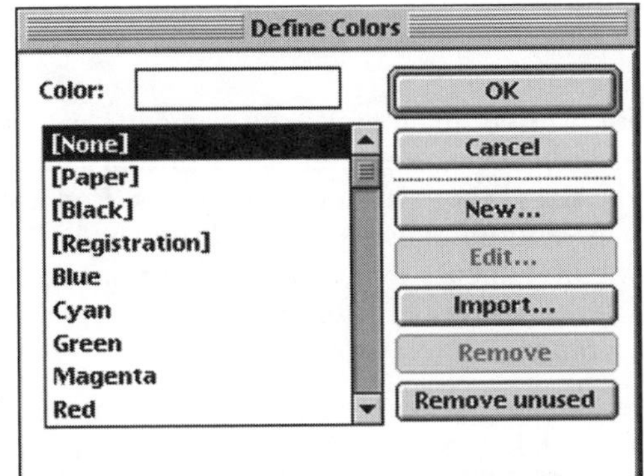

Figure 15-2: If you use Utilities⇨Define Colors, you get this dialog box en route to creating your new colors.

The Define Colors menu option has been moved in PageMaker 6.5 to the Utilities menu; the option had been in the Element menu in previous versions.

PageMaker next displays the Color Options dialog box, shown in Figure 15-3, which contains all the controls you need to create new colors, or edit existing ones.

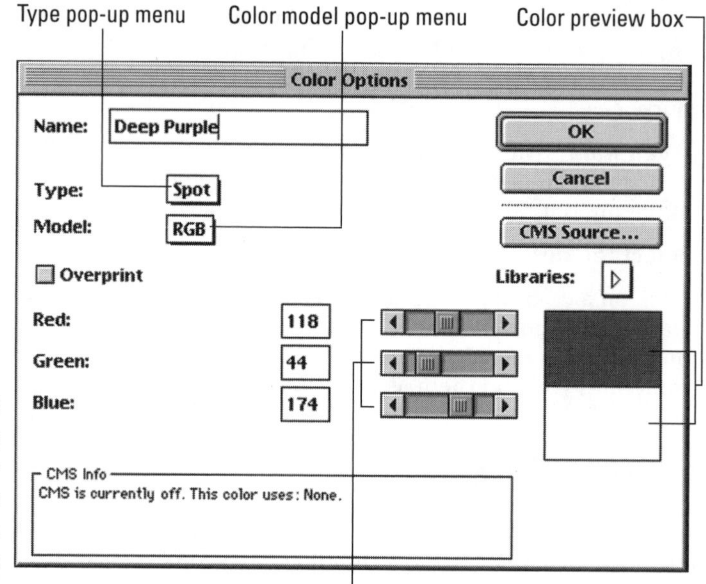

Figure 15-3: The Color Options dialog box.

To define a color, select a color model from the Model pop-up menu and then define the color by adding and subtracting primary colors. The *color model* determines what the primary colors are. You can select from three options:

- **RGB:** In the world of printed pigments, cyan, magenta, yellow, and black rule the day. But in the world of light, the primary colors are red, green, and blue. All colors mix to form lighter colors. Red and green, for example, mix to form yellow. Believe it or not! Choose the RGB model when you're creating documents that will be output on a slide printer or be distributed over the Internet or office network, where people will view them on their computer monitors.
- **HLS:** Here's a model you don't have to worry about. You may call this the television color model. You know those knobs on a TV that control tint, brightness, and color? Well, they work just like this model. HLS stands for hue, lightness, and saturation. *Hue* changes the color, just like the tint knob on a TV. *Lightness* makes the color lighter or darker, just like the brightness knob. And *saturation* controls whether a color is vibrant or a little diffused, just like the color knob. If you want to get to know these options, experiment with your TV set. But don't use HLS in PageMaker.

- **CMYK:** The printer's color model of choice! CMYK stands for our old friends cyan, magenta, yellow, and black —the process colors. Any time your publication is printing to a printing press or to any color printer than uses CMYK inks, choose CMYK.

You may have noticed some icons in the Colors palette to the right of the color names (back in Figure 15-1). The first column tells you what color model the color uses: the RGB icon indicates an RGB color, while the CMYK icon indicates a CMYK color. The second column tells you what the color type is: the Spot Color icon indicates a spot color, and the Process Color icon indicates a process color.

When you create colors in the RGB model, you get three slider bars in the Color Options dialog box (see Figure 15-3) — one each for red, green, and blue. If you set all three sliders to 255 (the maximum value), you get white. A value of 0 for all three sliders produces black.

If CMYK is selected, the Color Options dialog box displays four option boxes, one each for cyan, magenta, yellow, and black. To the right of each option box is a scroll bar. Move the scroll bar to the right to add a primary color; move it to the left to delete that color. You can also enter values between 0 and 100 percent in the option boxes. As you may expect, 100 percent is full-intensity color, 0 percent is no intensity, other percentages are somewhere in between. Remember that RGB colors mix differently than CMYK colors do —having all four values set at 100 percent gives you black, not white as it does in RGB.

For your Web pages, make sure that the Spot option is selected from the Type pop-up menu in the Color Options dialog box. For print publishing, select the Process option if you're sending your work to a commercial printer or using a CMYK printer.

The preview box in the lower-right corner of the Color Options dialog box automatically updates to reflect your changes. The top half of the preview box shows the new color you're creating. The bottom half shows the color that was selected, if any, in the scrolling colors list in the Define Colors dialog box.

After you mix the desired amounts of primary colors together, enter a name for your color in the Name option box. Then click on the OK button or press Enter to finish the job.

If you got to the Color Options dialog box through Utilities⇨Define Colors, PageMaker returns you to the Define Colors dialog box. You can now create more colors, edit them, and so on. Or you can press Enter to exit the dialog box. Your new colors appear in the Colors palette.

To add a new color to the Colors palette, you don't have to go through all the rigmarole of entering the Define Colors dialog box. You can enter the Color Options dialog box directly by Ctrl+clicking or ⌘+click on any of the [Black], [Registration], or [None] colors in the Colors palette. Because these colors aren't editable, PageMaker lets you add a new color instead.

Checking Out Color Libraries

The Libraries menu in the Color Options dialog box (in Figure 15-3) is a handy little thing. This menu puts a whole bunch of colors that have already been defined at your fingertips. If you want to import a predefined color from a library you've selected, just scroll through the library's palette of colors and then double-click on the one you want. All of that color's settings appear in the Color Options dialog box, and all that's left for you to do is make sure that the right Type option (Process or Spot) and the right Model option (CMYK or RGB) have been selected. Figure 15-4 shows the Color Picker dialog box that appears when you select a library.

PageMaker 6.5 comes with a color library designed expressly for documents being published to the Web. Color issues specific to the Web are covered later in this chapter.

Most libraries contain hundreds of colors, so don't expect to see all the colors at the same time. To locate a color, use the scroll bar at the bottom of the palette or enter a number into the option box.

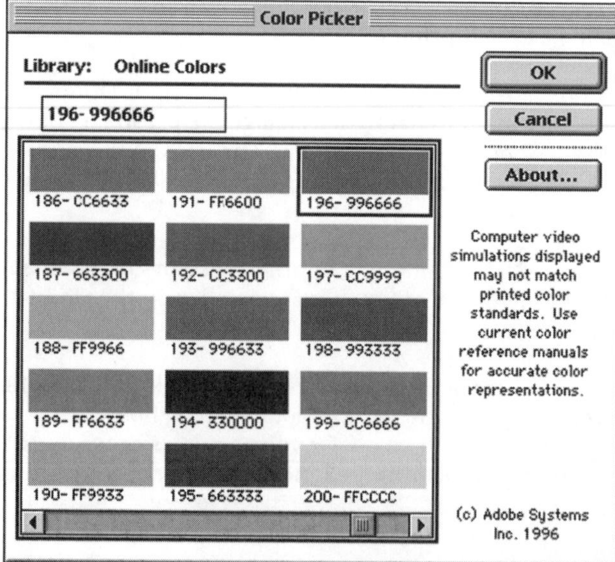

Figure 15-4: Color libraries can contain hundreds of predefined colors that are yours for the clicking.

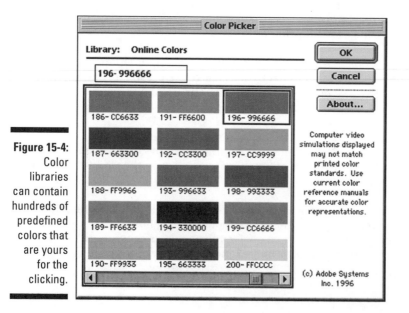

To add two or more colors at once, Ctrl+click on each color you want to select, or Shift+click to select a range of colors. For example, for the range of colors shown in Figure 15-4, click on color 196 and then Shift+click on color 200, which also selects colors 197, 198, and 199. Then Ctrl+click on colors 188 and 192, which selects each of those colors separately from its neighbors. To deselect a color, simply Ctrl+click on it again.

After you select the colors you want to import, click on the OK button to return to the Color Options dialog box and click on OK again to return to the layout window. All of your selected colors now appear in the Colors palette.

You can create your own color libraries by using the Create Color Library plug-in (access it through Utilities➪Plug-ins). You're asked for a name and a preferred number of rows and columns. The library includes all colors defined in the Colors palette — it's a great way to establish and save project-specific color libraries.

Changing Colors

After you create a color, that color is by no means permanent. You can edit a color long after you create it and, while doing so, change the color of all text and graphics to which the color has been applied. In this sense, colors are a lot like style sheets for text, enabling you to edit elements globally.

Suppose that you created a document using the colors Pantone 3385 Teal and black. After you've sweated over the document for several days, your boss says, "Gee whiz, this is great. But, I want something brighter, you know, something you may find in Oz. Yeah, that's it, I want Oz Green!" In the old days, you would have had to hire a hit man to knock off your boss and just hope that the next one was more open to teal. Nowadays, you can change the color of your teal items with almost no effort. Pick your preferred method of doing so:

- Choose Utilities➪Define Colors, select the color from the scrolling list, and click on the Edit button.
- Use the Color Options menu from the Colors palette's menu list.
- Save time and effort by Ctrl+click or ⌘+click on the color you want to edit in the Colors palette. Ctrl+clicking or ⌘+click bypasses the Define Colors dialog box and opens the Color Options dialog box directly.

- Double-click the color you want to edit in the Colors palette. PageMaker 6.5 opens the Color Options dialog box directly.

If you want to change a color by determining the new values yourself, just muck about with the CMYK or RGB option boxes and press the Enter key when you're finished. If you want to use a predefined color, select the appropriate collection from the Libraries pop-up menu, select one — and only one — color from the scrolling list and then click on OK twice to close all the dialog boxes. PageMaker changes your color and all elements colored with that color in less time than it took to read this sentence.

On the Macintosh only, a menu option on the Colors palette gives you the ability to edit colors quickly. Select an object, then select MacOS Color Picker from the Colors palette menu. You get the usual color wheel (the Apple HSL option) and slider bars (the Apple RGB option) common in Mac programs. Change the color and click OK — your color is now changed in your document. The keyboard shortcut — a real finger twister —to jump directly to the Mac color picker is Shift+⌘+click on a color in the Colors palette.

In addition to editing the appearance of a color, you can change it from process to spot or vice versa. To convert a color quickly, use the Colors palette's menus to change a color's type, rather than go through the Color Options dialog box.

Deleting Colors

The previous sections in this chapter introduce most of what you need to know about creating and editing colors in PageMaker. You may want to file away these tidbits to get rid of colors you don't want:

- To delete a color from the Colors palette, choose Utilities⇨Define Colors, select the color from the scrolling list, and then click on the Remove button. Or use Delete from the Colors palette's pop-up menu to remove the currently selected color. If the color is applied to some text or a graphic, PageMaker displays a message at the bottom of the dialog box to warn you that these elements will be changed to black. If that's okay with you, press Enter.
- If you've been experimenting with colors and now want to clean up your color palette, use the handy-dandy Remove Unused Colors menu option in the Colors palette. You can also use the Remove Unused button in the Define Colors dialog box (Utilities⇨Define Colors). Any color not applied to an item disappears.

Importing Colors from Other Documents

All colors that you create are saved with the current document. This means that colors created in one document are not necessarily available to another. To transfer colors from Document A to Document B, begin by opening Document B. Then choose Utilities⇨Define Colors and click on the Import button. (You can also use the Import Colors menu option from the Colors palette to do this.) Locate Document A on the disk and double-click on it. Then click on Open to return to the layout view. The colors from Document A are now available in the Colors palette.

If no document is open when you define or import colors, those colors that you define or import become the default colors for all new documents.

You can also import colors from EPS files. In fact, this is the default behavior. If you want to be certain that your EPS files' colors are being imported, make sure that the following two boxes are checked in the EPS filter dialog box: Add Process and High-Fidelity Color Names to Palette and Add Spot Color Names to Palette. To see the dialog box, make sure that Show Filter Preferences is checked in the Place dialog box when you import an EPS file. The filter dialog box appears as the graphic imports.

Specifying Colors for the Web

Color "printing" is pretty much a given on the Internet. (When was the last time you saw a monochrome monitor?) Colors on a computer screen and colors on paper are two separate breeds, and this section explains some peculiarities about using color in Web publishing.

How many colors can I use?

How do you pick colors that are guaranteed to look the way you want them to on the Web? The answer is in the Online color library that comes with PageMaker 6.5 (on the Mac, this feature is called Online Colors).

While your monitor can probably display thousands, if not millions, of colors (especially if it's beefed up with a graphics card running 16-bit, 24-bit, or 32-bit color), you have no idea what kind of monitor your reader has. Plus, the GIF graphic image format (the kind commonly used on the Web) has a palette limited to a fixed set of 256 specific colors. (The people who created the GIF standard decided to stick with 256 colors — also known as 8-bit color — because practically every computer sold since 1987 supports at least this many colors.) Because PageMaker exports your images to the GIF format (as well as the more color-rich JPEG graphic file format, which supports thousands of colors), you should get in the habit of sticking within the safe-and-certain Online color palette.

The Web palette in Windows 95 is actually limited to 216 specific colors, because Windows reserves 50 colors to use for its operating system interface. If you have ever changed your monitor's desktop colors via the Display control panel, you've selected one of those 50 colors. Because those desktop colors can be also changed by users on their computers, you want to avoid using those colors in your Web page. You have no clue how they may end up looking on the Web.

The creators of Web browsers such as Netscape Navigator and Microsoft Internet Explorer decided right from the start to support just 216 colors. While all 256 colors are available on the Mac (you can't redefine colors for the desktop's appearance), chances are you have both Windows- and Mac-based readers of your Web pages and, even if you didn't, the Mac browsers are designed with the same 216-color limit as their Windows counterparts. The PageMaker 6.5 Online library takes the safe route and offers only the colors that are guaranteed to work on both Windows and Mac.

If you do use colors beyond the 216 tried-and-true ones, not to worry. Web browsers substitute the nearest match from the 216 colors they support. (And, if you are using a browser that supports more than the specified 216 colors — for example if you're using the new Web-TV products or a specialized computer system such as UNIX — the browser also picks the nearest match from the colors it supports.)

Nothing's stopping you from using any other colors in your page (such as for text), but they'll probably shift to the closest one of the 216 Web-safe colors anyhow, so you may as well make use of the Online color library and eliminate some surprises.

Where can I use colors?

Because the Web doesn't always use the full range of PageMaker formatting and design capabilities (a subject covered in previous chapters of this book), you may wonder when it's worthwhile to specify color, or when you may as well just leave it alone. You can apply color to the following elements; the colors will be retained when the PageMaker file is exported to the Web's HTML format:

- Text
- Gray-scale and black-and-white TIFF files
- Black-and-white EPS files and other vector graphic files

Color graphics imported into PageMaker from another program retain the colors applied to them in the program in which they were created. You can't change their colors by attempting to apply a color to them in PageMaker.

No matter what the sources are for the colors in your Web page document — a color image imported into PageMaker, or text or black-and-white images colored within PageMaker — your Web-site readers see colors only as accurately as their Web browsers can display them.

Part VI
Weaving a Web Page

"HONEY! OUR WEB BROWSER GOT OUT LAST NIGHT AND DUMPED THE TRASH ALL OVER MR. BELCHER'S HOME PAGE!"

In this part . . .

This part of the book covers Web-specific stuff and how it fits into the world of publishing with PageMaker (and how PageMaker 6.5 deals with some of these strange new Web-publishing functions). This may be foreign territory for you, and it may even be why you bought this book in the first place.

The new Web-publishing tools in PageMaker are pretty neat, but the truth is PageMaker alone often isn't enough to create snazzy Web pages. With that in mind, this part of the book covers how to create hypertext links (using the foreign, sometimes invisible coding that Web browsers feed on and that lets you skip from Web page to Web page in a click). You also find out about tweaking your pages in an HTML editor.

If you want to produce Web pages that look as good as the printed thing, take advantage of a helpful partner that comes packed inside your PageMaker 6.5 box. With the Adobe Acrobat 3.0 software that comes with PageMaker 6.5, you can create online documents that have the appearance of typographically rich printed pieces. But don't jettison HTML — it has its benefits, too. HTML? PDF? Which is which? How do you pick? You'll just have to keep on reading.

Chapter 16

Hop to It! Creating Hypertext Links

In This Chapter

- Selecting online preferences
- Using the new hyperlinks palette
- Setting up hyperlink sources and destinations
- Making changes to hyperlinks
- Importing hyperlinks from other places

Links. Hyperlinks. Hypertext links. Whatever you call them, they're what give you the ability to traverse the Internet with a click, skip, and a jump. If you've ever spent much time reading documents on a computer screen, you can appreciate how indispensable hyperlinks are to navigating the millions of pages on the World Wide Web. Just click into a hyperlink, wait a few moments, and bingo! The information you want materializes on screen for you. See another link for a topic that interests you? Click again and you jump to another new page. You can cover more new territory more quickly than a foreign diplomat flying a Concorde jet.

When a viewer on the Internet clicks on a word or phrase designated as a line of hypertext, the on-screen display "hops" to related subject matter somewhere else in the document, or to another page on the same Web site, or to a page located anywhere else in the world on another Web server.

Hyperlinks are easy to spot on a Web page, as they should be. They typically appear as a bit of text highlighted in color (usually blue), and underlined so that people with grayscale monitors can also recognize them. (Graphics, boxed off Web-style in blue or some other color, can also perform double-duty as both illustrations and hyperlinks.)

The formal name for a spot on a Web page that connects you to other Web pages is *hypertext link,* but most people simply call them links. I use the term *hyperlinks* in this book because the word *link* in PageMaker refers to the relationship between imported text or graphics and their original sources (links are described in Chapter 11).

Hyperlinks are not new to PageMaker. Version 6.0 had basic hyperlink and HTML export capabilities but, frankly, they were grafted onto the program, almost as an afterthought. Version 6.5 does it right, with a redesigned HTML export capability, the ability to import URLs (Internet addresses) directly, and more sophisticated, better-integrated hyperlink-management tools. The enhancements to HTML support from PageMaker 6.0 to PageMaker 6.5 are so extensive that you should simply forget any PageMaker 6.0 HTML stuff you know and think of Version 6.5 as an introduction to HTML for the Web.

The previous chapters of this book give you the lowdown on how to put together a Web-worthy PageMaker layout. This chapter tells you how to add hyperlinks to your document to make it perform like a publication destined for the Internet.

Setting Up Hyperlink Preferences

Before you leap into adding hyperlinks to your document, you have to get yourself set up properly, which makes the process much more efficient when you get into the thick of creating your Web pages.

First, you need to select some preferences for working online. (Your *online* work consists of those documents that people read on their computers, as opposed to reading off of a sheet of paper.) To do this, select File⇨Preferences⇨Online and the new Online Preferences dialog box appears, as shown in Figure 16-1. You can set up your preferences once (with no documents open to make the settings the default for all new documents) and forget about them from there on out.

The following are my highly recommended settings for the Online Preferences dialog box:

- The top two boxes in the dialog box should always be checked.

  The first option, Outline Link Sources When Hand Tool ( ) Is Selected, ensures that any time the grabber-hand tool is active in your PageMaker layout, the hyperlinked items display boxed off and in blue so you can find them easily. To see the hyperlinks, the grabber hand tool must be selected. Figure 16-2 shows the effect of this. (The hyperlink always appears in blue unless a browser has been configured by the user to display a different color, or if you manually override the link color, as explained in Chapter 22.)

  You may notice that the cursor (or pointer, in Mac speak) in Figure 16-2 looks a little different than the regular Hand cursor. When you pass over a hyperlink, the cursor changes from an open hand ( ) to a pointed index finger ( ). If you click on the hyperlink with the pointed finger, PageMaker jumps you to the appropriate destination within your PageMaker document — just as if you were online!

Figure 16-1: Use this dialog box to set up your default online preferences.

The second option, Center Upper-Left of Anchor When Testing Hyperlinks, places the upper-left corner of a hyperlink destination front and center on your screen. This makes it easy to see if a link jumps the reader to the correct destination within your document. (Once your pages are exported from PageMaker to the Web, the location of the destination hyperlink is based on the reader's browser-display settings.)

- Most of the options in the URL information portion of the dialog box are best left to your network administrator (these options establish the network connection information that PageMaker, as well as your browser, use to access the Internet). You should nevertheless set the Download to Folder information, because that's where PageMaker puts any Web pages you download from the Internet for import into PageMaker (using the new PageMaker 6.5 ability to import Web pages).

If you have to set up the rest of the URL information, you must access your browser's configuration dialog box(es). In Microsoft Internet Explorer, for example, go to View⇨Options⇨Connections⇨Settings. Unless your Internet service provider or network administrator tells you otherwise, leave the Ports setting at 80. (If you use Netscape Navigator 1.1 or later, PageMaker doesn't require you to enter this information.)

- If you want to be able to access the Web from within PageMaker to test your hyperlinks as you do your layout, enter the name of the browser you're using in the Web Browser field (or use the Browse button to find the browser program you have on your hard drive, then click on its name).

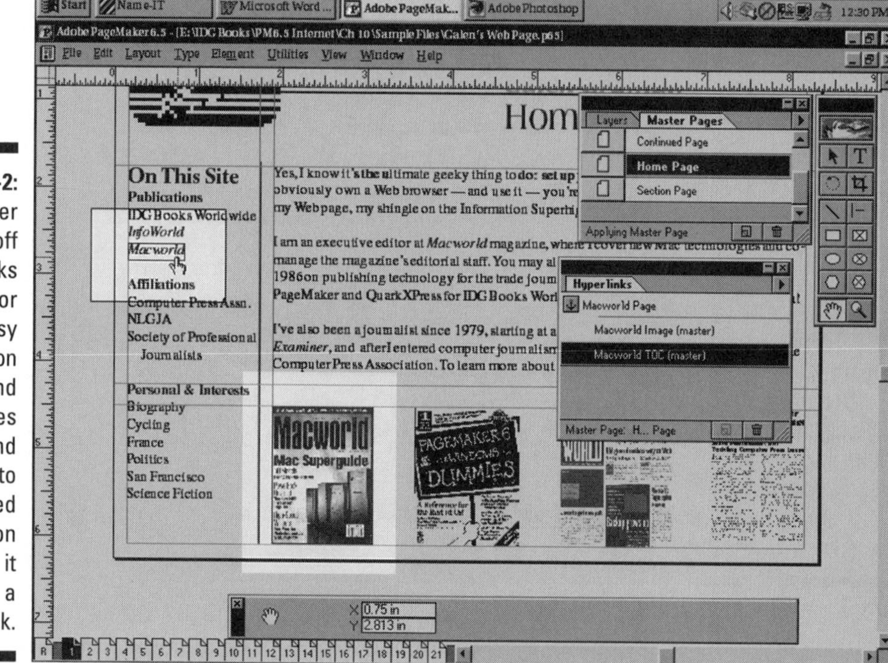

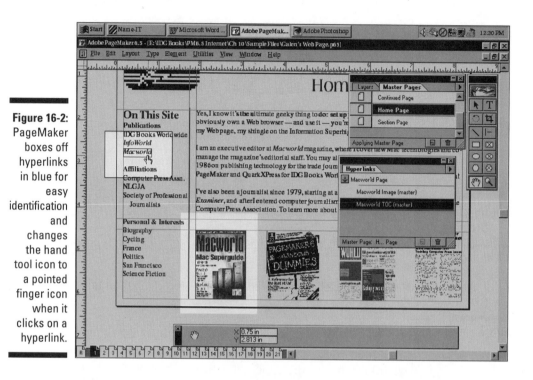

Figure 16-2: PageMaker boxes off hyperlinks in blue for easy identification and changes the hand tool icon to a pointed finger icon when it clicks on a hyperlink.

When you test your hyperlinks, PageMaker launches your browser and displays the page — assuming your online preferences in PageMaker are set correctly and you have a browser that can connect to the Web through your network or modem. You get an error message if the browser can't be launched or the Internet can't be accessed.

Creating Hyperlinks

In fine hyperlink fashion, you probably skipped to this part, already jumped ahead to the stuff on how to make changes to your hyperlinks, and then flipped over to the sidebar on URLs. Or, maybe you're a good, old-fashioned, one-page-at-a-time reader, in which case you're about to find out how to create hyperlinks.

Displaying the new hyperlinks palette

Just about all the commands you need to create and manage hyperlinks are in this palette, so expect to become best buddies with it. Select Window➪Show Hyperlinks to display the Hyperlinks palette, or use the shortcut Ctrl+9 (in Windows) or ⌘+9 (on the Mac). Figure 16-3 shows the palette with its menu options displayed.

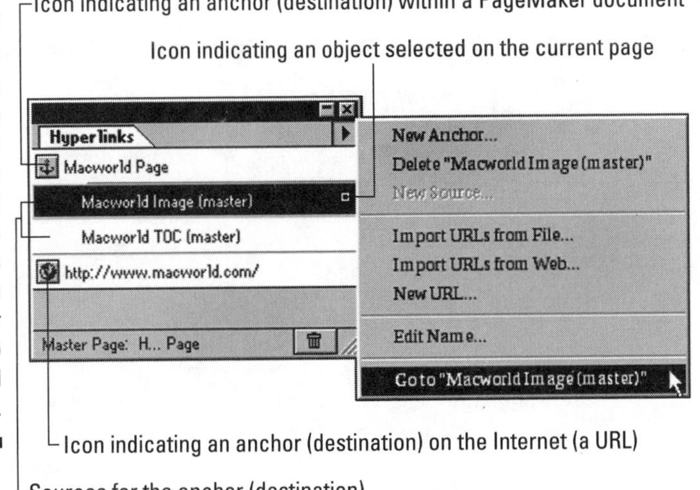

Figure 16-3: The Hyperlinks palette lets you create and manage hyperlinks within PageMaker or to external URLs.

Hyperlinks allow readers of your Web pages to jump from one item of interest to another without have to go on an endless scrolling search through screen after screen and file after file. Each hyperlink has a *destination* (the place you are hyperlinking to; also called an *anchor* in PageMaker) and a *source* (the clickable word or image of the hyperlink). In PageMaker, you can mark an object as one or the other: as an anchor or as a source. You can see both in the Hyperlinks palette in Figure 16-3, which arranges items by anchors first and then by the sources linked to them.

The small square to the right of a source or destination name in the Hyperlinks palette indicates that the hyperlinked object is selected on the current page.

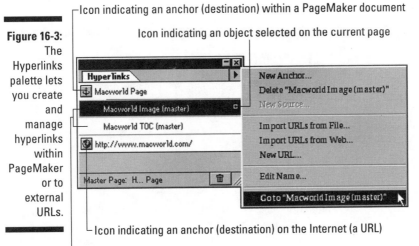

Linking to destinations

Establishing an object as a hyperlink destination or hyperlink source is a fairly easy process. In PageMaker, you have to first set up your destinations. An *anchor* is a destination within your PageMaker publication — another page in your current document, for example. An anchor can also be a destination on a different Web site.

To set up external destinations, you have to define a URL. (That's the fancy term for an Internet address. For more information, see the nearby sidebar, "Deciphering the URL.") As shown in Figure 16-3, PageMaker uses two different kinds of icons to indicate which destination you're working with — an anchor within the PageMaker document or a URL anchor.

Deciphering the URL

The Internet is full of acronyms (like WWW). Here's another: URL, usually pronounced as "you are el" and sometimes like "Earl." Whichever way you say it, URL means Uniform Resource Locator, and it's the unique address for a page or file on the Internet. The URL has several components.

On the Web, most URLs start with the *protocol indicator* (or prefix) `http://`, often (but not always) followed by `www`. The `http://` stands for *HyperText Transfer Protocol*, which tells the Web browser that it's dealing with hypertext. You may also see prefixes such as `ftp://` for File Transfer Protocol (used for software library locations) and `gopher://` (used for connecting to Internet search tools). The `www.` code means, of course, *World Wide Web*, but some addresses use `www2.` (the Web is filling up!) or no code at all.

Following the prefix is the *domain* (also called the *host name)*. Here are a couple of examples: `www.pcworld.com` or `www.idgbooks.com`. A domain is the site's main address — sort of an online equivalent of a building number and street name.

The domain can also be divided into directories (or sections), such as `pcworld/may1997/`. Think of them as floors or sections in a building. You can have several directories, with each subsequent directory being a subdirectory of the previous directory. The last directory in a sequence is followed by a closing slash (/), for example `/may1997/extra/`.

Finally, the URL can also include the names of actual pages in a document or names of files, such as `/extra/industrynews.htm`. The suffix `.htm` (common for PC-generated pages) or `.html` (common for Mac-generated pages) indicates an HTML page, as opposed to, for example, `.exe` for a program file or `.pdf` for an Acrobat file.

String it all together, and you get a URL that ends up reading something like this: `http://www.pcworld.com/may1997/extra/industrynews.htm`.

Each of those chunks of underlined (and usually blue) text and the boxed graphics (also usually in blue) you see in a Web page are connected to a URL; clicking into them tells your browser to load the information resource from a specific URL onto your computer.

Whenever you enter a URL to create a hyperlinks destination, remember to type it exactly as it should appear — just one typo means the link won't work.

You can have multiple sources pointing to an anchor (destination), but a single object (selected text or graphic image) can be a source to only one anchor (destination). Otherwise, if an object could be associated with multiple sources, your browser wouldn't know where to go when you click on a hyperlink!

The following steps tell you how to establish an object as an anchor (a destination within your PageMaker document):

1. **Select the destination object.**

   Select any graphic or piece of text from your PageMaker document that you want the reader to jump *to* when they click on the source hyperlink. If you want them at the top of the destination page, select a graphic in that spot or select the page's heading. If you want them to go to a specific place on the page, select a graphic or piece of text within that place.

   To select a graphic, click on it with the Arrow tool. To select text, use the Text tool to highlight a part of the destination text (selecting a few characters is sufficient).

2. **Select the New Anchor menu option from the Hyperlinks palette by clicking on the palette's right-pointing triangle (see Figure 16-3).**

3. **Enter a name for the anchor in the dialog box that appears (shown in Figure 16-4).**

   Enter a descriptive name. Otherwise, your Hyperlinks palette will be jammed with the names of dozens of destinations and you won't have a clue as to what they're about. In this example, the name indicates that this anchor leads me to a page about IDG Books.

4. **Click OK.**

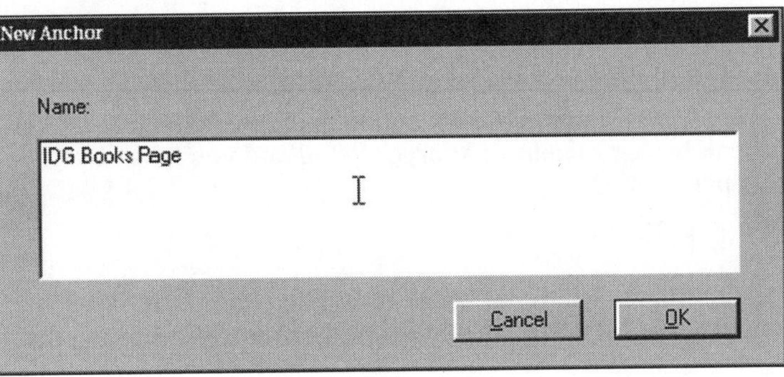

Figure 16-4: The New Anchor dialog box is where you name your hyperlink anchors.

That's all there is to it. Your Hyperlinks palette now lists the new anchor.

Here's how to create a URL destination:

1. **Select the destination object.**

   Follow the same procure that you would for creating a destination within your PageMaker document.

2. **Select the New URL menu option from the Hyperlinks palette (see Figure 16-3).**

3. **Enter the URL for the address destination.**

4. **Click OK.**

Establishing hyperlink sources

Setting up a source (the chunk of text or graphic the reader clicks on to jump to another page) is similar to setting up a destination, with an extra important step at the beginning:

1. **Select the destination.**

   In the Hyperlinks palette, select the name of the anchor or URL you want the source to be linked to.

2. **Select the source object.**

   Select any graphic or piece of text that you want the reader to jump *from* when they click on the source hyperlink. To select a graphic, click on it with the Arrow tool; to select text, use the Text tool to highlight the words that you want to appear in blue and underlined on the reader's computer screen. (When readers click on any part of the source text or graphic in your Web page, the hyperlink jumps them to the destination you specified in PageMaker.)

3. **Select the New Source menu option from the Hyperlinks palette (it appears dimmed in Figure 16-3) or double-click on the anchor or URL (destination) in the palette.**

   A dialog box similar to the one shown in Figure 16-4 appears.

4. **Enter a name for the source.**

   Enter a meaningful name. You'll be glad you did when your Hyperlinks palette has dozens of sources listed and you'll be able to tell them apart.

5. **Click OK.**

The Hyperlinks palette in Figure 16-5 shows the source and destinations defined. (The source names indicate that they appear on a master page.)

Placing objects on master pages and using them as sources can save you a number of repetitive steps. You can use a recurrent object as a source and not have to set it on each and every page that contains that object. (Chapter 12 explains how master pages make it easy for you to repeat objects on all document pages that are based on a particular master page.)

Altering Hyperlinks

The Hyperlinks palette that you use to create hyperlinks is also the place where you edit and delete them. So, fire up the palette now and follow along.

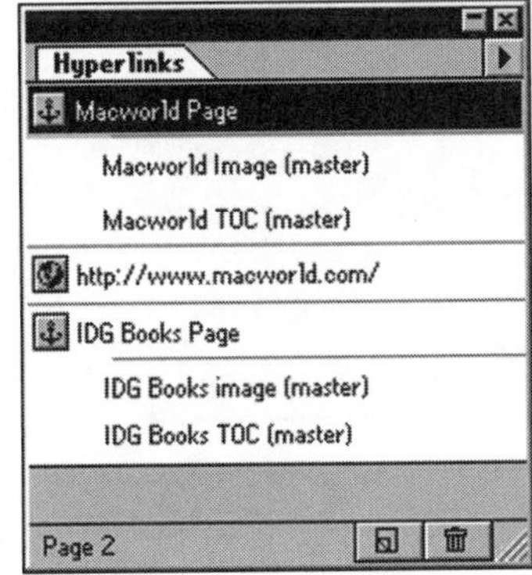

Figure 16-5: The Hyperlinks palette, with two anchors and one URL defined, and sources defined to the two anchors.

Changing the name or source

Two types of changes are typically made to hyperlinks: editing the hyperlink name and changing the source destination.

The easiest way to edit a source, anchor, or URL name is to double-click on the hyperlink name in the Hyperlinks palette. You get an Edit Source, Edit Anchor, or Edit URL dialog box similar to the New Anchor dialog box in Figure 16-4. Enter the new name, and click OK. That's it!

You can also select the hyperlink you want to edit by clicking on its name in the Hyperlinks palette and using the palette's Edit Name menu option.

To change the source destination — in other words, to hyperlink it to a different anchor or URL — follow these steps:

1. **Select the source.**

   In the Hyperlinks palette, click on the name of the source that you want to assign a new destination.

2. **Select the new anchor or URL.**

   Click on the anchor icon or URL icon for the new destination. Note that you must click on the new destination's icon, not on its name, to make the destination change.

3. **Confirm the change.**

   The dialog box in Figure 16-6 appears, asking you to confirm the change. Click on OK.

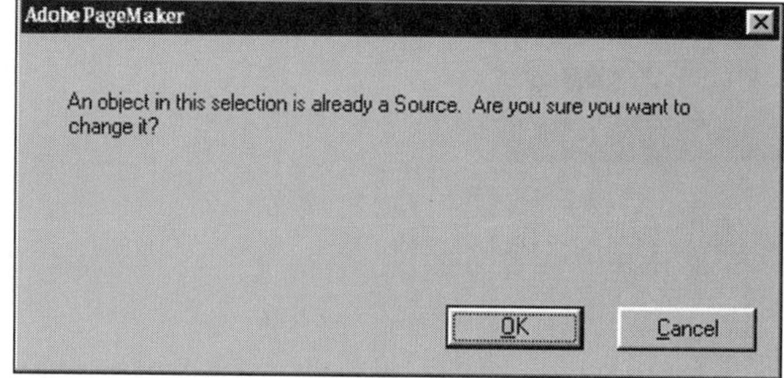

Adobe PageMaker
An object in this selection is already a Source. Are you sure you want to change it?
OK
Cancel

Figure 16-6: After changing a source's destination, you must confirm the change.

Deleting hyperlinks

To delete a hyperlink, click on its name in the Hyperlinks palette and select the palette's Delete menu option. Before you select that option, make sure that the name of the correct hyperlink appears after the word Delete in the menu. If not, reselect the correct hyperlink name in the palette.

If you delete an object from your PageMaker layout that is a source, the source hyperlink is automatically removed from the Hyperlinks palette. If you paste the object back in, the hyperlink is added back with it, too.

Importing Ready-Made Hyperlinks

You don't have to create every URL hyperlink yourself. PageMaker offers an easier way: Simply import hyperlinks from other HTML documents or from your browser's *bookmark documents* (a file of URLs that most browsers let you create to quickly go to Web pages you use frequently, sort of like having a telephone with a memory-dial feature). Think of this as the URL equivalent to the PageMaker Library feature, which lets you store collections of frequently used text and images that are available to all PageMaker documents. (Libraries are covered in Chapter 12.)

Importing from a document

To import URLs from an HTML document, use the Import URLs from File option in the Hyperlinks palette menu (see Figure 16-3). The URLs from the HTML document get added to the Hyperlinks palette as URL anchors.

You can import URLs when you place an HTML document into your PageMaker layout. That's right — you can place HTML documents just as if they were word-processed files, including the graphics and hyperlinks that are in the documents. You can place entire files either directly from the Web or from a local source.

Figure 16-7 shows the HTML Import dialog box you get when you place an HTML document through the File➪Place command. (The Show filter preferences check box must be selected in the Place dialog box for this filter dialog box to appear. The Place dialog box is accessible by the shortcut Ctrl+D or ⌘+D, which is covered in Chapters 7 and 13.)

When you place an HTML document into PageMaker, you can choose whether to import its graphics and hyperlinks by checking the appropriate boxes. Just make sure that the Keep Hyperlinks check box in the HTML Import dialog box is selected (see Figure 16-7). Placing an HTML document into your layout also brings all the URLs in that HTML document into the Hyperlinks palette.

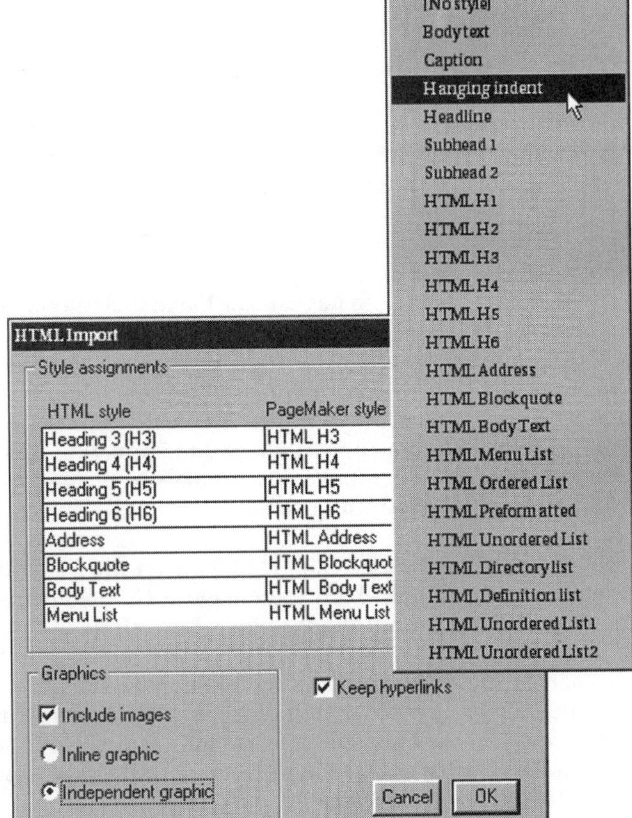

Figure 16-7: Use this dialog box to set up HTML import options.

You can also specify which PageMaker styles are substituted for the HTML document's HTML styles. For example, you may have a PageMaker style called Main Title that you are using for your largest headlines, but the HTML document may not have that style. To override the default substitutions, search the left column of the HTML Import box for the HTML style name you want to assign a different PageMaker style, then click on the PageMaker style name in the list to the right. You then get a pop-up list like the one in Figure 16-7. Just select the new PageMaker style that you want substituted for that HTML style.

Don't expect perfection from this HTML import capability. For example, you may find that the HTML document that started out as multiple tables is converted to single columns. That leaves you with significant rework on imported material for anything but the most rudimentary Web page design.

If you want to import just the text style and hyperlinks from an HTML document, simply import an HTML document and then delete the text and graphics. This is less work than entering the URLs and styles by hand, and probably less work than even importing the URLs as described earlier in this section and then manually creating the styles.

Importing from the Web

You can import URLs from a Web site by using the Hyperlink palette's Import URLs from Web menu option (see Figure 16-3). It works like the Import URLs from File menu option except that you will be asked to provide a Web address.

You can import pages from Web sites in the same way you would import them from HTML files by using the PageMaker Place dialog box (shown in Figure 16-8). Click on the Place URL button, which is highlighted in the figure. PageMaker then asks you for the appropriate Web address. Be sure to have your browser identified in the Online Preferences dialog box, as described earlier in this chapter (see Figure 16-1), and make sure you're connected to the Web. The same limitations in the importing capability described for placing HTML documents also applies to placing Web pages — some page formatting simply doesn't make it over.

Once you specify the URL you want imported, you get the HTML Import dialog box (shown here in Figure 16-9, and in Figure 16-7) which is where you tell PageMaker how you want the Web page imported:

- Graphics can be imported by checking the Include Images checkbox, and you can specify whether the graphics are kept separate from the text (by clicking on the Independent Graphics radio button) or are inserted into the text to match their placement on the Web page (by clicking on the Inline Graphics radio button).

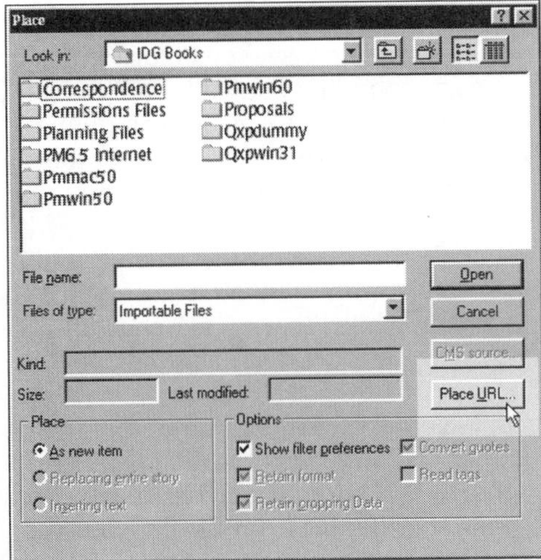

Figure 16-8: You can place Web pages into your PageMaker document by using the Place URL button, highlighted here.

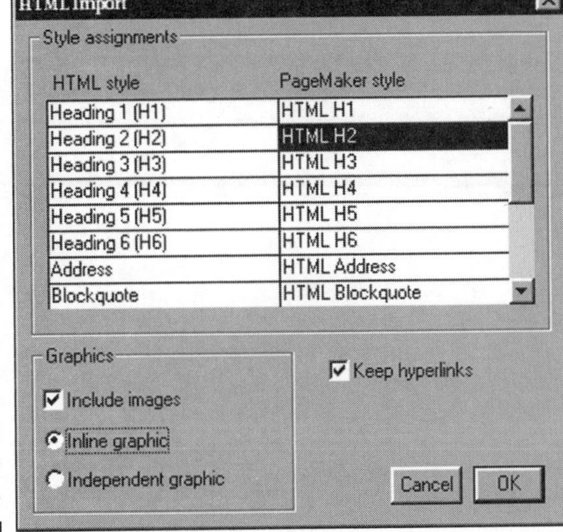

Figure 16-9: The Import HTML box is where you define how Web-page elements are imported into PageMaker.

- Click on the Keep Hyperlinks check box to retain the imported Web page's hyperlinks. They are added to the Hyperlinks palette in the document into which you are importing the Web page.
- You can assign the Web page's HTML styles to the styles defined in PageMaker. For example, if the main headlines on the Web page use the HTML style Heading 1, and you have defined a style called Main Headline in PageMaker, you can specify in the dialog box that you want PageMaker to use the style Main Headline wherever the Web page used the HTML style Heading 1.

To change a style, find the HTML style to which you want to assign a specific PageMaker style in the Style assignments list (see Figure 16-9). To the right of the HTML Style list is the corresponding PageMaker Style list. Click on the name of the PageMaker style you want to change. A pop-up menu appears listing all defined PageMaker styles (see Figure 16-7). Select the style you want to use, and release the mouse button. (See Chapter 9 for more on styles.)

Importing a Web page into PageMaker often results in a very different-looking document than what you saw on the Web. Figure 16-10 shows an imported Web page in PageMaker, while Figure 16-11 shows the original Web page. Big difference, huh?

WEIRDNESS

When importing Web pages, PageMaker strips out much of the document formatting. Many Web pages use HTML codes that PageMaker doesn't recognize, so PageMaker ignores that formatting. That's why the imported Web page in Figure 16-10 looks so different from the original Web page in Figure 16-11. This can also affect whether graphics are successfully imported, because if they are embedded in HTML codes that PageMaker doesn't recognize, they get stripped out.

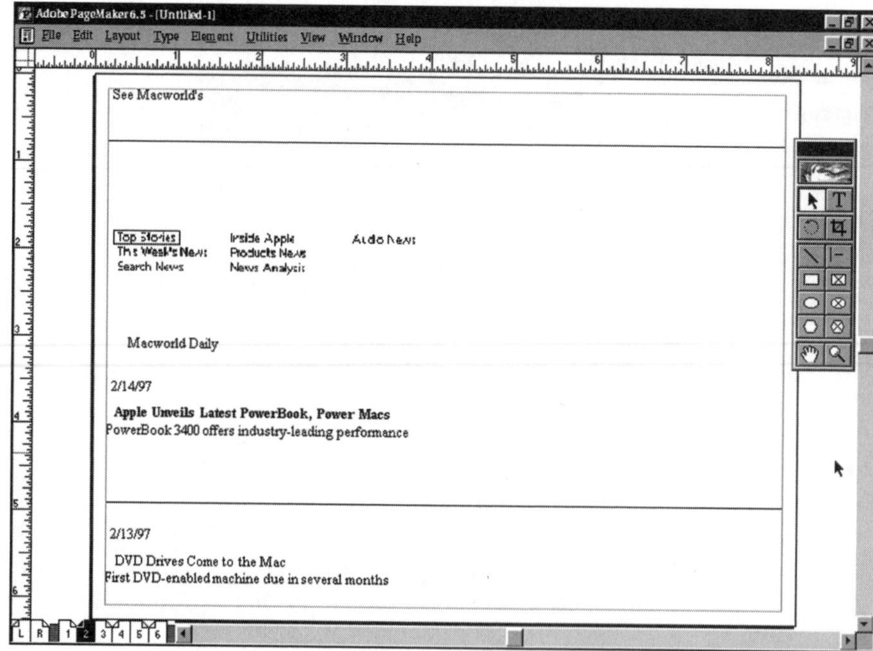
Adobe PageMaker 6.5 - [Untitled-1]
File Edit Layout Type Element Utilities View Window Help
See Macworld's
Macworld Daily
2/14/97
Apple Unveils Latest PowerBook, Power Macs
PowerBook 3400 offers industry-leading performance
2/13/97
DVD Drives Come to the Mac
First DVD-enabled machine due in several months

Figure 16-10: A Web page after it's imported into PageMaker (see the original in Figure 16-11).

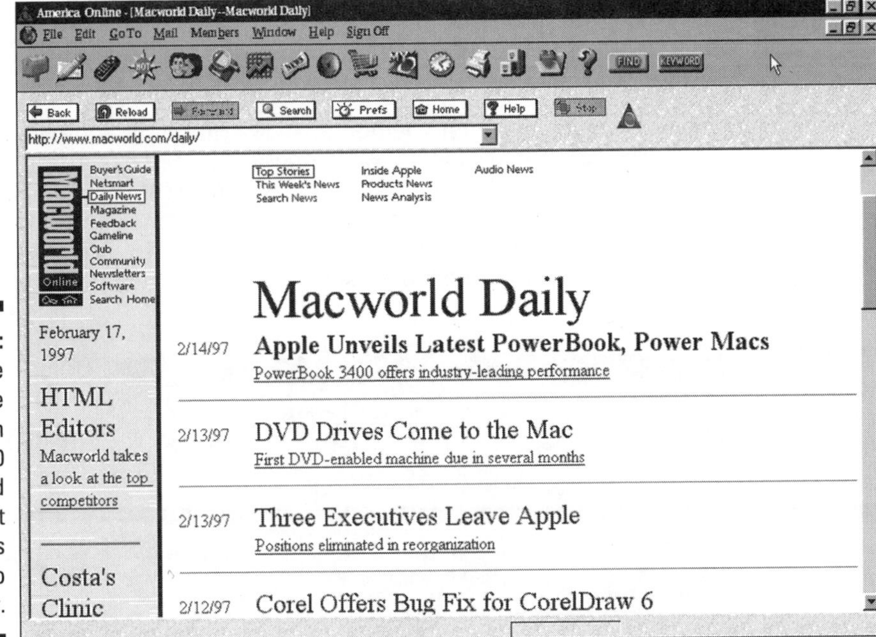

Figure 16-11: How the Web page shown in Figure 16-10 looked before it was inported into PageMaker.

Fortunately, PageMaker doesn't remove the actual text inside HTML code it doesn't recognize, but the formatting for that text can be lost. The bottom line is this: Don't expect Web pages to retain their layouts when imported into PageMaker. My advice is to use this function to import the text, and not the design, into your pages.

I found that importing Web pages using America Online as your Web connection is a very iffy proposition if you're using the Windows 3.1 version of AOL 3.0 (that's still the case even if you're running Windows 95). The Web import takes several minutes even if you have a high-speed link to an Internet service provider. With AOL, the transfer speeds are so slow that the import usually aborts, and the Web page is not imported.

Both the Macintosh and Windows 95 version of AOL work fine for importing Web pages. (You can download the Mac or Windows 95 version of AOL by using the keyword `Upgrade`.)

Using copyrighted materials

In this age of electronic data transfer, it's become increasingly easier to swap and share information. But be careful: You almost always need written permission to reuse someone else's work. When you import something from a Web site, be aware that you may be appropriating copyrighted information. In fact, you get a warning to this effect (shown in Figure 16-12) when you import URLs from a Web site or import Web site pages.

The few situations in which you don't need permission — known as *fair use* — typically involve small extracts that are quoted exactly and credited to their source (often done in book reviews or news stories). *Sampling* — the inclusion of snippets of a someone else's composition, a practice common with recording musicians and visual artists — falls into a gray area, with the bigger the snippet used the more likely that it's a copyright violation.

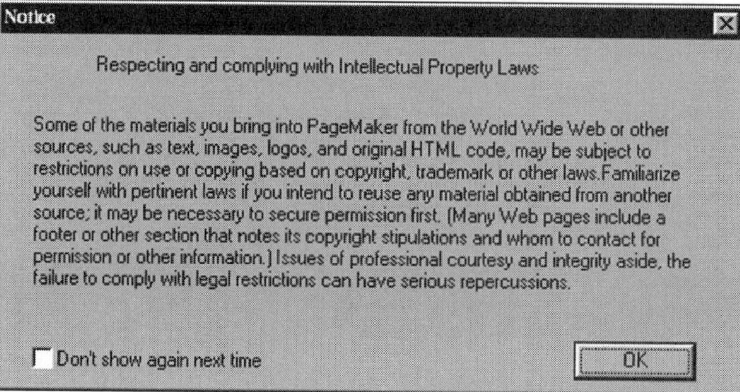

Notice
Respecting and complying with Intellectual Property Laws
Some of the materials you bring into PageMaker from the World Wide Web or other sources, such as text, images, logos, and original HTML code, may be subject to restrictions on use or copying based on copyright, trademark or other laws.Familiarize yourself with pertinent laws if you intend to reuse any material obtained from another source; it may be necessary to secure permission first. (Many Web pages include a footer or other section that notes its copyright stipulations and whom to contact for permission or other information.) Issues of professional courtesy and integrity aside, the failure to comply with legal restrictions can have serious repercussions.
Don't show again next time
OK

Figure 16-12: When you import Web pages or URLs, you get this warning about possible copyright infringement.

Chapter 17

Turning a PageMaker Page into a Web Page

In This Chapter

- Setting up master elements
- Placing text and graphics
- Adding hypertext links
- Creating and saving export styles
- Selecting graphics formats
- Exporting the document to HTML

You've heard that the formula to a successful project is 10 percent inspiration and 90 percent preparation? Or, is it 90 percent perspiration? Well, whatever the combination is, if you're not well-prepared, you'd better be prepared for trouble. As for the perspiration part, if you've read the previous chapters of this book, it's time for the payoff. You finally get to flex your layout muscles and put together some Web pages.

In Chapter 10, you can see how I laid out pages for my personal Web site. I use the same example pages in this chapter to take you through the full process of creating Internet-bound pages. What follows is a good example suited for PageMaker's abilities, because it mixes graphics, text, layers, and lots of hyperlinks, without getting into high-end Web publishing effects such as animation or interactive forms. (If you want to add some special effects to your PageMaker-created Web pages, you need to do some further work in an HTML editor, a subject covered briefly in Chapter 18.)

The following sections provide some basic steps to create actual Web pages, with references to other chapters that provide more specific details on these steps.

Set Up the Master Elements

Think of the following options as the foundation for your Web page documents. This basic setup is the place to start before filling in your pages.

1. **Create a new page.**

   Use File⇨New, or the shortcut Ctrl+N (in Windows) or ⌘+N (on the Mac) in the Document Setup dialog box, as described in Chapter 5.

2. **Choose a page size.**

   If you intend to preserve the basic PageMaker layout when you export the document to HTML, you want to pick the page size of Browser Large – 600 × 450, which matches the window size that most monitors can fully display. If you don't need to preserve the layout, any page size works.

3. **In the Document Setup dialog box, indicate how many pages you think you need to fill; then click on OK.**

   You can always add or delete pages later.

4. **Define any styles you intend to use for your text, as described in Chapter 9.**

   Styles are what tell PageMaker the kind of formatting to apply to your text. Using styles is essential to successful Web page creation in PageMaker, because HTML (the language used to create Web pages) relies on styles for most of its text formatting. If styles don't exist in your PageMaker document, all your text comes out looking the same on the Web.

5. **Create your master pages, a process described in Chapter 12.**

   Each individual page layout on your site should have its own master page. For example, you probably have a master page for your opening (home) page, and one for each different kind of inside page. In the sample site shown in Figure 17-1, I created a master page for the home page and another master page for the content pages (where I describe the publications I work for, my affiliations, my hobbies and interests, and so forth). For my personal Web site, just two master pages are sufficient, but you may need more for your site, depending on how widely the appearance of each page differs.

6. **On every master page, place all of the text or graphics that you want to see displayed on each Web page based on that master page.**

   Chapter 7 explains how to enter text, Chapters 13 and 14 explain how to add graphics, and Chapters 9 through 12 explain how to design your pages and manage their elements.

7. **Define any colors to be applied to text and graphics, as described in Chapter 15.**

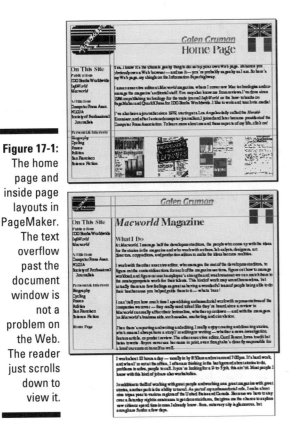

Figure 17-1: The home page and inside page layouts in PageMaker. The text overflow past the document window is not a problem on the Web. The reader just scrolls down to view it.

You may be wondering why the page headlined "Macworld Magazine" in Figure 17-1 shows text extending below the document window. I'm demonstrating that the text for that page runs longer that one screen length. Unlike print publishing, in which you'd simply create a second page rather than allow text to run past the margin, for the Web it's okay to extend text beyond the page boundary. The online reader merely has to scroll down to see the rest of the page. (See Chapter 10 for more on working with overflow text.)

I was able to easily create a bilingual Web site in both English and French with the new PageMaker *layers* feature. Layers come in handy for creating multiple versions of one document. I used the new feature to create one common layer for graphics, a second layer to hold English text, and a third for French text. To export the English versions of the pages, the common layer and English layers are displayed. To export the French versions of the pages, the common layer and French layers are displayed. If you're using layers, be sure to specify and name the layers *before* you add text and graphics. (Chapter 11 has more information on layers.)

Fill the Individual Pages

After you set up the standing elements on your master pages, you need to place text and graphics specific to each page. In the example in Figure 17-1, that would mean creating an individual page for each of the three publications, three affiliations, and six interests and hobbies listed in the "On This Site" column on the left of the page.

Any graphics you create within PageMaker, except for horizontal lines, do not export to HTML, so you won't see them once they hit the Web. If you want graphics to appear in your pages, you need to use an illustration pro-gram (such as CorelDRAW) or image-editing program (such as Adobe Photoshop).

Do Some Cleanup Work

After you add your text and graphics, run your pages through the following quality-control steps. The Internet can be very efficient at distributing embarrassing mistakes to millions, so the time spent doing this is well worth it.

1. **Spell-check your pages with PageMaker's built-in spelling checker, as described in Chapter 8.**
2. **Proofread a hard-copy printout of your document.**

   A spell-checker can't find mistakes in meaning or correctly spelled words that are used incorrectly.
3. **Inspect the overall appearance of your pages.**

   Do so with a printout, not on screen, to make sure that each page as a whole looks the way it should.
4. **Apply any special effects to your graphics.**

   Do this step now, unless you already did so when you placed the graphics in the document. Chapter 14 explains how to work with graphics, while Chapter 15 explains what kinds of graphics can have colors applied to them.

All graphics must fit within the boundaries of the document page; otherwise, they disappear once the page is exported to HTML, and all text must *begin* within the page. (Text can extend into the pasteboard, but don't jump text to a new page if you are preserving the PageMaker layout when exporting to the HTML format.) For more details on laying out elements for use in a Web page, see Chapter 10.

Add the Hypertext Links

Once your page content is complete, you need to add hypertext links that allow readers to jump to related subject matter within your document or to anyplace else on the Web. Chapter 16 describes the process for creating hyperlinks.

Save creating hyperlinks for the end of the page composition process. You can then review the entire site to determine which items or subjects should be linked. Attempting to create hyperlinks as you go along could result in time-consuming rework. You may move things around several times and end up with hyperlinks you no longer want or that no longer make sense.

You can use graphics, as well as text, for hyperlink connections. Sometimes it helps to use a mix of both text and graphics source hyperlinks, as I did by featuring text hyperlinks in my "On This Site" contents box and graphic image hyperlinks — the magazine covers — at the bottom of the home page (once again, see Figure 17-1). The Union Jack and French tricolor flag in the upper right corner of the pages function as source hyperlinks to English- and French-language versions of my home page.

Be sure to give meaningful names to your hyperlinks, rather than cryptic ones such as the default names *Anchor1* and *Source 1*. For example, in Figure 17-1, I called the source hyperlink (the clickable hyperlink) from the *Macworld* icon on the home page *Macworld home image*, and I called the anchor (or destination) hyperlink on the *Macworld* Magazine page *Macworld page*.

Export the Document to HTML

After you've completed assembling your pages with master page elements, frames, text, graphics, and hypertext links, you're ready to convert them from the PageMaker format to HTML format. (HTML is the language that makes your hypertext links act like hypertext.)

To export to HTML, select File⇨Export⇨HTML. Unfortunately, I can offer no keyboard shortcut for this step. You get the Export HTML dialog box shown in Figure 17-2. It takes a few tries to get the hang of this dialog box and its options, so you may want to pay close attention to the rest of this section.

During the course of the page-creation process, export your pages to HTML once in a while so you can see how they look through a browser. Doing so helps to avoid any surprises or disappointment when you view your final pages on the Web.

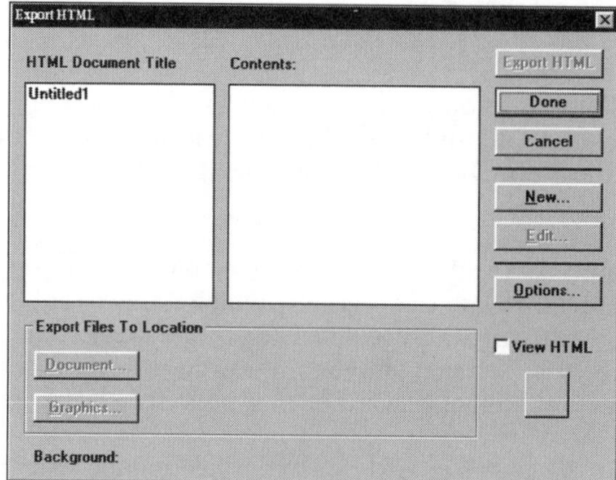

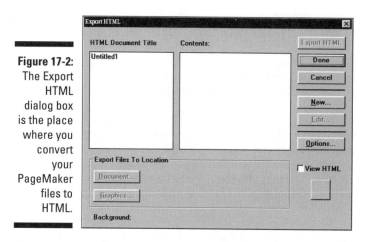

Figure 17-2: The Export HTML dialog box is the place where you convert your PageMaker files to HTML.

Create an export style

Each PageMaker document can have several HTML *export styles,* which are sets of instructions for what should be exported to HTML and how the exported text should look when displayed on a browser. Export styles are similar to paragraph styles for formatting text, or printer styles for controlling output settings. But unlike paragraph styles and printer styles, you won't find anything in the PageMaker program explicitly labeled an export style. But they do exist. See the entry Untitled1 in the Export HTML dialog box in Figure 17-2? That's a default export style (although not a very descriptive one).

To export your document to HTML, you must first create a new export style or edit an existing one:

1. **To create an export style, click on the New button.**

   Alternatively, if you want to edit an existing export style, select the export style name from the HTML Document Title list and click on the Edit button.

   Whether you create a new export style or edit an existing one, you get the dialog box shown in Figure 17-3. The title bar of the dialog box is either Export HTML: New Document or Export HTML: Edit Contents, depending on whether you clicked New or Edit, but otherwise the boxes are identical.

2. **Assign a name to the export style.**

   Enter the name into the Document Title box. Be sure that the name is descriptive enough so you know exactly what the style refers to. (In Figure 17-3, the name Macworld Page tells me that I've assigned a

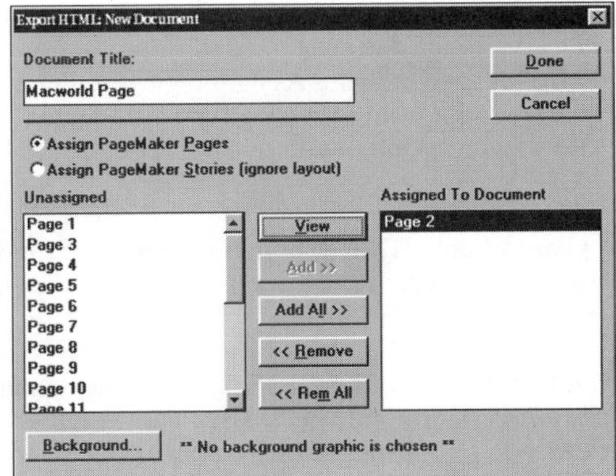

Figure 17-3: This dialog box is where you choose the pages and stories to be exported to HTML.

particular style to a page about *Macworld* Magazine.) As you build your Web site, each style name eventually appears in the HTML Document Title box (shown in Figure 17-2), and you want to be able to distinguish one from another.

Select stories or pages for export

In the Export HTML: New Document and Export HTML: Edit Contents dialog boxes (see Figure 17-3), you have an important choice to make: Do you want to export full pages or just stories? (A *story* is a text block or text frame, or a linked series of text blocks or text frames.) If you want the HTML document to look like your PageMaker layout, choose Assign PageMaker Pages; otherwise, choose Assign PageMaker Stories (an option that tells PageMaker to ignore your layout and just export text and graphics in the order you choose).

- If you choose the Assign PageMaker Pages option, a list of pages appears in the window under the Unassigned heading. (See Figure 17-3.) To add all of the pages, just click the Add All >> button; to add specific pages, click on the desired page number and then click on Add >>. Added pages are moved to the Assigned to Document window. You can also remove pages from the Assigned to Document Window by selecting the desired page and clicking on the << Remove button (which removes the selected page) or click on the << Rem All button, which removes all pages.
- If, along the way, you've forgotten what a particular page looks like, use the View button after selecting the page name in either the Unassigned or Assigned to Document windows. Doing so causes PageMaker to jump to that page, which will be visible on your screen, although you may need to move the dialog box (which remains visible) around to get a sense of the contents of the entire page.

- If you choose the Assign PageMaker Stories option, a list of all PageMaker stories appears in the area headed Unassigned. Use the buttons between the Unassigned and Assigned To Document boxes to add stories or remove them from the Assigned to Document window. Just select the story to be added or removed and click on the appropriate button.

Pages and stories appear in your HTML document in the order in which they are added. It's also the order in which they are listed in the Assigned to Document box.

When you export from PageMaker to HTML, all pages in the Assigned to Document window are merged into one big HTML page, which you may find cumbersome to work with in an HTML editor. To export one page at a time, select just one page and then follow the rest of the export steps in this chapter — and then repeat the process for every other page you want to export. If you export all your pages into one big HTML page, you can separate them in an HTML editor (how this is done depends on the HTML editor you're using), but that's more work than exporting the pages one at a time in PageMaker.

Don't let the export limitations get you down — there is a way to export multiple pages to HTML that keeps them as separate HTML pages and also retains any hyperlinks among them. This technique is not documented in your PageMaker 6.5 manual, but it works like a charm! Here's what you do:

1. **Create the HTML styles as described earlier in this section.**

   You'll typically have one PageMaker page assigned to each HTML style.

2. **In the Export HTML dialog box, select each HTML style you want to export.**

   Use Shift+click to select a contiguous range of styles, and Ctrl+click or ⌘+click to select noncontiguous HTML styles (selected styles are shown in Figure 17-4).

3. **Click on Export HTML to export the multiple pages.**

   That's it!

If, instead, you want several PageMaker pages to be merged into one HTML page, specify multiple pages for the HTML style that is to be composed of those multiple pages. Do not assign multiple PageMaker pages to one HTML style if you want your pages to remain separate when exported to HTML.

Typically, you would export one page at a time, especially if you've designed your pages as single units of information. I prefer to work with individual pages and use hyperlinks to let readers click from page to page, rather than scroll up and down through a lengthy string of text and images (which is what you get when several PageMaker pages are exported together). In

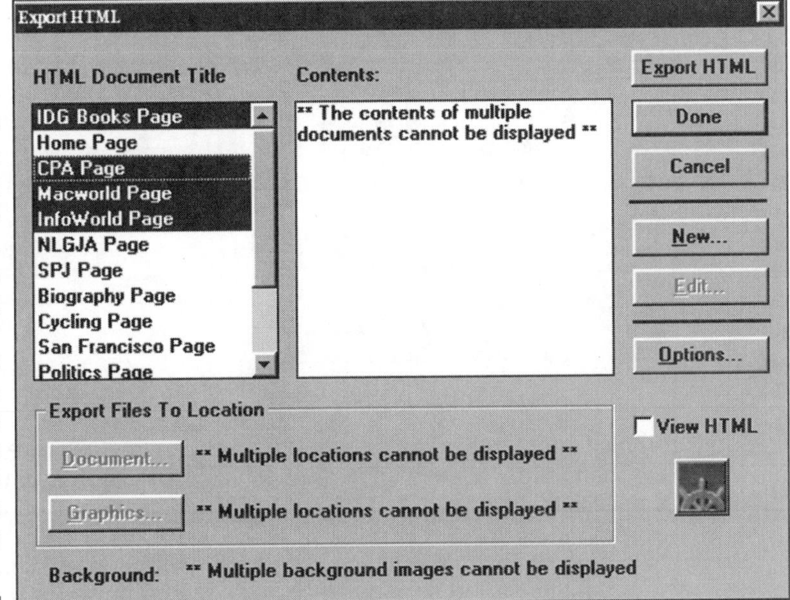

Figure 17-4: Select multiple HTML styles to export PageMaker pages that remain separate yet retain the hyperlinks among them.

some cases, however, combining several related pages may make sense so readers have the option of scrolling through the sequence of pages rather than jumping from page to page. If you string pages together, PageMaker automatically inserts a horizontal line between the pages. (Chapter 18 has more information how pages link up after export.)

Add background graphics

PageMaker can automatically add a background graphic to a page that's been exported to HTML. Click the Background button in the Export HTML: New Document or Export HTML: Edit Contents box. and use the dialog box that appears to select the JPEG or GIF image you want to use as the background image. (See Chapter 13 for an explanation of these two commonly used Web graphics formats.) The GIF or JPEG image you select is then placed behind every page listed in the Assigned to Document window, shown in Figure 17-3. (If you want the background on only one page, you have to export the background separately.) If you select a background graphic for stories instead of pages, the image is placed behind the entire page containing those stories. Figure 17-5 shows the dialog box where you choose a background image file. In Windows, the dialog box is called Choose a Background Image, while on the Mac it has no name.

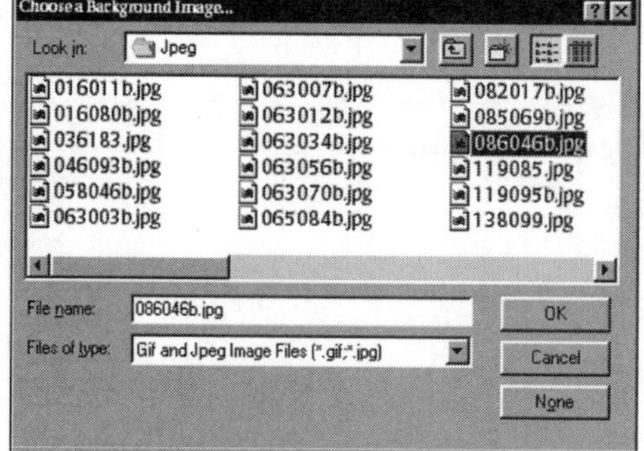

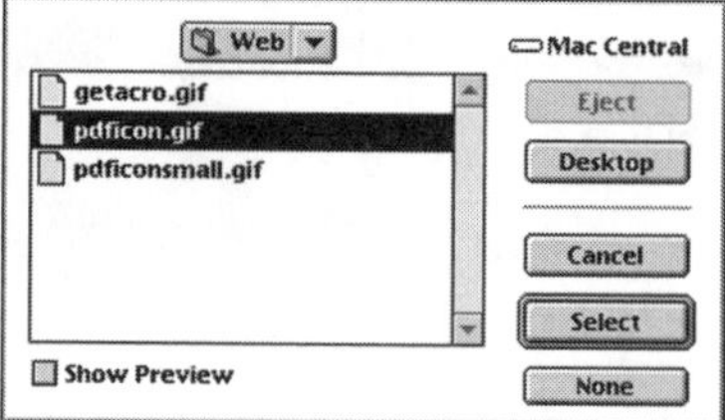

Figure 17-5: The dialog box for choosing a background image for your Web pages (Windows at left, Mac at right).

If the graphic is not large enough to fill the HTML page, the image is *tiled* (copied as many times as needed and repeated across and down the page until the page is filled).

Don't try to place Web page background graphics within PageMaker. Text wrapped around or placed on top of a graphic in PageMaker ends up adjacent to or below the graphic when the page is exported to HTML — which is not exactly what you have in mind. The only way to make text overprint graphics is by using the Background button when exporting to HTML — and then the background graphic is used for the entire page, not just for a particular piece of text.

To remove a background graphic, click on the Background button in either of the Export HTML dialog boxes in which you're working and click on the None button in the dialog box that appears.

Save the export settings

When you're finished using the Export HTML: New Document or Export HTML: Edit Contents dialog box (one of which is shown in Figure 17-3), click on Done to save the settings. You've now created or modified an export style.

If you click on the Export HTML button or the Done button, that export style is saved (provided you also save your original PageMaker document). The style remains available for later use when you work with the Export HTML dialog box in the future. But don't click on that Export HTML button just yet. You may have defined your export style, but you haven't done everything necessary to make sure that the export works properly — the next section explains those last steps you need to take before you should click on the Export HTML button. (If you want to modify or create a style without actually exporting it, click on the Done button in the Export HTML dialog box instead of the Export HTML button.)

You may be wondering how to get rid of an export style you no longer want. You looked for a Remove button, and found none. To remove an unwanted style, simply select the export style from the list in the HTML Document Title box in the Export HTML dialog box, and press the Backspace key. Adios style!

Choose export options

Next, you have to set up export options, such as paragraph style mapping and page width. When you click on the Options button in the Export HTML dialog box, you get another dialog box (shown in Figure 17-6) where you can select the options crucial to successful HTML export.

Figure 17-6: Use this Options dialog box to select the settings that determine the appearance of your exported HTML pages.

Decide if you want to preserve layout

To preserve (or at least approximate) column settings and relative position of text and graphics during export to HTML, check off the box titled Approximate Layout Using HTML Tables When Exporting Pages (shown in the Options dialog box in Figure 17-6). You also need to select the Assign PageMaker Pages option in the Export HTML: New Document (shown in Figure 17-3) or Export HTML: Edit Contents dialog boxes.

If you don't want to preserve the layout, but you selected the Assign PageMaker Pages option (as described in the earlier section "Choose export options") leave the Approximate layout box unchecked.

If you chose the Assign PageMaker Stories option, the Approximate layout checkbox is grayed out, because assigning stories rather than pages for export automatically eliminates layout approximation.

Assign style attributes

A list of all PageMaker styles and a second list containing their corresponding HTML styles are side by side under Style Assignments in the Options dialog box (see Figure 17-6). If you've defined more than seven styles, a scroll bar appears at the right of the Style Assignments window, which you use to scroll through the list of styles. (Chapter 9 covers the subject of styles in depth.)

If you select an HTML style name, a pop-up list appears, like the one shown in Figure 17-7. Use this list to change the HTML style assigned to a particular PageMaker style. Select the new style by clicking on the new style name in the list. Then be sure to double-check all of the PageMaker-to-HTML style translations before exporting the document.

Why would you want to change the default style translations? Because PageMaker doesn't know which HTML style you want substituted for each of the PageMaker styles you've used. For example, assume you have a style called List in your document. PageMaker doesn't know whether you want to export it as the HTML Unordered List style (with automatically generated bullets), the Ordered List style (with automatically generated numbers), or one of the other HTML list styles.

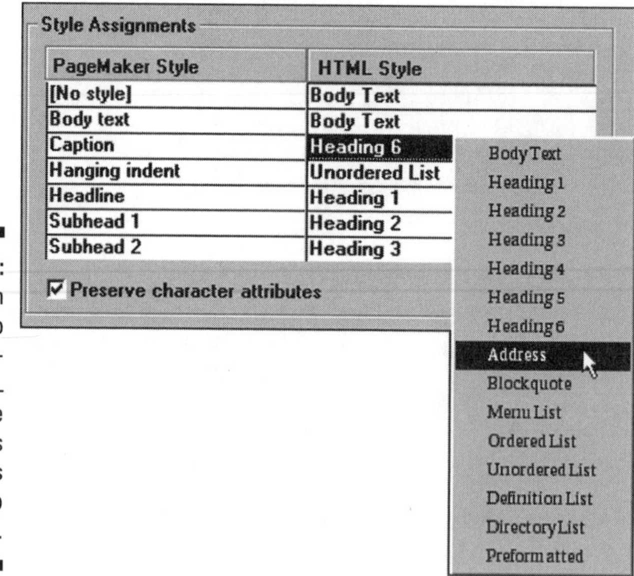

Figure 17-7: You can remap PageMaker-to-HTML style translations with this pop-up menu.

Any remapping of styles is saved if you click on the Export HTML button or click on the Done button in the Export HTML dialog box. This remapping remains available for future use when you call up the Export HTML dialog box. This remapping is tied not just to the current export style — it is used no matter which export style is active.

One other option that affects character formatting during output is Preserve Character Attributes, which you should always have checked. Doing so ensures that text specified as boldface always comes out bold on the Web. (Chapter 6 covers text formatting in detail.)

Select a graphics format option

The set of options that affect how graphics are displayed after export is shown in the Graphics section at the bottom of the Options dialog box. (See Figure 17-6.)

- In the Export As options, check off the button labeled PageMaker Chooses and keep it checked. This selection lets PageMaker do all the work for you. PageMaker automatically selects the best conversion option for each of your images, selecting either the GIF or JPEG file format on an individual basis. Or, you can select All in GIF or All in JPEG, if you need to have every image in one format.

- Set the File Names option according to the requirements of the file server that hosts your Web site. Choose the Use Long Name option if your *server* (the computer that makes your Web pages available for use on the Internet) is a Macintosh or a Windows 95-based or NT 4.0-based PC. If your server is a DOS-based, Windows 3.1-based, or UNIX-based PC, or if you don't know what kind of computer the server is, choose the Use Short Name (8.3) option. If you choose the Use Short Name option, PageMaker renames all of the graphics files to conform to the 8.3 naming standard, which is explained below. (This renaming won't affect the original graphics files, which the PageMaker document continues to use.)

  In DOS, UNIX, and many other older computer systems, filenames must contain a limited number of characters following a rigid pattern. The 8.3 pattern is the most common: It requires from one to eight letters or numerals for the filename, followed by a period, followed by one to three letters or numerals for the *extension*, the suffix that identifies the file type. The extension .HTM is used for HTML files in the 8.3 scheme. Examples are FILENAME.EXT, EST#JB.4, and 2FILE.R1.

- One other very important option — Downsample To 72 dpi — should always remain checked. This changes the resolution of each exported graphic to 72 dpi, matching the resolution of the typical computer monitor. It also makes graphics in HTML documents take up less space, which speeds downloading time — something your readers greatly appreciate. If you neglect to check this option, graphics are exported at their full resolution, which is a waste because most monitors can't display a resolution higher than 72 dpi.

Execute the export

Now with everything set up properly, you're almost ready to export your pages. Just a few details need to be wrapped up first.

Take a look at the Export HTML dialog box in Figure 17-8 and compare it with the one in Figure 17-2. In Figure 17-8, a couple of buttons are undimmed, a number of styles now appear in the HTML Document Title box, a page number is listed in the Contents box (which is now labeled Contents: PageMaker Pages), and the Export Files to Location box now shows two filenames.

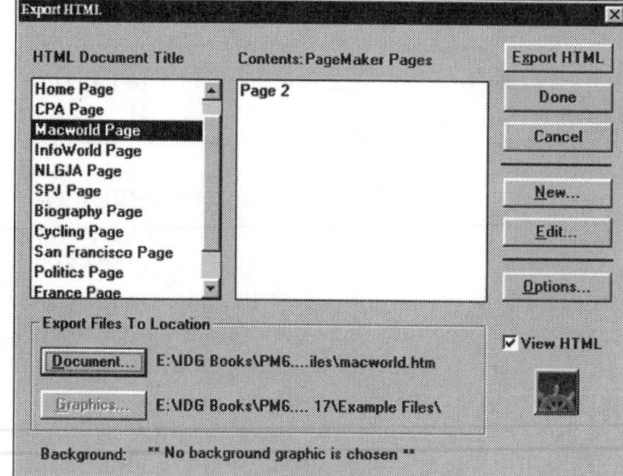

Figure 17-8: The Export HTML dialog box, with all settings entered.

Now look at the list of export styles in the HTML Document Title window. The page to be exported for the selected export style (in this case, Macworld Page) is displayed in the Contents: PageMaker Pages window (if you export stories instead of pages, this window is titled Contents: PageMaker Stories).

Notice that the View HTML checkbox is selected in the figure. When checked, this option launches your Web browser after exporting your HTML pages and opens those pages in your browser. (You need adequate system memory to have both PageMaker and your Web browser open at the same time.) To select a browser, click on the square button below the View HTML checkbox. You get a dialog box that lists your browser program. Select your browser. The browser's icon then appears in that square button, such as in Figure 17-8.

The Export Files to Location section contains file locations for the HTML document to be exported, as well the graphics that go along with that document. To tell PageMaker the export destination of your HTML documents, click on the Document button. PageMaker then displays the Document Save As dialog box shown in Figure 17-9.

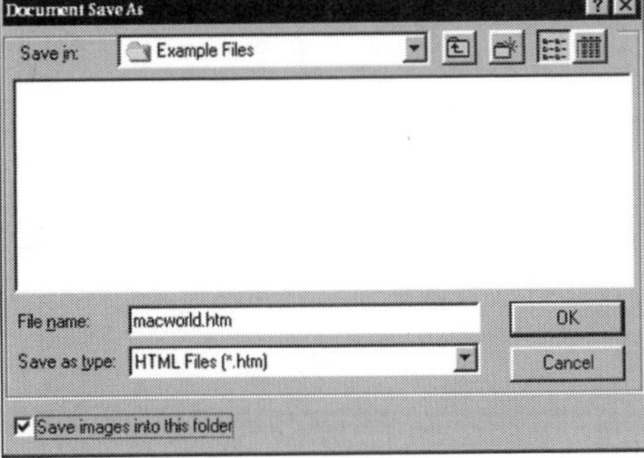

Figure 17-9: The Document Save As dialog box for HTML export.

Use the dialog box in Figure 17-9 the same way you would if you were saving a file folder in PageMaker. This dialog box works like any other Windows 95 or Macintosh Save As dialog box.

After you select the destination folder and assign a filename to the HTML document to be exported, select Save images into this folder in the Document Save As dialog box. Doing so ensures that all images associated with the HTML document are in the same folder as the HTML document itself. Having all the files in one place greatly simplifies transfer of files to the Web server — you just copy all the contents of the folder at once. Doing so also reduces the risk of not having everything you need when you're ready to make the page available on the Web.

When you select Save Images Into This Folder, the Graphics button in the Export HTML dialog box's Export File to Location section is dimmed (see Figure 17-8). If you don't check the Save images box, you can click on the Graphics button to specify the export destination of the graphics files. Do so only if you have a reason to put graphics in folders separate from the HTML pages to which they are linked. The Webmaster at your organization, or some other Web publishing expert, can tell you which option is best for your site's setup.

At this point, you're finally ready to export the HTML pages with the selected export style. Click on Export HTML in the Export HTML dialog box, and give PageMaker a few minutes to do its thing. Either your browser will launch (if the View HTML checkbox is selected), or you'll find yourself back in your PageMaker layout. Your HTML file is now exported to disk.

You lose all of your work in the HTML Export dialog box, and in the other dialog boxes within it, if you don't also save your PageMaker file. When you quit PageMaker, the program asks if you want to save the publication. Answer Yes every time. Even if you haven't changed the layout since you last saved the document, you still need to take this step. The settings in the HTML Export dialog box are part of your document and anything you do to them PageMaker regards as a change.

Chapter 18

Techniques for Taming HTML

In This Chapter

- Turning to HTML editors for help
- Creating hyperlink hierarchies
- Adding hyperlinks to HTML documents
- Resizing table cells to adjust your layout

Remember the good old days of print publishing? You put your word processing into PageMaker, brought in your to-die-for graphics, tweaked the pages, proofed them, turned them into PostScript files, and then sent them off to a service bureau that whisked them away to a printer who delivered a shiny printed product.

Publishing to the Web is a different story. You have no service bureau to rely on (although you can hit up your local Webmaster for guidance) and no printer to deliver your final product. After you've done your thing with text and graphics, and tweaked and proofed your pages, you then have to grapple with HTML, a somewhat arcane markup coding that's about as intuitive to use as instructions written in ancient Greek.

HTML isn't very pretty but that's okay, because how it makes a document behave is the beauty part of using the Web. HTML uses *hypertext,* the concept behind your being able to click and leap around online documents rather than having to search, and scroll, and scroll.

Making Use of HTML Editing Tools

PageMaker on its own is okay for creating your Web pages, if your page design is super-simple. But the more complex your Web site layout, the more work you need to do in HTML code to get the page to look the way you want it to. Chances are you also need help from a dedicated HTML authoring tool (more commonly called *HTML editors*) or even Adobe Acrobat, a program covered in the next chapter.

You can use a slew of tools for editing HTML, programs as simple as a word processor or as sophisticated as a Web-site builder and covering all of these tools would fill a book of its own. Dozens of HTML tools are now available for Mac and Windows users, as well as a bunch that run in UNIX.

Most Web publishers use a special kind of program called an HTML editor that is designed to work with HTML documents in several ways:

- In a preview view that lets you see your page as you work on it, just as PageMaker does for print publications
- In an under-the-hood, secret-innards view that shows the actual HTML code — somewhat like raw data in a PostScript file, something PageMaker politely hides in print documents (Figure 18-1 shows this raw, unvarnished HTML code as seen in Adobe Systems PageMill 2.0 HTML editor for Macintosh.)
- In an editable view that shows you a graphical version of your Web page but with special characters, boxes, and colors to indicate Web-specific features like hyperlinks and HTML frames (Figure 18-2 shows an example of this editable view in PageMill 2.0.)

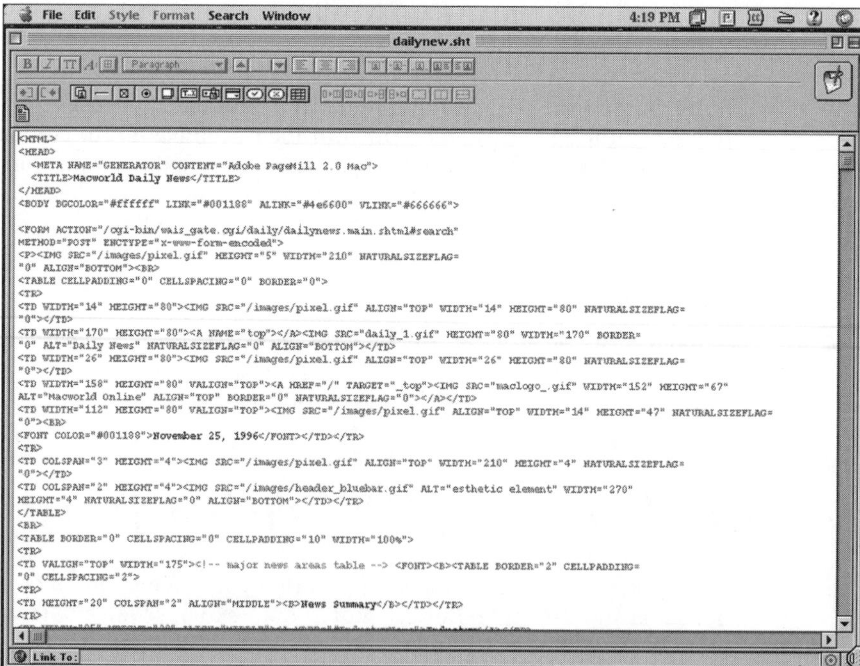

Figure 18-1: HTML code as seen in the Adobe PageMill 2.0 HTML editor.

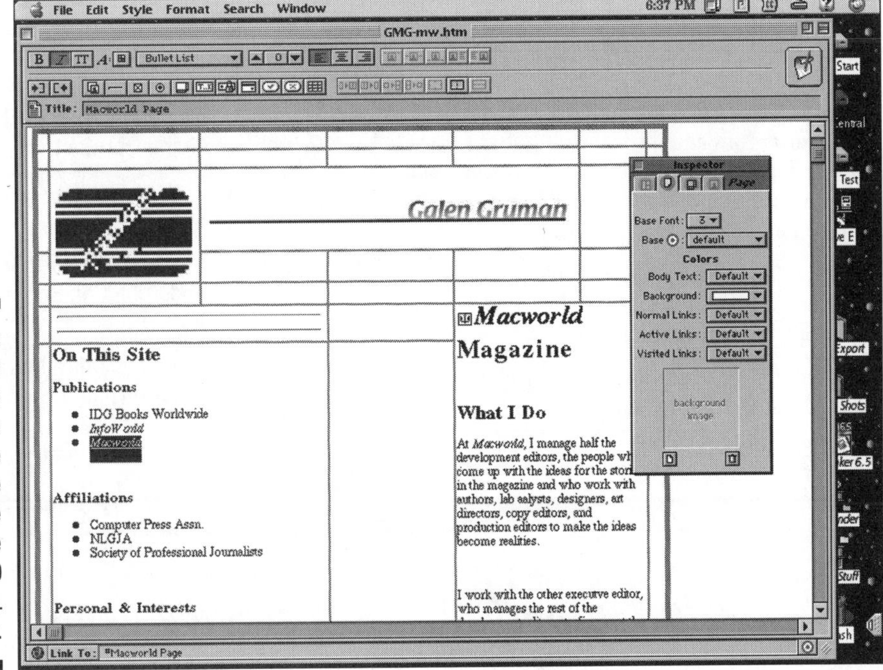

Figure 18-2: The editable view of a sample Web page in the Adobe PageMill 2.0 HTML editor.

The examples shown in this chapter are created in a popular HTML editor called PageMill. (As I mentioned earlier, a number of good HTML editors are available, I just picked the one I know the best.) If you don't use PageMill, what you see on screen in your HTML editor will likely look different than what you see here, and some of the commands and steps used to fine-tune your pages may vary as well. The concept is the same; the only difference is in how you accomplish some tasks.

Managing Hyperlinks

Managing hyperlinks makes up the bulk of your post-PageMaker Web-page work. Even though you can — and should — define hyperlinks in PageMaker, PageMaker isn't meant to be an all-in-one Web-page factory. You may think that because PageMaker has powerful features to manage links across multiple pages and chapters in a print document, PageMaker ought to be able to treat a collection of Web pages as a whole. But it can't. PageMaker exports files to the Web's HTML format — not PageMaker's internal format. PageMaker itself is clueless about Web-site management. After you've exported pages to HTML, that task is up to you.

HTML editing books to the rescue

If you're new to HTML authoring, the following books are a helpful resource. It just so happens they're all available from this book's publisher, IDG Books Worldwide (the last two titles are specifically on HTML editors):

- *HTML For Dummies,* 3rd Edition, and *MORE HTML For Dummies,* 2nd Edition both by Ed Tittel and Steve James
- *HTML For Dummies Quick Reference* by Deborah S. Ray and Eric J. Ray
- *Creating Cool HTML 3.2 Web Pages,* 3rd Edition by Dave Taylor
- *FrontPage Web Publishing & Design For Dummies* by Asha Dornfest
- *Creating Cool PageMill 2.0 Web Pages* by Bud E. Smith
- *PageMill 2.0 For Dummies* by Deke McClelland and John San Filippo

If you're looking for information on the best HTML editor to buy, check out the reviews in *Macworld* and *PC World* magazines, or on the magazines' Web sites at `http://www.macworld.com` and `http://www.pcworld.com`.

Using hyperlinks that survive export

Depending on how you export your pages to HTML, you may have to reestablish hyperlinks that you already identified in your PageMaker document (see Chapter 16 for more on creating hyperlinks). That's because PageMaker retains only two kinds of hyperlinks during export:

- Hyperlinks to Web pages and other Internet locations (these locations are *URLs,* or Internet addresses)
- Hyperlinks to other PageMaker pages being exported at the same time. For example, if you have a 15-page document in PageMaker and export only the first five pages to HTML, hyperlinks to pages 6 through 15 are lost during export (of course, links from pages 1 through 5 to material within pages 1 through 5 are retained in the exported file). Keep in mind that pages 1 through 5 are merged into one big HTML page that your readers can scroll through as a single length or navigate by using any hyperlinks within that set of pages. (There's a way to get around this: Use the secret technique for exporting multiple pages described in Chapter 17.)

Why does PageMaker fail to export hyperlinks in any PageMaker page other than those being exported right then and there? In HTML, hyperlinks must be connected to specific destination locations. If you export only some of the pages of a document from PageMaker to HTML, the program comes up empty-handed when it tries to link to locations in those other pages. Because PageMaker doesn't know what those pages will be named or where they will reside, it simply removes the hyperlinks during export (they do remain in the PageMaker file, however). That's why links to URLs are retained — you specify the final destination when setting up the URL in PageMaker.

What's in a (hyperlink) name?

On the Web, hyperlinks refer to actual file names. All those long URL addresses are nothing more than file names. If you've ever used DOS, you probably remember file names such as: `C:\MYFILES\FINANCE\1997\BUDGET.XLS` (this example is a spreadsheet file, .XLS, named BUDGET, in a directory for 1997 in a directory for financial files named FINANCE, in a directory for your personal files named MYFILES on a hard drive named C.).

Web addresses are set up in the same way. The URL `http://www.macworld.com/daily/prods/news919.html` follows the same pattern: An HTML document called news919 is in a folder for products stories (prods) which is in a folder for daily news (called daily) on the *Macworld* site (think of it as an Internet hard drive) on the Internet "Web channel" (http: HyperText Transfer Protocol). (In an HTML editor that displays raw HTML code, location hyperlinks — those within the same HTML page — use a naming convention such as *#Macworld News* rather than `http://www.macworld.com/news.html`, which is the format for hyperlinks to separate pages.)

You don't need to enter the entire URL (for example, `http://www.sitename.com`) of a hyperlink if all the HTML files for your site are on the same hard drive (and they usually are). I'll use a fictitious San Francisco real estate agent's site as an example: All of the agent's files are in a directory called `/realestate/sf/` on her Web server. In this case, a file name alone (such as `noe_valley.html`, for the houses in the Noe Valley neighborhood) would serve as an adequate hyperlink destination. However, if the agent wants to establish a hyperlink to another site with information on Noe Valley real estate, then she needs to enter the full file name. In this case the whole thing would read: `http://www.toprealty.com/sf/noe_valley.html`.

Setting up a Web page hierarchy

When you export your files to the HTML format (described in Chapter 17), you have a choice of exporting pages individually, in selected groups, or all together. The simplest way to preserve hyperlinks during HTML export is to export every page of your document all at once. But if you do that, PageMaker merges all of your individual pages into one very long page, separated with a line break between each page. Each of your hyperlinks from one page to another is retained, but they are actually hyperlinks from one location to another within that one very long Web page, not hyperlinks to other Web pages.

Most Web sites work better as a collection of separate pages hyperlinked to each other, rather than as a single length of text the reader has to scroll through endlessly. That's why I recommend exporting individual pages, or small groups of pages that demand to be read in sequence, and then using an HTML editor to hyperlink them together.

To save yourself some work, you may want to use the technique for exporting multiple pages described in Chapter 17 (but not documented in your PageMaker 6.5 manual). The multiple-selection technique ensures that your PageMaker pages are exported as individual HTML pages and all the hyperlinks are retained among them. (This may be how you'd expect PageMaker to work by default, but it doesn't.) With the multiple-selection process, you don't need to use an HTML editor to hyperlink the HTML pages exported from PageMaker — instead, all the hyperlinking you did in PageMaker is preserved.

Sometimes, it does make sense to have a few pages merged together during export from PageMaker into HTML. You should cluster pages to appear as one long HTML page when the information is closely related (for example, a list of information resources), and use hyperlinks to help your readers jump to another spot in the list quickly.

For example, if you were a real estate agent with a Web site, you may want a separate HTML page for each neighborhood in your territory, with each page hyperlinked to your home page. But if one neighborhood has several of your houses, you may want to put each street or price range on an individual page and export all the pages for that neighborhood together. That way, each neighborhood page is linked to the home page, and readers can scroll through information on all the houses in a particular neighborhood.

Figure 18-3 diagrams Web site pages strung together for sequential reading (the reader can move forward or backward in the chain) and a second Web site with both sequential and individual pages that link to one another in a nonlinear fashion. To get the type of hyperlink pattern shown at right in the figure, you need to export your pages from PageMaker to HTML one at a time, and then cluster a few pages together that you want the reader to scroll through.

You can create hyperlinks to more than just Web pages. If you want your reader to be able to download a file, such as the Acrobat viewer described in Chapter 19, you can link directly to that file. The process is almost identical to that for linking to HTML pages. The only thing that differs is that the file has an extension other than that for a standard HTML page (.htm or .html); the extension would be either .exe, .sea, .zip, .sit, or .hqx for a program or browser plug-in, or .pdf for an Acrobat file (see Chapter 19). The name of the file, including the extension, in the hyperlink address needs to match the name of the file you're linking to.

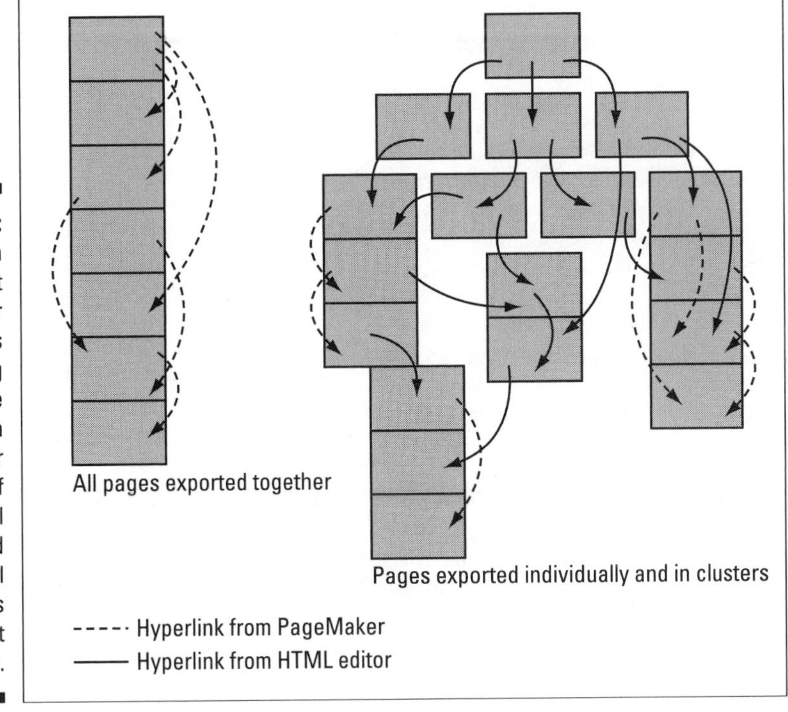

Figure 18-3: You can export PageMaker pages as one long HTML page (as shown at left), or as a mix of individual and sequential pages (as shown at right).

Adding hyperlinks in HTML

Although the process for adding hyperlinks in HTML differs somewhat from one HTML editor to another, the basic steps are the same. The process is essentially the same one you use when adding hyperlinks to your PageMaker documents (a subject covered in Chapter 16):

1. **Select the text or graphic that is the hyperlink source (the clickable hyperlink).**
2. **While in the appropriate dialog box or menu for your HTML editor, enter the name of the page the reader jumps to after clicking on the source hyperlink. (In Figure 18-4, it's shown as** `idgbooks.html`**.)**

If you enter an incorrect hyperlink in PageMaker, you don't need to reexport your pages to HTML. Instead, use your HTML editor to edit the hyperlink (or delete it and add the correct one). Be sure to also correct the hyperlink in PageMaker so that the next time you export HTML pages (perhaps when you update the site's information), the hyperlinks remain correct.

Putting the "hyper" in hyperlinks

If you're not using an HTML editor, you can enter or edit hyperlinks in a word processor or other text editor. HTML documents are really nothing more than text — essentially a program written in HyperText Markup Language. (Chapter 22 has more information on HTML codes used to set up hyperlinks.) The format for some basic hyperlink syntax follows, along with an actual example of how that syntax would read if you entered it in a text editor or word processor. (In the land of HTML, *syntax* describes how a Web browser should recognize and interpret instructions in the markup *tags* — the text contained within the angle bracket [< and >] characters.)

This example is from the Web site of a fictitious San Francisco real estate agent. The *text source* is the clickable hyperlink. The *anchor* is the place the reader ends up after clicking; you would insert the anchor code wherever you want that spot to be.

The text within parentheses is what you need to fill in for each specific hyperlink (the parentheses wouldn't be used in the actual codes).

- **Text source:** <A HREF="(URL address)">(text to click)</A>

  Example: <A HREF="homes/sf/noe_valley/listings.html">Noe Valley Homes</A> The <A> and </A> tags indicate the source for an anchor, while HREF="(address)" indicates the destination (the anchor itself).

- **Graphic source:** <A HREF="(URL address)"><IMG SRC="(file name)"></A>

  Example: <A HREF="/homes/sf/noe_valley/listings.html"><IMG SRC="/homes/sf/noe_valley/4487_24th.gif"></A>.

  The <IMG SRC="(file name)"> tag is a hyperlink to the name of a graphic file.

For hyperlinks within a page, the basic syntax is as follows:

- **Text source:** <A HREF="#(anchor name)">(text to click)</A>

  Example: <A HREF="#Noe Valley Listings">Noe Valley Homes</A>

  The # character indicates that the anchor is in the same HTML page as the source, not in a separate page; the # character must appear with the anchor name.

- **Graphic source:** <A HREF="#(anchor name)"><IMG SRC="(file name)"></A>

  Example: <A HREF="#Noe Valley Listings "><IMG SRC="/homes/sf/noe_valley/4487_24th.gif"></A>

- **Anchor:** <A NAME="(anchor name)"></A>

  Example: <A NAME="Noe Valley Listings"></A>

When you create a hyperlink to a separate Web page, enter the URL as part of the <A HREF-> code. For a hyperlink within the same page, the <A NAME-> tag is where you specify the destination, or anchor name, for the hyperlink.

In PageMaker, the anchor code is automatically placed at the location of the text or graphic that you set up as the anchor, as described in Chapter 16. No anchor is needed when hyperlinking to a separate page, because the anchor is that entire page, and the Web browser brings you to its beginning.

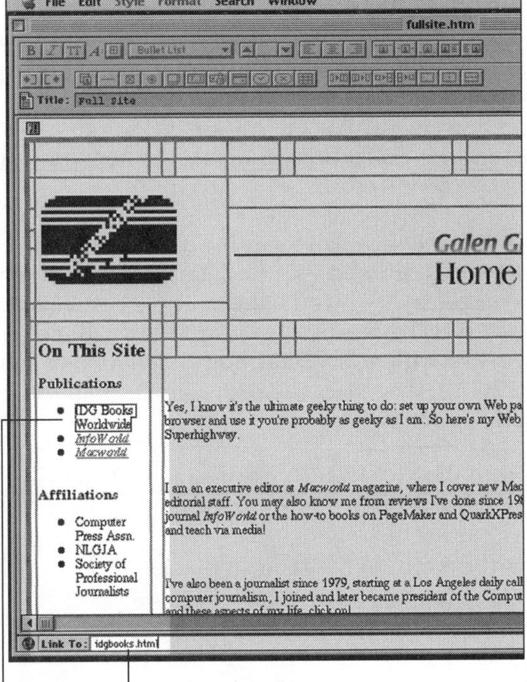

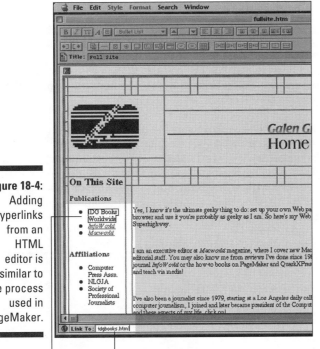

Figure 18-4: Adding hyperlinks from an HTML editor is similar to the process used in PageMaker.

Tweaking the Layout with Table Cells

During export to HTML, PageMaker superimposes a grid of sorts on your document to determine the relative position of text and graphics. It then creates a *table* — a series of cells such as you'd find in a spreadsheet — to contain the text and graphics. (Tables are a new capability in the latest version — 3.2 — of the HTML language, which PageMaker 6.5 takes advantage of to approximate layouts during HTML export.)

Tables are used to approximate the PageMaker layout when it's viewed on the Web. In Figures 18-2 and 18-4, you can see boundaries around objects. I didn't create those, and neither did my HTML editor — PageMaker did during export. This happened because I selected the option Approximate Layout Using HTML Tables When Exporting (found in the Options dialog box) when I exported the document to HTML (see Chapter 17 for more on this topic).

Resizing table cells

PageMaker does the best it can with approximating layout for export to HTML, but it tends to shortchange any material on the right side of a layout. Columns on the right tend to be allotted less space than those on the left, and they end up too narrow. To fix this problem, you need to adjust the cell width and height in your HTML editor.

In some HTML editors, you can resize the table cells by just clicking and dragging on the boundaries of the cells. In others, you have to edit the HTML code, which can get tricky if you have multiple columns and lots of PageMaker-generated cells. To do anything other than rudimentary resizing, spend some practice time with your HTML editor and a book specifically on that editor or on the HTML language. (Also check out Chapter 22 in this book for more on HTML coding.)

In HTML, all tables start with a `<TABLE>` command, in which you (or PageMaker) add statements for the table's attributes:

- `WIDTH="x"` sets the width of the table in pixels.
- `HEIGHT="x"` sets the height in pixels.
- `COLS="x"` sets the number of columns. (This statement is optional.)

These statements are inserted into the `<TABLE>` command in any order before the closing angle bracket (`>`), with a space between each statement, as well as a space after the word *TABLE*. For example: `<TABLE WIDTH="512" COLS="4">`.

At the very end of your table, in standard HTML fashion, is the second half of the table tag, `</TABLE>`, which designates the end of the table.

Although PageMaker specifies table widths in pixels, you can change pixels to percentages in an HTML editor to resize them proportionally. This is helpful if the page is viewed in a browser window smaller than the size specified during HTML export. To use percentages, insert the percent sign as shown in the following example (make sure that the number is a percentage of the screen width you want that column to have):

```
<TD WIDTH="x%">(text or graphics)</TD>
```

The first occurrence of a cell usually has a defined width. If no width is defined, the Web browser simply gives the cell as much space as remains in the table. This means you can size specific cells to be a certain width and let the browser set the width of the other cells.

Each cell requires a <TD> </TD> tag pair — if your table is five cells wide, you need five <TD> </TD> commands.

You can modify the width of a cell by changing the value shown in the HTML code (the value shown as *x* in the earlier example; in reality, *x* would be a real number). You can also use a HEIGHT="x%" statement in the <TD> command to adjust the height.

The browser looks for a <TR> command to know when to begin the next row in a table. If you have a table generated by PageMaker that has lots of cells, including merged cells, keep an eye out for the <TR> commands to know when you're in a new row. The other half of the tag pair, the </TR> command, signals the end of a row.

Merging table cells

You may see the command COLSPAN="x" inside a <TD> command. This command merges two or more cells in a row, not a column (the *x* is replaced in an actual COLSPACE statement by the number cells being merged).

Adding lines around cells

Tables on the Web are often boxed off with lines around the cells. But any boxes put around text in PageMaker to create this effect are ignored during export to HTML. If you want lines around cells, you have to add them in an HTML editor or add the appropriate HTML coding in a text editor.

You can insert any of the following three HTML statements in the <TABLE> command at the beginning of the table to specify the appearance of lines around a cell or the amount of space to allow between text or graphics and the cell:

- BORDER="x" adds a border around the table (replace *x* with the width in pixels for the border).
- CELLSPACING="x" determines the thickness in pixels of the lines around cells (the border must have a width of at least 1 for this command to work).
- CELLPADDING="x" determines the spacing in pixels between the cell boundary and the cell contents.

Examining some real table code

The following is a list of HTML table code for the fairly simple table shown in Figure 18-5. The table has no actual contents; if it did, you'd see text and graphic file names after the <TD> commands where the null space code ($nbsp;) now appears in the list. This example uses all the commands described earlier:

```
<TABLE WIDTH="448" BORDER="1" CELLSPACING="2"
          CELLPADDING="0" HEIGHT="221">
<TR>
<TD WIDTH="43%" HEIGHT="74"> </TD>
<TD WIDTH="17%"> </TD>
<TD> </TD>
<TD> </TD>
<TD WIDTH="40%"> </TD></TR>
<TR>
<TD HEIGHT="68"> </TD>
<TD> </TD>
<TD COLSPAN="2"> </TD>
<TD> </TD></TR>
<TR>
<TD> </TD>
<TD> </TD>
<TD> </TD>
<TD> </TD>
<TD> </TD></TR>
</TABLE>
```

Figure 18-5: An example of a table in HTML.

Finishing Up

To do the final edits to your page — fix typing errors, delete unwanted text, or add missing information — you need to edit the text in an HTML editor or word processor. Be sure to also update your PageMaker document so that the next time you export your HTML pages the text changes don't have to be redone. Unfortunately, any editing you do to HTML commands can't be brought into PageMaker for reexporting later.

When you're done making changes, remember to save the HTML pages in *ASCII format,* a standard text file format. An HTML editor does so automatically. In a Windows word processor, you must save the file in text format (it probably has the file extension .txt, but rename the file extension to .htm now or after you're done saving). If you're using a Macintosh word processor, save the file in text-only format.

Chapter 19

Creating Web Pages with Adobe Acrobat

In This Chapter

- Understanding the Acrobat option
- Exporting PageMaker files to Acrobat
- Obtaining the Acrobat reader program
- Setting export preferences
- Selecting hyperlinks preferences
- Adding special features

Here you are, itching to create a Web site — your calling card in the Internet global village — and you want it to be just as brilliant and exciting as you are. But then you find yourself mucking around with HTML, a markup language whose limited formatting powers are positively stifling your creativity. You figure that there must be some way to create Web pages that isn't so tedious, so restrictive, so totally squaresville. What you probably need is Adobe Acrobat.

Acrobat is a formatting alternative to HTML that lets you replicate your PageMaker pages so they can be viewed on a Web browser exactly as you created them. Acrobat uses the Adobe *Portable Document Format* (PDF) that produces online pages called *portable documents* that look just like your files for print publishing — with all the fonts, pictures, graphic elements, and text configurations you'd want. With PageMaker 6.5's Acrobat export option, you can create high-fidelity documents for use on your Web site. (These documents are variously described as Acrobat, Adobe PDF, and PDF files.)

You may be wondering, if Acrobat is able to do this, why go through the process of coding a document with HyperText Markup Language (HTML) at all? HTML is limited when it comes to fancy formatting (as described in earlier chapters of this book) but that's not an entirely bad thing. Elaborate formatting results in huge files that move slowly through the Internet (which is getting clogged up as it is). Those big files force Net surfers to wait and wait until your document becomes available for viewing on their screens.

HTML may be limited, but its a simple and straightforward formatting language that can be easily managed by Web browsers.

When to Use the Acrobat Option

Adobe PDF documents come in handy in several instances. Maybe you need lots of flexibility to create a multipurpose order form for your readers to download, print, and fax back to you. Or, maybe you want to include a list of prices or phone numbers that have to be printed in space-saving small type. Or, maybe you want to include pictures, as well as detailed product specifications, in an online catalog.

If you're creating a document for an intranet rather than the Internet, the complexity of the formatting and the size of your files and their effect on downloading time become less of an issue. Intranet documents are accessed over a fast network (usually within a company) rather than over the slower phone network via sluggish modems.

Using the Acrobat export option means you can use any kind of formatting you'd use in a print document, including many features that don't work in HTML. This gives you the freedom to make your Acrobat document as visually enticing as it needs to be for its content. (Previous chapters of this book provide ideas for page design, or you can turn to a print-oriented title, such as *PageMaker 6 For Windows For Dummies* or *PageMaker 6 For Macs For Dummies,* both from IDG Books Worldwide, Inc.)

Formatting options that do not export from HTML to the Web, but can be preserved with the Acrobat format include:

- All special symbols, including the bullets in bulleted lists
- All font formatting, including typefaces and text styles
- All spacing (tracking, kerning, and baseline shifts) and line endings
- Tabbed text and tables
- Layout formatting such as column widths, element placement, and text wrap around graphics
- All graphics created within PageMaker
- All special image effects available in PageMaker — such as masking, image controls, and filters
- Image bleeds, although only the portion that appears in the layout page appears in the Acrobat document (when exporting to HTML, on the other hand, if an image bleeds off the page, the entire image is removed from the HTML document)
- All page numbering

In addition, any hypertext links you create within your PageMaker document are preserved when exported to Acrobat format, so readers can still click and jump from page to page as they would with an HTML document — even to other HTML documents on the Web or on your intranet.

The document in Figure 19-1 is a simple PageMaker layout, the first two pages of a guidebook to France. But it has several features that don't survive HTML export, including an image that bleeds off the page (at right), graphics created in PageMaker (the bars to the left and underneath the word "Paris"), large italicized text and multiple fonts, footers at the bottom of the left-hand page, and tabbed text in the index. If you want your readers to view these pages with formatting left intact, you need to export the document to Acrobat format. Figure 19-2 shows the Acrobat version of the pages in Figure 19-1.

Several elements are shown in Figure 19-2 that are part of the Acrobat Reader program that displays Acrobat pages, including a search dialog box and thumbnails of all pages in the Acrobat file. Web surfers reading your Acrobat pages through a browser don't see those elements, but people using the Acrobat Reader software do. (The Acrobat Reader is covered later in this chapter.)

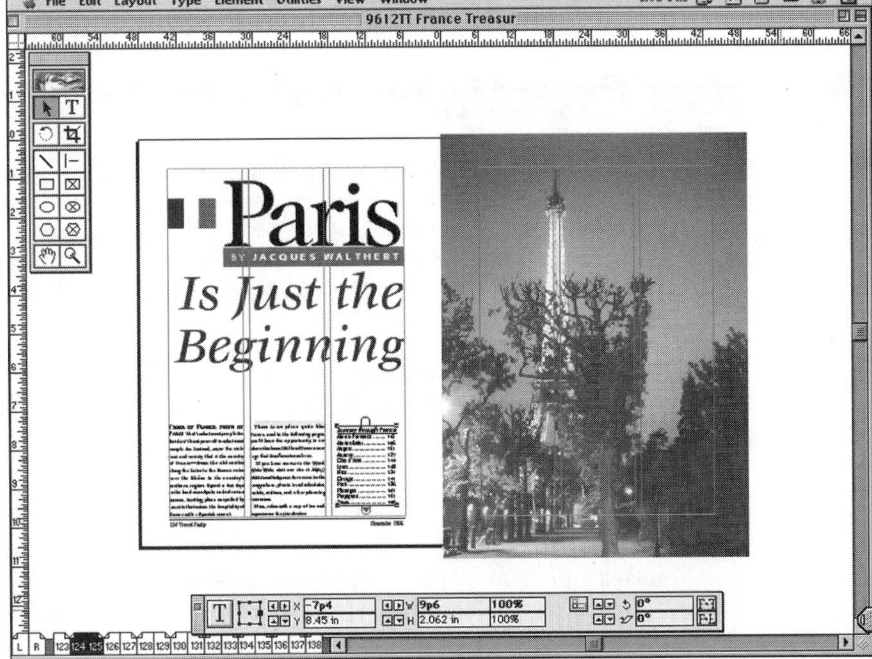

Figure 19-1: A layout featuring formatting that would be lost if exported to HTML but retained if exported to Acrobat.

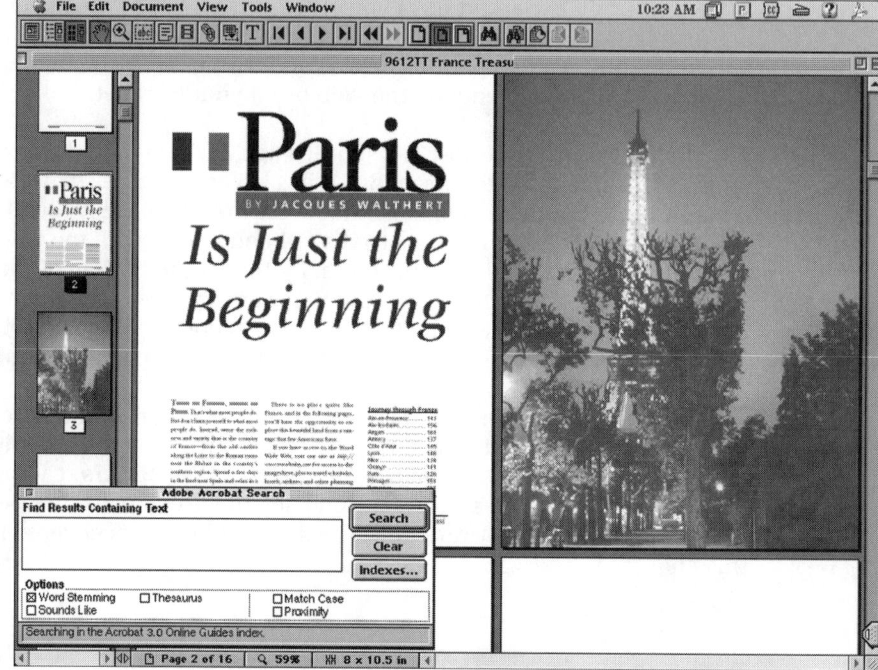

Figure 19-2: A working view of the page from Figure 19-1, shown in the Acrobat Reader program.

Exporting PageMaker Files to Acrobat

Once you've created your PageMaker pages, you're ready to export to Acrobat format — no special preparation is needed. To do so, select File⇨Export⇨Adobe PDF to open the Export Adobe PDF dialog box shown in Figure 19-3. The settings for creating Acrobat files really aren't as complicated as they first seem, so hang in there as we go through them.

You need to decide whether you want to export the Acrobat file immediately (by clicking on the Distill Now button) or create an interim file from which the Acrobat file is exported later (by clicking on the Prepare PostScript File for Distilling Separately button).

Several good reasons exist to pick the Prepare PostScript File for Distilling Separately option:

- You lack sufficient RAM to run both PageMaker 6.5 and the Distiller program at once. Chances are you encounter this memory shortage on a Mac more often than under Windows. On a Mac, you need about 40MB of RAM and the RAM Doubler program from Connectix installed, or a high setting for virtual memory (more than 80MB) in your Memory control panel.

To read Acrobat files, you need Acrobat viewers

To view Acrobat files, Web users need a tool called an Acrobat *viewer.* Viewers are available for the Macintosh, Windows, and another system called UNIX, and a viewer for any of these platforms can read an Adobe document from any other platform, even if it was created on a different type of computer. For example, a Mac viewer can read an Acrobat document exported from the Windows version of PageMaker.

You can get Acrobat viewers in any one of several ways:

- Buy the full Acrobat program, called Acrobat Exchange, from Adobe Systems (which lets users create and annotate Acrobat files as well as view them). Call Adobe at 800/642-3623 (in the United States and Canada) or access the Adobe Web site at `http://www.adobe.com/acrobat/`, or check out your favorite computer store or mail-order catalog.
- Download a free viewer-only program called Acrobat Reader from the Adobe Web site at `http://www.adobe.com/acrobat/`. Readers on your site can hyperlink to it from your Web page.
- Whether you've purchased the full Acrobat Exchange program or not, you have permission to make the viewer programs available to your readers who can download them directly from your Web site. This is a handy way for your readers to get the files when they need them. (Chapter 18 explains the process of adding a hyperlink to other locations.) Adobe provides an icon you can place into your Web pages to indicate that you have the Acrobat Reader files available. For more information on how to distribute the Acrobat Reader programs from your Web site, read the instructions provided by Adobe at `http://www.adobe.com/prodindex/acrobat/distribute.html`.
- Get the Acrobat viewer that works within Netscape Navigator 3.0 or Microsoft Internet Explorer 3.0, which lets you view Acrobat pages as you're browsing a Web site, rather than having to download the Acrobat file and view them in a separate program. The Navigator Acrobat plug-in comes with both the full Acrobat Exchange program and Acrobat Reader. It cannot be downloaded separately from the Adobe or Netscape Web sites, but you can make it available for downloading the same way you make the Acrobat Reader file downloadable from your site. (The Acrobat plug-in for Navigator also works with Internet Explorer.)

RAM Doubler is a great program to have if you use a Mac, so I suggest you get it no matter how much RAM your Mac has (but make sure you have at least 16MB of real memory, and preferably 24MB). Be aware that memory-doubling programs on Windows 95 don't live up to their claims, so you're better off buying real memory. Memory is now very inexpensive, so don't skimp on it, whether you use a PC or a Mac.

- You are creating lots of Acrobat files. It's faster to create all the PostScript files and then use the Acrobat Distiller program that comes with PageMaker 6.5 to batch-convert them to Acrobat files all at once.

Export Adobe PDF

Workflow
Distill now
View PDF using: Acrobat™ Exchange 3.0
Location: Mac Test:
Prepare PostScript file for distilling separately
Use Distiller's "Watched Folder" Select...
Current selection: None
Include downloadable fonts
Override Distiller's options Edit...
PageMaker's printer style: Acrobat
Paper size(s): Same as page size(s)
Pages: All Ranges: 123-
Export... Cancel PDF Options... Control... Save Settings Load Settings Reset Settings

Figure 19-3: The Export Adobe PDF dialog box is where you set up your Acrobat export settings.

- You are on a network that has a Watched folder for Distiller to use. A *Watched folder* is one that the Distiller program checks periodically for PostScript files to convert to Acrobat format. A network administrator at your organization is the one to set this up, so if you haven't used this folder yet, don't worry about it. If you do have to set up this folder, click on the Use Distiller's Watched Folder checkbox and then click on the Select button to specify where that folder should be located (on your hard drive or network). If this option is not selected, PageMaker asks you for the destination of the Acrobat file you're exporting.

Selecting output settings

The following explains the three control buttons at the bottom of the Export Adobe PDF dialog box in Figure 19-3. The settings of the first two should never change, while the third you can reselect as needed.

- The PageMaker's Printer Style pop-up menu (set at Acrobat in Figure 19-3) lets you select the printer drive used to create your Acrobat file. (You define printer styles by selecting File ⇨ Printer Styles⇨Define.) My advice: Just leave it at the default setting, which is Acrobat. Any other settings are just too technical to mess with.
- The Paper Size(s) pop-up menu lets you specify how the page size for your Acrobat file is determined: either by the actual size of the page (the default setting Same as Page Size[s], shown in the figure), or by the size of each page in a multiple document (used with the PageMaker Books multidocument feature, which doesn't apply to Web publishing), or by the printer style settings (if you create printer styles with

nonstandard page sizes or reductions/enlargements). Leave it at the Same as Page Size(s) default to keep things simple.

- For the Pages option, select All if you want all of the pages in your document converted to Acrobat format, or choose Ranges and specify the page numbers for the range of pages you want output to an Acrobat file.

Managing fonts

For accurate font exporting, select Include Downloadable Fonts in the Export Adobe PDF dialog box. This option copies all the font information necessary for accurate on-screen reproduction into your Acrobat file. If you don't select it, the Acrobat Reader tries to simulate your fonts on the reader's computer — a hit-or-miss proposition — and special symbols are completely lost. Be aware that selecting this option increases the file size, but that's the price you have to pay to deliver print-like quality documents over the Web.

Several other controls for managing fonts are located in the Distiller PDF Job Options dialog box, shown in Figure 19-4. To access it, select Override Distiller's Options in the Export Adobe PDF dialog box (in Figure 19-3) and then click on the Edit button.

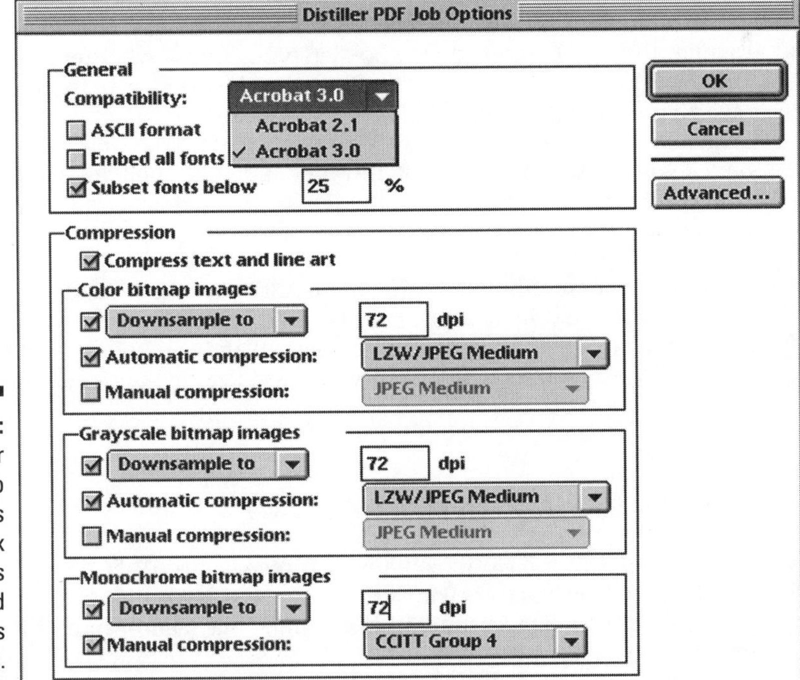

Figure 19-4: The Distiller PDF Job Options dialog box controls font and graphics settings.

- Selecting Embed All Fonts under the General options tells Acrobat to include all fonts used in your document, even those that reside on every PostScript printer (Helvetica, Times, Courier, Zapf Chancery, and Zapf Dingbats). Use this if your document uses Zapf Chancery or Zapf Dingbats, which non-PostScript printers may not have. (In Windows, non-PostScript printers automatically use Arial instead of Helvetica and Times New Roman instead of Times. These printers support Courier as well.)
- Subset Fonts Below is a useful option to conserve file space, so make sure it's checked. This option works by storing in the Acrobat file only the characters used in a document, rather than the whole font. The default is 25 percent, but you can change it.

You might think you should set the Subset fonts option to 100 so that all of the characters used are stored, but don't. When this option is selected, just the characters used for each page are stored with each page — in a multipage document, this can easily add up to storing the whole font more than just once. (When the whole font is stored, its characters are available to every page, but when Subset fonts is selected, stored characters are available only to their pages.) As it turns out, 25 percent is the best setting for maximum efficiency in storing font information.

Setting file compatibility

Because Adobe Systems just recently released Acrobat Version 3.0, the Distiller PDF Job Options dialog box lets you choose whether to create Version 2.1 or Version 3.0 Acrobat files with the Compatibility pop-up menu (see Figure 19-4) . I recommend selecting Acrobat 3.0 and make this version available to users browsing your Web pages. Select the Acrobat 2.1 option only if you're publishing over an intranet and your company has invested in supplying everyone with the full version of Acrobat 2.1 and hasn't yet upgraded them to Version 3.0.

Another file-compatibility control is the ASCII Format checkbox. Some printers have trouble handling the standard binary format for PostScript files (Acrobat PDF is a version of PostScript) and can better handle the ASCII format. If your readers won't print your files, use this option; otherwise, leave it unchecked.

Compressing graphics

The Distiller PDF Job Options dialog box (see Figure 19-4) gives you compression controls for three kinds of graphics — color bitmap images, grayscale bitmap images, and monochrome (black-and-white) bitmap images.

- Select the Downsample To option, which reduces the resolution from the image's original setting to whatever you specify in the dpi option box.
- If you expect readers to view your Acrobat files on screen only, set all three types of bitmaps to 72 dpi, which is the resolution of a computer monitor. (When you export to HTML, your bitmaps are downsampled automatically to 72 dpi.)

- If you think your readers are going to print your Acrobat files, select either 72 dpi or 150 dpi for the color and bitmap images and either 150 dpi or 300 dpi for the monochrome images. In most cases, the lower of the settings is acceptable, but you may want to use the higher number if your readers are using printers at 600-dpi or higher. Optimal resolution is one that matches the user's printer, but it does increase file sizes dramatically.
- With the Automatic compression option, PageMaker chooses the best compression option for each image; the Manual compression setting lets you select the compression option for each file of that type.
- For color and grayscale bitmap images, choose the most suitable compression quality. The default is LZW/JPEG Medium (shown in Figure 19-4). The JPEG compression scheme removes some detail in images to better compress them; however, the more detail that's removed, the murkier an image is. You can set the quality from high to low in five increments with the pop-up menu that appears next to the Automatic compression checkbox. Choose one of the high options only if your images have a lot of subtle details; otherwise, use the default setting.
- Vector files, such as EPS figures, and the text itself in your document can also be compressed. Just click on the Compress Text and Line Art checkbox.

Using compression means that files take less time to download (and use up less disk space) but take a little longer to open and display in the Acrobat Reader. The slightly slower display is well worth the saved download time, so you should routinely use compression options.

The Advanced button in the Distiller PDF Job Options box may either intimidate you or peak your interest. Suffice it to say, I don't cover those advanced options in this book.

Handling hyperlinks

One of the neat things about the Acrobat format is that it preserves hyperlinks created in PageMaker as well as preserving print-like visual attributes. The Acrobat default export retains hyperlinks within a document and hyperlinks to other documents or Web sites. You do have the option of disabling the hyperlink function through the PDF Options dialog box shown in Figure 19-5. This box can be accessed by clicking on the PDF Options button in the Export Adobe PDF dialog box.

Why do I need to override the Distiller?

You may wonder why an option to override the default Distiller settings appears in the Export Adobe PDF dialog box. This override option comes in handy in a couple of instances:

- Override the default if you expect to change the settings at least twice in a single work session. It's easier to do this in PageMaker than to launch Distiller, change its settings, go back into PageMaker, create the Acrobat file, then go back to Distiller and reset its settings.
- Override the default if you share Distiller with other users, all of whom are working on different kinds of documents with different kinds of Acrobat-processing needs.

You may be using a networked copy of Distiller for processing PostScript files. Or, you may be generating PostScript files that someone else processes on a PC or Mac using their own copy of Distiller. Or, several users may be creating Acrobat documents on your machine, all with different processing needs.

Check the Distiller settings to make sure the defaults are set according to your needs. After opening Distiller, select Distiller ➪ Job Options, or the shortcut Ctrl+J (Windows) or ⌘+J (Mac) to open a dialog box similar to the Distiller PDF Job Options dialog box in PageMaker.

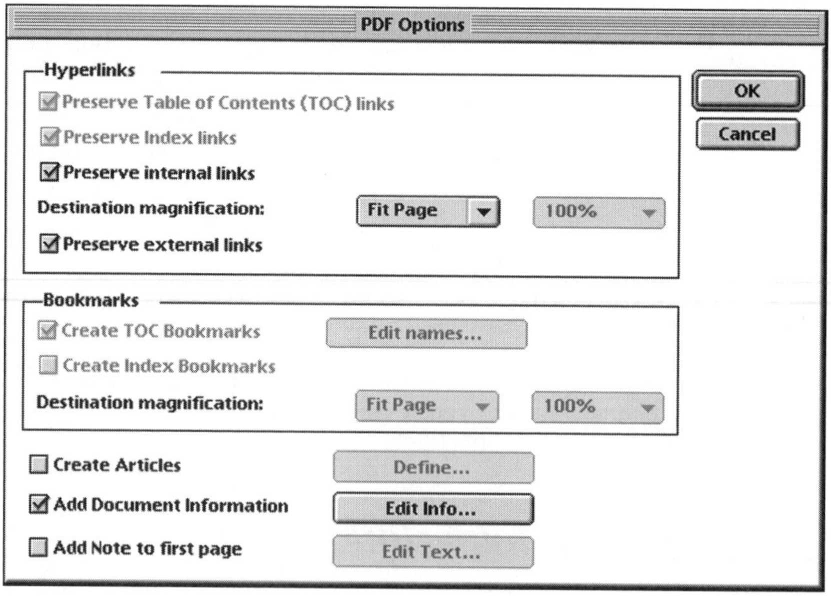

Figure 19-5: The PDF Options dialog box controls hyperlinking and document outlining.

The Hyperlinks section of the dialog box lists four kinds of hyperlinks. Select the ones you want preserved when creating the Acrobat file:

- Preserve Table of Contents (TOC) Links retains links from a PageMaker-generated table of contents to the source text in a document. This option is grayed out if the document has no table of contents.
- Preserve Index Links retains links from a PageMaker-generated index to the source text in a document. This option is grayed out if the document has no index.
- Preserve Internal Links preserves hypertext links from one page to another in a document. Chapter 16 shows how to create these hyperlinks.
- Preserve External Links preserves hypertext links from your document to a Web page in another document (see Chapter 16).

Destination Magnification, shown in the Hyperlinks box, determines the way a linked page is displayed in the Acrobat reader. Its pop-up menu displays five options:

- Fit Page ensures that the entire page that is the hyperlink destination displays in the window when the reader clicks on the hyperlink.
- Fit Page Contents ensures that the contents of the page that is the hyperlink destination displays in the window when the reader clicks on the hyperlink. Any margin between the page border and the contents is cropped out.
- Fit Top Left ensures that the top left of the destination (the text or graphic that contains the hyperlink anchor) appears along with as much of the rest of the page that fits within the browser window. You can set a percentage of magnification or reduction for what is displayed.
- Fit Top Left Page ensures that the top left of the destination page appears along with as much of the rest of the page that fits within the browser window. You can set a percentage of magnification or reduction for what is displayed.
- Fit Context ensures that the specific information being hyperlinked to an image or a string of text displays in the browser window when the reader clicks on the hyperlink to it.

Creating outlines

If you used PageMaker's index and table-of-contents features (which many print-oriented documents do), the Acrobat export function can convert them to an electronic outline — which it calls *bookmarks* — that the Acrobat Reader displays to readers so they can quickly find their way through your document. It essentially creates a hyperlink version of the index and table of contents so they can click the relevant word or phrase in an outline view and jump to the appropriate text.

Creating articles

When you export a PageMaker layout to HTML, you can choose to preserve the layout or you can export your document as one long stream of text arranged by order of the stories (text blocks) in the PageMaker document. (You can find more information on this in Chapter 17.) Exporting to Acrobat format always preserves the layout, but you also have the option of exporting the stories in a layout as separate articles by using the Create Articles option (seen in Figure 19-5).

In the Acrobat Reader or Acrobat Exchange program, you can get a list of the stories to export as articles through the View menu's Articles option (or press Ctrl+Shift+A or Shift+⌘+A) — a much quicker way to find stories than scrolling through pages.

After you select Create Articles, click on the Define button to select the PageMaker stories you want included in the list of articles in Acrobat. Each independent text block or frame is listed as a separate story; if several text blocks or frames are linked, the first block or frame is the beginning of that story.

Saving settings

In the Export Acrobat PDF dialog box (in Figure 19-3), three options can be used to help you manage your preferences:

- Save Settings saves the current settings you selected through the Adobe Acrobat PDF dialog box to disk, and these settings appear the next time you open the dialog box. However, you cannot create a bunch of different settings to select from later — each time you use this option, the saved settings file is overwritten with the current settings.
- Load Settings applies the latest settings saved through Save Settings.
- Reset Settings applies the default PageMaker settings.

Adding Extra Features

If you want to include special features in your Acrobat files after you export them from PageMaker, and if you own the Acrobat Exchange program, you can do any of the following to your Acrobat files:

- Create thumbnails of each page, which are then displayed in a window in the Acrobat Reader or Exchange to make it easier for the user to find a desired page
- Add "sticky notes" and highlight text with an electronic highlighter
- Add additional hyperlinks within the document or to other documents and Web pages
- Insert QuickTime movies
- Create buttons and fields that manage the behavior of the Reader or Exchange program, such as jumping from one page to another, printing a page, playing a sound, or submitting a form to a Web address (for use in interactive Web pages)
- Reformat text
- Rotate and crop pages
- Insert pages from other Acrobat files and export specific pages to new Acrobat files

Part VII
The Part of Tens

The 5th Wave
By Rich Tennant
Andy soon began to think he shouldn't have opted for the cut-rate Web hookup after all.
©RICHTENNANT

In this part . . .

You know the problem with most computer books? (*Besides* the fact that their turgid prose violates all known measures for soporific tedium.) They don't offer enough sound bites. When you set the book down, you should be humming the tunes, as it were, conjuring up images of pages gone by, psyched to the gills to put a few techniques to the test. In other words, you should be raring to use PageMaker.

That's what the "Part of Tens" is all about. In preceding chapters, we discussed a few thousand issues pertinent to PageMaker and Web publishing in context; the rest of the book hurls factoids at you completely out of context. The idea is that if we hurl enough of them hard enough, a few are bound to get stuck in your brain. It is our supreme wish that on your deathbed you say something completely meaningless to surviving relatives like, "You can specify a fixed-width font with the <TT>, </TT> HTML tag code," as they wait expectantly to hear who's mentioned in your will. If you do, try to videotape it. We may be able to use it in a marketing campaign; you never know.

Chapter 20

Ten Shortcut Groups You'll Always Use

In This Chapter

- Choosing commands in the File menu
- Zooming in and out of a page
- Navigating around pages
- Controlling object placement
- Displaying PageMaker palettes
- Activating tools from the keyboard
- Choosing the Undo command
- Choosing Clipboard commands
- Using Story Editor — the PageMaker word processor
- Applying formatting attributes
- Creating and editing styles and colors
- Using the Windows super shortcut

The amount of money spent on computers and other hardware that operate faster than previous hardware is amazing. For a mere thousand dollars, you can shave seconds off your working day. But while your computer pushes new frontiers in speed, you're working at the same old pace you always were. Imagine this from your computer's perspective: Here it is stuck with this same old-model user with no chance to update, *ever*.

The point is that you get a lot more work done a lot more quickly without spending a single penny if you learn to work more efficiently. And the best way to save time is to learn the essential shortcuts, which are laid at your feet in this one-of-a-kind, efficiency-building chapter. No seminars, no weight-lifting, no pyramid schemes. No more excess mousing around and wading through boxes and menus. Just a couple quick flicks of the keyboard gets you what you want in a flash. Take time to memorize these shortcuts, and you'll witness the most amazing transformation your computer has ever seen.

Opening, Saving, and Quitting

Use these shortcuts to navigate through the basic File menu commands:

- **Windows: Ctrl+N; then Enter**

  Mac: ⌘+N; then Enter

  To create a new single-paged, letter-sized document (assuming you don't mind default settings), press Ctrl+N (in Windows) or ⌘+N (on the Mac) and then press Enter. You're good to go. If you want to customize the document here and there, press Ctrl+N or ⌘+N and change the settings in the dialog box as desired.

- **Windows: Ctrl+O**

  Mac: ⌘+O

  To open a document that you created previously and saved to a floppy disk or your hard drive, press Ctrl+O.

- **Windows: Ctrl+S**

  Mac: ⌘+S

  To save your document to a disk or drive, press Ctrl+S. Save your document early and often to avoid the heartbreak of lost work.

- **Windows: Ctrl+Q**

  Mac: ⌘+Q

  To escape the generous clutches of PageMaker and return to the Windows Start button or the Macintosh Finder, press Ctrl+Q or ⌘+Q. If you haven't saved your most recent changes, press Enter to do so when PageMaker asks.

- **Windows: Ctrl+D**

  Mac: ⌘+D

  Chances are that you'll be placing a lot of pictures and text files into your documents during your career as a PageMaker user. Use Ctrl+D or ⌘+D to quickly go to the Place dialog box.

- **Windows: Ctrl+K**

  Mac: ⌘+K

  PageMaker 6.5 buried its Preferences dialog box well within several menu layers. You can quickly dig it out and access it by using Ctrl+K or ⌘+K.

Zooming with Keyboard and Clicks

These shortcuts come in handy for enlarging or reducing your viewing selection quickly:

- **Windows: Ctrl+plus (+), Ctrl+hyphen (-)**

  Mac: ⌘+plus (+), ⌘+hyphen (-)

  No need to reach for the Zoom tool — just use Ctrl+plus (+) or ⌘+plus (+) to magnify the screen or Ctrl+hyphen (-) or ⌘+hyphen (-) to reduce the magnification.

- **Windows: Ctrl+ 0, Ctrl+1 , Ctrl+2, Ctrl+5**

  Mac: ⌘+0, ⌘+1, ⌘+2, ⌘+5

  If you want to zoom in or out on a selected bit of text or a selected graphic, press Ctrl+0 (zero) or ⌘+0 (zero) for the fit-in-window size that lets you see the entire page, Ctrl+1 or ⌘+1 to access 100 percent of the actual page size view, Ctrl+2 or ⌘+2 for the 200 percent view size, and Ctrl+5 or ⌘+5 for the 50 percent view size.

- **Windows: Ctrl+spacebar+drag, Ctrl+Alt+spacebar+drag**

  Mac: ⌘+spacebar+drag, Option+⌘+spacebar+drag

  To magnify the screen beyond 400 percent — without first switching to the Zoom tool — press and hold Ctrl+spacebar or ⌘+spacebar to select the magnifying glass cursor and then drag around the portion of the page you want to magnify. The surrounded area you select grows to fill the window.

- **Windows: Ctrl+Alt+spacebar+click**

  Mac: Option+⌘+spacebar+click

  Pressing Ctrl+Alt+spacebar or Option+⌘+spacebar reduces the current magnification.

- **Windows: Alt+click with Zoom tool**

  Mac: Option+click with Zoom tool

  If you have the Zoom tool selected, you can just drag over an area to enlarge your view, and Alt+click or Option+click to reduce your view.

Navigating inside Your Document

Use these shortcuts to move around inside your document without having to resort to tedious scrolling:

- **Windows: Alt+drag**

  Mac: Option+drag

  To move your page around inside the window, Alt+drag or Option+drag with any tool except the Zoom tool. Your cursor changes to the cute little grabber hand for the duration of your drag.

- **Windows and Mac: Page Up, Page Down**

  Press Page Up to move to the previous page or set of facing pages. To move forward a page, press Page Down.

- **Windows: Ctrl+Alt+G, p#, Enter**

  Mac: Option+⌘+G, p#, Enter

  If you want to go to a specific page, press Ctrl+Alt+G or Option+⌘+G, enter the page number, and press the Enter key. To go to a master page, press the same shortcut, select the Master Page radio button, choose a master page from the pop-up menu, and press Enter.

- **Windows and Mac: Shift+choose Layout⇨Go to Page**

  To peruse every page of your document, press the Shift key while choosing Layout⇨Go to Page. PageMaker shows the next page or spread, waits a few seconds, and then shows the page or spread after that. PageMaker continues cycling, displaying the first page after the last page, until you click your mouse button. Give it a try!

Locking and Grouping Objects

These key combinations come in handy to make sure objects don't stray from their appointed place or to group them as a unit:

- **Windows: Ctrl+L, Ctrl+Alt+L**

  Mac: ⌘+L, Option+⌘+L

  To make sure that you don't accidentally move something once you have it exactly where you want it, select it and use Ctrl+L or ⌘+L to lock it into place. Ctrl+Alt+L or Option+⌘+L opens the lock.

- **Windows: Ctrl+G, Ctrl+Shift+G**

  Mac: ⌘+G, Shift+⌘+G

  Similarly, once you have placed several items together and want them to stay together, select them and use Ctrl+G or ⌘+G to group them. PageMaker then lets you treat them as if they were one object. Ctrl+Shift+G or Shift+⌘+G breaks up the group.

Displaying Palettes

Palettes make selecting PageMaker options as simple as pointing and clicking. Here's how to make palettes appear and reappear in a snap:

- **Windows: Ctrl+quote ('), Ctrl+J, Ctrl+B, Ctrl+8, Ctrl+Shift+8, Ctrl+9**

  Mac: ⌘+quote ('), ⌘+J, ⌘+B, ⌘+8, Shift+⌘+8, ⌘+9

  You can display or hide six palettes by pressing key combinations. Press Ctrl+quote (') or ⌘+quote (') to hide and show the Control palette. To access the Colors and Styles palettes, press Ctrl+J or ⌘+J and Ctrl+B or ⌘+B, respectively. Ctrl+8 or ⌘+8 displays and hides the Layers palette, while Ctrl+Shift+8 or Shift+⌘+8 accesses the Master Pages palette. Finally, you can get to the new Hyperlinks palette easily with Ctrl+9 or ⌘+9.

- **Windows and Mac: Tab with open palettes**

  When the Arrow tool is active and a document is open, pressing the Tab key does a very neat thing: It turns off all open palettes, giving you a clear view of your document. Pressing Tab again reactivates the palettes that had been visible.

Selecting Tools

PageMaker puts loads of powerful tools at your disposal. Use these key combinations to call them up in a hurry:

- **Windows and Mac: Shift+F2, Shift+F3, Shift+F4, Shift+F5, Shift+F6, Shift+F7**

  If your mouse gives you the eeeks, here's a tip you're going to love: how to access tools from the keyboard. Several of PageMaker's tools are accessible by pressing Shift plus a function key. The function keys correspond to the tools in the order that they appear in the toolbox's left side (no shortcut exists for the Arrow tool, unfortunately). The Rotate tool is Shift+F2, the Line tool is Shift+F3, the Rectangle tool is Shift+F4, the Ellipse tool is Shift+F5, the Polygon tool is Shift+F6, and the Hand tool is Shift+F7.

- **Windows: Shift+Alt+F1, Shift+Alt+F2, Shift+Alt+F3, Shift+Alt+F4, Shift+Alt+F5, Shift+Alt+F6, Shift+Alt+F7**

  Mac: Option+Shift+F1, Option+Shift+F2, Option+Shift+F3, Option+Shift+F4, Option+Shift+F5, Option+Shift+F6, Option+Shift+F7

  The toolbox's right side has a similar sequence. Just add Shift+Alt (Windows) or Option+Shift (Mac) to the following function keys to invoke the specified tools: F1 for Text, F2 for Crop, F3 for Orthogonal Line, F4 for Rectangular Frame, F5 for Elliptical Frame, F6 for Polygonal Frame, and F7 for Zoom.

- **Windows: Ctrl+spacebar or F9**

  Mac: ⌘+spacebar or F9

  A function key shortcut for the Arrow tool does not exist. But you can toggle between the Arrow tool and the currently selected tool by pressing F9, or Ctrl+spacebar or ⌘+spacebar. For example, if the Text tool is selected, pressing F9 or Ctrl+spacebar selects the Arrow tool. Pressing F9 or Ctrl+spacebar again takes you back to the Text tool. Go ahead, give it a try. You'll fall in love all over again.

  Ctrl+spacebar is also the shortcut to temporarily access the Zoom tool. If you press and hold the two keys, you get the Zoom tool cursor. But when you release the two keys, you get the Arrow tool. Fancy that, two shortcuts for the price of one!

Undoing Mistakes

You'll probably use this shortcut more than any other. It undoes goofs and other undesirable operations:

- **Windows: Ctrl+Z**
- **Mac: ⌘+Z**

  If you want to eliminate the last action you performed, press Ctrl+Z or ⌘+Z. Unfortunately, PageMaker can't undo as many operations as it should — it can't undo text formatting, for example — but sometimes the Undo feature comes in handy. For example, if you delete an entire text block, Ctrl+Z or ⌘+Z brings it back to life.

Windows 95 super shortcuts

While Adobe made the Mac and Windows versions of PageMaker virtually identical, in one area the two programs are merely fraternal twins. By taking advantage of the Windows right mouse button, PageMaker 6.5 gives you quick access to a number of helpful options with the right mouse button+click action. The following figure shows a bunch of these on a screen (although only one can be active at a time). Particularly useful items to right+click on are:

- The master page icon to switch master pages
- The page icons to add or delete pages
- Graphic images to apply effects or to copy or paste them
- Text to edit, spell-check, copy, or paste
- The pasteboard to zoom in or out

In most cases, the Arrow tool should be selected. But, if you are working with text, you can have the Text tool active when you're right-clicking to get text-oriented options. If another tool is selected, right-clicking displays only the general PageMaker options, such as zoom settings.

PageMaker 6.5 for both Windows and Macintosh does have those new, handy menus on all of its palettes, which gives Mac (and Windows) users right+click-like quick access to many options.

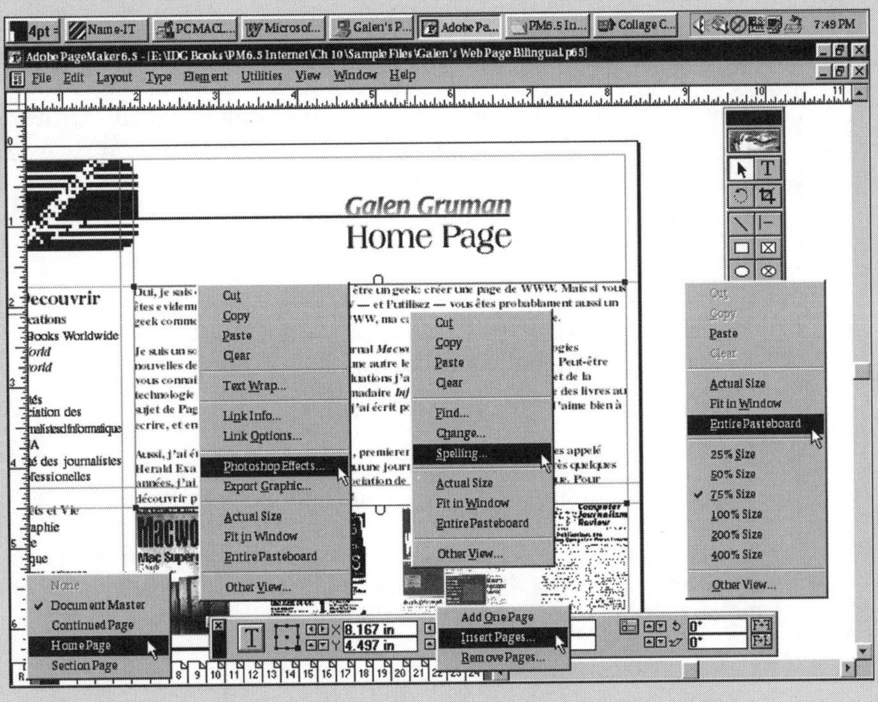

Making Copies

The following shortcuts are quick ways to transfer or replicate text and graphic elements:

- **Windows: Ctrl+X, Ctrl+C, Ctrl+V**

  Mac: ⌘+X, ⌘+C, ⌘+V

  To cut some selected text or a selected graphic and transfer it to the Clipboard, press Ctrl+X or ⌘+X. (If you use your imagination, the *X* looks like a pair of scissors, hence its use for *cut.*) To copy a selection, press Ctrl+C or ⌘+C. And to paste the contents of the Clipboard into your PageMaker document, press Ctrl+V or ⌘+V. (The *V* is supposed to look like an insertion wedge, hence its use for *paste.*)

Editing Text in the Story Editor

Story Editor is kind of like PageMaker's built-in word processor. The following shortcuts quickly shift you to Story Editor view:

- **Windows: Ctrl+E**

  Mac: ⌘+E

  To enter the Story Editor, select some text with either the Arrow or Text tool and press Ctrl+E or ⌘+E. Pressing Ctrl+E or ⌘+E again takes you back to the layout view.

- **Windows: Ctrl+L; then Enter**

  Mac: ⌘+L; then Enter

  Inside the Story Editor, you can press Ctrl+L or ⌘+L and then Enter to check the spelling of your text. (The Enter key activates the Start button inside the Spelling dialog box.)

- **Windows: Ctrl+H; then text; then Enter**
- **Mac: ⌘+H; then text; then Enter**

  To search for some text while working in the Story Editor, press Ctrl+H, enter the text, and press Enter. To search for one bit of text and replace it with another, press Ctrl+H or ⌘+H, enter the text your want to search for, press Tab, enter the text you want PageMaker to substitute, and press Enter.

- **Windows: Ctrl+A**

  Mac: ⌘+A

  To select all text, press Ctrl+A or ⌘+A. If you choose this shortcut in layout view when the Text tool is inside a text block, all text in the story is selected. If the Arrow tool is selected, PageMaker selects everything in your document.

Formatting Text

PageMaker provides lots of ways to change the formatting of text from the keyboard. The following are just a few of the most popular shortcuts appropriate for Web publishing:

- **Windows: Ctrl+Shift+B, Ctrl+Shift+I, Ctrl+Shift+U**

  Mac: Shift+⌘+B, Shift+⌘+I, Shift+⌘+U

  The shortcuts used most often are for your most basic formatting: You get boldface with Ctrl+Shift+B or Shift+⌘+B, italics with Ctrl+Shift+I or Shift+⌘+I, and underlining with Ctrl+Shift+U or Shift+⌘U.

- **Windows: Ctrl+Shift+period, Ctrl+Shift+comma**

  Mac: Shift+⌘+period, Shift+⌘+comma

  To increase the type size to the next menu size — 10, 11, 12, 14, 18, and so on — press Ctrl+Shift+period (.) or Shift+⌘+period (.). Press Ctrl+Shift+comma (,) or Shift+⌘+comma (,) to reduce the type size. Both shortcuts are applicable only to characters selected with the Text tool.

  While size changes don't export to the Web, this shortcut is handy when you're trying to fit copy into a text block above a graphic. You can avoid jumping text to a new page and forcing an unwanted break in your Web page. (See Chapter 10 for more details.)

Making Styles and Colors

Styles are indispensable PageMaker tools. These shortcuts allow you to edit and create colors and styles in just a few steps:

- **Windows: Ctrl+click, double-click**

  Mac: ⌘+click, double-click

With the Styles palette on-screen, you can edit styles and create new ones by Ctrl+clicking or ⌘+clicking, or by double-clicking the style name. Ctrl+click or ⌘+click, or double-click, on No Style at the top of the palette to create a new style sheet.

This same technique allows you to edit colors in the Colors palette. Ctrl+click or ⌘+click, or double-click, on any color name to edit it. To create a new color, Ctrl+click or ⌘+click, or double-click, on the [Black] or [Registration] color.

- **Windows: Ctrl+3**

  Mac: ⌘+3

  To define a series of styles, use the shortcut Ctrl+3 or ⌘+3 to enter the Define Styles dialog box.

Chapter 21

Ten Ways to Avoid Web Publishing "Gotchas"

In This Chapter

- Stick to Web-friendly formatting
- Get a grip on using graphics
- Avoid the jump-happy syndrome
- Always link to required programs
- Label sources and anchors properly
- Set your global preferences
- Keep page elements in bounds
- Make safety precautions a habit
- Check your work online
- Use the correct tool for the job

Web publishing, like any other task as complicated and intensely creative, has its share of "gotchas" — those missteps and oversights that can result in aggravating rework to correct dumb little mistakes, or that leave you stymied instead of gratifyingly finished (this, of course, is guaranteed to happen when you're on a deadline). This chapter can help you avoid some Web page gotchas by describing the ten most vexing but nevertheless avoidable missteps. Gotchas may always getcha sometime, but hopefully none of the following will be among them.

Stick to Web-Friendly Formatting

Don't be tricked into thinking text formatting in PageMaker for the Internet is as free-wheeling as it is for print. Many features, such as fancy type faces, text wrap, precision placement of elements, and drawings made with PageMaker graphics tools, simply don't translate to the Web. Focus on specific advantages, features, and limits of HTML and the Web. A browser, not a sheet of paper, should be the mental model as the container for your layout.

Get a Grip on Using Graphics

Graphic images can take a long time to download off the Web and display on a user's computer screen, so avoid filling up your pages with pictures for the sake of pictures. Pick images for their impact and information value, and use them sparingly. A few carefully selected graphics carry more weight than a jumble of multiple images, and fewer images won't drive your readers away with lengthy waiting times.

Avoid the Jump-Happy Syndrome

One of the Web's great features is the *hyperlink,* which lets readers quickly skip from topic to topic in any order they want. But an excessive number of links can wear out even the hardiest Net surfer. Group related information in one place on your site. Limit using hyperlinks to other pages for when the topic changes. Think of a link as the electronic equivalent of starting a new chapter or introducing a main heading.

Always Link to Required Programs

If your Web site uses special features, such as embedded Acrobat files, Java script, or ShockWave animation, be certain to include hyperlinks to the Web pages or program files Internet rovers visiting your site will need in order to use these special features.

Label Sources and Anchors Properly

Use descriptive names in the Hyperlinks palette for your hyperlink sources and destinations. After you've defined a few dozen links, you really appreciate having names that give you a clear idea of what's being linked to what. This practice saves you the frustration of puzzling over the names in a long list of links with no idea of the content behind them.

Set Your Global Preferences

Save yourself the effort of applying preferences each and every time you create a new document. PageMaker lets you set up preferences that are automatically applied to all of your future pages. Simply open PageMaker with *no* documents open; then set the preferences you want to have each time. Examples of time-saving preferences are HTML-friendly paragraph styles (see Chapter 6) and colors (see Chapter 15).

Keep Page Elements in Bounds

Make sure that graphics don't run past the page boundary (or else they're removed during HTML export), and make sure that text blocks start within the page margin (text blocks can extend past the margins as long as the upper-left corner of the text block is inside the page boundary).

Make Safety Precautions a Habit

"Better safe than sorry" is more than a scouting motto. They're words to live by when publishing to the Web.

- When exporting your documents to HTML or Acrobat, double-check the entries in the dialog boxes to ensure that you're exporting the correct pages.
- Make sure that you've properly mapped PageMaker styles to the equivalent HTML styles.
- Double-check that the correct page size is selected.
- Check that the preserve layout option is on or off, according to your preference.
- Always spell check your document before you export it.
- Back up your work to a second hard drive or to a removable drive (Zip, SyQuest, or tape).

Check Your Work Online

Always preview your Web pages in the browser or browsers the majority of your readers probably use themselves. To have both Netscape Navigator and Microsoft Internet Explorer, by far the two most popular browsers, at your disposal is worth the nominal investment.

Use the Correct Tool for the Job

Sometimes, you may need to work on your HTML or Acrobat pages in a program other than PageMaker. That's okay — PageMaker wasn't designed to be an everything-is-possible, all-in-one Web-page factory. Think of PageMaker as the hub of your operations and the following tools as skilled hired hands you may need to employ:

- A word processor to write long blocks of text
- An HTML editor to fine-tune your Web pages after exporting them from PageMaker
- An image editor to fine-tune graphics before using them in PageMaker
- A site-management tool if you're also managing the site, not just creating pages
- The Acrobat Exchange program if you're creating many Acrobat pages
- Any tools required for creating special elements, such as ShockWave animation, QuickTime movies, and others

Chapter 22

The Ten Most Useful HTML Tag Groups

In This Chapter

- Basic text formatting
- Breaks in text
- Paragraph styles
- Heading styles
- List styles
- Text alignment
- Hyperlinks
- Color specifications
- Housekeeping codes
- Special type symbols

Wouldn't it be nice if you could ride the waves of online publishing, comfortably astride the back of PageMaker, and never have to encounter the ugly snoot of that Web publishing creature called *HyperText Markup Language* (and shortening it to HTML doesn't make it sound any prettier). "PageMaker is a visual tool, so it should hide all that stuff from me," you say indignantly. Sorry, bucko, but HTML is the programming language that gives you the power to create and publish your Web pages. Learn to love it, because that ugly snoot is staring you straight in the face.

You're going to have learn at least the basics of HTML to fine-tune your Web pages. It's not a hard language to learn, mostly because it's so primitive in some respects. (On the other hand, HTML is what makes it possible to just click on the screen to flip to the topic you want.)

If you want to go beyond the basics, I recommend a few books, all from the publisher of this fine tome: *HTML For Dummies Quick Reference,* by Deborah S. Ray and Eric J. Ray, is a fast and easy summary of how to use

HTML; *HTML For Dummies,* by Ed Tittel and Carl de Cordova, goes into more detail on the language and how to use it; and *Creating Cool Web Pages with HTML,* by Dave Taylor (also available in a Mac-oriented *Macworld* edition), covers HTML use from your perspective — that of a designer, not a programmer. (All of these titles are published by IDG Books Worldwide, Inc.)

It helps to keep a couple things in the back of your mind before you begin to read the information in this chapter:

- HTML codes are not case-sensitive, so don't bother using the Shift key if you don't want to.
- Most codes need to be turned on and then off. The *off* version is almost always the same as the *on* version, except a slash (/) begins the code. For example, <B> turns boldface on, and </B> turns boldface off.
- You won't be entering or seeing these codes in PageMaker. You only deal with them if you fine-tune your HTML files in a text editor or HTML editor after you export your PageMaker document into HTML format.

Text Formatting

Use the following codes for basic type styling, such as boldface, italics, and underlining:

- <B>, </B>

  These codes turn boldface on and off, respectively.

- <I>, </I>

  These codes turn italics on and off, respectively.

- <U>, </U>

  These codes turn underlining on and off, respectively.

- <TT>, </TT>

  Use these codes to specify a fixed-width font, like Courier that resembles typewriting. The code stands for *teletypewriter,* recalling the old days of fixed-width computer printing.

  You can combine these codes. For example, the HTML code <B>Bold <I>italic</I> is nice</B>, don't you think? would appear as **Bold *italic* is nice**, don't you think?

Breaks in Text

Breaks in paragraphs and pages require special codes in the land of HTML. Use the following three codes to make sure your text breaks the way it should:

- <P>

  To indicate a paragraph break, HTML requires the <P> code. The hard returns in an HTML file are ignored — for all that HTML knows, all of your text could be just one big sequence of characters. For our sake, most HTML editors and programs that create or export HTML (including PageMaker) also put hard returns before the <P> codes so you can more easily see the paragraph breaks in your code. Note that a </P> code exists to indicate the end of a paragraph break, but it is optional and rarely used.

-

  If you want a soft return — a forced line break that does not create a new paragraph (in other words, you don't want a paragraph space after the return), use the <BR> code to insert a soft return — the equivalent of Shift+Enter in most word processors and in PageMaker. In fact, the PageMaker soft return gets translated to <BR> during HTML export.

- <HR>

  To insert a horizontal rule (that is, a line), use this code.

Paragraph Styles

Paragraph styles are critical in distinguishing various types of information. See Chapter 9 for more about PageMaker and HTML styles.

- <BODY>, </BODY>

  The basic text in a document should be specified with the <BODY> style.

- <BLOCKQUOTE>, </BLOCKQUOTE>

  These codes are similar to <BODY>, except the entire paragraph is indented on the left; this tag pair is usually used to set off citations and extended quotes.

- <ADDRESS>, </ADDRESS>

  This small-size, italic style is often used for legal information, such as copyrights and disclaimers, as well as for information on how to contact the author or Web master. It's also great for captions.

- `<PRE>, </PRE>`

  This tag, short for *Preformatted,* tells the browser to format the text exactly as it appears, which means you must specify line breaks with the `<BR>` command. It also uses a nonproportional font (similar to a typewriter font), so text aligns character by character, making it handy for tables and lists.

Heading Styles

Headline styles are somewhat limited in HTML. Use this code to distinguish between headline levels in your Web pages:

- `<H#>, </H#>`

  Six levels of headings are available, specified with the numbers 1 to 6 (use the actual number instead of the # symbol above), with `<H1>` being the biggest headline and `<H6>` the smallest.

List Styles

Several kinds of list tags exist, which are covered in detail in Chapter 9, but the ones you use over and over again are the following two pairs:

- `<UL>, </UL>`

  To get an unordered list (a bulleted list), use this pair tag. The browser inserts the bullets automatically. Each item within a list needs to be tagged `<LI>` at the beginning of the paragraph, but you don't need to insert a paragraph break (`<P>`) after each item.

- `<OL>, </OL>`

  If you can have *unordered* lists, you should be able to have *ordered* lists, and by golly you can. These work exactly like unordered lists except that instead of ending up with bullets, you see the items automatically numbered by the browser.

Text Alignment

The following codes allow you to center-align or right-align text (although right-aligning takes a little more work):

- `<CENTER>, <CENTER>`

  These codes are used to center-align text (they work in Internet Explorer and Netscape Navigator, only). When you turn off centering, the text goes back to being left-aligned.

- `ALIGN=RIGHT, ALIGN=CENTER`

  No tag for right-alignment exists, but you can add either the `ALIGN=RIGHT or ALIGN=CENTER` commands (called *attributes*) inside a style tag such as `<BODY>` or `<H1>`. Make sure to add a space before the attribute. The attribute is turned off when the style tag (such as `</BODY>` or `</H1>`) is turned off. For example, `<H1 ALIGN=RIGHT>`Free Software!`</H1>` would create a big headline aligned to the right of the browser window saying *Free Software!* The alignment of the text following the `</H1>` code would go back to being left-aligned. Note the wordspace before the attribute.

Hyperlinks

Hyperlinks are formed with hypertext, the HT part of HTML. Use the following code to create hypertext links:

- `<A HREF="URL">`**text to be highlighted as a hyperlink**`</A>`

  To code a hypertext link, HTML includes in this tag pair both the URL link and the text to be highlighted on screen as the hyperlink for the browser to use. Information that must be contained within the quotation marks is the URL for the Web page you want to link to. The portion between the second and third brackets is the highlighted text.

Color Specifications

Colors are great, but be advised that the following color commands work only in Netscape Navigator and Internet Explorer:

- Why are there letters in the following numeric values? The values are part of a *hexadecimal* numbering scheme, in which numbers from 10 to 15 correspond to the letters A to F: A = 10, B = 11, C = 12, D = 13, E =14, and F = 15. To figure out a hexadecimal value, multiply the left digit by 16 and add the right digit. Thus, 0E = 14, since (0 x 16) + (14) = 14. Likewise, 1E = 30 (1 x 16) + (14), EE = 238, FF = 255. That means there are 256 possible values (00 to FF) per color. It might have been simpler for this command to use the decimal numbers 0 through 255 that we are all familiar with, but it doesn't.

- TEXT=#rrggbb

  To apply color to text, insert this attribute inside a style tag. This is similar to the way the ALIGN= attribute, described earlier in this chapter, is used. Replace the *rrggbb* with the red, green, and blue color values that make up your color. For example, <OL TEXT=#041EFF> applies to an ordered list (the TEXT= attribute is an <OL>, or Ordered List style, code), with a color made up of 4 parts red (04), 30 parts green (1E), and 255 parts blue (FF). That result is a dark aqua.

- ALINK=#rrggbb

  To determine the color for active links (the ones that have yet to be used), add this attribute inside each style tag that has hyperlinks you want to color. For example, this attribute inside a hyperlink code would make that hyperlink dark aqua rather than the normal pure blue.

- VLINK=#rrggbb

  You can determine the color for links that have been used (those that have been visited) by using this attribute. This works in the same way as the two color attributes described earlier.

Housekeeping Codes

PageMaker and other programs that generate HTML add the following codes automatically. Just so you don't make the mistake of deleting them accidentally, I've listed them for you:

- <HTML>, </HTML>

  Every HTML document must begin with <HTML> and end with </HTML> so that the browser knows when it is working with HyperText Markup Language and when it isn't.

- <HEAD><TITLE>, </TITLE></HEAD>

  Every HTML document has a header enclosed in the <HEAD> and </HEAD> tags; the header immediately follows the <HTML> tag. Usually, a <TITLE> and </TITLE> tag pair are nested inside the header tags. While these tags are not absolutely required by some browsers, other browsers need them, so I'd leave them in.

- <BODY>, </BODY>

  Immediately after the </HEAD> tag, you need to indicate where the document itself (the material displayed to the reader) begins. That's where the tag <BODY> comes in. At the very end of the HTML document, right before the </HTML> tag, the </BODY> tag must appear to tell the browser that the part of the file to display is finished.

- `<!- text -> or <COMMENT>, </COMMENT>`

  You can embed comments with either of these tags. The only difference is that if any HTML code appears within the `<COMMENT>` pair, the browser implements that HTML code, while the browser ignores everything between a <!— and a —>.

Special Type Symbols

The table on the following pages gives you the HTML codes for special symbols that PageMaker can both generate and export in HTML format. Notice how the HTML codes are essentially the same as the ANSI codes used in Windows? (ANSI codes are the ones you type in on the numeric keypad while holding down the Alt key.)

Not all browsers can display all of the characters and symbols that either Windows or the Mac have available. Try this test: If you can't see a keyboard symbol you've used when browsing your page on the Web, you can assume your reader probably won't see it either. But if you are confident that most of your readers have the latest in browsers (maybe they're looking at your pages on a corporate intranet), feel free to use these characters.

Table 22-1 Accessing Special Symbols

Symbol	*Windows ANSI Code or Keyboard Shortcut*	*Macintosh Keyboard Shortcut*	*HTML Code*
Financial			
¢	Alt+0162	Option+4	¢
£	Alt+0163	Option+3	£
¥	Alt+0165	Option+Y	¥
Legal			
©	Alt+G or Alt+0169	Option+G	©
®	Alt+R or Alt+0174	Option+R	®
¶	Alt+7 or Alt+0182	Option+7	¶
§	Alt+6 or Alt+0167	Option+6	§
Mathematical			
°	Alt+0176	Option+Shift+8	°
±	Alt+0177	Option+Shift+plus	±
x	Alt+0215	Option+Y in Symbol font*	×
÷	Alt+0247	Option+Shift+P in Symbol font*	÷
International Punctuation			
¿	Alt+0191	Option+Shift+/	¿
¡	Alt+0161	Option+1	¡
«	Alt+0171	Option+\	«
»	Alt+0187	Option+Shift+\	»
International Alphabet**			
À à	` then letter or	Option+` then letter	À à

Symbol	Windows ANSI Code or Keyboard Shortcut	Macintosh Keyboard Shortcut	HTML Code
Á á	´ then letter	Option+E then letter	Á á
Ä ä	Shift+´ then letter	Option+U then letter	Ä ä
Â â	Shift+6 then letter	Option+I then letter	Â â
Ã ã	Shift+` then letter	Option+N then letter	Ã ã
Å å	Ctrl+Alt+Shift+W, Ctrl+Alt+W	Option+Shift+A, Option+A	Å å
Æ æ	Ctrl+Alt+Shift+Z, Ctrl+Alt+Z	Option+Shift+´, Option+´	Æ æ
Ç ç	´ then letter	Option+Shift+C, Option+C	Ç ç
È è	` then letter	Option+` then letter	È è
É é	` then letter	Option+E then letter	É é
Ë ë	Shift+´ then letter	Option+U then letter	Ë ë
Ê ê	Shift+6 then letter	Option+I then letter	Ê ê
Ì ì	` then letter	Option+` then letter	Ì ì
Í í	´ then letter	Option+E then letter	Í í
Ï ï	Shift+´ then letter	Option+U then letter	Ï ï
Î î	Shift+6 then letter	Option+I then letter	Î î
Ñ ñ	Shift+` then letter	Option+N then letter	Ñ ñ
Ò ò	` then letter	Option+` then letter	Ò ò
Ó ó	´ then letter	Option+E then letter	Ó ó
Ö ö	Shift+´ then letter	Option+U then letter	Ö ö
Ô ô	Shift+6 then letter	Option+I then letter	Ô ô
Õ õ	Shift+` then letter	Option+N then letter	Õ õ

(continued)

Table 22-1 *(continued)* **Accessing Special Symbols**

Symbol	*Windows ANSI Code or Keyboard Shortcut*	*Macintosh Keyboard Shortcut*	*HTML Code*
International Alphabet**			
Ø ø	Ctrl+Alt+Shift+L, Ctrl+Alt_L	Option+Shift+O, Option+O	Ø ø
ß	Alt+0223	Option+S	ß
Ù ù	` then letter	Option+` then letter	Ù ù
Ú ú	´ then letter	Option+E then letter	Ú ú
Ü ü	Shift+´ then letter	Option+U then letter	Ü ü
Û û	Shift+6 then letter	Option+I then letter	Û û

**Does not translate correctly to HTML because of font change.*

***The United States-International keyboard layout must be used for keyboard sequences (no Ctrl or Alt keys used) to work correctly. Use the Keyboard control panel to set the desired layout. Alternatively, use the Alt+ANSI codes (0 plus the number in the HTML code) to generate the characters.*

Chapter 23

Ten Web Pages Worth a Good Look

In This Chapter

- Apple Computer QuickTime
- Walter S. Arnold
- Delphi
- Fine Arts Museums of San Francisco
- Heidsite
- IDG Books Worldwide
- Macworld Daily
- PC World
- Thunder Lizard Productions
- U.S. Robotics Pilot

Thousands of great-looking pages are yours for the browsing on the Internet — and an equal number that probably shouldn't have left home.

To help you get a sense for good Web-page composition, I gathered together ten well-designed pages to close out the "Part of Tens." I made my choices from Web pages already familiar to me that I know are frequently visited, or that were recommended by my Webhead colleagues and friends, or that just simply appealed to my personal taste. I recommend that you browse the Web periodically to see how others have designed their pages. They may provide some inspiration and guidance on how to put one of these things together.

The following ten pages all share the following attributes, and you should keep them in mind for your pages, as well:

- **Simplicity.** A common tendency among amateur designers is to overdo it. Keep the design simple, and your readers can both enjoy your pages and be able to use them easily.
- **Clarity.** Clean lines in text columns and picture arrangement, coupled with a clear association between elements (such as news stories situated under a news icon or headline) help the reader to grasp information more quickly. Avoid clustering elements into a confusing jumble and remember to leave enough space around items to clearly separate them.
- **Variety.** While a jumble is annoying, an overly uniform design risks becoming monotonous. Introduce some variety into your document — different shapes, sizes, and colors — to break up the page. Just be sure that variety doesn't sacrifice simplicity or clarity.

Now that you know the key ingredients for a well-designed Web page, take a look at the following examples. I limited my selection to Web pages that provide capsulized information — not a gallery's worth of pictures or text the length of a serialized novel. I selected primarily home pages, because they set the visual tone for the rest of the site and offer the most opportunity to combine graphics and text (once inside a Web site, readers are less interested in eye-catching graphics and more interested in quick information). I also listed each site's URL (address) in case you want to see these pages online.

Inclusion of a Web page in this book is not an endorsement of its contents or offerings, nor does it necessarily mean the pages were created with PageMaker. Web sites change frequently, so the pages shown here may no longer be on the Web, may have been edited to some degree, or may not look exactly as they do here because each browser affects the appearance of a Web page.

Apple Computer QuickTime

```
http://www.quicktime.apple.com
```

This page balances a block of interesting graphics at the top against a somewhat text-heavy bottom half, which is broken up with columns of varying widths. The result is an information-packed page (shown in Figure 23-1) that doesn't seem jammed together.

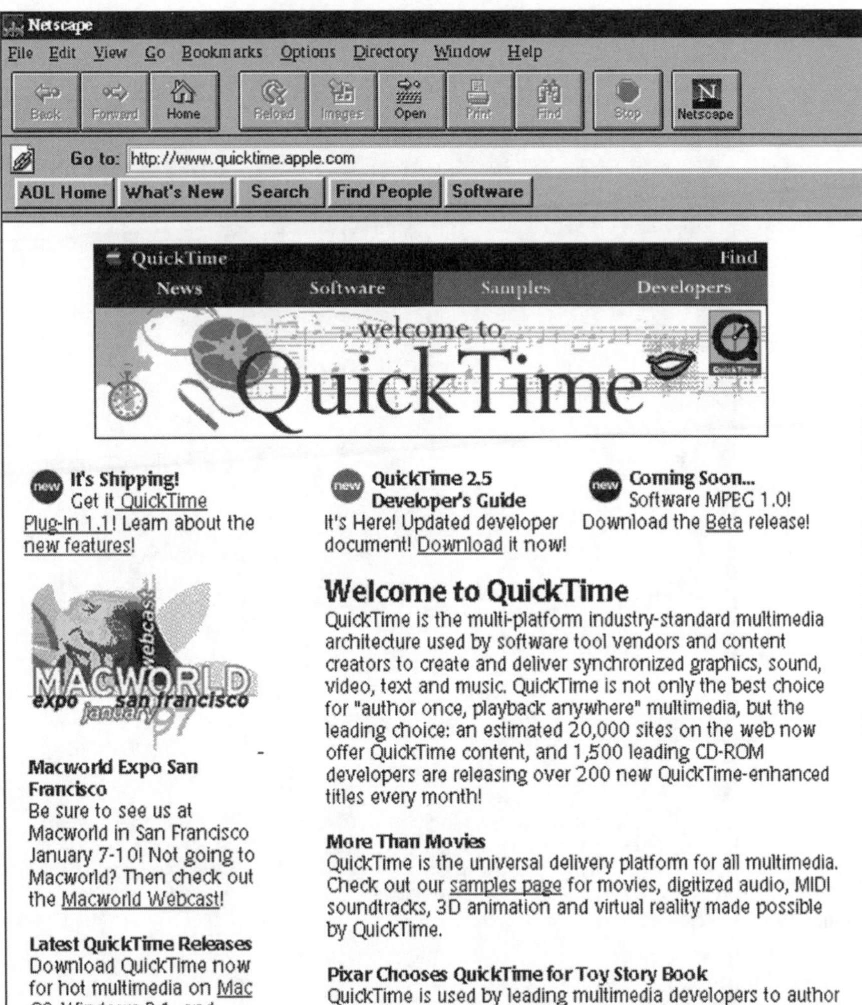

Figure 23-1: The Apple Computer QuickTime page.

Walter S. Arnold

`http://www.mcs.net/~sculptor/ and http://www.stonecarver.com`

A strong image can go a long way, as the page in Figure 23-2 shows. But also notice the use of multiple columns and text wrap (something you need to do in an HTML editor, after exporting your document from PageMaker). The magazine-like layout gives this page the instant identification of a brochure, which is exactly what it is.

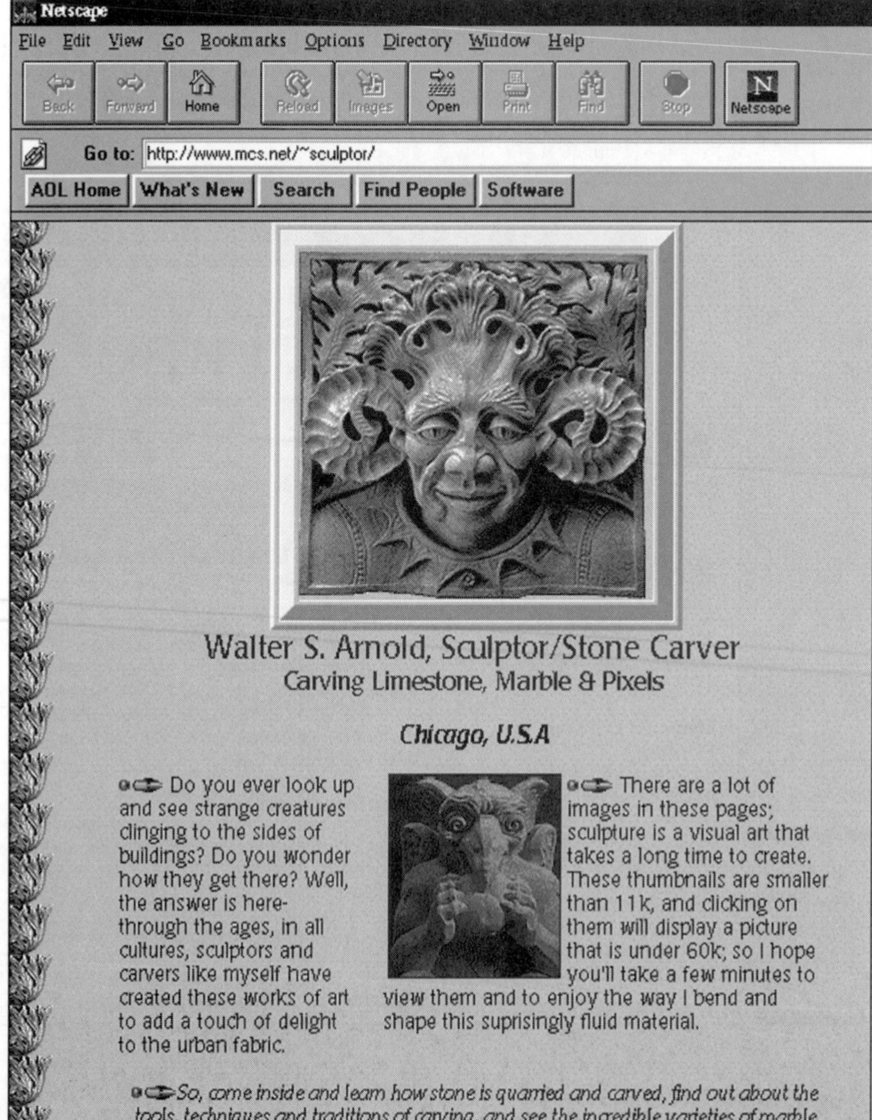

Figure 23-2: Sculptor Walter S. Arnold's page (© 1997 Walter S. Arnold).

Delphi

`http://www.delphi.com`

The unusual middle-of-the-page placement of the main index, and its contrasting background, give the page in Figure 23-3 a striking look but doesn't overwhelm the rest of the page's sections. The use of the small graphics help to make each section distinct while also adding a little whimsy.

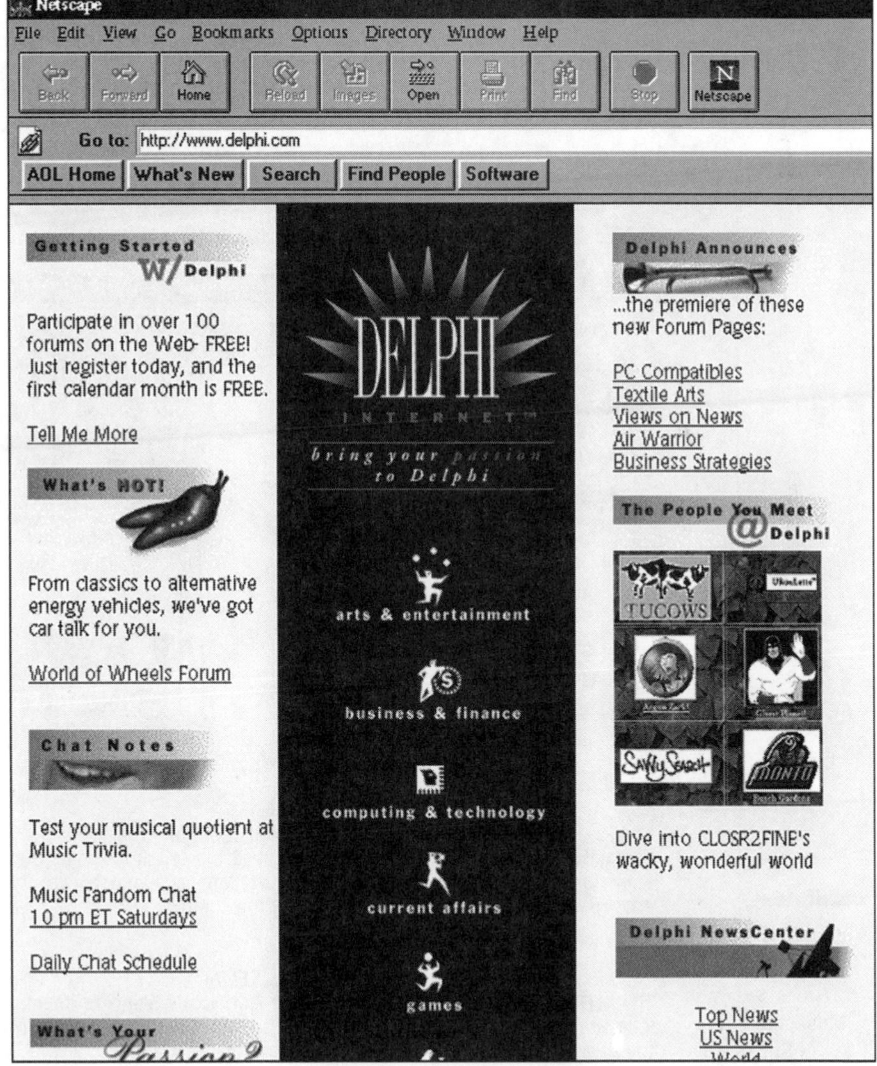

Figure 23-3: The Delphi page.

Fine Arts Museums of San Francisco

`http://www.thinker.org`

This is an example of a simple yet powerful one-column Web page. Figure 23-4 distinguishes itself by relying on the graphic to function as the index to the rest of the site. Each part of the arch is actually a separate hyperlink! (*Note:* You need an HTML editor to set up multiple hyperlinks such as these in a graphic; PageMaker alone doesn't give you the ability to do this.)

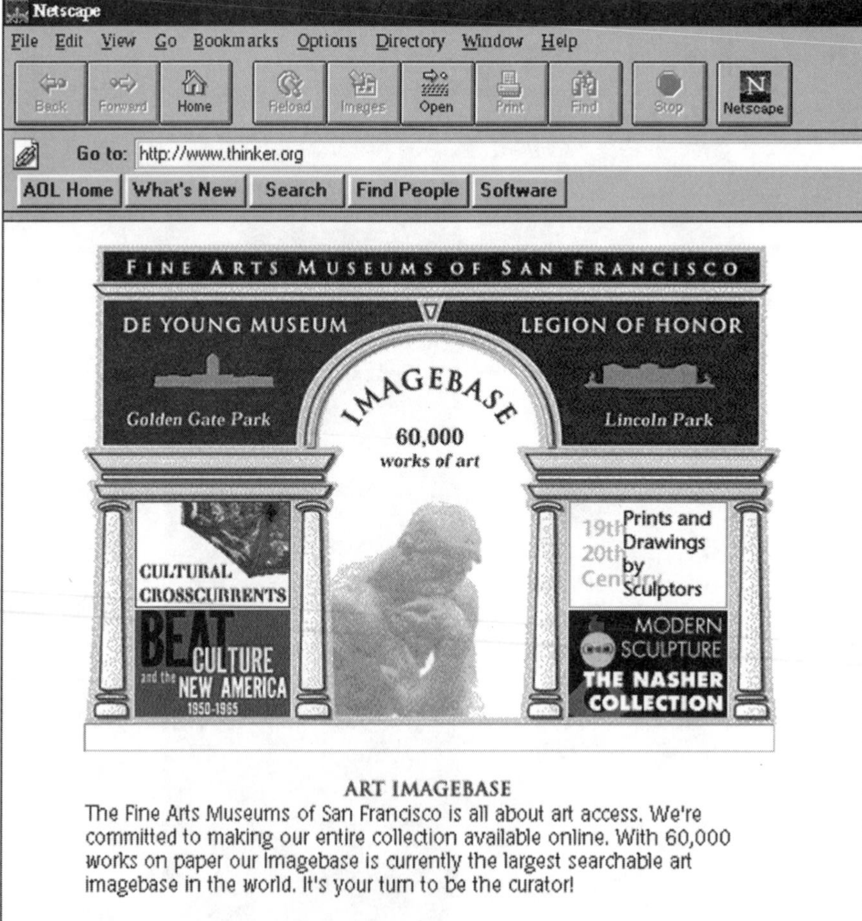
Netscape
File Edit View Go Bookmarks Options Directory Window Help
Back Forward Home Reload Images Open Print Find Stop Netscape
Go to: http://www.thinker.org
AOL Home What's New Search Find People Software
FINE ARTS MUSEUMS OF SAN FRANCISCO
DE YOUNG MUSEUM
LEGION OF HONOR
Golden Gate Park
IMAGEBASE
60,000 works of art
Lincoln Park
CULTURAL CROSSCURRENTS
Prints and Drawings by Sculptors
BEAT CULTURE and the NEW AMERICA 1950-1965
MODERN SCULPTURE THE NASHER COLLECTION
ART IMAGEBASE
The Fine Arts Museums of San Francisco is all about art access. We're committed to making our entire collection available online. With 60,000 works on paper our Imagebase is currently the largest searchable art imagebase in the world. It's your turn to be the curator!
DE YOUNG MUSEUM
The M.H. de Young Memorial Museum, San Francisco's oldest museum, is located in Golden Gate Park and dates to the 1894 Midwinter Exposition. In the past 100 years, it has become the repository for the most comprehensive collection of American paintings on the West Coast, as well as major collections of African art, Oceanic art, art from the pre-Columbian Americas, and textile arts.

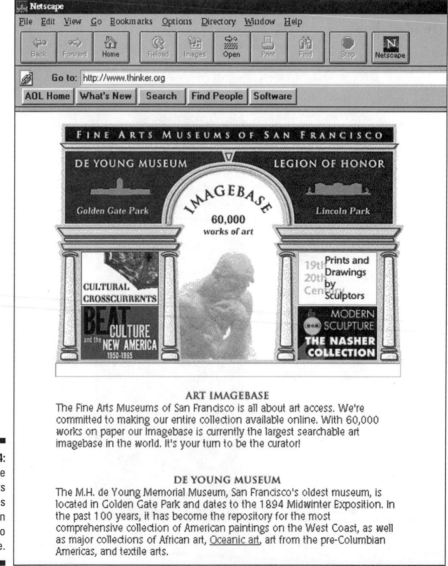

Figure 23-4: The Fine Arts Museums of San Francisco page.

Heidsite

```
http://www2.heidsite.com/heidsite/
```

A simple design enlivened with clever use of imagery, and with sufficient space for text and graphics, makes the page in Figure 23-5 an easy read with lots of personality.

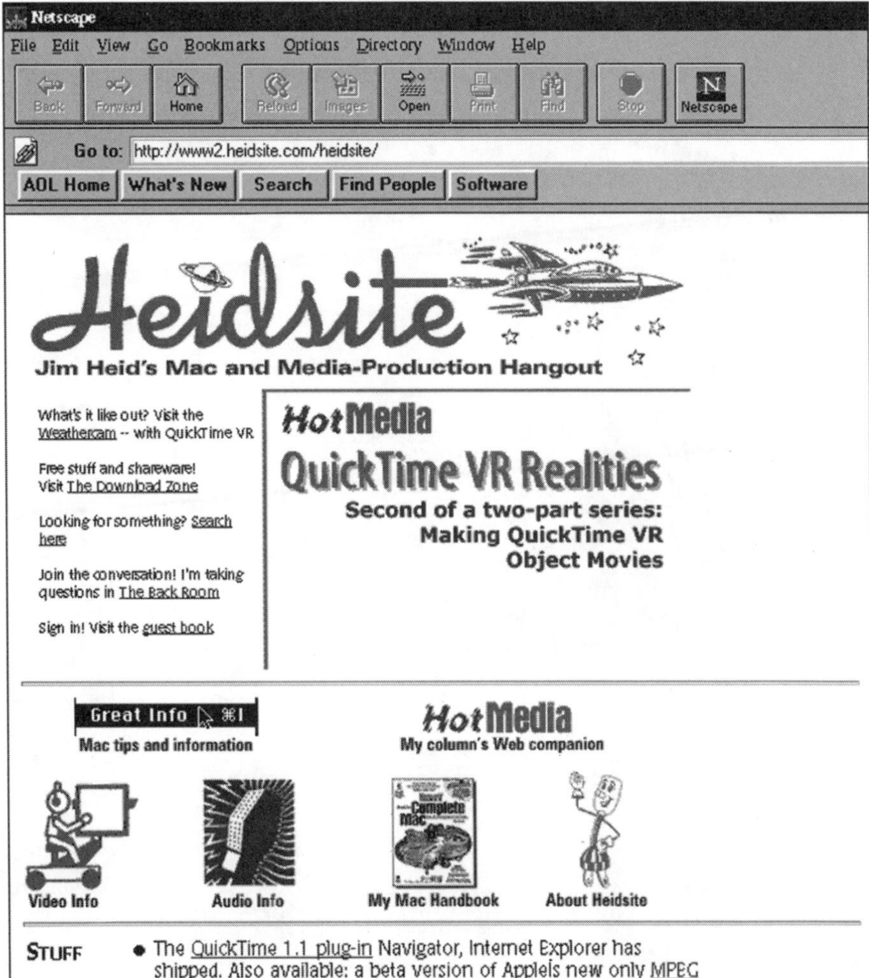

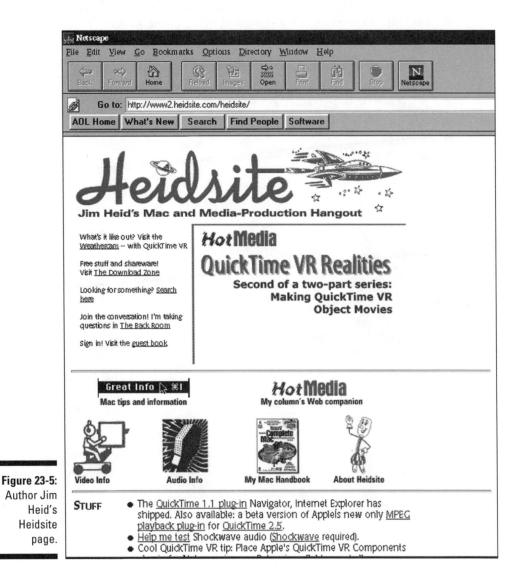

Figure 23-5: Author Jim Heid's Heidsite page.

IDG Books Worldwide

`http://www.idgbooks.com`

The use of graphical columns on the outside of the page — one for the site's table of contents and the other to highlight specific content — coupled with a wider middle column for text give the page in Figure 23-6 a crisp, assertive look. Loads of hyperlinks fill a fairly small space, but enough information is provided to let readers know where they're going before they click.

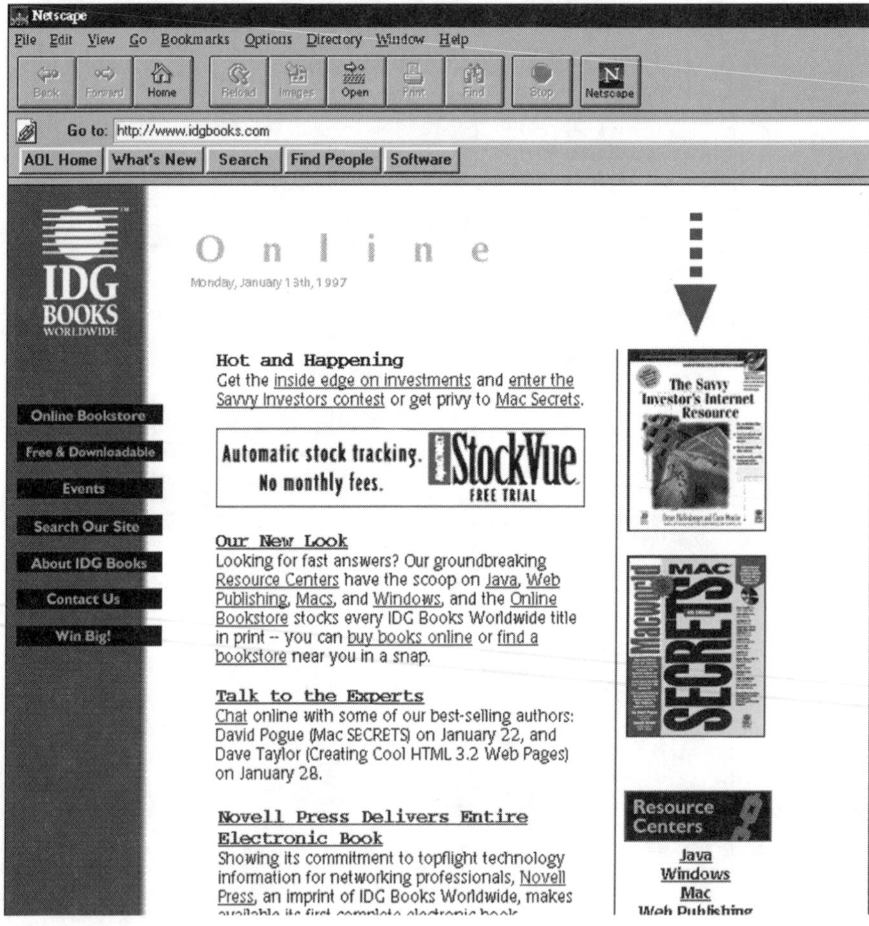

Figure 23-6: The IDG Books Worldwide page.

Macworld Daily

```
http://www.macworld.com/daily/
```

The page shown in Figure 23-7 uses large type, a clear division between the stories and index, straightforward organization, and an effective use of shading to indicate your location in the *Macworld* site.

Figure 23-7: The Macworld Daily page.

PC World

`http://www.pcworld.com`

Three-column layouts seem to be as popular on the Web as they are for print magazine layouts. What distinguishes the *PC World* home page shown in Figure 23-8 is the banner at the upper left that extends across two columns. This banner gives the page a little variety and makes the elements included within it easier to read and more prominent — a subtle but effective way to call attention to specific content.

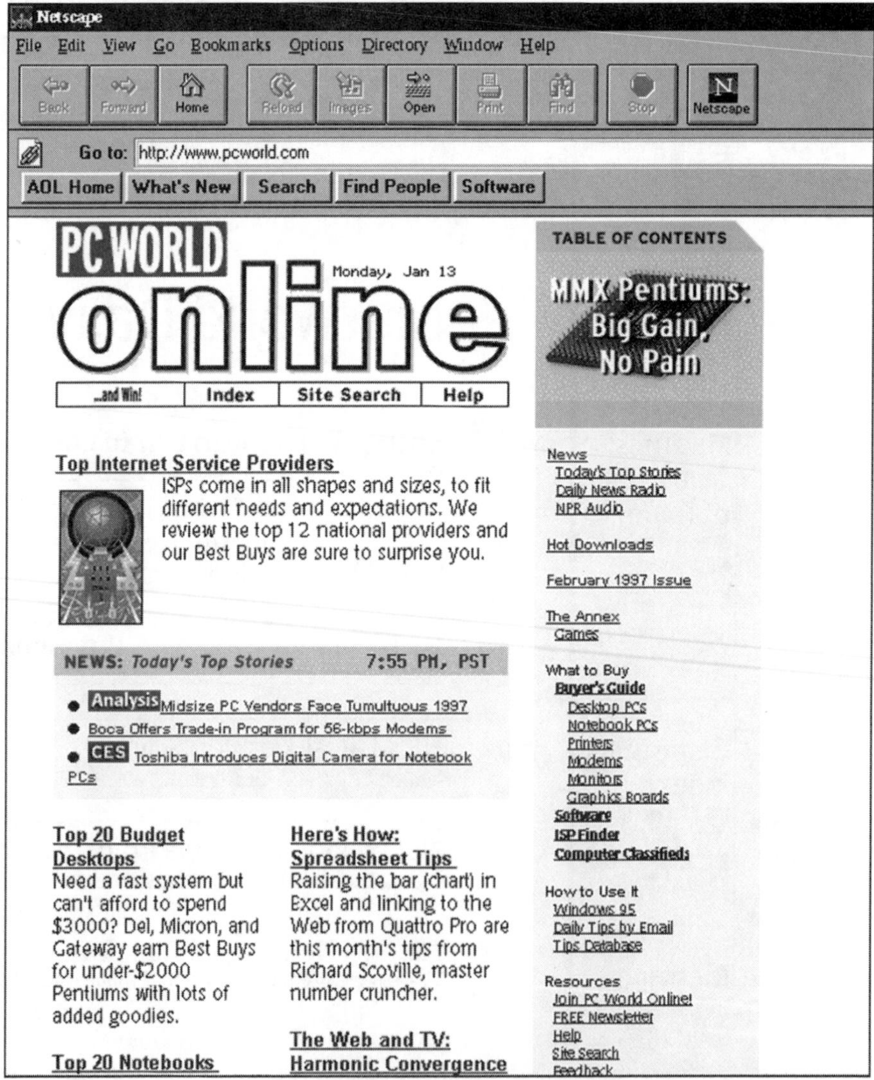

Figure 23-8: The PC World page.

Thunder Lizard Productions

`http://www.thunderlizard.com`

Not all Web pages need multiple columns of text. The page in Figure 23-9 does quite nicely with one column, thanks to the graphical button index on the left and the high-impact, large headline size.

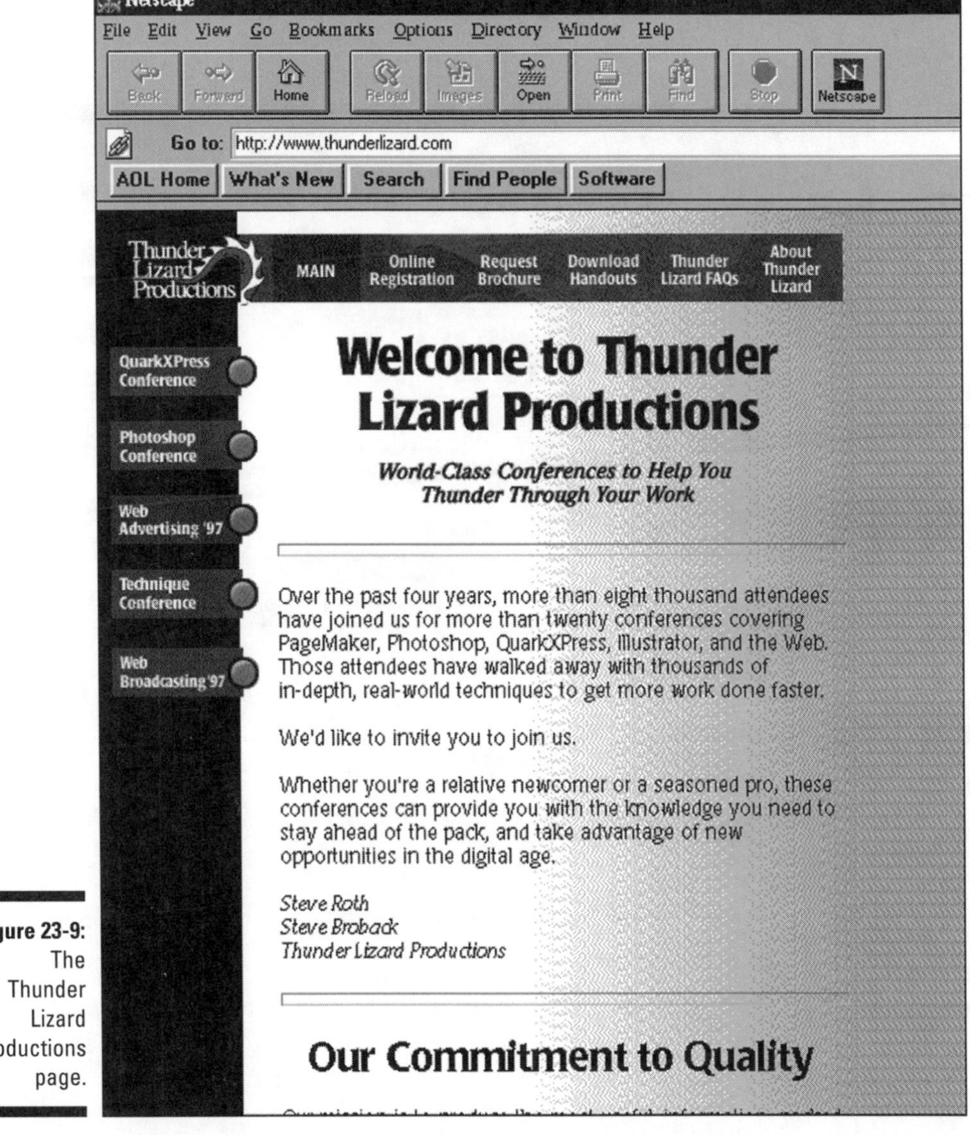

Figure 23-9: The Thunder Lizard Productions page.

U.S. Robotics Pilot

```
http://www.usr.com/palm/500.html
```

Effective use of blank space (also known as *white space*) can attract a reader as readily as any jazzy photo image. The Web page in Figure 23-10 uses such a technique to draw your eye to the graphic, buttons, and text. The design is simple but not completely stark. The positioning of the buttons and index at the top of the page, rather than on the left margin where you may expect them to be, creates visual interest and movement on the page.

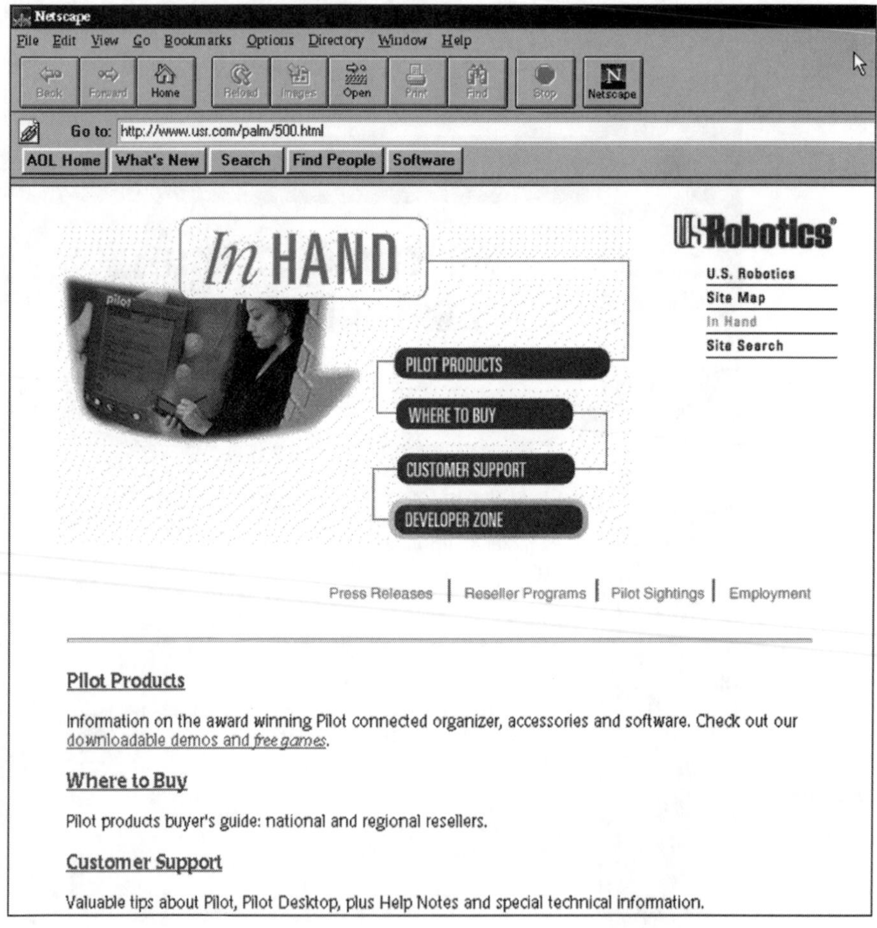

Figure 23-10: The U.S. Robotics Pilot page.

Appendix

How to Install PageMaker 6.5

Software installation seems to get easier all the time — just pop in a CD, find the Setup or Install program, and double-click on it. This beats the days of inconsistent installation programs and, horror of horrors, the ancient `A:\ALDSETUP C:\` commands from the Windows PageMaker of just a few years ago.

While getting install programs up and running is simpler than ever, you still need to select from many options to get optimal use out of the program after it's set up. PageMaker is a complex program with many components that also supports a variety of devices (printers, scanners, monitors, and so forth), which means you need to specify your system needs and preferences to allow PageMaker to install the right combination of features for you.

Basic Installation

Unless stated otherwise, the installation steps for Macintosh or Windows are the same:

1. **Insert the installation CD into your computer's CD-ROM drive.**

   If you don't have a CD-ROM drive, mail the coupon inside the PageMaker box to order the installation software on 3.5-inch floppy disks. You should receive them from Adobe within a few weeks.

2. **With the CD (or floppy) inserted, double-click on your hard drive icon.**

   Open up the My Computer icon (your hard-drive icon, in case you renamed it from My Computer) if you're in Windows; then double-click on the CD-ROM drive icon. If you're on a Macintosh, the CD icon appears on your desktop; just double-click on it to access the contents.

   If your copy of Windows 95 is set up with Autorun enabled, you get a menu after inserting the CD into your CD-ROM drive. Click on the Install PageMaker 6.5 option, and skip to Step 5.

3. **Look for the installation program folder and open it.**

   On the Windows CD, the folder is called `_Pm65`; on the Mac, it's called `Adobe PageMaker 6.5`.

   Now you're almost ready to begin the actual PageMaker installation.

4. **In Windows, double-click on the setup.exe icon; on the Mac, double-click on the Install Adobe PageMaker 6.5 icon.**

5. **The PageMaker installation program now launches.**

6. **Close any programs that are running.**

   In Windows, you get a Welcome screen telling you to close any other programs that are running. Although the on-screen instructions tell you to click on Cancel to do this, you can just go to the Windows task bar (where the Start button is), click on the button for a program you want to shut down, and then press Alt+F4. Do so for each program that is running. When you're done closing other programs, click on the Next> button in the Welcome screen. On the Mac, you don't get the Welcome screen.

Basic Custom Setup

Now that you have the basic installation steps out of the way, it's time to select your option preferences to customize some PageMaker operations.

1. **Select which language you want to install.**

   Select the language you want PageMaker to use for its menus and main spelling and hyphenation dictionaries. In Windows, you get language choices in the Language Selection dialog box that appears after the Welcome screen. On the Mac, you get language choices in the Installer window that displays when you first launch the PageMaker installer. The choices vary based upon the country where you bought PageMaker. (In North America, you get a choice of U.S. English, Canadian English, and International English — the British English used outside of North America.)

2. **Click on Next> in Windows to move to the next installation option.**

   On the Mac, selecting a language automatically moves you to the next installation option.

3. **Select your choice of setup options.**

   In Windows, you have three options, which are displayed in the Setup Type dialog box that appears after you're done making your selections in the Language Selection dialog box. The Typical option installs what the folks at Adobe think most people would prefer to use. The Compact option installs the most basic features only, which comes in handy if you're short on disk space. The Custom option lets you decide what to install. I recommend choosing Custom, even though it involves more work up front, because you can select the PageMaker setup that works best for you.

On the Mac, you have two options in the PageMaker Install dialog box that appears after you choose your language: Easy Install and Custom Install. Easy Install is the same as the Typical option in Windows. To get the equivalent of the Windows Compact option on the Mac, choose Custom Install. Later on in the installation process, you can select an option for Minimum Memory Install that's equivalent to the Windows Compact option if you're short on disk space.

4. **While you're still in the Setup Type dialog box (in Windows) or Install Adobe PageMaker 6.5 dialog box (on the Mac), decide where you want to install PageMaker.**

In Windows, click on the Browse button to select the hard drive (if you have more than one) and the folder where you want to install PageMaker 6.5. If you're in Windows and you want to put PageMaker in a new folder, enter the new folder name in the Path name box in the Choose Directory dialog box that displays after you click Browse. PageMaker asks if you want to create a new folder. Select Yes. PageMaker then confirms that you want to create a new folder (which it calls a directory), as Figure A-1 shows.

On the Mac, click on the Switch Disk button in the Install dialog box or the pop-up menu of drives above it to select a hard drive. That pop-up menu also has an option called Select Folder that lets you pick a specific folder after you've chosen the hard drive. (The installation program will create a folder named Adobe PageMaker 6.5 on your hard drive; if you selected a specific folder to install PageMaker in, the installation program will put the Adobe PageMaker 6.5 folder inside that specific folder you selected.) If you want to put PageMaker 6.5 in a new folder, click on the New Folder button that appears in the dialog box that comes up after you choose the Select Folder option. Make sure that Adobe PageMaker 6.5 is the application selected in that dialog box. Then click on the Select button once you've found (or created) the desired destination folder. (Figure A-2 shows the series of dialog boxes.)

Do *not* install PageMaker 6.5 in the same folder as PageMaker 6.0 if you have the older version. Doing so overwrites several custom files (such as tracking values, new and custom scripts, custom color libraries, user dictionaries, and custom printer-description files). I cover upgrading from Version 6.0 to Version 6.5 later in this appendix.

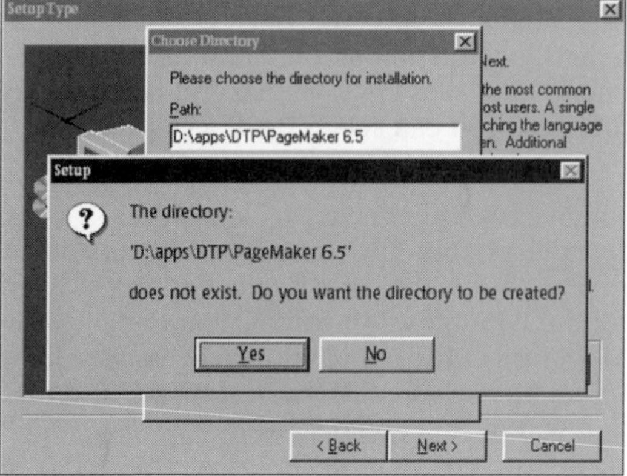

Figure A-1: Windows PageMaker confirms your desired action when you ask to install the program into a new folder.

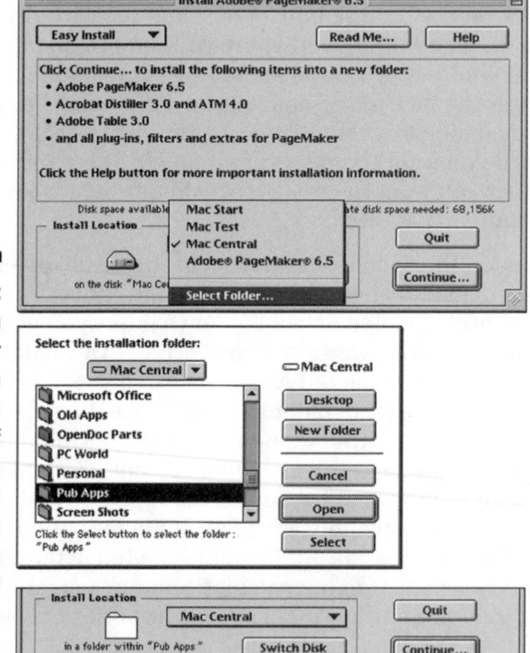

Figure A-2: Macintosh PageMaker moves you through a series of dialog boxes and menu items to choose the installation folder.

5. **After you select the folder where you want to install PageMaker, click on Next> in Windows or click on Continue on the Mac.**

More Custom Setup Options

If you select the custom setup option described earlier in this appendix, you get the Select Components dialog box in Windows. On the Mac, your PageMaker Install dialog box changes, as shown in Figure A-3. This is where you specify what you want PageMaker to install.

Keep in mind that you can always rerun the installation program later to add or delete components, so don't panic about not knowing in advance everything you want. (I explain reinstallation later in this appendix.)

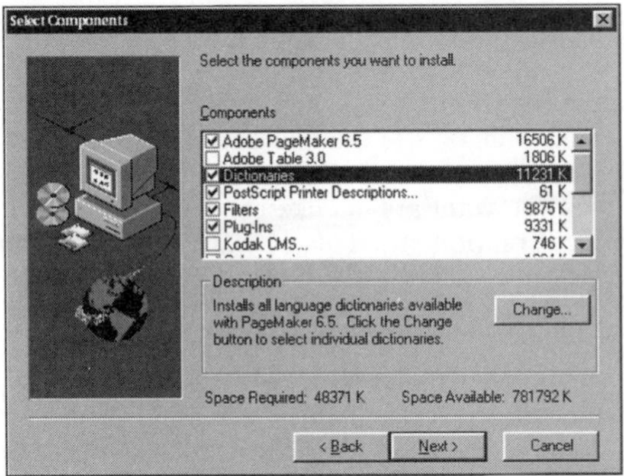

Figure A-3: For a custom setup, PageMaker gives you a set of features to select. (Windows dialog box is at top, Mac at the bottom.)

- If you chose the Typical or Compact setup option in Windows, or the Easy Install setup option on the Mac, you can skip the rest of this section and go straight to the "Registering and Restarting PageMaker" section in this appendix. Otherwise, continue on.

- To get the equivalent of the Windows Compact installation option on the Mac, select the Minimum Memory Install option and then click on the Install button in the Install Adobe PageMaker 6.5 dialog box.
- Select the Adobe PageMaker 6.5 option on both the Mac and Windows. If that is the only option checked in Windows, it is the same as choosing the Compact setup mentioned earlier.
- Adobe Table 3.0 is a separate program that lets you create tables. The problem with this program is that the tables get converted into an uneditable graphic when imported into PageMaker. I suggest not installing it, and if you find you need it later, re-run the installation program and select it at that time.
- Select the spelling and hyphenation dictionaries for the languages you need.

- In Windows, select the Dictionaries option in the Select Components dialog box and then click on the Change button to get the Select Sub-components dialog box that lists available languages. Make sure that only the languages you want are checked and then click on Continue to return to the Select Components dialog box.

  On the Mac, just click on the triangle to the left of the Dictionaries item; you then get a drop-down list of dictionary options from which you can select.
- If you use a PostScript printer — including an imagesetter for final output of print documents — select the PostScript Printer Descriptions option.
- Select the Filters option. It determines what kinds of files (text and graphics) that PageMaker can import and export.

  After selecting this option in Windows, click on the Change button to get the Select Sub-components dialog box with a list of filters. Select only the filters you want and then click on Continue to return to the Select Components dialog box.

  On the Mac, just click on the triangle to the left of the Filters item; you then get a drop-down list from which you can select filter options.
- Plug-ins add special features to PageMaker. Most plug-ins are available in the PageMaker Plug-ins menu under Utilities, and the rest appear in other PageMaker menus.

  In Windows, check off the Plug-ins box and then click on the Change button to get the Select Sub-components dialog box with a list of plug-ins. Select only the plug-ins you want and then click on Continue to return to the Select Components dialog box.

  On the Mac, click on the Plug-ins box and then click on the triangle to the left of the Plug-ins item; you then get a drop-down list from which you can select plug-in options.

For Web publishing, I recommend selecting the following plug-ins:

Acquire Image (if you have a scanner attached to your computer), Align Objects, Balance Columns, Change Case, Create Color Library, Export Adobe PDF, Global Link Options, Grid Manager, HTML Export, HTML Import, Library Palette, ODBC Import (if you are importing files from databases), PageMaker 4.0 – 6.0 Publication Converter, Photoshop Effects, QuickTime Media, and Scripts Palette.

If you're publishing to print, also install: Add Continued Line, Bullets and Numbering, Drop Cap, Edit Tracks, EPS Font Scanner, Expert Kerning, Keyline, Running Headers & Footers, Save for Service Provider, Sort Pages, and Word Counter.

- If you're a Mac user, select the Microsoft OLE option, which PageMaker 6.5 requires. (In Windows, this option is part of the operating system itself, so you don't need to install it.) You should select this option even if you have another program (such as Microsoft Excel or Word) that uses OLE. Installing this option ensures that your Mac has the latest OLE version.

- Select Kodak CMS only if you are doing color print publishing. You won't need this level of color matching for the Web. If you select Kodak CMS on a Mac, also select Color Management Device Profiles. (In Windows, selecting the Kodak CMS option enables the profiles automatically.)

  Once you're done choosing options to install, click on Next> (in Windows) or Continue (on the Mac). PageMaker then asks you what type of devices it should color-manage. In Windows, one scrolling list covers basic kinds of devices (monitors, scanners, and so forth), while another list covers specific models for the device type currently selected. On the Mac, this information is in just one list. For scanners and monitors, so few types exist that you should just choose Generic.

- Color Libraries provide a set of libraries with predefined colors for various kinds of printing presses. For Web publishing, the only library you need to select is Online Colors. For print, you need several of the Pantone-brand color-ink libraries, including Coated, Coated Pastel, Metallic, Process, ProSim, Uncoated, and Uncoated Pastel. Ask your publishing guru if your company uses any of the other color libraries (which are for brands of color inks less commonly used or used regionally).

  In Windows, select Color Libraries and then click on the Change button to get a list of libraries. In the Select Sub-components dialog box that then appears, select only the libraries you want and then click on Continue to return to the Select Components dialog box.

  On the Mac, select Color Libraries and then click on the triangle to the left of the Color Libraries item; you then get a drop-down list from which you can select color library options.

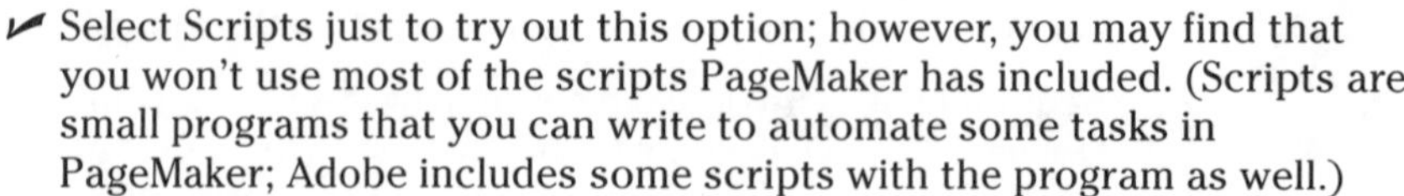

- Select Scripts just to try out this option; however, you may find that you won't use most of the scripts PageMaker has included. (Scripts are small programs that you can write to automate some tasks in PageMaker; Adobe includes some scripts with the program as well.)

Unfortunately, in the Windows version, you aren't able to select which sample script to install — it's all or none. But on the Mac version, you can select specific scripts by clicking on the triangle to the left of the Scripts item; you then get a drop-down list from which you can select script options.

- Select the Tutorial option if you are new to PageMaker. Otherwise, don't bother.
- The Extras option gives you the chance to install several utilities:

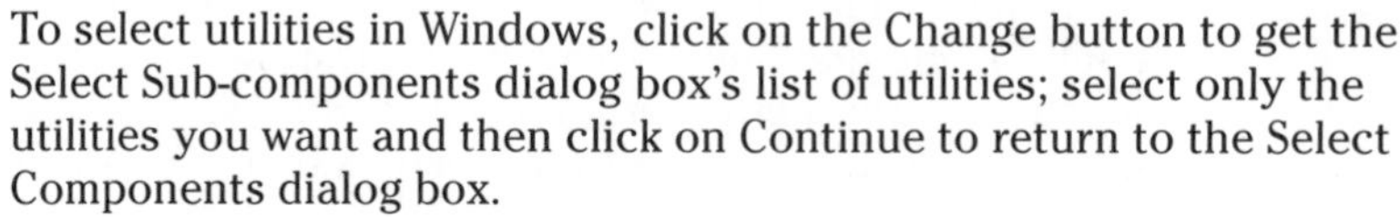

To select utilities in Windows, click on the Change button to get the Select Sub-components dialog box's list of utilities; select only the utilities you want and then click on Continue to return to the Select Components dialog box.

On the Mac, click on the triangle to the left of the Extras item; you then get a drop-down list of utilities from which you can select. Calibration Table and Kodak Monitor Installer are useful only if you are using the Kodak CMS color-management system.

Character Set lets you print out symbol lists — an unnecessary utility for Web publishers.

Dictionary Editor is a must for easy updating of the spelling and hyphenation dictionaries.

QuarkXPress Converter is useful if you are moving from QuarkXPress to PageMaker.

Update PPD Utility is a must for print publishers and service bureaus who deal with lots of brands and types of printers; for Web publishers, it's not necessary.

- Select Acrobat Distiller 3.0 if you don't own the full Acrobat 3.0 package and want to create Acrobat pages from PageMaker. (This feature is automatically installed if you chose the Typical setup option.)
- In Windows only, select Apple QuickTime 2.1 for Windows to install support for motion-video. You may use QuickTime 2.1 for more than just PageMaker, because it's the standard motion-video software for both PCs and Macs. (This feature is automatically installed if you chose the Typical setup option.) On the Mac, QuickTime 2.5 comes with the Mac System 7.6; the PageMaker CD has a separate installer for QuickTime 2.5 for earlier Mac systems.

- Select Adobe Type Manager (in Windows) or ATM 4.0 (on the Mac) if you don't own Adobe Type Manager 4.0. This option gives you more control over font appearance and makes it easier for PageMaker to print accurately to any kind of printer and to display fonts on screen more legibly. Note that this program is used by the entire Windows or Mac system, so it enhances all of the programs you run, not just PageMaker. (This feature is automatically installed if you chose the Typical setup option.)

- If you selected the PostScript Printer Descriptions option, PageMaker asks you to select the printer support files, known as PPDs (for PostScript printer descriptions). In Windows, you get two lists: one on the left for brands of printers, and one on the right for models in that brand. For example, if you own an Apple LaserWriter IIg, select Apple from the list at left, and then select LaserWriter IIg from the list of Apple printers at right. The Mac has just one list of brands; click on the triangles to display a particular brand's models. You may need to scroll to find your printer make or model.

  Be sure to select every printer you or your colleagues use — and don't forget to include the imagesetter, such as a Linotronic or Agfa device, that produces your final print publications.

- On the Mac, you are asked for the printer-description and color-matching options after you complete the program-registration form (covered in the next section of this appendix); in Windows, you complete the program-registration form after you've been asked for the printer-description and color-matching options.

Registering and Restarting PageMaker

On the Mac, PageMaker gives you a dialog box telling you to restart your Mac after it completes the installation. (Restarting a Mac or PC forces all programs to close.) You can choose Cancel to abort the installation (and finish whatever work you were doing in another program and don't want to lose by restarting) or click on Continue to finish the installation.

Before installation begins, PageMaker asks you for your name, company, and serial number (which is on the CD envelope). In Windows, you'll get the User Information dialog box in which to enter this information; on the Mac, you get a dialog box with no name that asks for this same information. Enter the information and click on Next> (oddly, in this case, the Windows and Mac versions use the same button name, rather than the usual Continue for the Mac). In Windows, you are asked for registration information *after* you've selected any printer-description and color-calibration settings; on the Mac, you are asked for registration information *before* you've selected any printer-description and color-calibration settings.

At this point, PageMaker does its installation magic. Installation takes a few minutes, so you've got time to get up and stretch your legs.

In Windows, you may get dialog boxes for QuickTime and Adobe Type Manager installation once PageMaker is installed. The dialog boxes are routine, with no options to worry about. Move through them by pressing Enter.

Now you're ready to wrap everything up.

- After PageMaker has installed everything you've selected, it displays a dialog box that gives you the option of registering your PageMaker software via modem. In Windows, select the PageMaker 6.5 online registration option and click on Finish. On the Mac, you have the option of online registration once you fill in your name, company, and serial number, which you're asked for *before* the actual program files are installed. Then fill out the form that displays on the screen. (If you don't register by modem, mail in the printed registration form in the PageMaker box.)

  In Windows, you may be asked if you want to restart your computer. If nothing else is running, go ahead and let PageMaker shut down your machine. If something else is running that you don't want to close, choose the option No, I Will Restart My Computer Later and then click on OK.

- You can't run PageMaker 6.5 until you have restarted your computer. To restart it, select the Start⇨Shutdown⇨Restart the Computer? sequence. On the Mac, you have no choice but to click the Restart button once the installation is complete.

- After your system restarts, you can eject the CD and put it away for safekeeping. In Windows, right-click on the CD-ROM drive icon in your My Computer window and choose Eject from the pop-up menu. On the Mac, select the CD icon on the desktop and press ⌘+Y.

Reinstalling to Change Options

If you want to change PageMaker options later — add or remove PPD files, color libraries, utilities, plug-ins, filters, and so forth — you just need to rerun the PageMaker installation program and pick the Custom installation option. Any option that you deselect that was previously installed is removed, and any new option that you select is added.

The PageMaker installation program doesn't display in the checkboxes what was already installed. Every option appears to be unselected except the PageMaker 6.5 program itself. To be on the safe side, check off everything you need, whether or not it was already installed.

Upgrading from PageMaker 6.0

For many programs, an easy way to upgrade to a new version is to install it over the old version in the same directory. But *don't* attempt to do that with PageMaker 6.5, or else you'll lose a series of custom settings, including tracking values, new and user-defined (custom) scripts, user-defined (custom) color libraries, user dictionaries, and customized printer-description files (edited through the Update PPD Utility).

You do need to install PageMaker in its own folder, as described in the "Basic PageMaker Options" section. Then copy the custom-setting files from their PageMaker 6.0 folders into the PageMaker 6.5 folders of the same name. (Within the PageMaker 6.0 and 6.5 folders is a series of additional folders that contain these custom settings, among other things.) Neither version of PageMaker should be running.

The starting points for all of these custom-setting files is the Rsrc folder (in Windows) or the RSRC folder (on the Mac), which is inside the folder that contains the PageMaker program. The locations for each file in Version 6.0 and in Version 6.5 are the same, so be certain to copy each file to the same location within the PageMaker 6.5 folder hierarchy as it is within the PageMaker 6.0 folder hierarchy. That hierarchy is as follows:

- Tracking values are stored in the file Traksval.bin in the Usenglsh folder in the Rsrc folder (in Windows) or in the file Tracking Values in the RSRC folder (on the Mac).
- For scripts folders, select the Rsrc or RSRC folder⇨Plugins folder⇨Scripts folder⇨specific scripts folders. In Windows, the script files have the file extension .txt. Copy the scripts folders, or the individual scripts, to the Scripts folder. The folders display in the Scripts palette as folders and are a handy way to keep similar scripts together (such as Type Scripts and Color Scripts).
- Color libraries are stored in the Color folder in the Usenglsh folder in the Rsrc or RSRC folder. On both Windows and Mac, they have the file extension .acf. Copy only the color libraries you created with the PageMaker Define Colors dialog box.

- In Windows, user dictionaries are stored in the appropriate language folder (such as Usenglsh or Francais). These folders are located inside the Prx folder, which is inside the Linguist folder, which is inside the Rsrc folder. On the Mac, they are stored in the appropriate language folder (such as Usenglsh or français), which is inside the Proximity folder, which is inside the Linguists folder, which is inside the RSRC folder.

On both Windows and Mac, the user libraries have the file extension .UDC. Copy only the dictionaries you created with the Dictionary Editor utility (whose file name is deapp.exe in Windows and Dictionary Editor on the Mac).

- In Windows, PPD files are stored in the Ppd4 folder in the Usenglsh folder in the Rsrc folder. They have the extension .ppd. Copy only the PPDs you modified with the Update PPD Utility (whose file name is Ppd.exe in Windows).

On the Mac, you don't need to worry about PPD files — they are used by the entire Mac system and stored in the Printer Descriptions folder in the Extensions folder within the System Folder. As long as you gave the modified PPD files (modified via the Update PPD program) different names than they had originally, they won't be overwritten when PageMaker 6.5 (or another program) installs PPD files.

Index

• Symbols •

• A •

• B •

• G •

• H •

• M •

• O •

• P •

• Q •

• R •

• S •

• U •

• W •